Speak Like Singing

Speak *Like Singing*

Classics of
Native American Literature

Kenneth Lincoln

University of New Mexico Press | Albuquerque

© 2007 by the University of New Mexico Press
All rights reserved. Published 2007
PRINTED IN THE UNITED STATES OF AMERICA
13 12 11 10 09 08   1 2 3 4 5 6
First paperbound printing 2008
PAPERBOUND ISBN: 978-0-8263-4170-9

LIBRARY OF CONGRESS CATALOGING-IN-PUBLICATION DATA
Lincoln, Kenneth.
Speak like singing : classics of Native American literature / Kenneth Lincoln.
p. cm.
Includes bibliographical references and index.
ISBN-13: 978-0-8263-4169-3 (CLOTH : ALK. PAPER)
1. American literature—Indian authors—History and criticism.
2. Indians of North America—Intellectual life.
3. Indians in literature. I. Title.
PS153.I52L55 2007
810.9'897—dc22

2006029138

Thanks for permission to reprint from Hanging Loose Press
for Sherman Alexie's *The Summer of Black Widows* (1996) and
One Stick Song (2000); University of Arizona Press for Sherwin Bitsui's
Shapeshift (2003); HarperCollins Publishers for Louise Erdrich's
Original Fire (2003); Joy Harjo for *She Had Some Horses* (Thunder's
Mouth Press 1983) and *In Mad Love and War* (Wesleyan University
Press 1990); Coffee House Press for Linda Hogan's *The Book of
Medicines* (1993); N. Scott Momaday for *In the Presence of the Sun*
(St. Martin's Press 1992); Greg Sarris for *Mabel McKay* (University of
California 1994); University of Arizona Press for Luci Tapahonso's
Sáani Dahataal (1993) and *Blue Horses Rush In* (1997); Penguin Group
(USA) Inc. for James Welch's *Riding the Earthboy 40* (1971, 1976, 1990).

Cover photograph "Ruin in a Cave" © Tom Till
Book and cover design and type composition by Kathleen Sparkes
This book is set in Adobe Sabon OTF STD 10/13, 26P
Display type is Adobe LinoLetter OTF STD and Adobe Silentium OTF PRO

For the Children

of My Children

Gabriel, Julia, and Chloe

And she knew their thoughts and said in a
voice that was like singing. . . .

> With visible breath I am walking.
> A voice I am sending as I walk.
> In a sacred manner I am walking.
> With visible tracks I am walking.
> In a sacred manner I walk.

And as she sang, there came from her mouth a white cloud
that was good to smell. Then she gave something to the
chief, and it was a pipe with a bison calf carved on one side
to mean the earth that bears and feeds us, and with twelve
eagle feathers hanging from the stem to mean the sky and
the twelve moons, and these were tied with a grass that never
breaks. "Behold!" she said. "With this you shall multiply
and be a good nation. Nothing but good shall come from it.
Only the hands of the good shall take care of it and the
bad shall not even see it." Then she sang again and went
out of the teepee; and as the people watched her going,
suddenly it was a white bison galloping away and snorting,
and soon it was gone.

> —*Black Elk Speaks*

> To say the name is to begin the story.
> —*Swampy Cree*

> I
> the song
> I walk here
> —*Modoc*

Contents

---

* My model is the writer's *way* to a native homeland, rather than an MLA Handbook. To reduce distracting footnotes, I have embedded references in the text. Any scholar wanting to track my sources can consult the bibliography.

Preface

Okíya wowahwa

I told my vision through songs.
—Nicholas Black Elk, *The Sixth Grandfather*

Sundown, and a drained blue from the sky so long,
                                    ghost whispers, lost voices,
Dry wind in dry grass, our bitter song.
                    —Charles Wright, "Mondo Orfeo,"
                    A Short History of the Shadow

"He spoke like singing," Hehaka Sapa remembers the "make-live" prophet of his Lakota Ghost Dance vision. The *wanékia* "all-colors" voice goes everywhere (Neihardt, *Black Elk Speaks* 188). "As I sang one song," the purblind holy man told John Neihardt in 1931, son Ben Black Elk translating, "there were older men there to tell what they meant to the others. Before I told this everyone took out his pipe filled with kin-nikinnick to make offers to the sacred man that I had seen. Then I told my vision in song and I sang this song three times" (DeMallie, *The Sixth Grandfather* 264). *Then I told my vision in song:* visionary tribal song, no less than Homeric hymn or Hebraic psalm, stories a people's history down through the ages, from the beginnings of Earthmaker and White Buffalo Calf Woman, to Nicholas Black Elk and Mabel McKay, into the twenty-first century.

By contrast, Euro-American literacy has receded from tribal orality—origin myths, spirit journeys, cautionary tales, healing chants, morality tales, communal prayers, and ceremonial dances drawing the people together through song and story. In postwar shock, twentieth-century poets vex the kinship of tribal music and personal song-poem, beginning with the fragmented blank verse in T. S. Eliot's "The Love Song of J. Alfred Prufrock," through Sylvia Plath's fractured *Ariel,* to Carolyn Forché's postcolonial *Poetry of Witness.* Ancient measures break modernly free to lament, to howl, to dissent—rarely to connect musically. Charles Wright laments the animistic losses in "Mondo Orfeo":

> Our song resettles no rocks, it makes no trees move, it
> Has come to nothing, this sour song, but it's all we've got
> And so we sing it
>   being ourselves
> Matter we have no choice in.

The Greek root of lyric means "to give accent to speech," but the metric step, the dance measure, is all but erased in recent poetry, and indeed, free verse is a long way from intoning song. Wright elegizes laconically:

> For us, however, it's box canyon and bad weather
>   and what-comes-next.
> It's wind rasp.
>   It's index finger to puckered lips. It's Saint Shush.

Chanted Lakota visions trace with saving tribal grace to collective beginnings that bless all. Long, long ago, the tribal matrix White Buffalo Calf Woman brought the medicine pipe and so, too, *spoke like singing;* Black Elk's people still hear and chant her songs, as John Neihardt recorded in 1931, only four decades after the Wounded Knee Massacre nearby. As with the grandfather stallion songs, everything listens and dances—the leaves, grasses, waters, leggéds, wingéds, and crawling beings. "They were better able now to see the greenness of the world," Black Elk says after *heyoka* curing songs, "the wideness of the sacred day, the colors of the earth, and to set these in their minds" (*Black Elk Speaks* 149).

Speak Like Singing honors talk-song visions for all relatives. The study seeks to plumb, if not to reconcile, Native and American poetics, tribal chorus and solitary vision. Against the grain of historical fission, America has fusional need for cross-cultural voices, forms, spirits, and dialogues. *Okiya wowahwa,* the Lakota say to "make peace" where I come from, also meaning to court a partner. Nick Black Elk recalls the grandfather spirit in "The Great Vision":

> His voice was not loud, but it went all over the universe and filled it. There was nothing that did not hear, and it was more beautiful than anything can be. It was so beautiful that nothing anywhere could keep from dancing. The virgins danced, and all the circled horses. The leaves on the trees, the grasses on the hills and in the valleys, the waters in the creeks and in the rivers and the lakes, the four-legged and the two-legged and the wings of the air—all danced together to the music of the stallion's song.
>
> And when I looked down upon my people yonder, the cloud passed over, blessing them with friendly rain, and stood in the east with a flaming rainbow over it. (*Black Elk Speaks* 35)

Addressing the crossing genres of poetry and prose, *Speak Like Singing* offers an appreciation of words, first and foremost, from the cultures that shape them into literacy. As with ancient petroglyphs or codices, my approach tries to touch the texts regeneratively in a mutually shared American language today. The book does not sidetrack in schools of theory or academic scaffolding. Writers write, rather than rap ideologically. "As long as I can remember," N. Scott Momaday says in *The Man Made of Words*, "I have been enchanted by words" (*MMW* 1). So after forty years of reading literary texts, writing my own, and teaching American literature, I resist post-colonial scat trailing the Trojan horses of psychological realism, gender wars, sign-making semiology, nationalist essentialism, or spiritual crusading to save the holy land. The stampede to theory has been dizzying and dismaying. Back to lingual origins, this study looks at what's there from beginning to end, *words*: sound as syllable; syntax as song measure; structure as woven textual pattern; sign as an idea seen (image) or things in motion (metaphor) or motions with roots and wings (symbol); style as the wo(man); sense as catlike thought moving about the tribal body's house. Critical tools are the makings of the text itself.

A non-Indian scholar, I want to come as close as possible to the translated Native literary classics and their tribal contexts, the contemporary writings of five women and five men as selected crossing texts—the Sappho and Homer through Dickinson and Heaney of Native oral and literary traditions, all the way from rock art and purblind singing forward to modernist literacy and WordPerfect. This study does not regard Native cultures ethnocentrically *reserved* ("out of sight and out of mind," Russell Means said in the Wounded Knee AIM days) or ghettoized, as in some academic settings—let alone off-limits to responsible outsiders. Beginning and continuing with the Lakota where I was raised in northwest Nebraska during the 1950s, evolving through formations of Native American Studies at UCLA for going on four decades, residing for fifteen years now an arrow's flight from the Institute of American Indian Arts in a Native fertile crescent of the Rio Grande Valley, I consider tribal peoples to be human beings with languages and literatures long-living that cross the alleged Buckskin Curtain. Native Americans are speaking and singing across the land today, both grounded Native ceremonialists and emerging American writers. *Hétchetu aloh!* Hear them out.

Consider how tribal words compose a cultural text.

Acknowledgments

My gratitude and respect for UCLA colleagues in American Indian Studies: Paula Gunn Allen (Laguna/Metis) in English, Paul Apodaca (Apache-Mexican) in Folklore and Mythology, Charles Ballard (Quapaw) in Folklore and Mythology, William Bright in Linguistics, Duane Champagne (Ojibwe) in Sociology, Vine Deloria Jr. (Lakota) in Political Science, David Draper (Choctaw) in Music and Folklore, Allegra Fuller-Snyder in Dance, Hanay Geiogamah (Kiowa) in Theater Arts, Carole Goldberg in Law, Joy Harjo (Creek/Cherokee) in English, Charlotte Heth (Cherokee) in Ethnomusicology, Felicia Hodge (Pomo) in Public Health Care, Jennie Joe (Navajo) in Public Health Care, Paul Kroskrity in Linguistic Anthropology, Melissa Meyer (Cherokee) in History, Ken Morrison (Cherokee) in History, Pamela Munro in Linguistics, Peter Nabokov in World Arts and Cultures, Gary Nash in History, Monroe Price in Law, James Porter in Ethnomusicology, Douglas Price-Williams in Anthropology, Alfonso Ortiz (San Juan Pueblo) in Anthropology, John Red Horse (Cherokee) in Public Policy, Velma Salabiye (Navajo) in Library Science, Greg Sarris (Miwok/Pomo) in English, Melvin Seeman in Sociology, Ernest Siva (Kahweah) in Ethnomusicology, Allogan Slagle (Cherokee) in Federal Indian Law, Kogee Thomas (Cherokee) in Library Science, Russell Thornton (Cherokee) in Sociology, Rebecca Tsosie (Yaqui) in Federal Indian Law, Concepción Valadez (Hispanic-Aztec) in Education, Johannes Wilbert in Anthropology. Cal Bedient knew where to caulk this craft, and Kathleen Washburn helped trim the sails. UNM editor Elizabeth Hadas had the salt to pole my raft upstream to port.

Pilamaya, dok-shá.
Kenneth Lincoln
La Cieneguilla,
New Mexico

Native

Dialectics

"Why do you insist on calling yourselves
Indians?" asked a white woman in a nice hat.
"It's so demeaning."
   "Listen," I said. "The word belongs to us now.
We are Indians. That has nothing to do with
Indians from India. We are not American Indians.
We are Indians, pronounced In-din. It belongs to us.
We own it and we're not going to give it back."

—Sherman Alexie,
1994 Manhattan PEN panel

WE ARE OUR OWN HISTORY

"An emigrant never knows what he wants," W. H. Auden claims in *The Dyer's Hand* (362), "only what he does not want." Compared with the pioneer erasure of local history and ethnic identity in an émigré New Land, Native ancestral traditions grant tribal peoples lasting lyric heritage in the Americas, and they refuse to sacrifice that ceremonial sovereignty. The fact that Western Hemispheric tribes have survived a 97 percent extermination compels Natives to talk and to sing themselves anew. From Harold E. Driver's estimate of 30 million to Henry F. Dobyns arguing 60 million pre-Columbian Indians, the demographic numbers keep rising, as does the U.S. Native population, doubling in the 2004 census to 4.4 million. Some are listening—survival carries future responsibility for all.

Native culture hinges on tribal endurance, indeed renewal; intercultural fusion is not erasure or co-option, but renascence. As Americans have seen through the twentieth century, neither killing fields nor suburban malls, extermination camps nor cultural trashcans in an existential cul-de-sac have snuffed out regenerated Native traditions. The old ways are being continually renewed through ongoing ceremonies and acculturated literacy. "We don't see ourselves alone," Luci Tapahonso says from a Navajo perspective. "We have a whole past, our own history. You know, we are our own history, we are our own history" (Joseph Bruchac interview, *Survival This Way* 276; unless noted, cited interviews are in this collection). Literacy is cultural history from a tribal perspective.

This, then, is not a book about bygone ethno-literacies in other tongues and times. Instead, *Speak Like Singing* offers a cross-cultural study of Native voices speaking through American literature today, especially the fusions of poetry and prose in Western English. The books I read are read by Native writers, the authors known on both sides of the Buckskin Curtain: Bakhtin and Carver, to Momaday and Basso, to Simic and Erdrich. Birthright and bloodline notwithstanding, Natives grow up and evolve into bicultural citizenship, and many are born of crossings. Americans are mixed into this tribal fusing, even when some choose to recuse themselves from the dialogue. As one reviewer prodded that this study sample the "field of discourse" these days, consider the call for segregated ethnic literacy.

RED STICK LIT CRIT

In the last year of the millennium, Craig Womack stumps for a Muskogee nationalist essentialism in *Red on Red: Native American Literary Separatism*. According to his Red-like-me doctrine, only local-color Creeks can truly understand what Womack calls "Creekness," so *Red on Red* assumes the privileged witness on Alexander Posey, Louis Oliver, Joy Harjo, and Lynn Riggs—himself not Creek, but a Cherokee working in Hollywood musicals and writing *Oklahoma*.

Red on Red trumpets a regressive model for "Muskogee-centric" ethno-literacy borrowed from the 1813–14 Red Stick War, as Womack postulates, "against both internal traitors and outside oppression" (*RR* 52). Historically in the Southeast, U.S. agents exacerbated land claims and blood quantum disputes to set off a civil war between traditional "white" and mixed-blood "red" villages. Creek purists with red-painted war clubs murdered hundreds of their own suspected tribal collaborators and all the Whites they could lay hands on. After a decade of bloodshed and the violent intervention of Andy Jackson's federal militia, the internecine civil war guttered in a disputed 1825 Treaty of Indian Springs, the execution of Chief William Macintosh by his own people, and pyrrhic tribal meltdown. Tragically, the Creeks lost their own fratricidal cleansing pogrom, along with thousands of Trail of Tears clanspeople on forced removal to Oklahoma, and signed away their territorial rights to 23 million acres of ancestral homelands. Womack parallels this civil war with the current culture wars in academia: "Integration, acceptance, and assimilation to literary norms will no longer be our highest goal. Native critics will turn toward more disruptive tactics" (*RR* 303). Reader beware. Could Puritans burn the wrong witches, or as fictionalized in Leslie Silko's *Ceremony*, skinwalker veteran essentialists terrorize locals? "You drink like an Indian," a teeth-rattling Emo taunts Tayo in a bar, "and you're crazy like one too—but you aren't shit, white trash. You love Japs the way your mother loved to screw white men" (*C* 63). "Don't trust all Indians," the makeshift medicine man Betonie warns against essentialism, or "write off all white people" (*C* 128).

Sovereign nations do not stand on isolation, to challenge Womack's asserted separatism by way of Deloria and Lytle's *The Nations Within: The Past and Future of American Indian Sovereignty*, but on mutual independence and interpersonal (indeed, intercultural) recognition. Sovereignty would serve as a cross-national way for peoples to acknowledge and to respect each other across differences. In an academic civil war, the tribe's own people get trapped behind the Buckskin Curtain or outside its essentialist tarp, since many (including Womack by his own admission) are not Muskogee-literate speakers, let alone readers, and in light of relocation are not indigenous to southeast Oklahoma. According to recent tribal elections, more Creeks live in southern California than in Oklahoma. Eighty-two percent of all Native America lives off-reservation today, by 2004 census figures, and few are bi-literate professors.

Dissing others, Muskogee colleague Joy Harjo says, poisons her own Red-White bloodlines of Creek, Cherokee, French, and Irish tributaries. "I've gone through the stage where I hated everybody who wasn't Indian, which meant part of myself," she tells Joe Bruchac. "We're not separate. We're all in this together" (96). Regardless of motive, essentialism defeats Native and American cultural discourse. *Talking stink,* as they say on the streets, fouls the common air people share exploring mutually sovereign literacies. Beyond Indian Country and Nobel, National Book, and Pulitzer prizes notwithstanding, can only a Mississippi sharecropper appreciate race relations in Faulkner, an Ohio Black singly understand local dialect in Toni Morrison, or a New Jersey shopkeeper exclusively scan the variable foot of William Carlos Williams? Using cultural monopoly for private witness rules out all other tribal classics than one's own, including the Bible and the Great White Roots of Peace, Homer and the Code of Handsome Lake, Dante and the Popol Vuh, and Shakespeare and Blessingway Ceremony. Do Native writers want to be appreciated by audiences inside and outside their own kin, or misunderstood behind the screen of separatist privilege?

Red Stick purges, all too often personal vendettas, profit the self-appointed prophets. "Reconciliation," according to Elizabeth Cook-Lynn's *Anti-Indianism in Modern America*, remains "Dishonest in its Inception, Now a Failed Idea." Whether promoted by IRA sellouts in Belfast, Cook-Lynn snaps at soft-hearted liberals, or in South Africa by Robert Mandela and Bishop Tutu, South Dakota reconciliation is bicultural trash to be dumped on the "scrap heap of dumb ideas." For ongoing polemics of the drummed up culture wars—debates over real and virtual Natives, rez and academic Indians, oral and literary texts, self-determination and multi-culturalism—see Robert Warrior, Jace Weaver, and Crag S. Womack's recent *American Indian Literary Nationalism* (New Mexico 2005), essentially an attack on "outsider" Elvira Pulitano's *Toward a Native American Critical Theory* (Nebraska 2003). Harold Littlebird, Laguna/Santa Domingo Pueblo, offers a word of reflection:

> But in all the things that I remember, I hear it said all the time
> that it's for all people. They say that all the time: All People.
> The way you would say it in Laguna, "Opa," that's what it means,
> "All People." It's not just here in North America that you're
> praying for, but it's all people. You don't make any distinctions
> of color, or race, of anything. (*Survival This Way*, 163)

ALLIES

Over forty years of work in Sioux Country and elsewhere, no matter how hot the seat, I heard little self-promoting separatism from Lakota healers like Dawson No Horse, John Fire, Robert Stead, or Leroy Poor Bear; witnessed no token essentialism from traditionals like Jennie Lone Wolf,

Ed Fills-the-Pipe, or Lawrence Antoine; smelled rare in-crowd stink from artists like Oscar Howe, Kevin Locke, or Arthur Amiotte; faced few slammed doors from community leaders like Bill Iron Mountain in Pine Ridge, Lionel Bordeaux at Rosebud's Sinte Gleska College, or my brother Mark Monroe in our hometown American Indian Center of Alliance, Nebraska. Tough talk, yes. We traded critical skills and hard truth-telling among the Lakota of my hometown, growing up locally with Felix Goodshot, Jack Long Pumpkin, Connie Stairs, and Edison Richards—regionally with Joe American Horse, the Pine Ridge tribal chair; Winnebago Reuben Snake, Your Humble Serpent; and recently deceased Vine Deloria Jr., the grumpy Lakota litigant.

True dog soldiers know friends from enemies. Seasoned warriors know that tribal resources are precious, blooded or otherwise, and talking stink is seldom *washtay*. In the fractious 1970s, Pine Ridge vigilantes snarled bad mouth on the rez—Dick Wilson's GOONs, hotheaded AIMsters, drugged-out thugs, rifle-toting rednecks, FBI assassins terrorizing Wounded Knee citizens—but decent folk of conscience took cover, and academics hid over the next hill. Vine Deloria crossed the lines into the standoff and talked and listened. To his death, Deloria worried that ethnic scholars would sell out in an academic "ghetto," promoting themselves as "house pets of universities" ("No More Free Lunches," in Shanley, ed., *Paradoxa*, 2001).

In my Wasichu time, I was heckled at a home-state Nebraska conference twenty years ago by an irascible Sioux hell-raiser, reviewed nastily by carping critics, hassled in class by born-again activists red-lining Sherman Alexie's *Indian Killer*, and ridiculed by Anglophilic colleagues who deep-sixed me to the social sciences. This all goes with the tribal sweat suit, into classroom culture wars, to academic deceleration. No one told me it would be easy or that I could not do the needed work. More to the essentialist hatchet: Cook-Lynn chooses not to read Wallace Stegner, Michael Dorris, or Adrian Louis, as she bugles in print. Indigenist Ward Churchill cries fascist over the 9/11 tragedy, and Wendy Rose trashes UC Berkeley anthropologists in *Academic Squaw*. Sherman Alexie banters in the *New York Times Magazine* that White Men can't drum—but do these cultural snipers speak for all Indians, even a pan-tribal minority?

The major Native American texts in print, published in English by coast-to-coast literary and university houses, are open to the public. If Russell Means crows separatism on the shoulders of a non-Indian ghost writer in *Where White Men Fear to Tread*, why does he keep appearing in kitschy movies like *Pocahontas* and *The Last of the Mohicans*, fifteen Hollywood films in just as many years ("The Ways of Means," in *Santa Fean*, November 2005)? Aren't these attitudes so many self-defensive gripes or academic rumbles or career aggrandizements, rather than rez issues of land, language, sovereignty, spirit, and cultural survival? A witness ponders what will be left after Womack's Red Stick purges run their course, or Cook-Lynn rubs out all hope of reconciliation, or Means and Alexie milk the last of liberal guilt, and the cross-cultural remnants have to live together, especially the 82 percent off-reservation survivors. Beyond the rez, more than three-and-a-half million intercultural mixers, mestizos, and translators must be counted among the few thousand purist bloods, ethnic nationalists, or academic essentialists drumming up a Red Stick purge. Who speaks pan-tribally for any or all Indians? Louis Owens argues in *Here First*, "The descendant of mixed-blood sharecroppers and the dispossessed of two continents, I believe I am the rightful heir of Choctaw and Cherokee story-tellers and of Shakespeare and Yeats and Cervantes. Finally, everything converges and the center holds in the margins. This, if we are to go on" (Krupat and Swann, 270).

INTERCULTURAL BRIDGES

Speak Like Singing is neither insider-privileged nor outsider-objective. My critical advocacy is addressed to intercultural readers trying to understand Native literacy through fusional song-poetry and story-narrative. Cultural diversity marks local variance among tribes. Bloods, skins, traditions, and literatures have been mixing for centuries; isolation is not an option, though co-option may be a clear and present danger. I do not advocate Native erasure through White acculturation, or White arrogation of tribal rights, but intercultural dialogue. The crux is how writers remain Native while writing American literature, and there are no simple fixes.

Given a history of warfare, betrayal, dispossession, and land swindle, American Indians insist on their differences and ask the country's cross-cultural respect for tribal sovereignty. "Maybe any life of resistance to mainstream culture is traditional Indian," Linda Hogan muses to Joe Bruchac (126). Native writers reflect on distinctions and original differences, but speak to a common reader. Wild rice to Uncle Ben, fry bread to Big Mac, how do Americans accept the variances, even admire and learn from differences without homogenizing original cultures?

Generic crossings of song and story, poetry and prose interconnect Native and American voices and visions in given tribal settings, as major writings evince from *Black Elk Speaks* to *House Made of Dawn*, from

Ceremony to *Shapeshift*. Traditional tellings, ceremonial prayers, and ritual chants beyond the culture wars cross with modernist, postmodernist, and supra-realist modes. Songs tone stories. From Sequoyah and Sitting Bull through Louise Erdrich and Sherwin Bitsui, Native tongues play off mainstream American voices in the Western canon, Chaucer to Chekhov, that many writers, Indians and non-Indians, studied in college. Scott Momaday was a Stanford doctoral student when I was an undergraduate there in the early sixties. Only a few years later, Simon Ortiz and Joy Harjo attended the prestigious Iowa Writers Workshop, as Jim Welch was studying with Richard Hugo and William Kittredge at the University of Montana. Leslie Silko was teaching Joy Harjo at the University of New Mexico in the 1970s, where Silko's second cousin Paula Gunn Allen, working with Robert Creeley, was completing a doctorate in American Studies. Luci Tapahonso was enrolled at UNM as a writing single mother. In the late 1970s, Louise Erdrich studied literature at Johns Hopkins and Dartmouth with Michael Dorris, while Greg Sarris was working with me at UCLA, eventually to receive a Stanford Ph.D. in Modern Thought and Literature and join our faculty in 1990. Linda Hogan completed an MFA at the University of Colorado, where she now teaches, and Sherman Alexie received his literary degree from Eastern Washington State in 1991. Sherwin Bitsui blazed through the Institute of American Indian Arts in Santa Fe, then finished a creative writing major in American Literature at the University of Arizona in the spring of 2005.

Over three decades the writers Paula Gunn Allen (Laguna Pueblo/ Metis), Greg Sarris (Miwok/Pomo), Hanay Geiogamah (Kiowa), and Joy Harjo (Creek/Cherokee) have been my Native American Studies literary colleagues, among scores of interdisciplinary UCLA scholars credited in the opening. When I joined the faculty in 1969, the Lakota activist Roger Buffalohead was founding the UCLA American Indian Center. People learn in both directions. Across my own interdisciplinary pastures, tribal literacies root American writers in the Native: Thoreau, Melville, Whitman, Austin, and Sandburg; to Faulkner, Williams, Hemingway, Penn Warren, and Snyder; down through Kesey, McMurtry, Oliver, Berry, and Merwin—as discussed in *Sing with the Heart of a Bear* (Lincoln, 2000). "I fooled around with the language," the Mohawk poet Karoniaktatie says, "because the language and the culture of English and America fooled around with me and my life" (Bruchac, *Survival This Way* 140). *Speak Like Singing* argues that classic Native artists today—Momaday, Silko, Tapahonso, Welch, Erdrich, Harjo, Sarris, Hogan, Alexie, and Bitsui—fuse tongues, bloodlines, literacies, genres, and local cultures across a permeable Buckskin Curtain.

LANGUAGE AS PERCEPTION

> Every word must express in unmediated and direct
> fashion the poet's design; there must be no distance
> between the poet and his discourse.
>
> [The prose writer] speaks *through* language, as it
> were, a language that has gained in thickness, become
> objectivized, and moved away from his mouth.
>
> —Mikhail Bakhtin, *The Dialogic Imagination*

Some thoughts about form, since words and their constructions ground this study: The poet sings within a personal tongue to the self, Bakhtin posits; the prose writer speaks through words to a projected other. Singer and storyteller in Native America cross these dialogical modes—within and through ceremonial or spoken language—in voices that carry inside to out, and back again. Tribal writers are mutually conversant about aesthetic forms. Speaking of his Acoma father singing about an old man dancing, Simon Ortiz recalls: "the song was the road from outside himself to inside— which is perception—and from inside himself to outside—which is expression. That's the process and the product of the song, the experience and the vision that a song gives you. The words, the language of my experience, come from how I understand, how I relate to the world around me, and how I know language as perception. The language allows me vision to see with and by which to know myself" ("Song, Poetry, and Language—Expression and Perception" 118). Language as perception: no stranger to literary talk or cultural theory, Natives know their own ideas through words—lyric song to narrative story—as Keith Basso shows with Apache raconteurs revered for their iconic speech (*Western Apache Language and Culture*). Native writers see themselves experientially in and through words as embodied insights— an outer world internalized perceptually, an inner world vocalized objectively. "An idea is a thing seen," Robert Duncan says of Plato in *The Poets' Dante* (Hawkins and Jacoff, 2001). Lakota elders, John Fire or Jennie Lone Wolf, said people learn by watching and doing.

Few stable definitions of poetry and prose cross cultures, space, and time. *The Princeton Encyclopedia of Poetry and Poetics* circles genres in an attempt to collate Western aesthetics. "There is no uniquely valid way to classify theories of poetry," the experts say; "that classification is best which serves the particular purpose at hand" (639). Stressing diversity, the scholars pound one linchpin: "All theorists recognize that poetry is a fabricated thing, not found in nature." How does a reader correlate this Western sense of the *made* artifice with Lakota "breath in the pipe" (sacred words passing *through* a person) or "sing with the heart of a bear" (a guardian voice *shaping the singer*)? Can N. Scott Momaday "make" a modern poem as a Kiowa *man made of words*? Can Nicholas Black Elk speak as a purblind Lakota "word sender" and survive literary translation in an ethnographic text by John Neihardt, the poet laureate of Nebraska and president of the Academy of American Poets? If Alexander Pope's Augustan verse finds "Nature to advantage dressed," scholars must reverse *nurture/nature* terms to solicit Navajo *Talking God*, to regard *Diné* speech as the "in-standing wind-soul," or to honor Luci Tapahonso's tribal invocation, "Sacred begins at the tip of my tongue" (all discussed later). Clearly readers must calibrate the distance between sacred and secular, mused and made, natural and fabricated. Begin with the given, not the made: Natives consider song-poetry as the breath of life itself, the word an animate spirit, the lyric sacred, narrative social bonding, and harmony natural *in all things*.

Arguing by way of Aristotle's *Poetics* that meter is not poetry, but inversely that "the word 'poetry' has always meant primarily 'composition in meter,'" the Princeton arbiters posit that "Prose is ordinary speech on its best behavior" (*PEPP* 885). With inconsistent rhythm, discursive syntax, fewer images, and less density, prose breaks free of poetry, the scholars say, "when the sentence structure takes the lead and all patterns of repetition are subordinated to it and become irregular." These wooly definitions do not take a reader very far toward imaged detail, carved diction, measured syllable, natural structure, word tare, tonal texture, or the song-dance origins of poetry as differentiated from talk-prose. Academically safe, does a scholar state something so general that few dispute it, "a fabricated thing," or stir the embers, light a fire, and spark the mind to *think with and through* generic differences in oral to written traditions?

Lyric—*to give accent to speech*—comes from Greek *lyra*, musical instrument, so it is "a poem written to be sung," the *Princeton Encyclopedia* concludes (462). Asking where words, texts, and song-poems originate, John Miles Foley in *How to Read An Oral Poem* documents that Middle Eastern "tokens" of numeracy appeared around 8000 B.C. and Mesopotamian cuneiform about 3200 B.C., Indus script by 2500 B.C., Semitic script in 2000 B.C., and Phoenician script at 1200 B.C. (23–24). The Greek alphabet dates to 775 B.C., Mayan and Mesoamerican scripts to 500 B.C., the Alexandrian Library to 250 B.C. Yhen Chinese print technology appears by 750 A.D., Gutenberg's printing press in 1450 A.D., Sequoyah's Cherokee script in 1821 A.D., and the C. L. Scholes typewriter in 1867 A.D.

At least a radiocarbon-dated millennium before all of these diverse literacies, Clovis Man was fluting spearheads and marking stone walls in the Blackwater Draw of eastern New Mexico (David Grant Noble, *Ancient Ruins of the Southwest* 7).

And the word set to music as lyric? Egyptians left elegy, ode, hymn, and tomb inscriptions of work songs from shepherds, fishers, and chairmen in the Pyramid Texts ca. 2600 B.C. The Hebrews evolved rhythm, harmony, and meter with Moses among the Egyptians in the tenth century B.C., historians posit, resulting in David's trimeters and pentameters, Old Testament parallelism and alliteration, musical psalms (Greek *psallein*, "to pull upon a stringed instrument"), folk proverbs, moral epigrams, wisdom literature, and Job's lyric dialogues with Yahweh. The Greeks perfected lyrics of chant, song, and dance into the fifth century B.C., primarily organized in *stichic* meter that was recited, and *melic* meter that was sung and danced. Over eleven thousand years ago, Paleo-Indians hunted mastodons in the Rio Grande Valley and incised ceremonial images on basalt cliffs.

With no entry for *narrative* as such, the Princeton experts define a "narrative poem" as lyric that "tells a story," often associated with magus, bard, scop, or troubadour magic (*PEPP* 542). The scholars conclude that a prose poem is a "poem in prose" (664).

What about Native American literary forms, aesthetic histories, artistic genres, cultural premises, and spiritual muses back thirty to forty thousand years in the Western Hemisphere? Three *Princeton Encyclopedia* pages cover North and South "American Indian Poetry" as oral tradition by way of linguistic anthropology—no word on contemporary Native writing.

WISDOM SITS IN PLACES

Less so over formal definitions, Native lyricists and tribal narrators are more concerned with how ancestral traditions and ceremonial complexes feed into today's cultural literacy. So, too, pre- and postmodern theory tempests seem short-lived to tribal artists, and remain *academic* to on- and off-reservation peoples working for daily survival. Indians are more involved with how their own history anchors tradition, and where evolving culture holds tribal values fast. The genius of Native voices has been around for tens of thousands of years, long before Greco-Roman or Hebraic-Christian literary history—oral cultures with ancient adaptive wisdoms geographically embedded in the stones, trees, rivers, and plains of tribal origins. *Wisdom sits in places*, the Cibecue Apache tell Keith Basso. Theirs are not so much twice-told tales as ceremonial sites countlessly revisited, no less than the thousand-year-old Ancestral Pueblo petroglyphs standing watch over the Santa Fe valley where I live today—basalt dictionaries of stone-carved texts, oral and more recently written, that bear a revisionary, indeed a retranslative look via ongoing Pueblo ceremonies (more on this in the next chapter). Newly expressed in English, working tribal *languages* and literary experiences frame the subjects of this study, local *language as perception* its critical premise. *As it used to be long ago may I walk*, the Navajo timelessly sing their Beautyway ceremonies in the fingertip trail of the wind and scalp whorls of hair. The Grand Canyon Havasupai pray for everyday blessings: *Make me always the same as I am now*. Both chants translate in reverse blank verse (see Washington Matthews, *Navajo Myths, Prayers, and Songs* 55; and Leslie Spier, *Havasupai Ethnography* 286).

One language or culture invigorating another catalyzes translative fusion, what microbiologists call *symbiogenesis* or symbiosis, evolving over 50,000 years with *homo sapiens* (to be discussed later as SET theory, pioneered by Lynn Margulis in *Symbiotic Planet* 1999). Beyond the days of ethnic cleansing, other-baiting, patriotic Creationism, and imperial reinvasion, a coevolutionary paradigm counters the misread Darwinian *survival of the fittest*. Rather than superior or convulsive "fit," the word once meant song, ballad, or story. Old English *fitt* was a canto of singing or speaking.

CROSS-CULTURAL FUSIONS

> . . . the problem of white novelists creating black
> characters and, by extension, male writers creating
> female characters, old writers creating young
> characters and so on. Are we at heart insular and
> self-absorbed creatures or boundary-crossers capable
> of compassion?
>
> —David Chanoff, *The Writing Life*

Speak Like Singing focuses on early books of poetry and prose by select Native writers, foregrounding the distinct voices and tribal diversities of living Indians. Rather than scan the renewed dawning of a Native American Renaissance, this study focuses on carefully chosen paradigms among ten Indian artists in working daylight, a follow-up to Andrew Wiget's finely edited *Handbook of Native American Literature* (1994).

Eight grandparents and tribal elders by now, plus two younger literary luminaries, today's Native classicists deserve canonical respect among global literacies. Other critics might choose other models. I want to track the crossing of lyric into narrative over three generations of Native literacy. Through the pan-tribal medium of English—a second language for some, now a mother tongue for most—these Native writers begin as poets and often go on to write novels. How lyric pitch blends into narrative pace flows through many tongues and into many fusions of song and speech, poetry and prose, orality and literacy.

Traversing Li Po to Pablo Neruda to Richard Hugo, tribal writers work at arm's length from other American writers globally today. This crossing does not augur any sacrifice of cultural integrity or tribal sovereignty in some draconian law of the excluded middle. The Bering Straits were crossed both directions, the Canadian researcher Elaine Dewar documents in *Bones: Discovering the First Americans*. Crisscrossing can benefit both sides of cultural interface. Take the long view. Back three and a half billion years, as discussed later in Linda Hogan's evolutionary poetics, symbiogenetic speciation coevolved mutually as microbiological adaptations, bacteria to protoctist, advancing the survival and success of fusing gene banks (Lynn Margulis, *Symbiotic Planet*). Joy Harjo reminds Bill Moyers in *The Power of the Word* 1989 PBS Series that "at one point we were *all* tribal people. Europeans were tribal people; all around the world the roots of all human beings were tribal" (*The Spiral of Memory* 39). *All My Relatives*, the Lakota call ceremonially, tribalizing the Gaia hypothesis of James E. Lovelock—that the living are all in this together, one interdependent global organism of coexisting cell complexes, Lynn Margulis estimates, more than 30 million connected living species, microbiology to macroeconomics, including atmospheric gases and surface rocks and water. Natives have always prayed to the spirits in all living things—Grandmother Mountain, Grandfather Stone, Mother Earth, Father Sky, Guardian Bear, Trickster Coyote, Wind Breath, Lunar Spirit, Brother Sun and Sister Moon. All life is one Hypersea of living matter as "animated water," Russian mineralogist Vladimir Vernadsky posits, an ecosystemic biomass of plants, animals, fungi, bacteria, and protoctists (Margulis, *Symbiotic Planet*). No call for ethnic cleansing or blanching, no forced assimilation to privilege. Global tribal peoples ask volitional bi-acculturation, ideally speaking, sharing skills and knowledge systems. No co-option, cooperation. Essentialism on either side proves self-limiting. Either humans evolve responsibly by this Native paradigm of extended kinship to every living being, *All my relatives*, or xenophobia will destroy all life on the planet.

Discussing isolationist limitations with Bruchac, the Chickasaw poet and novelist Linda Hogan considers the mandate: "Rather than people cutting themselves off from white communities to be traditional, the more I think about it in my life the more I have thought that breaking down those barriers is much more important than building them up. Any kind of racism at this point is not good for any people. And to become anti-white is a mistake. It's self-destructive for those who do." Her own fusional ancestries, a Nebraska pioneer grandmother and an Oklahoma Chickasaw horse trader, grant Hogan reversible flaps through the Buckskin Curtain. "Talk about a balance of things—talk about head and heart or head and soul—somehow I think that merging the two cultures in a really *healthy* way, not as done in the past, might be an integration in the way that we were talking about earlier. Indians have already begun that process. Years ago. Now I see white people integrating in that way. Mostly women at this point" (132). How do people suture these old fractures and come together symbiotically?

Ancestral Translations

Live poetry is a kind of singing. It differs from prose,
as song does, in its complexity of stress and intonation.
Poetry demands a human voice to sing it and demands
an audience to hear it.

—Jack Spicer, "On Spoken Poetry"

This study needs to talk cultural and formal shop for a moment. Specific to endangered literacy and cultural crossing these days, a reader might consider the transition between storytelling and writing stories—whether a speaking voice can be written down accurately on paper to be reconstructed in a reader's hearing. What is lost or gained in the leap from speech into print? "Truly fine poetry must be read aloud," Borges says of Dante. "Poetry always remembers that it was an oral art before it was a written art. It remembers that it was first song" (Hawkins and Jacoff, *The Poets' Dante*). Storytellers may be nearly extinct, Larry McMurtry worries in *Reading Walter Benjamin at the Dairy Queen*, "like whooping cranes." And is modern prose fiction, say William Faulkner's *The Sound and the Fury* or Jonathan Franzen's *The Corrections*, more individually personalized, more self-isolating than tribal oral narrative? The novelist may be existentially slanted and voiced, less tribally or historically communal than village crier or folkloric raconteur. These are some of today's Native concerns as tribal cultures evolve translatively through print to non-tribal, English-literate readers. Beyond Harold Bloom's fulminations on the Western canon or Liz Cook-Lynn's irreconcilable crankiness, *Speak Like Singing* must track literature to its beginnings. The fusional crossings of Native oral and written literacies could be graphed as coevolving:

"Text" comes from Latin *texere*, meaning "to weave," and "write" derives from Old English *writan*, that is, "to cut or incise," usually in stone. As discussed, the word poem follows from Greek *poiein*, "to make, create," and "read" mutates from Old English *rædan*, literally "to offer advice or counsel" (Foley, *How to Read* 53). Literature in a text-centered age, from Latin *litera* or "letter" and Medieval Latin *litteratus* or "lettered man," implies "works composed in letters by a lettered person" (Foley 27).

Where does this leave translated oral song-poetry? Dennis Tedlock calls for a "performative translation" of oral texts, a dialogical anthropology mediating between artist and scholar, and offers working recreations of Zuni and Quiché ceremonial chants in *The Spoken Word and the Work of Interpretation* (13). In cultural crossings, Tedlock asks for "good speaking" texts over "bad writing." Surveying the history of linguistic anthropology in *Native American Verbal Art*, Williams M. Clements resists translations that "freeze expression." Whether "to oralize writing or to literalize speaking," Clements argues, "translation proper always involves an attempt to familiarize the Other" (19, 10–11). The translator of Navajo oral texts Paul Zolbrod takes on genres and modes of song-poetry and story-prose in *Reading the Voice*. He ponders the translated crossings of lyric and narrative, oral culture and poetic texts: "What are the measured qualities of the singing voice? Where in the spoken voice do they [readers] see the internal rhythm, and what looser patterns do they see in the so-called prose that would give it poetic dimensions when recited verbally? Is there thematic rhythm that resonates in partial repetition or topical reiteration?" (122). A. L. Soens gathers and annotates classical poetry of Native North America in *I, the Song* to help readers see the New World through pre-Columbian lyric eyes, a tradition of the ethnographic anthology going back through George Cronyn, Natalie Burlin Curtis, Alice C. Fletcher, Margot Astrov, and Arthur Grove Day to more recently William Brandon, John Bierhorst, Frederick Turner III, Jerome Rothenberg, and Brian Swann, among fine anthologists.

Brian Swann and Arnold Krupat cross linguistics, literature, social sciences, performing arts, folklore, religion, and philosophy in Swann's collected essays on traditional Native literatures, *Smoothing the Ground*; later in Krupat's *Recovering the Word*; then a Smithsonian series, *On the Translation of Native American Literatures* (Swann). The translation debate ranges over vast terrain—from Daniel Brinton, Natalie Curtis Burlin, Mary Austin, and populist associates a century back; through turn-of-the-century ethnographic linguistics of Elsie Clews Parsons, Ruth Underhill, Knud Rasmussen, Alfred Kroeber, and hundreds of other scholars for the Smithsonian Bureau of American Ethnology and the American Anthropological Association; to Michael Castro, Dell Hymes, Barre Toelken, Dennis Tedlock, William Bright, and modern-day linguists; now taken up by Native writers Gerald Vizenor, Craig Womack, Greg Sarris, Paul Apodaca, Ofelia Zepeda, John E. Smelcer, Rex Lee Jim, Kimberly M. Blaser, Gloria Bird, and hundreds of others (see the autobiographical essays in Krupat and Swann's *Here First*). In 2005 Joy Porter and Kenneth Roemer edited a handbook of thematic and contextual essays on tribal writings *The Cambridge Companion to Native American Literature*.

Joseph Bruchac, Abnaki translator/editor/writer-at-large for Greenfield Review Press, notes in interviewing Native poets for *Survival This Way*: "American poetry—still talking about the European side—seems to be characterized very often by a longing and a loneliness, a sense of being on the edge of a kind of wilderness, a frontier, and trying to force that into a mold which you create on your own. That idea of changing the natural world, of changing everything around you to reflect your image, also seems to be counter to the vision of the American Indian writer" (276–77). The elder Navajo poet Luci Tapahonso responds to the lonely American:

"I also think that this loneliness, this clamoring for some sort of security, leads a lot of people to become 'Wannabes,' who suddenly decide that this is it, that they're going to be Indian and that sort of thing. That's always struck me as funny, but then it's sad in a way. I don't know, I can't imagine what it would be like to be in that position. To me, I think it would be like Hell, to be without family, to not know where you came from, not know who your relatives are, and to not be able to have a place and say, 'This is, now this is who I am or this is where I came from'" (277).

Tales to Sing

Canto y cuento es la poesia.	Poetry is song and telling.
Se canta una viva historia,	A live story sung
contando su melodia.	its melody told.

—Antonio Machado,
De mi cartera

WALKED SINGING AND TOLD OLD STORIES

"Earth and I gave you turquoise," Momaday chants syllabically to a beloved, "when you walked singing." Rooted in tribal context with people and place, mimesis and metaphor bracket this study. Most often the mimetic language of prose can be taken for what it *says it is*, or at least tries to say: the storyteller has a point to make. "We live laughing in my house / and told old stories." So, too, the poet has a tale to sing. The metaphoric language of poetry tries to be concrete and explicit, but it doesn't hit the head on the nail, as John Berryman decenters the poet's "thinky death" in *The Dream Songs*. While prose masters try to nail their targets, poets may feel more, know less about less, and speak in tongues—groping their way across a broken plain of silence like a blind man tapping hardpan with a stick.

Novelists know what they want from a character or scene, or at least they know to *listen for* hints that will clue the reader into what's going on by the end. Poets don't edit or e-mail action. They go searching by instinct, by timing and training, by a kind of seventh sense that precedes thought and word (a bladeless knife without a handle, Jean Arp says). In Bruchac's interview, the Acoma poet Simon Ortiz speaks of

absorbing culture orally: "Listening to people, to wind, whatever is murmuring, has been an important part of how I perceive and how I learn"
(214). Beyond the immediate catalyst, poetry anticipates the heart's
deed before it's done, and just after, a kind of attentive nimbus around
things—instinctual intention and intimate innuendo. This feel for poetic
things hovers near the lover's touch—to say all without having to say too
much, or much at all. "At once, accordingly you knew," Momaday writes
of giving a small brown stone to the blind painter Georgia O'Keeffe, "As
you knew the forms of the earth at Abiquiu."

Not so much lover as conspirator, the novelist can work the crowd
like a carny barker—fishing for the price of admission, staging the sword
swallower, the (almost) naked lady, the fat woman singing, the bearded
dwarf, the fire eater and two-headed calf. It's a show, folks. Not so for
the poet, who goes on guts, heart, and soul—countertenor, not preacher.
Petroglypher, not megaphonist. Psalmist, not prophet. The prose narrator
reaches across the space between reader and writer; the poet reaches into
reality through metaphor. King David, not Ezekiel. Queen Sheba, not
Sarah. Son Isaac ("she laughs"), not father executioner.

Verse builds to pitch before the clarifying curtain rises, then carries
over when the scrim of certainty falls. The listener does not know which to
prefer, Stevens ponders, "The blackbird whistling / Or just after." Lyric is
pre- and postcoital, anticipatory and after-pensive. "I always see the world
from a corner," Paula Gunn Allen, the Laguna poet-novelist, admits—
"from a slant, so to speak" (Bruchac, *Survival This Way* 16). And slant
light does not allow the reader to ignore or to forget; as Dickinson says,
"Success in Circuit lies."

Poetry can only be *about* anything, Heather McHugh claims of her
trade, the way a cat is about the house—not the thing, but tonally the
space it stalks (*Broken English*). Simon Ortiz puts liminal presence in a
Pueblo perspective: "Poetry is a way of reaching out to what is reaching
for you. Poetry is that space in between what one may express and where
it is received. Where there is another energy coming toward you—it's that
space in between" (Bruchac, *Survival This Way* 223). Prose addresses the
moving stage, back- and front-lighted, propped, costumed, cue-marked
in action. The opening gun on the wall, Chekhov says, fires by the story's end. In poetry a turf shovel becomes a writer's squat pen, "snug as a
gun" in a writer's hand—Seamus Heaney digs into his homeland Troubles
with it ("Digging," *Death of a Naturalist*). Think narrative overvoice
and lyric undervoice. Some *things* to hear and hold through what's being
said, something whispered within what's being sung in the shadows.

"I heard songs when the cactus wren sipped nectar from the tongue of a cricket," Sherwin Bitsui shapeshifts in Navajo arroyos ("The Noose in My Dream," *Shapeshift*). Poetry draws on a (private) language that draws into itself. "We can find no scar," Dickinson rhymes, "But internal difference, / Where the Meanings, are—" (#258). Prose samples a conversation stepping through its medium to ask, What do you think *about* that?

DEEP SOUND OF SENSE

> Even when we read a poem silently, we tend to read
> it differently from prose, paying more attention to
> its rhythm and pitch and pace, its interplay of vowels
> and consonants, its line-by-line progression of subtle
> harmonies and discords corresponding with variable
> states of feeling or the flow of the mind itself.
>
> —Stanley Kunitz, *Next-to-Last Things*

Poetry is rhythmic, prose runs on, and sometimes the differences fuse. Lyric and narrative can differentiate modes, or they can cross into each other and blend, especially in the poetry and prose continuums of Momaday, Welch, Silko, and Erdrich. "I continue working in syllabics," Momaday says. "I have written what is called 'free verse,' though to my mind that is a contradiction in terms. I'm greatly interested in the so-called 'prose poem,' another contradiction in terms, but what I mean is, I like writing what is essentially a lyrical prose in which I'm not concerned with meter, but with rhythms and fluencies of sound, primarily" (Bruchac, *Survival This Way* 178). Woven into Native or Red English as spoken lyric is the notion that binary rhythms cadence a shared language—iambic and reverse iambic, that is, trochaic feet. Mallarmé said there was the alphabet and iambic measure, nothing in between. Cross-cultural magic cants through the rhythms. "The Anglo-Saxon who uttered spells over his fields," Momaday posits to Bruchac, "so that the seeds would come out of the ground on the sheer strength of his voice, knew a good deal about language. That man's faith—and may I say, wisdom—has been lost upon modern man, by and large. It survives in the poets of the world, I suppose, the singers" (183). Prayer and chant survive the oldest extant poetics.

"Also, we don't have to do anything special," Linda Hogan assures Joe Bruchac, "to have contact with the spirit world. It's just natural if you stop and listen. Just there, always. Like your own heartbeat" (132). Regardless of ethnic bias or linguistic bent, heart-beating humans are bipedal beings, that is, two-footed. Humans tend to favor one foot (or accent) over another. This binary paradigm is surely different, no doubt, with a horse or spider, fish or snake, but the rhythmic human heart goes tha-*rump*, tha-*rump*. When agitated, it reverses the rhythm: *tha*-rump, *tha*-rump. In arrhythmic conditions the heart syncopates its beat—tha-*di*-rump, or wilder variations, tha-di-*rump*-ty. Radically irregular rhythms don't bode well for the human heart in the long run.

So humans are bipedal, Natives and newcomers, and the poetic feet of a shared English language tend to be binary—clusters of unaccented and accented feet that gather in dyadic coveys, anapestically tha-di-*rump*, or dactylically *tha*-di-rump. The retired poet laureate Robert Hass argues, "We are pattern-discerning animals, for whatever reason in our evolutionary history. We attend to a rhythm almost instinctively, listen to it for a while, and, if we decide it has no special significance for us, we can let it go; or put it away, not hearing it again unless it alters, signaling to us—as it would to a hunting or a grazing animal—that something in the environment is changed. . . . It is the first stage, wakeful, animal, alert, of the experience of rhythm. And it is the place to which we are called by the first words of any poem or story. *Once upon a time; how many dawns chill from his rippling rest; it is a law universally acknowledged . . . , fishbones walked the waves of Hatteras*: it calls us to an intense, attentive consciousness" (*Twentieth Century Pleasures* 112–13).

Heartbeat, breath, vision, hearing, walking, holding and handling, nasal intake and oral outrush all exhibit binary balancings, Native a-rightings. Add a caveat in translateral mind-body torque; that is, right-brain hemisphere cross-ties diagonally to left body, left hemisphere diagonally to right. Trickster's skitter-step cannot be left out of the slant equation. "To be assisted of Reverse," Emily Dickinson says, "One must Reverse have bore—" (#799). It is no small matter that Momaday has long promised a study of Dickinson, that Joy Harjo switched from painting to poetry after reading the closeted singer-poet, that Mary TallMountain named her cat Emily Dickinson, that Linda Hogan and Louise Erdrich list the New England bard as a primary influence, that Lucy Tapahonso expresses her debt, and that Sherman Alexie parodies Emily Dickinson in a cross-cultural sign of respect.

Rhythmic cadence is all. Song-poetry accents the *im* in the pulse, the *oom* of the phapha. The Makah chanted their ongoing culture, translated trochaically, *Mine is a proud village, such as it is, / We are at our best* when *dancing* (Frances Densmore, "Nootka and Quileute Music," in Bierhorst, *In the Trail of the Wind* 45). Current as a daily newspaper, tribal song ranks next to hunting as the distinguishing trait of Arctic culture. The Inuit dance house anchors village life, Margot Astrov writes in *The Winged Serpent*. Tribal lyrics migrate around Native America, as the Navajo moved from western Canada to the Southwest. "There's a song for everything," Navajo poet Luci Tapahonso tells Joe Bruchac down west. "There are songs for nothing and there are songs for anything. I think it's just natural that it would work itself into the poetry because the poetry, too, is a song—in the sense that it stirs one's mind or that it creates a dance within a person's imagination. It creates movement, so that song is movement not only physical, but spiritually, emotionally. Good poetry is that, is motion and relates to the whole thing of dance and prayer because they are all one motion. They are all together. There is no separation." (279–80). The Arizona Papago Maria Chona told Ruth Underhill seventy years ago in *Singing for Power* (46):

> It was good at cactus camp. When my father lay down to sleep at night he would sing a song about the cactus liquor. And we could hear songs in my uncle's camp across the hill. Everybody sang. We felt as if a beautiful thing was coming. Because the rain was coming and the dancing and the songs.
>
> > *Where on Quijota Mountain a cloud stands*
> > *There my heart stands with it.*
> > *Where the mountain trembles with the thunder*
> > *My heart trembles with it.*
>
> That was what they sang. When I sing that song yet it makes me dance.

Dancing is to poetry, Paul Valéry posits, as walking is to prose ("Poetry and Abstract Thought," in *The Art of Poetry* 70). And the traditional Native dancing instruments—drum, rattle, and flute—have taken on strings today. Pha-pha-pha, goes the insistent heartbeat of life, and the drumbeat oscillates like breath, oom-pha oom-pha. The syllabic heartbeat may be more often breathlike, an iambic cadence, slack-stress, slack-stress—which in turn follows a rising syntax, an iambic pattern at the heart of Anglo-Saxon English. "These figures moving in my rhyme," N. Scott Momaday meters a tetrameter couplet in Kiowa-English time. "Who are they? Death and Death's dog, Time." When breath speeds up the heartbeat, body in motion, a trochaic heave pushes against the iambic cadence. Here the patterned beat slides, reverses measure—<u>oom</u>-pha, <u>oom</u>-<u>pha</u>, <u>stress</u>-slack, <u>stress</u>-<u>stress</u>—as musical note leans into spondaic accent. Patterns bend and invert, torquing metrics. While the tempo fires up, the foot begins to tap out a *rhythmus* or "flow," Greek root for rhythm and rhyme: oom-pha-<u>pha</u>, oom-pha-<u>pha</u>, slack-slack-<u>stress</u>. This anapestic stride picks up the beat, generating the power to lift a body off the ground. A fleet-throated flute carries the melody into the air—lyric birdsong riding across metric torque like wings over an undulating meadow. James Welch writes "In My Lifetime": "I <u>run</u> these <u>woman</u> <u>hills</u>, <u>trans</u>late <u>wind</u> / to <u>mean</u> a <u>kind</u> of <u>life</u>, the <u>children</u> of <u>Speakthunder</u> / are <u>never</u> <u>wrong</u> and <u>I</u> am <u>rhy</u>thm to <u>strong</u> <u>medicine</u>" (*Riding the Earthboy 40*, 23).

As the shift, feint, and slide of the dance go full out, laterally moving downfield with the gracile power of a broken field runner, a dactylic stutter step takes over: <u>oom</u>-pha-pha, <u>oom</u>-pha-pha, <u>stress</u>-slack-slack. As in Frost's "abrupted" lines, sense plays off sound in Welch's "Surviving," the plucked notes bending, counterpoint shadowing point. "That <u>night</u> the <u>moon</u> <u>slipped</u> a <u>notch</u>, <u>hung</u> / <u>black</u> for <u>just</u> a <u>second</u>, just <u>long</u> <u>enough</u> / for <u>wet</u> <u>black</u> <u>things</u> to <u>sneak</u> <u>away</u> our <u>cache</u> / of <u>meat</u>. To <u>stay</u> a<u>live</u> this <u>way</u>, it's <u>hard</u>. . . ." Form must give as it goes, release as it girders the line. Frost says of metric ballast and fugal argument, "We enjoy the straight crookedness of a good walking stick" ("The Figure a Poem Makes," in *Complete Poems* vii). And the impulse to sing is accent to witness, as the urge to talk hankers to tell. "It's very difficult for me to separate song and legend and myth," Harold Littlebird says to Bruchac. "History, Pueblo history, has been passed on orally . . . and lots of them have to do with song, chant, and sound. The way you express different cloud formations, for example; when you listen to that word being said, it has its own sort of song with it, just by the way you would say it and by the way you pronounce it. . . . Even your own personal name that someone gives to you, your Indian name, it has a certain sound. It sounds like a song" (160).

Spoken measure plays against metric scansion, whether in Dickinson's ballad meter or Momaday's syllabic verse. Translateral cross-play helps to illustrate the counter-rhythmic argument for syncopated metric feet— what Frost called the "sound of sense" crooked across the regularities of meter (*Complete Poems* v–viii). "One <u>had</u> to be <u>versed</u> in <u>country</u> <u>things</u>" reverses metrically, "<u>Not</u> to be<u>lieve</u> the <u>phoebes</u> <u>wept</u>." In the terrible lyric "Desert Places," expected iamb is reversed in trochaic *heave*, Pound said of modernist poetics ("<u>cannot</u> <u>scare</u> me"); slack syllable compounds an anapest ("with my <u>own</u>"), or the trisyllabic foot turns over on itself in a dactyl ("<u>stars</u> where no"); spondaic arrest or pyrrhic slack suspends movement ("Be<u>tween</u> <u>stars</u>—<u>on</u> <u>stars</u> where <u>no</u>"); and other minor variations tweak the binary metric pattern that Frost plays like an open-tuned dulcimer: "They <u>cannot</u> <u>scare</u> me <u>with</u> their <u>empty</u> <u>spaces</u> / Be<u>tween</u> <u>stars</u>—<u>on</u> <u>stars</u> where <u>no</u> <u>human</u> <u>race</u> is. / I <u>have</u> it <u>in</u> <u>me</u> <u>so</u> much <u>nearer</u> <u>home</u> / To <u>scare</u> my<u>self</u> with my <u>own</u> <u>desert</u> <u>places</u>." Point and counterpoint—Robert Hass thinks that pattern and rupture thicken strong verse rhythms. "Repetition makes us feel secure and variation makes us feel free" (*Twentieth-Century Pleasures* 115). Ezra Pound in *ABC of Reading* says all art boils down to pattern and variance, no less than Pueblo dance step or Lakota chant. Every American *native* poet has heard these rhythms and counter-rhythms in the heartbeat of the cultural landscape, the downbeat of ceremonial dance and tribal song.

Inquiring apprenticeship and instinctual genius begin at essential rhythmic levels. No master creates without mastering the basics; no novice starts with fine-tuned mastery. Carter Revard, the Osage poet and medievalist scholar, feels that a loping Oklahoma inflection grounds his voice, Native distinctly through Sooner: "Well, it's for me the rhythms and sounds of Osage County people, Indian and others. . . . It was talk about things that mattered, that were part of their own lives; just the way people actually sounded when they were talking about things that mattered to them there" (Bruchac, *Survival This Way* 242). Consider prescript and practice, the rules of the game and playing an original tune, whether American talk or Native song. "The stories have gone out of a lot of poems," Revard worries with Bruchac, "along with the rhymes and the song, the tears and laughter, but this is less true in every case with those we call minority writers. There's a live force and strength there. You can hear in the poetry of American Indian writers a genuine felt concern for what is going on. . . . The stories have got to come back, the sound stuff, the rhyme, all of that, more of it and better" (248). What premises this lyric narrative imperative in Native worldviews? "The whole worldview of the Indian is predicated upon the principle of harmony in the universe," Momaday believes (180). Pattern and variation, "a fixed element and a variable," Pound reminds readers of balancing forms in *ABC of Reading* (201). *Hozhó*, the Navajo insist, balances goodness and beauty, ethics and aesthetics in the holy four winds. "The Navajo phrase sa' qh naagháí bik'eh hózhó, while its meaning has been subjected to diverse interpretation," James Kale McNeley writes of *Holy Wind in Navajo Philosophy*, "is thought to symbolize the idea or goal of beauty, harmony, order and well-being" (citing Haile 1930; Reichard 1970; and Witherspoon 1977, 57).

Speaking Forms

> The word must have been in the beginning a magic
> symbol, which the usury of time wore out. The mission
> of the poet should be to restore to the word, at least in
> a partial way, its primitive and now secret force. All
> verse should have two obligations: to communicate
> a precise instance and to touch us physically, as the
> presence of the sea does.
>
> —Jorge Luis Borges, *La Rosa Profunda*

Design crosses cultures, a fusional critic argues, and literacy translates orally. "The poem's form is the sound it makes when spoken," H. S. McAllister offers of tribal translations in either direction ("The Language of Shamans" 299). Factor in base-line metrics and rhythmic irrationals, American lyrics and Native through-lines. Add a grounding caveat: as in sculpture, symphony, or dance, audiences appreciate artistic forms trans-culturally. "Rhythm is a form cut into TIME," Pound argues of pan-global aesthetics, "as a design is determined SPACE," music and story to sculpture and ballistics (*ABC of Reading* 198). Temporal choreography, cultural architecture: consider the American Indian Dance Troupe as flesh-and-blood poetry in motion, or Allan Houser's animate sculpture as projected tribal culture—Apache ceremonial singer, mother and child, stone dancer and drummer. And the limits of workshop talk? In art some things are known, some imagined, a few at hand and others beckoning just out of reach. Ray Young Bear, the Mesquakie poet and novelist, brings the argument around personally: "But I sort of tie in dreams, some of my own imagery and my thoughts and, on rare occasions, something I heard which my Grandmother said—how we are connected to the past. Once in a great while, whether I am socializing in a university or an Indian tavern with my friends, I sometimes find out that some of my friends are great bearers of poetic images, even though they don't realize it. So I listen with keen interest and, in a sense, I can see that everyone in an Indian community is a poet of sorts" (Bruchac, *Survival This Way* 343).

Natives traditionally voice their verse-making through song and dance. Writers diverse as the political Lakota pundit Vine Deloria Jr., the Navajo poet Luci Tapahonso, and the Spokane media maverick Sherman Alexie title millennial works *Singing for a Spirit: A Portrait of the Dakota Sioux*; *Sáanii Dahataal/The Women Are Singing*; and *One Stick Song*. Simon Ortiz tells Joe Bruchac, "I was talking about song as poetry, song as motion and emotion. Song as the way in which I can feel those rhythms and melodies and how those things give me energy. . . . song is poetry and poetry is the way in which those images become possible. . . . poetry is the way in which we make the connection between all things" (223). Musical note connects to lyric foot. Particle moves through passage in writing, syllabic sound units tonalize speech (forty English phonemes), syntax *flows* through speaking (the meaning of Greek *rhythmus*, as cited, generating metric rhythm and echoic rhyme). "I think with Roethke it was to pay attention to the ear, to hear the song aloud," the Klallam poet Duane Niatum remembers of his training at the University of Washington. "The poem aloud, the poem leaving the page becoming a spirit outside, a song in the air" (207).

Via Roethke's Seattle workshop, this study circles back to Simon Ortiz's reflections on his father singing about an Acoma man dancing: "the song was the road from outside himself to inside—which is perception—and from inside himself to outside—which is expression" ("Song, Poetry, and Language" 118). Bridging into modern lyric, W. C. Williams distinguished American speech from British by considering *pace*. Idiomatic measures of particle-and-pause balance comma to caesura, hyphen or colon to arrested line enjambment in poetry. The ear is tuned for syllabic *pit-pat* in motion and what Frost dubbed "abruption" twisting within the given line. Attending to matters of voice, W. H. Auden listened for *pitch*, and Ezra Pound heard *periodicity*: tone, tare, heft, and texture against shifting patterns of inflection and innuendo, syntactic pitter-patter. Discussing stress, duration, and pitch, Stephen Dobyns writes in "Aspects of the Syllable": "The three primary intonational features form the basis for three different metrical systems throughout the world. The Germanic languages use a prosody based on stress system, the Romance languages use a prosody based on duration, as does Arabic poetry, while two thousand of the world's four thousand languages, many of them Asian, use a system based on pitch" (*The Writer's Chronicle* 59).

Pound sculpted the lucid natural object in Imagism, precise naming and musical phrasing, running tensile sense. "I listen carefully, but I listen for more than just the sound," Simon Ortiz recalls, "listen for more than just the words and phrases, for more than the various parts of the song. I try to perceive the context, meaning, purpose—all these items not in their separate parts but as a whole—and I think it comes completely like that" ("Song, Poetry, and Language" 115). Lyric tonalizes narrative when the musical image sets characters in motion. Particles flow in pattern, syllables move toward syntactic meaning.

Walk and Dance

> . . . the word *hymn* is of eastern derivation and the
> Greek word *hymnos* relates to the word for *woven*
> or *spun.* . . . [Charles] Boer says: "in its primal sense,
> a hymn was thought of as what results when you
> intertwine speech with rhythm and song. And it is in
> this sense precisely that the word 'hymn' appears in its
> oldest recorded usage, in the *Odyssey* (VIII, 429) when
> Alcinoos invites Odysseus to 'enjoy dinner and listen
> to the spinning of a yarn'" (*oides hymnon*).
>
> —Michael Schmidt, *The First Poets*

Poetry leaps and illuminates the world along a woven vertical path (see Lincoln, *Sing with the Heart of a Bear*). Prose characterizes and travels the world along a horizontal track or way. For a Native writer, as noted in Ortiz, Tapahonso, and Welch, lyric and narrative details lay the ground where people come from. Carter Revard recalls, "Where I come from, in fact, is the cross-timbers and Flint Hills country. I grew up in a valley with hills and trees all around, but the valley itself is mostly bluestem meadow. Out to the west is the great prairie, and over to the east past Bartlesville is prairie and plains again. I was in hilly, rolly country something like the Ozarks with shallower hills. It's also a country of slow streams and muddy stream not the spring-fed streams of eastern Oklahoma. Winding, slow bottom land. A land of sandstone hills and limestone prairie, and black-jack oak and hickory, redbud, dogwood" (Bruchac, *Survival This Way* 244). A poetry of local names speaks itself in cultural landscape—hilled "stone" of sand, prairie "lime" in stone, spondaic *"blackjack oak"* and dactylic *"hick*ory," reddened "bud," or canine "wood."

As Paul Valéry suggests, poetry dances, prose walks. Richard Howard spins the difference in *Alone with America*: "prose proceeds, verse reverses." Of course, these are binary constructs. There's no better way, I suppose, to think about such things cross-generically or intercul-turally. George Bent hears a Southern Cheyenne on a war horse challenge cholera in 1849: "If I could see this thing, if I knew where it was, I would go there and kill it" (George Hyde, "Life of George Bent," in Nabokov, *Native American Testimony* 89). The Papago Owl Woman sang when her best friend died in the 1930s, "In the great night my heart will go out. / Toward me the darkness comes rattling. / In the great night my heart will go out" (Frances Densmore, "Papago Music," in Margot

Astrov, *The Winged Serpent* 196). Red Jacket, the Seneca, questions missionaries in 1805: "Brother, you say there is but one way to worship and serve the Great Spirit; if there is but one religion, why do you white people differ so much about it?" (B. B. Thatcher, "Indian Biography," in *Native American Testimony* 58). The Plains commander Sitting Bull chanted his death song in 1890: "So I have been a warrior / And now the war is over so / I know to bear against hard times" (Frances Densmore, *Teton Sioux Music*, translation in Lincoln, *Sing with the Heart of a Bear* 37). And Chief Joseph the Nez Percé leader told General Miles in 1877, "Hear me, my chiefs, I am tired. My heart is sad and sick. From where the sun now stands I will fight no more forever" (1877–78, 45th U.S. Congressional document, in Nabokov, *Native American Testimony* 181). Words in translation still eloquent, memorable, truthful—the lyrics rise and fall on voices dissolving into their own rhythms. The narratives state who and what terms direct the speakings.

Song-poetry may be more like Sun Dance circle, compared with talk-story around a night campfire: kiva and council house, prayer and potlatch, naming ceremony and gambling game, making "powwow" medicine and talking-stick circle, corn meal and horno bread. These eidetic binaries pair in the spirit of playful gaming, as with Navajo *correspondences* echoing the folk idiom of Apache *wise words* distinguishing elder speakers. Jerome Rothenberg translates the Diné image sequences in *Shaking the Pumpkin* (309–11): *arrow / Wind / Cicada / arrow-crossing / life*. Or lingually, *Big Fly / feather / Wind / skin at tip of tongue / speech*. Cultures are seasoned with temporality: *Old Age / ax / Frog*. Confucius gave an editing ideograph, "renew the people," translated by Pound in the *Analects* (46): *ax / grinding stone / woodpile*. This kind of imagist thinking runs deep, "older than men can ever be—old like hills, like stars," Black Elk says, ancient as thought can be (*BES* 20).

Still in the spirit of cross-cultural imagining are Federico García Lorca's ideas on "deep song." The *duenda*, or dance spirit of the house, overtakes flamenco when singer, dancer, drummer, and guitarist are no longer playing, but are played by the musical genius of song, place, audience, and time (*In Search of the Duende* 49). Tracking the sundown migration of gypsies westward from India to Spain over millennia, García Lorca says that "Deep song is akin to the trilling of birds, the crowing of the rooster, and the natural music of forest and fountain. It is a very rare specimen of primitive song, the oldest in all Europe, and its notes carry the naked, spine-tingling emotion of the first Oriental races" (*ISD* 3). Emanating from the first sob and first kiss with "tears of narcissus and ice," deep song cries as it heals (*ISD* 57). Smashing all form and style, it burns viscera, wounds throat, and draws "blood like a poultice of broken glass" (*ISD* 51). A nightingale without eyes, the *duenda* sings blindly through the night. "Fortunately for the virgin Poetry and for all poets, there are still sailors who sing at sea, women who rock their children to sleep in the shade of grapevines, and rustic shepherds on mountain paths" (*ISD* 18). And there are still four-and-a-half million Native peoples chanting in the United States, hundreds of tribes singing ceremonially at births and deaths and healings, at prayer meetings and tribal gatherings, at Sun Dance and Beautyway honorings, at campfire and kiva sings: *Beauty all around us.*

The Chilean poet Pablo Neruda thinks about lyric less sacramentally, scratching for an "impure poetry" of common things and objects at rest—wheels, bags, barrels, baskets, handles, footprints and fingerprints, "worn as if by acid through the duty of our hands, steeped in sweat and in smoke, smelling of lilies and urine, spattered by the professions that we live by, inside or beyond the law." In Madrid, 1935, Neruda advances an elemental song-poetry, "impure as a suit, a body with soup-stains and shameful attitudes, with wrinkles, observations, dreams, vigils, prophecies, declarations of love and of hatred, beasts, convulsions, idylls, political beliefs, denials, doubts, affirmations, taxes" ("Towards an Impure Poetry" from *Caballo verde para la poesía* 1). Just so, Native poets talk-sing of treaties, vision quests, ritual clowns, powwows, Christian peyote meetings, tricksters, shamans, spiritual guardians, and one-eyed '49 Fords.

American modernists backlight the spoken and sung arts as narrative and lyric. Like "a piece of ice on a hot stove," Frost says, poetry rides on its own melting, its own fluidity ("The Figure a Poem Makes," in *Complete Poems* viii). Erdrich and Momaday rhythmically listen in. Frost's talk-song melts to the reader's touch, just as Welch's iambics amble across a Montana prairie. "His bones go back / so scarred in time, the buttes are young to look / for signs that say a man could love his fate, / that winter in the blood is one sad thing" ("In My Lifetime"). Wallace Stevens saw poetry as a pheasant disappearing into the brush of "green green's apogee"—iridescent, risible, iris-ring-necked—no less than Metis voices ghost Erdrich's jacklighted Dakotas verse: "Home's the place we head for in our sleep" ("Indian Boarding School: The Runaways"). Williams viewed his craft as "penetrant" and directly pleasurable—true to the world, word for word—unparaphrasable, as Auden said, no more or less than itself, and so it is with Joy Harjo's blues lyrics in "Alive": "I am free to be sung to; / I am free to sing. This woman / can cross any line." Pound saw the natural object as its own metaphoric cosine—correlative to itself, Eliot thought: the thing itself, selved through Hopkins's *inscape*, quick-lit, quick-witted, quick-silvered, quick-claimed, quick-wicked. Momaday's formalist and free verse draws on all these modernist tenets, as in the prose poem "The Colors of the Night" (*In the Presence of the Sun* 30):

> There was a woman whose hair was long and heavy and black and beautiful. She drew it about her like a shawl and so divided herself from the world that not even Age could find her. Now and then she steals into the men's societies and fits her voice into their holiest songs. And always, just there, is a shadow which the firelight cannot cleave.

Native Exercises

We are talking shop with singers of holy winds here: writerly issues of temperament and genre, tempo and instinct, talent and aesthetic. Rather than prove any theory or mire in a footnote, allow the imagination to play as Rothenberg shows the Navajo generate correspondences: *smoke / cloud / rain / acceptance / breathing in* (*Shaking the Pumpkin* 311). These are not so much impressions as *observations*, as Marianne Moore referred to her verse experiments between natural science and cultural studies. Stretch some literary muscles between bicultural high bars to loosen the academic safety net. If poetry is a nightingale, a meadowlark, a thunderbird, or a pheasant receding in the brush, imagine the winged possibilities, rather than carving up the bird.

We could say that prose appears, while poetry disappears.

"And silence is the long approach of noon
Upon the shadow that your name defines—"
(N. Scott Momaday).

Poetry takes away, as prose tacks on.

"I drank a long sucking bellyful of water from the tap"
(James Welch).

Prose multiplies, as poetry divides.

"She had horses who licked razor blades" (Joy Harjo).

Poetry decenters, prose centers.

"You have to know me to know what I'm talking about"
(Mabel McKay).

Prose adds, poetry subtracts.

> "When you have ten names for snow,
> what is the temperature of each vowel in photosynthesis?"
> (Sherwin Bitsui).

Poetry veils, prose unveils.

> "I could see that the old people were right when they
> insisted that Jesus Christ might do for modern whites
> in a good climate, but that the Hopi gods had brought
> success to us in the desert ever since the world began"
> (Don Talayesva, Hopi Sun Chief).

Prose swells, poetry shrinks.

> "The song is very short because we understand so much"
> (Maria Chona, Papago).

Poetry conceals, prose reveals.

> "A good road led on. So there was nothing to do but cross the
> water, and bring her home" (Louise Erdrich).

Prose as engraved Confucian stone, poetry a Heraclitean streamflowing.

> "I remember the sound of her glad weeping and the water-like
> touch of her hand" (N. Scott Momaday).

Poetry as a (double) rainbow, Noah to Beautyway. Confucius saw prose in carved wood grain.

> "That is what I love most in your writing, Jim, the gully and
> railroad track, the sumac and coal smoke—all could only
> be from the place you give us or that gives you to us, that
> Ohio country" (Leslie Silko to James Wright).

Silk sheet and hangman's rope, eclipse and solstice.

> "*whiskey salmon absence*" (Sherman Alexie).

Bow and rifle, verb and noun.

> "If I spoke / all the birds would gather / in one breath /
> in the ridge of my throat" (Linda Hogan).

INTERTRIBAL MODELS

In summary, allow for the literary measures of this Nativist study. Mikhail Bakhtin places the centripetal dialogic of intertextual fiction against the centrifugal monologue of self-referential poetry—social talk and soliloquy, heteroglossic field of speaking discourse against hegemonic choir loft (Todorov, *Mikhail Bakhtin* 65). Communal pageant and private prayer, the former addressed directly to an audience, the latter overheard. Bakhtin praised "primitive" carnival in its socializing admixtures of culture, religion, and society. A century before Bakhtin and welcoming prose fiction, Frederick Schlegel's 1800 *Literary Notebooks* argued the diversity of poetic brilliance profusely scattered through village culture—specifically the naturally mixed layers of unaffected verse forms, folktale and folksong, town gossip and hymnal, that made up the new genre of the romanza or novel. Socratic dialogist of the emerging bourgeoisie, Schlegel argued that the crossbred novel was "a poem of poems, a whole texture of poems" (Todorov, *Mikhail Bakhtin* 86). Clearly, lyric crosses into narrative across all cultures.

By 1913 in "A Station of the Metro," Ezra Pound was crystallizing Homeric hexameter, the talk-song meters of Greek musical feet, into Imagist English haiku:

The apparition of these faces in the crowd;
Petals on a wet, black bough.

The sweeping iambic cadences of the six-footed line scan in three musical phrases, *The apparition—of these faces—in the crowd*. The enjambed semicolon tilts to a reverse trochaic foot, *Petals*, ever so softly *on*, as the plosive triple spondee caps the line in deep Orphic image, *wet, black bough*. Crowd and bough suspend the couplet indefinitely as a ghostly off-rhyme through the semicolon, while the focal image of *Petals* springs from the fecund dark *bough* on which the prewar *faces* bloom. The couplet chants shamanic metamorphosis no less than W. B. Yeats's 1890 Innisfree vision, "I hear it in the deep heart's core," as Sitting Bull died singing the meadowlark's cadence. These are meters and motions, images and issues keenly remembered and worth modeling classically, more individually slanted and voiced as Native writers today make tribal use of Red English *rhythmus*.

Classic cadences reemerge in the works of tribal writers. N. Scott Momaday, no stranger to lyric metrics or modernist imaging, adapts the Homeric hexameter at the end of *The Way to Rainy Mountain*: "East of my grandmother's house the sun rises out of the plain" (*WRM* 83). This walking cadence meters much of the Kiowa writer's prose, giving it a plains stride and natural prairie cadence. In *Winter in the Blood*, James Welch elegizes a son discovering his father's frozen body in the shock-drainage of a highway ditch: "Was it a shoe sticking up, or a hand, / or just a blue-white lump in the endless skittering whiteness?" (*WIB* 19). The prose line, here lineated, reverses Pound's 6/4 metric enjambment and thrusts the trochaic spondees "<u>shoe</u> <u>stick</u>ing" and "<u>blue-white</u> <u>lump</u>" against the iambic urge to gentle the feet, only to fall away with the ghostly, questioning trochees and dactyls, "<u>end</u>less <u>skit</u>tering <u>white</u>ness?" This Blackfoot lyric novelist draws poetic measure through postmodern narrative, the grainy realism of postwar homecomings that land-mine the twentieth century. Finally, Louise Erdrich clusters syllables in metric cadences that recall a Homeric talk-singing line, Renaissance burst of blank verse, torqued inversions of modernism, and tribal aftershock— through a Native American rebirth of oral literacy. In lyric prose, *Love Medicine* cadences June Kashpaw's mythic walk through her own death into the dancing stars and aurora borealis of the northern lights: "The <u>snow</u> fell <u>deep</u>er that <u>East</u>er than it <u>had</u> in <u>for</u>ty <u>years</u>, / but <u>June</u> <u>walked</u> <u>over</u> it like <u>wat</u>er and <u>came</u> <u>home</u>" (*LM* 6). The lines echo the 6/4 metrics and reverse feet of Pound's 1913 Metro vision, but talk-story with Native American lyric narratives into the next century.

Translation, as Borges defines poetic *re-creation* in all languages, proves historical transition—tradition evolving through new tongues and literary forms. Natives *speak like singing* in their writings: "you walked singing," Momaday chants through turquoise syllables, "We lived laughing in my house, / and told old stories" ("Earth and I Gave You Turquoise"). Cultural fusion accents the call, making the most of diverse American resources, Native through émigré. These stories and songs are embedded in the ancestral stones of America.

Speech Like Song

Because it's that beat, that pulse. Everything is. Even in the drums back home, it is all heartbeat, just pulse that's going through everything. Everyone is singing and dancing.

—Diane Burns, Anishinabe/Chemehuevi

OTHER THAN HUMAN WORDS

Genres cross time, place, tongue, and discipline. Poetry, the most elusive of arts, stirs the impulse to sing—"a kind of twilight feeling before the moon is seen," Dickinson writes in an early letter to Jane Humphrey. "It was in song that I first found poetry, or it found me, alone at the breaking of dawn under the huge elm sheltering my childhood house," Joy Harjo says in *Ploughshares* (Winter 2004–2005). It is *about* to snow, before and after Stevens looks thirteen ways at a blackbird. The crowing of crows breaks the still space of Momaday's winter composition. And human song, as far back as the Orphic Odes, perhaps the first lyric verse recorded by Westerners, draws on birdsong—not so much the voweled notes, as the spaces between. With bears, insects, canids, whales, porpoises, birds, apes, and humans, *talk singing* crosses species. Indeed, biochemists have located the genes, called "transcription factors" FoxP1 and FoxP2, shared by humans and songbirds that allow people to speak and birds to sing (*The Journal of Neuroscience*, 31 March 2004). In *The Language of the Birds* the folklorist David Guss notes interspecies *talk-song* between animals and tribally based *homo sapiens* (the "third" chimpanzee, as the bio-anthropologist Jared Diamond notes our

98.6 percent ape-gene-compatible DNA). Guss quotes Mircea Eliade on shamanic "animal" or "secret" language:

> All over the world learning the language of animals, especially of birds, is equivalent to knowing the secrets of nature and hence to being able to prophesy. Bird language is usually learned by eating snake or some other reputedly magical animal. These animals can reveal the secrets of the future because they are thought to be receptacles for the souls of the dead or epiphanies of the gods. Learning their language, imitating their voice, is equivalent to ability to communicate with the beyond and the heavens. We shall again come upon this same identification with an animal, especially a bird, when we discuss the shaman's costume and magical flight. Birds are psychopomps. Becoming a bird oneself or being accompanied by a bird indicates the capacity, while still alive, to undertake the ecstatic journey to the sky and the beyond. ("Shamanism, Archaic Techniques of Ecstasy," trans. Willard R. Trask, in *Language of the Birds* 77–78).

Ikicize waon kon he, Sitting Bull sang in the 1880s, *wana henala yelo* he / *iyotiye kiya waon*. Sitting Bull's eight-syllable tercet in G-flat minor echoes the falling thirds and fourth of a Western meadowlark's call, a bird the Lakota call a "Sioux singer" because it trebles such good Lakota. The melody has become the Flag Song of the "Sioux National Anthem" (see *Porcupine Singers: Traditional Lakota Songs*; and Kevin Locke, *Lakota Wiikijo Olowan*). As discussed in *Sing with the Heart of a Bear* (35–37), a working translation should be singable by way of Frances Densmore's ethnomusicological notes, 1914 at Standing Rock: "So I have been a warrior / and now the war is over so / I know to bear against hard times." Is it the songbird that ghosts hearing, or the silence just after? The resonance of the moment, or its echoic shadow? Pattern and pause, repetition and variation, singers know, scallop lyric lines.

Poetry is a means of searching, a quickened attention, and too often mistranslated Native tongues lie silenced. "Blessed / are those who listen," Linda Hogan writes of Chickasaw ancestors, "when no one is left to speak" ("Blessings"). This acoustic seeking stirs expectation, not so much any *thing*, or even about anything, more tone, tare, and tempo. In *Preoccupations*, Seamus Heaney calls his Irish muse an alertness, a hankering, a readiness. In this spirit of anticipation Erdrich's Anishinabe ancestors once sang, *As my eyes / search over the prairie / I feel the summer in the spring* (Frances Densmore, *Chippewa Music*). Not on the surface, but down under, poetry strikes the promise of news, the way birdsong wakes a listener to the moment. Bobwhites alert, owls warn. Crows tease, nightingales console. Lyric does not speak for the song, but in the singing, so listen to the performance. When the bird and the book disagree, Audubon said, trust the bird. And lyric poetry is only "about" things as a bird is about to fly.

Talk would tell all, tell it anciently well. The medicine man Leonard Crow Dog told Richard Erdoes on Grass Mountain at Rosebud, South Dakota, March 18, 1981: "This story has never been told. It is in no book or computer. It came to me in a dream during a vision quest. It is a story as old as the beginning of life, but it has new understandings according to what I saw in my vision, added to what the grandfathers told me—things remembered, things forgotten, and things re-remembered. It comes out of the World of the Minds" (*American Indian Myths and Legends* 129). Prose jogs the *run run* of narrative, Jorie Graham notes, babbling somewhere to go, a space-time continuum A-to-Z rivered with temporality. Poetry, on the other hand, has nowhere to go, nothing in particular to do that can be summarized or paraphrased or graphed in story line. Like the dance, poetry exists for itself unfolding through form, a pattern of witness in motion. *In the great night my heart will go out*, Owl Woman sang among the Papago, as quoted earlier. *Toward me the darkness comes rattling. / In the great night my heart will go out.* Strophe to antistrophe, self-willed courage to destined fate, the poet's voice goes to meet the rattling dark. Poetry breaks time, prose lives by and in time. *The water bug is drawing / the shadows of the evening / toward him on the water*, the Quechuan chant the encroaching night ("Frances Densmore and American Indian Music," in Brandon, *The Magic World* 96). The arcing voice, the smallest life will not be stilled. "The poet is a light and wingéd and holy thing," Plato says in the *Ion*. Poetry is leaping and luminous, poets chant, vertically ascendant and descendant, rising and plumbing the darkness and light. *Down west, / Down west we dance*, the California Wintu Harry Marsh sang with the sun setting over the Big Waters. *We spirits dance, / We spirits weeping dance* (Dorothy Demetracapoulou, "Wintu Songs" 493). Even grief may be cadenced with grace, tempo, and understanding.

Narrative *run run* moves as prose contours; lyric *row row* flows as poetic rhythm. *Run run* courses restlessly through tangled passages; *row row* rises-and-falls with pulsing cadences. Things come together narratively to answer the searching movement of the story; details scatter lyrically soaring and descending, breaking linguistic form in singing tongues. *Schwarze Milch der Frühe wir trinken dich nachts*, Paul Celan wrote his holocaustal "Death Fugue" or "*Todesfuge*": *wir trinken dich mittags und morgens wir trinken dich / abends*. "Black milk of dawn we drink you nights / we drink you noondays and mornings we drink you / sundowns" (*Paul Celan: Poems*, trans. Michael Hamburger 60–63). A Holocaust Jew writing in German haunts the struggle of what Joy Harjo and Gloria Bird see as Native Americans *Reinventing the Enemy's Language*. All great poetry shatters the self in performance—much of it dangerous, Plato thought, a terrorist threat to state norms. Poetic epiphany breaks through plot point and releases its scattering light; narrative plot gathers its momentum to settle a point.

Novelists aspire to generative clarity, but in the secular groundings and passages and gatherings of character, community, history, plot, action, and timing—all through the unremitting *run run* of words "to make you hear, to make you feel," Joseph Conrad says in the Preface to *The Nigger of the Narcissus*—"before all, to make you *see*." A novelist fully and explicitly senses a real world, the intercultural sea captain says, aspiring "to the plasticity of sculpture, to the colour of painting, and to the magic suggestiveness of music—which is the art of arts." And if he is lucky, "the old, old words, worn thin, defaced by ages of careless usage" will tell a moving story: "—all the truth of life is there: a moment of vision, a sigh, a smile—and the return to an eternal rest" (*NN* 10–12). The running cadence and lyric acoustics of this polylingual émigré are not lost on a Native "man made of words," N. Scott Momaday, a blank-verse novelist like James Welch, or a long-legged metricist such as Louise Erdrich.

Prose runs along horizontally filling in the spaces, explaining character through context. Readers take on time and space in prose—the import of speech, less the impulse to sing. "East of my grandmother's house the sun rises out of the plain," Momaday writes of his Oklahoma Kiowa origins. "Once in his life a man ought to concentrate his mind upon the remembered earth, I believe. He ought to give himself up to a particular landscape in his experience, to look at it from as many angles as he can, to wonder about it, to dwell on it. He ought to imagine that he touches it with his hands at every season and listens to the sounds that are made upon it. He ought to imagine the creatures there and all the faintest motions of the wind. He ought to recollect the glare of noon and all the colors of the dawn and dusk" (*The Way to Rainy Mountain* 83).

A four-winds, four-seasons, two- and four-legged, swimming, crawling, and flying rebirth of tribal kinship runs on like a river course through historical memory—the richly prosaic landscape of collective creation and ongoing relations with all things, all peoples and life forms. More simply put by Linda Hogan, "Outside was my church, my place of vision and dreaming" (*Survival This Way* 129).

So we can consider the *im* of port in this case, the portage from one place to another, prosaically carried along. "The moment passed, and the next and the next, and he was running still," Momaday writes of the grandfather Francisco in *House Made of Dawn*, "and still he would see the dark shape of the man running away in the swirling mist, like a motionless shadow. And he held on to the shadow and ran beyond his pain" (*HMD* 208). The story courier sprints forward, as the song porter hefts his baggage to the loft; and in collaboration, beyond aimless poetry or incessant prose, *this* lyric sound adds up to *that* narrative sense, a house made of talking dawn and singing light.

To recast the case, prosaically, *what about* a cat about the house? What can we say . . . about *talk* by talking? It's not just how we sing, "Ah!" but what we get when we get it, "Oh!" The Greek root of *character* helps to illustrate the point. Ezra Pound says in *ABC of Reading* that character means stone "engraved," as noted in petroglyphs physically incised with things; and good talk is characterized by people, place, time, and space spoken about—story, earth, history, and surrounding stuff. "Once upon a time, long ago—I am now telling a sacred story," begins the Cree Louis Moosomin, blind from childhood, for Leonard Bloomfield in 1925, "—once upon a time, of old, a certain man dwelt in a lone lodge with his wife and his two children" (*Sacred Stories of the Sweet Grass Cree* 14). To the point, an Adamic or first-person "one of us" sets the stage for human drama with Eve and others—Old Man, Old Woman, homeland and progeny. A Garden of Edenic origin inscribes a benchmark, a place of beginnings to begin. The seasons, weather, and calendric time trail arcs of temporality and mortality, going on going on. A biospheric setting grounds and details the context of all these—props, lighting, costumes, stage directions, cues—human and natural contexts. Notice with this given narrative that nouns and prepositions of place take precedence over verbs of motion and adjectival or adverbial imaging, the laurels of poetry. *Things* weigh in over acoustic searching, product over process. *Where will you and I sleep*, Dorothy Demetracapoulou translated a Wintu chant between world wars; *At the down-turned jagged rim of the sky you and I will sleep* ("Wintu Songs," *Anthropos* 1935).

A-HO! OLD ONES

> The art of narrative song . . . had no need of stylus
> or brush to become a complete artistic and literary
> medium. . . . One cannot lead Proteus captive; to bind
> him is to destroy him.
>
> —Albert Lord, *Singer of Tales*

Prose explains, poetry exclaims. The genres cover the distance between interjective (A-ha! or A-ho!) and interrogative (How to? and Why so?). Prose takes its own good time covering the ground to be known. Poetry grazes the earth from above and below. The crossings arrest time-space. *House Made of Dawn* ends in lyric narrative where it begins with Abel on his grandfather's sacred run: "He could see the rain and the river and the fields beyond. He could see the dark hills at dawn. He was running, and under his breath he began to sing. There was no sound, and he had no voice; he had only the words of a song. And he went running on the rise of the song. *House made of pollen, house made of dawn. Qtsedaba*" (*HMD* 212).

The old stories were told as elegantly as modernly crafted fictions—to wit, the opening lines of tribal oral texts taken from a single translative gathering, *American Indian Myths and Legends*, edited by Richard Erdoes, Lakota biographer, and Alfonso Ortiz, the San Juan Tewa anthropologist. Begin with a genesis not so far from Eden. "Earth Maker took some clay in his hands," the Pima say about the beginning, "mixed it with his own sweat, and formed it into two figures—a man and a woman." From earth to earth, the old legends hold, there are chthonic couples and procreative dyads, gender balancings and social completions. These conjunctive keys to tribal ways fill Scott Momaday's writings and Mabel McKay's weavings. "Long ago," the Southern Ute say, "a very old man and his wife lived alone and hunted for game, but it was scarce and they were hungry." The essentials—old age, marital unity, social continuity, food scarcity, and survival hunger—set the dramatic stage for something to happen, as James Welch retells the ancestral 1883 Winter of Starvation in his classic first novel, *Winter in the Blood*. "Long ago when all the animals talked like people," the White Mountain Apache recall, "Turkey overheard a boy begging his sister for food." The fable question begs a story: Why would a brother ask his sister to feed him? Linda Hogan carries gender kinship into interspecies crossings of *The Book of Medicines* and biodiversity of *Dwellings*. "Big Eater ate and ate," the Pequod say of the beginnings, both human definition and food-chain caution—a warning not lost on Leslie Silko's Southwest war-drought victims in *Ceremony*. "Man-Eagle, a frightful monster, had laid waste to the whole country," the Hopi open a creation story turning on devastation and re-creation, the Diné essentials of Sherwin Bitsui's fractal desiccations in *Shapeshift*.

"When Kloskurbeh, the All-Maker, lived on earth," the Penobscot recount, "there were no people yet." The last word *yet* leads the creation story on, as Momaday's grandmother Aho recalls the Kiowa emerging from a hollow log despite obstructions. "The earth was once a human being: Old One made her out of a woman," the Okanogan say of mother-right origins, the maternal clan basis of some 93 percent of all Native tribes. Silko's Grandmother Spider weaves "the belly of the story" that her granddaughter tells. "Before there was a man, two women, an old one and her daughter, were the only humans on earth," the Ojibwe say. Who was the first Mother and where did the men come from? Joy Harjo asks in *She Had Some Horses*.

TRIBAL KINSHIP

"Back in the great days of the Indians," the Brule Sioux recall, "a maiden and her five brothers lived together." Gender dramas—siblings, extended family, male and female dyads, exogamy, and epic beginnings—start here and tumble into Louise Erdrich's sagas of northern-plains kinship. "In the old days, when everything began," the Inuit recall, "a brother lived with his sister in a large village which had a dance house." So dancing graces the beginnings, certainly—dancing and singing the world into being, the sibling center of tribal culture—but where is the sister's suitor? The desire to couple brightens sunrise from Momaday's *House Made of Dawn* through Welch's *Winter in the Blood*; courtship fires passion from Harjo's *In Mad Love and War* through Erdrich's *Love Medicine*. There were magical things to behold, the Cheyenne say: "Sun had beautiful, wonder-working leggings which could set the prairie on fire and drive the game toward the hunter's bow." Feral herding skills meant survival to hunter-gatherers of the high plains, as Black Elk remembers the Lakota following bison and Momaday records his Kiowa ancestors tracking antelope.

"A man and his wife lived with their five-year-old son in an ugly-looking lodge in the woods," the Seneca say of early times—generational crossings that pass from one humble home to possibly better. Joy Harjo's saxophone lyrics turn such a tale into blues-poetry for her band *Poetic Justice*. "Late in the autumn," the Navajo say of the first days, "they heard in the east the distant sound of a great voice calling." Who is this spirit singing? Luci Tapahonso listens for Talking God's narrative verse in *A Breeze Swept Through*, where sacred begins at the tip of the tongue. The Pima record that "The Magician had made the world but felt that something was missing," a crucial plot point fermented in Sherman Alexie's restless poetics. And the Brule Sioux recount creation history, "One summer so long ago that nobody knows how long . . . ," as Aho tells her grandson beginning his way to Rainy Mountain, "You know, everything had to begin, and this is how it was." During those early difficult times, the Blackfeet recall, "In the days when people had only dogs to carry their bundles, two orphan children, a boy and his sister, were having a hard time." Who could answer their needs? The old plot points spark stories in the contemporary writings of Momaday, Welch, Silko, Erdrich, and Sarris. The descriptive language precise, the action encoded naturally, the words tensile, these ancient oral narratives are well-told works of art from first words to last.

The Yuma tell of creation: "This is how it all began. There was only water—there was no sky, there was no land, only nothingness. Then out of the waters rose a mist, and it became the sky. Still there were no sun, no moon, no stars—just darkness. But deep down in the waters lived Kokomaht, the Creator. He was bodiless, nameless, breathless, motionless, and he was two beings—twins." Most every Native creation story embraces twinning; "two by two," the Laguna sing, the connecting or coupling or doubling mode essential to tribal balance and survival. "In the beginning the earth was covered with water," the Jicarilla Apache say, "and all living things were below in the underworld. Then people could talk, the animals could talk, the trees could talk, and the rocks could talk." And they still do, many tribes say; just stand still and listen, truly listen. Linda Hogan would have survivors attentive when no one is left to speak. Orphic, extrahuman voices trace back to the creation of biospheric time and cross-species consciousness, even as the deer and blind grandfather of Welch's Blackfeet winter know things have gotten "cock-eyed."

PLOT POINTS

There were problems in the beginnings too. "Before there were people on the earth," the Modoc say, "the Chief of the Sky Spirits grew tired of his home in The Above World, because the air was always brittle with an icy cold." What to do about loneliness and suffering is a question old as Earthmaker or Yahweh, central to stories around Silko's Tayo, Erdrich's Lipsha, Momaday's Abel, Welch's No Name, or Sarris's own orphan-story. The Slavy people add, "In the beginning before there were people, there was a long winter." Tribes learned to live and to survive winter in the blood. And the Crow admit their struggles in telling origin stories— "How water came to be, nobody knows. Where Old Man Coyote came from nobody knows." Tersely informed, trenchantly circumscribed, not always certain. "Great Spirit, Wakan Tanka, was angry with us for some reason," the Brule Sioux recall, and conflict begs a story. Following the path of the sun, the Snohomish account for topographical variance and lingual diversity. "The Creator and Changer first made the world in the East. Then he slowly came westward, creating as he came. With him he brought many languages, and he gave a different one to each group of people he made." As Sherman Alexie glosses in *Old Shirts & New Skins*, today's bilingual Tower of Babel—off-rez Bellingham to the frontiers of Baghdad—is no less cacophonous. Originally from the Eastern seaboard, the Cherokee remember things this way: "Earth is floating on the waters like a big island, hanging from four rawhide ropes fastened at the top of the sacred four directions." From Black Elk to Bitsui, the four winds cadence the cardinal directions, *washtay* to *hozhó*, and always there comes the first descent and possible grace, as imaged in Erdrich's jacklighted sacrificial clearing. "Kamush, Old Man of the Ancients," the Modoc say, "went down with his daughter to the underground world of the spirits." Why she descended with Old Man is an Orphic story all in itself.

The Caddo remember blunders in the creation of all things, not unlike unresolved cruces in Erdrich's *Tracks* or Hogan's *The Woman Who Watches Over the World*. "Once there was a chief whose wife, to the fear and wonder of the people, gave birth to four little monsters." The inter-tribal Trickster sneaks into cautionary creation. "Coyote is a bad hunter who never kills anything," the Zuni say of antiheroics worth regarding in Alexie's *The Lone Ranger and Tonto Fistfight in Heaven* or Erdrich's Old Man Potchikoo tales in *Original Fire*. "Out walking, Old Man Coyote spied a group of good-looking girls picking wild strawberries," the Crow remember a homeopathic love medicine tale of feral berries. The Brule Sioux tell a how-*not*-to tale: "A pretty *winchinchala* had never been with a man yet, and Iktóme was eager to sleep with her." Intimacies have always been precariously situational, down through Welch's loveless No Name and Agnes, to Silko's impotent Tayo and Night Swan, to Erdrich's hapless June and Gordie. There lies the regenerative story. The Alsea recall, "Coyote had no wife, and nobody wanted him," and the Flathead remember, "Coyote was walking one day when he met Old Woman." Coyote is up to little good, but must be heeded, no less than the Ojibwe Nanabozho, Blackfeet Na'pi, or Pueblo *koshare* clowns. The Brule Sioux say, "Once in the middle of the night, Iktome woke up in a cold sweat after a bad dream"—a being with night sweats contemporary as ancient.

Times were not always paradisiacal. "Long ago," the Tlingit up north say with dramatic flourish, "there was a giant who loved to kill humans, eat their flesh, and drink their blood." Anyone who doesn't fear Windigo terror is crazy, the Cree say. Linda Hogan understands the hunger lust at the heart of male violence: they "had their way with them," she says of sailors molesting dolphins and killing whales, thirsting to "be held / in the thin, clear milk of the gods." The Caddo recall, "In the beginning of the world, there was no such thing as death." Somehow death came into being—a story retold many ways, from wintry blues, to trickster twists, to love toxins, to mad love and war. "This is a true story; I wish it weren't," the Brule Sioux say.

And the spirits can be equally difficult. "Now, there were four ghosts sitting together, talking," the Brule Sioux recount, "smoking ghost smoke, having a good time, as far as it's possible for ghosts to have a good time." Irony is no stranger to epic origins. Listening to Grandmother Spider, Leslie Silko overhears good and bad witches quarreling over making things up, including the White invasion in *Ceremony*. And the Chinook chime in a tale with no good ending: "One night the ghosts decided to go out and buy a wife." Some tales are not true, but real all the same. "Long ago and far away this did not happen," the Tewa Pueblos say. How would she know if it *really* happened? Mabel McKay says—she wasn't there.

AESTHETIC BEGINNINGS

These samplings of Native creation myths are concise, engaging, inventive, and arresting. They begin somewhere at the beginnings with the Creator making a pair of humans in cyclical rather than linear time, so the past is always present, the lessons timeless. Conjunction is key: tribal pairings. Not a word is wasted getting to plot points. There are generative problems to be traced, to be pondered and learned from—isolation, starvation, loneliness, resources, ghosts, monsters, temporality, interspecies crossings, ecological balancings—essential human and animal needs through all times. Gender equities are primary, and women often set the key to tribal harmonies. Family focuses all—the extended kinship of all relations to everything— ceremonialized in storytelling, singing, dancing, playing, talking, and praying. Paying daily attention is critical, as magic and miracle pervade ongoing origins. For every monster, beast, or witch appears a hero, a warrior, a guardian spirit-being. Everyone and everything has voice—humans, animals, stones, sun, moon, the earth and sky. Surviving winter and drought and famine and predator triggers cautionary parables, why-so tales, where-from myths, and how-to stories. And Coyote or a trickster motley of other magician-fools (raven, crow, rabbit, spider, deer, loon) feed across the liminal margins of tribal fire and forest dark. Sex and scatology season daily candors, and death is never far from home. Familial relations are always the first line of defense against threats from outside the tribal campfire.

These opening plot lines turn on *what* things could happen to humans, sequentially, rather than immersing the hearer in *how* things happen, lyrically. The tales account for causes, imaginatively. Sun and moon, sky and earth, husband and wife—the tellings key on coupling and balancing, order and harmony—twins, siblings, genders, even contraries as paired opposites. They tell of a time when all spoke one language: animals as human characters, stones and trees and streams responsive to Orphic voices, a creation all in common—the ideal, if not the reality, of history. The tales address peril with caution and example—darkness, winter, cold, hunger, danger, risk, courage, change, surprise. "Fear is What Quickens Me," the Ohio poet James Wright titles a poem (*Collected Poems* 115), and Joy Harjo gives fear back to its own origins in *She Had Some Horses*. And the tale-tellings include negative inversions, tricksters and their tricks, appetite and procreation, courting and duplicity, gathering and hunting, growing and stealing, warfare and betrayal, dishonesty and destiny, windfall and grace. All the human twists in choice and chance from Homer to Hemingway, Mencius to Momaday, tribally configure and reemerge in Native American writings today.

WHO WE ARE

At the heart of the American Indian oral tradition
is a deep and unconditional belief in the efficacy of
language. Words are intrinsically powerful. They
are magical. By means of words can one bring about
physical change in the universe. By means of words
can one quiet the raging weather, bring forth the
harvest, ward off evil, rid the body of sickness and

pain, subdue an enemy, capture the heart of a lover,
live in the proper way, and venture beyond death.
Indeed, there is nothing more powerful.

—N. Scott Momaday,
"The Native Voice in American Literature"

Songs and stories remind the Cibecue Apache, Basso's Nick Thompson says, *who we are*. From an Indian point of view, stories and songs tell a people who-the-people-are-becoming through time, across space, by way of words-as-cultural-carriers, yesterday to today. "Come, come, / Let us tell the sacred stories, / Let us sing the sacred songs," Momaday writes in the old camp voices renewing tribal culture every day in "Carriers of the Dream Wheel." The creation stories and ceremonial songs echo ancestors and foretell descendants, as told long ago and long into the future. They speak through people speaking to each other. "There were many people, and oh, it was beautiful," Aho tells her Kiowa descendants. "It was all for Tai-me, you know, and it was a long time ago" (*Way to Rainy Mountain* 4)

Just as *art* once meant "to connect," tribal literacy survives as an interactive organism, going on interconnectively. Story is the human container or "compartment," as in "floor" of an historical building from the ground up. Humans are *storied* as the living "tissue" or *history* of a people united across time and space. The old Laguna Ku'oosh tries to heal a war-shocked, mixed-blood Tayo in Silko's *Ceremony*: "He smelled like mutton tallow and mountain sagebrush. He spoke softly, using the old dialect full of sentences that were involuted with explanations of their own origins, as if nothing the old man said were his own but all had been said before and he was only there to repeat it" (*C* 34).

Lyric How-Why, Narrative What-Where

Poetry takes shape descending into the unknown and rising back up. W. S. Merwin reworks Robert Lowie's "Crow Texts," in *Selected Translations* (66):

I am climbing
everywhere is

coming up

Poetry kinetically drops and darkens, perceptually leaps and illumines. The lyric *italicizes* meaning, Dickinson says, as sheet lightning lights up shadowland. "We noticed smallest things— / Things overlooked before," the poet writes of her neighbor dying, "By this great light upon our Minds / Italicized—as 'twere" (#1100). Slant native daughter of New England when Senator Dawes of Massachusetts allotted Indian lands in severalty, Dickinson prefigures Hemingway's plain-style rule to "write hard and clear about what hurts."

Prose unravels across form in the slipstream of language; narrative traces meaning beyond the shaped words. The Chippewa novelist and poet Louise Erdrich closes *Love Medicine* with Lipsha coming home through an age-old Homeric paradigm: "The morning was clear. A good road led on. So there was nothing to do but cross the water, and bring her home" (*LM* 272). This is the epic *nostos* in a modern Native novel, homing anti-heroically acted out not by the father, but an illegitimate son.

Prose works on results; it is what form does, transcended by function. So narrative is *about what*, whereas lyric may be *what about?* As Anton Chekhov or Ray Carver or James Welch shows, the two genres cross from the ground up in the best writings or speakings. "We walk around and we wonder," poet Roberta Hill says, "where do these thoughts come from? And he [Lance Henson] said 'They come from your feet. When you're walking on the earth they come up through your feet.' Up, up, up into your head. And women, you know, in Oneida culture, in the traditional culture, have this close connection between their feet and the earth. This idea of being close to the earth. When you dance, you know, you're close to the earth. You don't jump around, you massage the earth. And I like to think of that connection, that the earth is telling us things" (Bruchac, *Survival This Way* 334–35).

In/sight: a reader sees into poetry as though looking down into an opaque pool. The (sometimes dark) crystals dance in patterns, light and shadowy images coming off the water. The Japanese monk Dogen Kigen spoke of lyric enlightenment by way of lunar pond reflections: the moon does not get wet, the water is not broken (Alan Watts, *The Watercourse Way*). Time stops while space deepens, as the mind dives into the moving reflections. "I rhyme to see myself," Seamus Heaney says, "to set the darkness echoing"— adding of Irish bogs, "the wet centre is bottomless" ("Personal Helicon" and "North"). In the sister depths of a mountain lion's eyes, Linda Hogan glimpses "the yellow-eyed shadow of a darker fear" ("Mountain Lion").

Out/look: readers see through prose, as though gazing through a transparent river. Prefiguring the narratives of Welch, Hogan, Silko, and Sarris, Ford Madox Ford saw the narrative truth of Hemingway's *A Farewell to*

Arms as though looking into a lyric trout stream: "Hemingway's words strike you, each one, as if they were pebbles fetched fresh from a brook. They live and shine, each in its place. So one of his pages has the effect of a brook bottom into which you look down through the floating water" (Alfred Kazin, *An American Procession* 373). Coins in a storied stream bed of running, clear water; nouns that one can take hold of; the technique of foreshortening—minimal form, maximal function—the narrative stream is deeper than it looks. Conversely, our songs are short, Maria Chona says of Papago ceremony, because we know so much (Ruth Underhill, *The Autobiography of a Papago Woman* 11). There is an art to lyric speech, a poetry of condensation and calculation.

The bush is sitting under a tree and / singing, the Ojibwe sing of tribal shadow and space necessary to nurture cultural lyric ("Frances Densmore and American Indian Music," in Brandon, *The Magic World* 96). Song-poetry translates ceremonial liturgy as culture-in-motion into print. There are close to a thousand published Native writers to date in the United States, over half of them poets. The rhetorics of speech and tribal debate feed into prose fiction and its related narratives—memoir, personal history, essay, biography, autobiography, public stump, cultural rally, and political fustian. *We Talk, You Listen*, Vine Deloria Jr. says of reactivist warriors, Lakota and otherwise. "There are so many illusions I need to believe," the Coeur d'Alene–Spokane poet-novelist Sherman Alexie lyricizes holocaustal aftershock in "Seattle, 1987."

IT MATTERS LIKE HELL

But I was not the last, for when I looked behind me
there were ghosts of people like a trailing fog as far
as I could see—grandfathers of grandfathers and
grandmothers of grandmothers without number.
And over these a great Voice—the Voice that was
the South—lived, and I could feel it silent. And as we
went the Voice behind me said: "Behold a good nation
walking in a sacred manner in a good land!"

—*Black Elk Speaks*

Why Native writers begin as poets and turn into novelists is anchored in ceremonial song tradition and historical dance ritual. Black Elk remembers his Great Lakota Vision as a ceremonial procession of past and future, of goodness and beauty crossing in the red and black roads of the sacred hoop, an ever-present Native definition. Given the history of Native dispossession, the quincentennial of the Discovery and after, Americans need to assess what is left of the cultural losses. "We're gonna make it as we go along, generation to generation," Dawson No Horse sang out in an all-night Lakota *yuwipi* ceremony in 1981 at Wakpamni Lake in South Dakota, "addin' on an' addin' on" (Lincoln and Slagle, *The Good Red Road*). As history moves on, Native cultures persist on their own terms. Note some four-and-a-half million American Indians, doubling their population counted from the 2000 census, mostly mixed-blood survivors of 4 to 6 million original Natives in the United States alone, Jack Forbes estimates—perhaps 25 to 30 million others in the country with traces of Indian lineage today (Jack Hitt, "The Newest Indians," *New York Times Magazine*, 21 August 2005). "Sometimes at evening I sit, looking out on the big Missouri," Buffalo Bird Woman the Hidatsa elder recounts. "The sun sets, and dusk steals over the water. In the shadows I seem again to see our Indian village, with smoke curling upward from the earth lodges; and in the river's roar I hear the yells of the warriors, the laughter of little children as of old. It is but an old woman's dream. Again I see but shadows and hear only the roar of the river; and tears come into my eyes. Our Indian life, I know, is gone forever" ("Waheenee," in Nabokov, *Native American Testimony* 182).

If changed, all is not lost. Down by the rivers of time, there are still some 40 million hemispheric kinspeople, out of a shadowed 40 to 60 million pre-Contact Natives representing two thousand language-cultures. The attrition, as stated, was about 97 percent by 1900, when U.S. tribal peoples numbered less than 237,000. The United States government declared war on Indians during the period from 1860 to 1890, and drove the survivors into POW relocation camps called "reservations." Many fled or hid or went away to die. "No one knows where they are— perhaps they are freezing to death," Chief Joseph said as he surrendered to Generals Howard and Miles in 1877 at the Canadian border. "I want to have time to look for my children and see how many of them I can find. Maybe I shall find them among the dead. Hear me, my chiefs, I am tired. My heart is sad and sick. From where the sun now stands I will fight no more forever" (45th U.S. Congress, in *Native American Testimony* 181). Chief Joseph swears by the sun, a student once said, the way Christians swear on the Bible. An eternal negative reversal—reversing the reversal of life itself—the sun eclipsed, then risen courageously again in a dignity of peace-making acquiescence. The old healer chooses a self-resolving power not to fight anymore, and seals the tactical surrender, forever. His is a double sense of tragedy and dignity, power broken and released, war and hostility ended, peace and integrity prayed.

"Among American Indians, Blacks, Chicanos, and others," Carter Revard argues, "they write because it matters like hell. You can say God is Dead, but not if your people have just been wiped out" (Bruchac, *Survival This Way* 248). Some 555 federally acknowledged tribes, another 200 filing for acknowledgment, survive in our contiguous forty-eight states alone, believing long-term in cyclical harmony—what goes around comes around. The old beliefs stay recurrent. There are distinctly, as with the winds, four seasonal "appearances" to all things (consistent with the seasonal modes of Monet's haystacks, or Andy Goldsworthy's seasonally photographed fields and streams). A modal calendar begins with spring as comic renewal, summer as romantic tryst, fall as tragic break, winter as ironic continuance, and so on—balance and symmetry, rightness and beauty prevailing through time. The cardinal powers of the directions also turn on this cyclical harmony: according to Black Elk's Lakota vision on the high plains, the sunrise east is red with pipestone and morning star (ancestral promise and daily renewal). The sunlight south is yellow with flowering tree and sacred hoop (the centering roots and integrating circle of life). The stormy west is black with sky-bowl of rain and lightning-bow of fire (the life-giving thunder powers to nurture and to defend). The snow-blind north is white with medicine root and goose wing (the homing powers to heal and to move). Binary pairings rule, a complementarity of contrast and completion. No one stands alone, every thing with a sun shadow, every being a spirit, every direction a meaning. And so with living languages and cultures. "The Swampy Cree say stories live in the world," writes the ethnographer Howard Norman, "may choose to inhabit people, who then have the option of telling them back out into the world again. This all can form a symbiotic relationship: if people nourish a story properly, it tells things about life. The same with dreams. And names" (*Who Met the Ice Lynx* I–II).

Tribal names are zoo- and biomorphic, not anthropomorphic: Black Bear or White Buffalo Calf Woman, Red Cloud or Grass Woman. Space is sacred through the etched power of image: *frog / hail / potatoes / dumplings*, the Navajo play with rhyming things, as noted in correspondences, *smoke / cloud / rain / acceptance / breathing in* (Rothenberg, *Shaking the Pumpkin* 311). Hundreds of tribes have hundreds of variations on powers of the word to see and to hear, to feel and to know—to sense the fourfold tonalized vision of a blessed world—but all believe in what anthropologists have come to call *sacred reciprocity*, that is, the *re* and *pro* of tribal giving and receiving. What goes out comes back.

Balancing Relatives

This key concept of communal sharing, the ongoing tribal exchange of gifts, as Lewis Hyde discusses ritual sharing in *The Gift*, leads to a second principle of extended kinship. We are all related. *Mitak' oyasin*, the Lakota cry, "all my relatives." All related, all relatives: certainly not news in the tribal world, but no less a cliché however often invoked, no less than good day or thank you or godspeed, in need of daily reconfirmation among the divide-and-conquer competitions of Western individualism. This universal interrelationship includes blood family, leggéd/wingéd/crawling/swimming life-forms, bones in the earth, spirits of all things, adoptive and adaptive receptions for outsiders, strangers regarded as reawakened selves, cosmic and intrinsic animism (sun, moon, stars, sky—down to quartz, thistle, cottonwood, and spider). "The whole damned tribe's one big family," say now-day Indi'ns like John Fire back home in the Dakotas (Erdoes, *Lame Deer* 45). Scientists call these interspecies and trans-spatial webs the Beijing Effect. When a butterfly flaps its wings in Buenos Aires, the reverberation is felt, however minutely, among blackbirds in Connecticut.

So in tribal thinking there is an interdependency of all beings, and all beings are alive, nothing inanimate. The universe is benevolent and life-giving, friendly, related to humans on a family scale. *I / the song / I walk here*: the Modoc chant the song's animacy (A. L. Kroeber, *Handbook of California Indians*, in Brandon, *The Magic World* 3). *Tunkáshila*, the Lakota address stones—"Grandfathers." The Navajo speak with the wind, breath coming in and out as spirit-life, the "in-standing wind" their soul, as James McNeley discusses in *Holy Wind in Navajo Philosophy*. *Hozhó*, the Diné say—before me, behind me, above me, below me, beauty and truth all around me—balance, goodness, harmony, happiness. All life is reciprocal and representative as democratic union. "We-the-people" is how Jefferson is said to have translated the word "Iroquois," a coalition of six nations variously united under the White Roots of Peace since the fourteenth-century time of Hiawatha and Deganawidah. A "United" States or Nations would configure ideally with parallel pairings of differences, male and female moieties, plant and animal clans, sacred and secular societies, speech and song, poetry and prose. Carter Revard, the Osage with an Oxford doctorate in Medieval literature, says: "Virgil needed Homer and Venus, Dante needed Virgil and Beatrice, we need Uncle Coyote and Grandmother Spider, Grandfather, Stone Boy. . . . The stories have gone out of a lot of poems, along with the rhymes and the song, the tears and laughter, but this is less true in every case with those we call minority writers. There's live force and strength there. You can hear in the poetry of American Indian writers a genuine felt concern for what is going on. . . . The stories have got to come back, the sound stuff, the rhyme, all of that, more of it and better" (Bruchac, *Survival This Way* 248).

Organisms balance, harmonize, and endure through history. Adaptive individualism or *symbiogenesis*, as evolutionary microbiologists now say—a "symbiotic alliance" of first bacterial cells to form nucleated cells—pools toward tribal inclusion, beginning in mythic or sacred times when men spoke with animals. Jenny Leading Cloud, not so long ago in 1967, told Richard Erdoes at White River Rosebud: "In the old, old days, before Columbus 'discovered' us, as they say, we were even closer to the animals than we are now. Many people could understand the animal languages; they could talk to a bird, gossip with a butterfly. Animals could change themselves into people, and people into animals. It was a time when the earth was not quite finished, when many kinds of mountains and streams, animals and plants came into being according to nature's plan.

"In these far-gone days, hidden from us as in a mist, there lived a rabbit—a very lively, playful, good-hearted rabbit. One day this rabbit was walking, enjoying himself, when he came across a clot of blood. How it got there, nobody knows. It looked like a blister, a little bladder full of red liquid. Well, the playful rabbit began toying with that clot of blood, kicking it around as if it were a tiny ball" (*American Indian Myths and Legends* 5–8).

And then, lo and behold, Jenny Leading Cloud, fully aware of her bilingual audience, interjects a note of cultural interface, offering a theological touch of critical discourse: "Now, we Indians believe in *Takuskanskan*, the mysterious power of motion. Its spirit is in anything that moves. It animates things and makes them come alive. Well, the rabbit got into this strange moving power without even knowing it, and the motion of being kicked around, or rather the spirit of the motion—and I hope you can grasp what I mean by that—began to work on the little blob of blood so that it took shape, forming a little gut."

The living spirit of the motion—*and I hope you can grasp what I mean by that*—the energy that forms the blood-gut being kicked around, trickster-fashion, will make things up according to cosmic play and temporal design. Here is a world still alive and in-the-making, always, larger than human life, kin with animal and vegetal life forms, spirited, as preternaturally and naturally magical as a kid kicking a ball of things around.

Jenny Leading Cloud's extraordinary moment of authorial intrusion, no less than George Eliot coming out of the wings of *Middlemarch*, signals a critical awareness of the storyteller talking about what she's talking about: the Lakota are not monotheistic God-the-Father worshippers, a reader may see, but pantheistic animists who believe in many, many spirit-gods, a four-by-four set of sixteen powers to start the spirits rolling (see DeMallie and Levenda on Lakota *Tobtob kin* in *The Anthropology of Power*). The Lakota say a *Power-that-moves(what)moves* moves through all this, kinetically unharnessable as an electron, but no less trackably deniable than Brother Rabbit. Just so, electromagnetic-gravitational forces as so-called string theory are said to move through all-that-is in the projected physics of our own cosmos. Just in case, Jenny might add, an outsider thought this was a modified Genesis or Jesus parable by way of Ovid's *Metamorphosis*.

She continues the Lakota creation story: "The rabbit kicked it some more, and the blob began to grow tiny hands and arms. The rabbit kept nudging it, and suddenly it had eyes and a beating heart. In this way the rabbit, with the help of the mysterious moving power, formed a human being, a little boy. The rabbit called him *We-Ota-Wichasha*, Much-Blood Boy, but he is better known as Rabbit Boy."

Rabbit Boy is taken home to be adopted by lapin parents, only to be told one day on growing up, "Son, I must tell you that you are not what you think you are—a rabbit like me. You are human. We love you and we hate to let you go, but you must leave and find your own people." So all dressed up by his furry kin, Rabbit Boy goes to a human village, falls in love with the beautiful maiden, and Spider Man or *Iktóme* the Trickster gets jealous.

"Let's cut this pretty boy up and eat him," he says; but Rabbit Boy has a power-song about battling the sun that will protect and revive him.

The people go ahead and *kill* Rabbit Boy, they think. A storm rises, eclipsing the sun, turning everything into "black night." When the cloud is gone, so are Rabbit Boy's meat chunks in the soup pot. A-ho! says a wise old healer, this Rabbit Boy has powerful sun medicine. We'd better marry him to the maiden. Wait, Spider Man protests, I'm more powerful than pretty boy, so cut me up and see my song-stuff work. But Iktóme forgets the song, and mixes the sun up with the moon, and once chopped up into the soup, he never comes back to life again. And so Trickster out-tricks himself, as he always does, concludes Jenny Leading Cloud, as she tells a Lakota creation story to a white man. The tale could be cousin to the Tewa-Hopi Jug Boy myth pecked into the basalt cliffs above my Santa Fe River home.

The lessons are obvious for interspecies rabbits and humans—indeed, for Indian-White relations. Collaboration is the fur of survival in evolutionary fusion. The technical term *symbiogenesis* turns on the adaptive crossings of species (a consortium of microbes or "microbial merger" living symbiotically). And non-Indians, who do not know the life-support tribal songs and stories, ought to be careful arrogating power in self-advancing situations. They might get chopped up, stewed, and eaten.

OTHER PERSONS

Humans cross with animal life-forms, as the Cree and Chippewa call diverse living organisms "other-than-human-persons." Things house spirits: the grandfather in the stone or sky, the grandmother in the earth or water. Biospheric connections prevail. "I see men as trees walking," the blind man told Christ, and Matthew says he was made to see. Plains tribes saw Christ as their make-live Savior during the Ghost Dance revival ending the nineteenth century. When his black-stallion grandfather speaks in song, cited in the beginning, Black Elk remembers the spirit spoke like singing: "The leaves on the trees, the grasses on the hills and in the valleys, the waters in the creeks and in the rivers and the lakes, the four-legged and the two-legged and the wings of the air—all danced together to the music of the stallion's song" (*Black Elk Speaks* 32).

Elegy and epic cross and fuse in Native American writing. "Earth and I gave you turquoise," N. Scott Momaday writes in 5/7/5/7/7 Sino-syllabic verse, "when you walked singing / We lived laughing in my house / and told old stories / You grew ill when the owl cried / We will meet on Black Mountain." Art is connective tissue in its oldest sense, conjunctive, as in the Indo-European root *ar-* or "link" of the words arm, army, archer, armor, architecture, articulate. Simon Ortiz told Joe Bruchac: "Poetry is the way in which we make the connection between all things. Poetry is a way of reaching out to what is reaching for you. Poetry is that space in between what one may express and where it is received. Where there is another energy coming toward you—it's that space in between" (223).

And language, the art of prose and poetry, appears to trail back two million years to interjective syllables like *Ah!* and *Ha!* and *Ho!* Stephen

Pinker says in *The Language Instinct*, advancing a syllabic string theory of human life syntactically evolving through language. "Words are intrinsically powerful, I believe," says Scott Momaday in a passage partially quoted earlier. "And there is magic in that. Words come from nothing into being. They are created in the imagination and given life on the human voice. You know, we used to believe—and I'm talking now about all of us, regardless of our ethnic backgrounds—in the magic of words. The Anglo-Saxon who uttered spells over his fields so that the seeds would come out of the ground on the sheer strength of his voice, knew a good deal about language. That man's faith—and may I say, wisdom— has been lost upon modern man, by and large. It survives in the poets of the world, I suppose, the singers" (183).

Syllables mature into syntax over a million years, the brain multiplying fourfold as *homo sapiens* comes forth natively, linked by song and speech, conversely silence and space. Still today words tie people together, the desire to relate, to tell, to sing, to dance, to couple, to join, to belong, longing to be. The impulse to sing, the import of speech are symbiotic ways of looking at Native literacy, oral and otherwise. The blind seer Black Elk chants of comic *heyoka* renewal (*Black Elk Speaks* 146):

> The day of the sun has been my strength.
> The path of the moon shall be my robe.
> A sacred praise I am making.
> A sacred praise I am making.

Words on Words

> He is a word sender. This world is like a garden. Over
> this garden go his words like rain, and where they fall
> they leave it a little greener. And when his words have
> passed, the memory of them shall stand long in the
> west like a flaming rainbow.
>
> —Nicholas Black Elk on John Neihardt,
> *Black Elk Speaks*

All *words* ("I shall say" in ancient Greek *muthos*) originally come from speech and were verbally charged, energized *things per se*, Latin *verbum*. Words were mouthed actions, leaping and luminous with the physical world, magical. What things *do*, where ideas *go*, how feelings *feel*—the shaggy Old English *Wort* bristled thick with Anglo-Saxon *scops*, *skellings*, *flytings*, *kennings*, and *sweords*. Seamus Heaney speaks of reading *Beowulf* as a bilingual "voice-right" in the struggle between Celtic and English cultural history, trafficking "this middle ground between oral tradition and the demands of written practice" (*B* xxiv). In translating the first epic verse written for Germanic tribal mead houses and *banfires*, Heaney crosses a thousand-year divide: *either/or* nationalist politics to *both-and* "multicultural odyssey" (*B* xxvi).

So when Tapahonso writes in "Joe Babe" syllabics, Silko center-margins her lyric insets in *Ceremony*, or Momaday writes verse in syllabics, heroic couplets, or Imagist icons—the texts cross old tribal ways into new literary forms. When Welch writes in pentameters and surrealist dream sequences, Erdrich in measured iambics and modernist etchings, Harjo in fusional lyrics that generate saxophone scores—song-poets fuse ancient tradition with literacy. When Alexie riffs off-rez, Sarris narrates plain-style life-story, Bitsui chants in fractal riffs, or Hogan sculpts min-imalist lines—Native writers are finding *equivalent* forms, ceremonial notes and song steps and lyric pitches, in Euro-American reexpressions of oral traditions carried over from ancestral heritages. Native writers live in present time. Whether Indians grow up traditionally or between cultures, their sense of balance and harmony, of cadence and measure, of people and place, of tribal speaking and ceremonial singing can trans-late *sui generis* into Western verse and prose, if readers handle them with care. Native literacies are national treasures, not without finely edged irony: the post-9/11 joke circulating by Moccasin Telegraph e-mail today features a photograph of Geronimo's armed Apache with the caption *Homeland Security Since 1492.*

TALK-SONG, SING-STORY

"This is what we know about our stories," Nick Thompson tells Keith Basso. "They go to work on your mind and make you think about your life" ("Stalking with Stories," in *Western Apache Language and Culture* 125). Songs voice feelings; stories objectify senses. Talk and song con-nect inside with outside—"the wind that gives us life," the Navajo say, inhaled and exhaled as the ex-pressed soul or "in-standing wind." Look at the trail of the wind in the fingertips, Diné say, and note tribal origins and continuing life-forces as breath. Intercollectively the wind moves all around and through humans as it shapes speech. Calling the wind *Taté*, one of the four primary spirits (with sun, earth, and stone), the Lakota honor *Takuskanskan* (literally "force" plus "sky-energy" reduplicated) moving through all things, the Power-that-moves-what-moves.

The Navajo believe that songs surround singers with a protective cloud or nimbus—before, behind, below, above, and all around. Stories raise a verbal shield, announcing, warning, defining, defending the people. "The shield is its own story," Momaday says of Plains cultures. "The shield is a mask." Both herald and defense orally encoded, the name *shield-as-mask* relates what's within a culture to outsiders. "The mask is an appearance that discloses reality beyond appearance. Like other masks it bespeaks sacred mystery" (*In the Presence of the Sun* 74). And with the bearer of a word-shield, the story-in-a-name articulates people to themselves and others (the Kiowa family name Mammedaty means "walking above"). Name-stories remind all of common beginnings, shared heritage, present tribal responsibilities, communal promises toward the future. Iconic names ring epic, no less than Achilles, Xerxes, Dido, Sheba, or Genghis Khan: Powhatan, Pocahontas, Sequoyah, Jacatacqua, Black Hawk, Sacagawea, Red Cloud, Sarah Winnemucca, Will Rogers, Wilma Mankiller, Ray Young Bear.

Songs and stories go to meet the unknown, the alterity of others and other things. Announcing the stranger, tribal words greet the outsider and elicit response, as with the Kiowa arrow maker saying casually to the man outside his Rainy Mountain tipi, "I know that you are there on the outside, for I can feel your eyes upon me. If you are Kiowa, you will understand what I am saying, and you will speak your name" (Momaday, *Way to Rainy Mountain* 46). Failure to respond proves fatal.

Prayer-talk petitions the spirit-powers to help those in need. And words can translate unknown movements and voices toward human recognition, as *meta-phor* bears the news (carried out and back), the word derived from racing a Roman chariot to the far marker and returning. Metaphoric news comes home from afar, tribally adopted, critical to survival.

Words voice a legacy—for the children's children—a history of who-people-are that helps descendants *be* who they are-to-become in the best sense of *related* people, from *time immemorial*, for all time. "Make me always the same as I am now," Pueblos sing. Old Ku'oosh in *Ceremony* explains to Tayo the fragile webs of words, stories, and songs holding the world together: "It took a long time to explain the fragility and intricacy because no word exists alone, and the reason for choosing each word had to be explained with a story about why it must be said this certain way. That was the responsibility that went with being human, old Ku'oosh said; the story behind each word must be told so there could be no mistake in the meaning of what had been said; and this demanded great patience and love" (C 35–36).

Speech & Actions

Oral tradition is the other side of the miracle of language. As important as books are—as important as writing is, there is yet another, a fourth dimension of language which is just as important, and which, indeed, is older and more nearly universal than writing: the oral tradition, that is, the telling of stories, the recitation of epic poems, the singing of songs, the

making of prayers, the chanting of magic and mystery,
the exertion of the human voice upon the unknown—
in short, the spoken word. In the history of the world
nothing has been more powerful than that ancient and
irresistible tradition of *vox humana*. That tradition is
especially and above all the seat of the imagination,
and the imagination is a kind of divine blindness in
which we see not with our eyes but with our minds
and souls, in which we dream the world and our
being in it.

—N. Scott Momaday, "A Divine Blindness:
The Place of Words in a State of Grace"

Public words address common concerns, speaking to events that affect
everyone. The evolution of human time through space is known as
history, from the Greek "tissue." When time thickens with history,
humans mark it lingually distinct, topo-epically descriptive as a *chronotope* or physical trope in time, says Mikhail Bakhtin (see *The Dialogic
Imagination*; and Bender and Wellbery, *Chronotypes*). The Crucifixion
or Sun Dance, Jamestown or Sand Creek, Plymouth or the Little Big
Horn, Gettysburg or Wounded Knee need no explaining to citizens of
the nation. Time takes on literal and symbolic value as a physical event
in space. The Apache see chronotopes in narrative topography, and as
translated by Keith Basso, *wisdom sits in places*: "It's like water that
never dries up," Dudley Patterson tells the linguistic anthropologist.
"You need to drink water to stay alive, don't you? Well, you also need to
drink from places. You must remember everything about them. You must
learn their names" (Basso, *Wisdom Sits in Places* 127).

And so time and event coalesce in a descriptive term as tribal "toponym," or topographical map engraved in a place name: a hill in which
Two Old Women Are Buried; a cornfield where *She Became Old Sitting*;
a butte designated *Trail to Life Goes Up*; an ephemeral spring marked
Fly's Camp. Dudley Patterson continues, "You must remember what happened at them long ago. You must think about it and keep on thinking
about it. Then your mind will become smoother and smoother. Then you
will see danger before it happens. You will walk a long way and live a
long time. You will be wise. People will respect you."

Much respected for his fluid recollections and inspired naming,
N. Scott Momaday writes of tribal monuments: "At Devil's Tower

or Canyon de Chelly or the Cohokia Mounds you touch the pulse of the living planet; you feel its breath upon you" ("Sacred Places," in *The Man Made of Words* 114). Momaday's own tribal birth name, *Tsoai-talee* or Rock-Tree Boy, comes from the Kiowa name for *Mato Tipi*, the Lakota House of the Bear, otherwise known as Devil's Tower in northeast Wyoming. The volcanic throat called a laccolith benchmarks the migration of Kiowas coming down onto the plains from Montana mountains.

Landscape translates into tribal event through signifying words, tribal politics. Political speeches focus and organize social power, civic responsibilities to others, leadership systems in war and peace. And they can be misused. Chief Joseph addressed Congress in 1879: "I have heard talk and talk, but nothing is done. Good words do not last long unless they amount to something. Words do not pay for my dead people. They do not pay for my country, now overrun by white men. . . . Good words will not give my people good health and stop them from dying. Good words will not get my people a home where they can live in peace and take care of themselves. I am tired of talk that comes to nothing. It makes my heart sick when I remember all the good words and the broken promises. There has been too much talking by men who had no right to talk. Too many misrepresentations have been made, too many misunderstanding have come up between the white men about the Indians" (Ramsey, *Coyote Was Going There* 38–39).

Speech educates kin in life skills, teaching the economics of planting and herding and gathering tribal livelihood. Talk tells a person how to do things right—a morality daybook. "So someone stalks you and tells a story about what happened long ago," Nick Thompson a.k.a. Slim Coyote says to Basso. "That story is working on you now. You keep thinking about it. That story is changing you now, making you want to live right. That story is making you want to replace yourself" (*Western Apache Language and Culture* 124–25). People advise and consent through what folklorists call inspired *speech acts*: religious warnings as omens, auguries, divinations; prophesies of spirits, gods, demons; visions that translate the ecstatic cosmologies of shared belief systems; defenses against poisons, threatening weapons, adversarial chants, or magic curses. Beyond prophesy, the old rhythms renew tribal kinship among the young. Old Francisco remembers the passing of the heated Pueblo drum in Momaday's novel *House Made of Dawn*: "And from then on he had a voice in the clan, and the next year he healed a child who had been sick from birth" (*HMD* 208).

A democracy and diversity in language allows humans to express what they think, feel, and see in a collective world. People learn to hear themselves, to listen to their own words among the words of others. "Listen to your children," a Pine Ridge Lakota said over *Native America Calling* national public radio in January 2004. "Then they will be better able to listen to you." Humans learn to decide their needs among others, each with a voice and vote, all an extended family. Not all will agree in democratic diversity; each agrees that all tender and transcend isolation. Momaday concludes "A Divine Blindness" with a call to tribal speech like singing: "If words are the intricate bonds of language, and if the spoken word is the first part of this ancient design, this construction that makes of us a family, a tribe, a civilization, we had better strive to understand how and why—and perhaps first of all, *that*—we exist in the element of language" (*Man Made of Words* 87).

WORKING WORDS

Storing grain and burying ancestors, Lewis Mumford says in *The City in History*, mark the first human cities along the Nile River 12,000 years ago. Words have been socializing and organizing Native American communities from about the same time, if we accept the 11,200-year-old archaeological evidence of Clovis Man, not to mention the Cohokia Mounds in Ohio, Chaco Canyon in New Mexico, Round Valley in California, or the Olmec, Toltec, Mayan, Incan, and Aztec empires south of the border. Corn was being hybridized in central America 12,000 years ago. A 12,500-year-old stone tool has been found at Monte Verde, Chile, and migrations from Daisy Cave, California, southward along the coast may date back as much as 30,000 years, given expansion rates along with genetic and linguistic analysis (Lemonick and Dorfman, "Who Were the First Americans?"). Written language systems, Jared Diamond reasons in *Guns, Germs, and Steel*, were a function of geography and species hybridization across the Mediterranean, whereas the Western Hemisphere with its north-south axis did not develop writing-for-trade since they didn't use an intertribal commodity system.

Words work to socialize people. Well-systemized group dynamics convey ways of getting along to get along, sorting out problems, sharing resources, settling disputes, debating public issues. *We-the-People*, the Iroquois called themselves in village councils and longhouses that led toward New England town meetings, as émigré Anglo-American exiles caught wind of democratic tribal behaviors alternative to despotic feudalism and hierarchic privilege. Over a hundred tribes called themselves humans, Vine Deloria Jr. documents in *God Is Red*. *Cherokee* means the Real People; *Lakota*, Allies; *Diné*, The People; or *Hopi*, People of Peace. The Winnebago called themselves *People of the Real Speech*. *Powwow* among the Algonkians meant to "make medicine" communally. The Inuit still settle disputes with organized public song-duels.

Plains tribes sun-dance and tell stories around campfires at night, play bingo and trade jokes in casinos. The Navajo love horse trading and gambling for high stakes, and the Pueblo gather ceremonially in underground kivas, socially in plazas on feast days, and even sportively on tribal golf courses at Cochiti, Santa Clara, Pojoaque, Sandia, or Isleta (the Navajo pro golfer Notah Begay was captain of the 1990s Stanford team including freshman Tiger Woods). The Pomo traditionally meet in sunken round-houses, going down into the earth, as in Plains vision-quest pits, to root the talk ceremony in grounded origins. Examples are endlessly specific to tribal groups, but all gather to play, to tell and sing of their common concerns. The healer Old Torlino told Washington Matthews a creation story for *Navajo Legends*, a chant that opens Margot Astrov's *The Winged Serpent* (3):

> I am ashamed before the earth;
> I am ashamed before the heavens;
> I am ashamed before the dawn;
> I am ashamed before the evening twilight;
> I am ashamed before the blue sky;
> I am ashamed before the sun.
> *I am ashamed before that standing within me which*
>   *speaks with me.*
> Some of these things are always looking at me.
> I am never out of sight.
> Therefore I must tell the truth.
> *I hold my word tight to my breast.*

WORDS OF WISDOM

Local knowledge, according to Clifford Geertz, regionally dictates, moderates, and edits understandings of self and others. No one knows a culture so well as those who live it, even when insiders don't always conceptualize or verbalize what it is they know about themselves. Gossip lets locals know they belong, Leslie Silko says of growing up on the edges of Laguna Pueblo. Loose talk, street lingo, goofy jive, even trash-talk bind clans across differences, positively or negatively grounded in one another. Folklore carries the legacy of common daily beliefs. *Spits straight up*, the Japanese say, *learns something*. The lesson needs no translation. *No pockets in a shroud*, the old-timers said back home. *Indians Scalp Their Enemies*, says a plaque in my Lakota brother Mark Monroe's Community Indian Center. *Whites Scalp Their Friends*.

Teasing words are a social corrective in all this, translating the cutting edge of local customs across age barriers or gender shifts or contesting clans. Teasing even opens the porous boundaries between distant intimates or differing cultures. Don Talayesva returned to Hopi in the 1920s after a White Man's education in New York City: "I had learned a great lesson and now knew that the ceremonies handed down by our fathers meant life and security, both now and hereafter. I regretted that I had ever joined the Y.M.C.A. and decided to set myself against Christianity once and for all. I could see that the old people were right when they insisted that Jesus Christ might do for modern whites in a good climate, but that the Hopi gods had brought success to us in the desert ever since the world began" (Leo W. Simmons, "Sun Chief," in Astrov, *The Winged Serpent* 248). The good humor of homecoming seasons human belonging.

"Let us examine the facts of your present eruption into our country," the Cherokee Corn Tassel says with seasoned reason to 1785 Tidewater colonists. "You talk of the law of nature and the law of nations, and they are both against you." The great leader is amenably equable, begging to differ with the newcomers' logic. "You say: Why do not the Indians till the ground and live as we do? May we not, with equal propriety, ask, Why the white people do not hunt and live as we do?" This is not mere affected injury, Corn Tassel argues, it is a grievance Indians equitably deplore. The insult demands reply and redress. "The great God Nature has placed us in different situations. It is true that he has endowed you with many superior advantages; but he has not created us to be your slaves. *We are a separate people!* He has given each their lands, under distinct considerations and circumstances; he has stocked yours with cows, ours with buffalo; yours with hog, ours with bear; yours with sheep, ours with deer. He has, indeed, given you an advantage in this, that your cattle are tame and domestic while ours are wild and demand not only a larger space for range, but art to hunt and kill them" (*Tatham's Characters Among The North American Indians* (1820), in Nabokov, *Native American Testimony* 122). As Keith Basso shows with Apache joking in *Portraits of the "Whiteman*," the buckskin can be stretched, worked, and softened to be of human use, up to the point of breaking.

Recipes are the most stable literacy of any culture, Johannes Wilbert, the UCLA South American anthropologist, insisted in personal conversation. Burn the books, smash the tablets, deface the petroglyphs, erase the records, trash the treaties, and tribal peoples will still prepare their daily food in the same ways over thousands of years. Buffalo stew on the plains, corn grits in the Southeast, eel and turkey bake in the Northeast, chile mutton stew in the Southwest, salmon potlatch in the Northwest, acorn mush in California—tribal is as people cook, place to place, consistent over time. And recipes, passed down generation to generation without cookbooks, whet the oral poetry of Native palates. Simon Ortiz, Luci Tapahonso, and Scott Momaday all write recipe poems about Southwestern chili.

Tall tales exaggerate dramatic wonder in a world that is always surprising, some think, in order to survive the numbing and dumbing-down of human torpor or arrogance. Disturbance, dazzlement, play, joke, corrective satire, essentializing caricature, debunking parody keep minds alive to the possibilities of human imagining against insurmountable mortal odds, death itself. The Nez Percé tell how Coyote borrows Farting Boy's asshole, tosses up his eyes, retrieves them, rapes old women, and tricks a young girl seeking power in *Shaking the Pumpkin*. Coyote Old Man's antics are most often blamed for the origin of death.

Collective memories honor origins, the days when grandparents were young: the way-it-was and how-it-is coming together as crossing generations passing on everything. Momaday celebrates his Kiowa birth name in anaphoric lyric, "The Delight Song of Tsoai-talee," the "whole dream" of local places (*In the Presence of the Sun* 16):

I am the glitter on the crust of the snow
I am the long track of the moon in a lake
I am a flame of four colors
I am a deer standing away in the dusk
I am a field of sumac and the pomme blanche
I am an angle of geese in the winter sky
I am the hunger of a young wolf
I am the whole dream of these things

Tribal stories record collective history—what combines and concerns peoples as a people: how to survive the present, learn from the past, and prepare for the future. *A people without a history*, the Sioux say, *is like a wind in the buffalo grass.*

WORDS FOR THE DAY

Occasional words figure as ceremonial talk when Natives treat with others "at the forest's edge" of cultural differences. Constance Rourke in "The Indian Background of American Theatricals" considers the plenary 1621 Plymouth Thanksgiving as the first recorded American literature—words could "play" between grateful pilgrims and generous Algonkians in dramatic pageantry, enacting dance, honoring talk, ceremonial song. Reversely treating Whites, all the agreements, promises, accusations, remedies, and apologies have served as so much bum fodder through the years, note cartoonists like Robert Freeman.

Solar-calendar anniversaries mark the passing of seasons, the spring-fall crossings of the equinoxes, the Pueblo *far-north* and *far-south corner time* of the summer and winter solstices. Cultures under the same sun, moon, and stars are not so annually different in these United States. Easter, Independence Day, Labor Day, and Christmas come about the same time as the spring ditching ceremonies, the summer world renewals, the fall harvests, or the winter feast days for many tribes. Agrarian cycles and animal migrations, Sun Dances and Rain Rituals all have a set organic text in the four-winds, four-seasons cycles of solar time. Not so long ago, and still in rural America, seasonal and directional quadrants help locals to quarter the lunar and solar flow of time through yearly cycles. Check the annual *Farmers' Almanac*.

The lunar calendar of waxing and waning light at night (the night *red-light-sun*, Lakotas call the moon) illumines specific daily lives of expanding and contracting human organisms. The Aztec year is composed of thirteen 28-day months. And global human calendars are marked lingually from birth through death. Infants develop through ceremonies charting first breath, first smile and laugh, first teeth, first crawl and walk and talk—on into childhood games passed on, pubescent rituals and initiations, male and female societies youth to adulthood, commemorations of menstruation and maturation, courting and sports, prowess and agility. Stories and songs run thick with these human passages.

"You know, in the old days," Black Elk says of High Horse courting, "it was not so very easy to get a girl when you wanted to be married." This story appears right after The Great Vision and the coming of the "fat-takers" into Lakota country, as told by *Watanye* (Poor), a trickster with sore lips who winced when he laughed. "Then High Horse went back to the old man and said he would give four horses for the girl—two of them young and the other two not hardly old at all. But the old man just waved his hand and would not say anything.

"So High Horse sneaked around until he could talk to the girl again, and he asked her to run away with him. He told her he thought he would just fall over and die if she did not. But she said she would not do that; she wanted to be bought like a fine woman. You see she thought a great deal of herself too" (*Black Elk Speaks* 52). Attracting, courting, mating, marrying, coupling, caring for, birthing, educating, putting up with, nursing, lamenting, burying—all tribes carry tall tales, ritual chants, and song ceremonies particular to their cultural definition.

Adult responsibilities settle into what humans call *work*, the inherited parental labor to care for and feed families. Women have traditionally kept the homes of Indian people: tribal matriarchs manage their homes communally, exercise power through mother rights and guardian clans, as their men go out and come back across boundaries of maternal privilege. With variant exceptions men hunt, travel, war, plant, herd, harvest, and store grain, more or less traditionally. Helpful and empowering words go with all these workings. A. Grove Day notes in *The Sky Clears* (4–5) that Indians made songs and stories for many reasons: To petition, to pray, and to praise their spirit-powers. To invoke the gods through seasonal ceremonies. To cure and to ask help in hunting, planting, and breeding. To chronicle history and to trace tribal origins. To teach morality, to mourn, to inspire warriors, to court, to amuse. To ridicule or to bewitch opposition. To honor heroes, to express the soul, to praise nature, to boast, to mark a vision. To enact folk dramas, to quiet the young, to ease work, to color games, to play, and to celebrate. William Brandon in *The Magic World* (xii) speculates that if Indians ran General Motors, they would have a song for every car assembly step.

Social organizings involve speaking through group behaviors, the why and how and when to do . . . *the way we do things*, they say back home. "But you won't forget that story," Nick Thompson tells Basso. "You're going to see the place where it happened, maybe every day if it's nearby. . . . That place will keep on stalking you like the one who shot you with the story" (*Western Apache Language and Culture* 125).

Religious groupings and observances are marked with right and wrong words: morality is decided and agreed upon through voicing forgiveness, grace, atonement, and acceptance. Visionary words give a culture spiritual uplift, the inspiration literally to get up in the morning and ask the sunrise blessing for the day's journey through local space and time. And certain well-chosen words encapsulate the advice of leaders, advised by powers greater than self—the priest-leader-visionary women

and men honored as the spoken and sung best of the people: Chief
Joseph, *Zitkala-sa* or Gertrude Bonin, *Ohiyesa* or Charles Eastman,
Buffalo Bird Woman, Handsome Lake, Pretty Shield, Vine Deloria Jr.,
Lucy Thompson, Reuben Snake, Helen Sekaquaptewa, Clyde Warrior.
"I am here by the will of the Great Spirit," Sitting Bull told reservation
bureaucrats in 1885, "and by His will I am a chief. My heart is red and
sweet, and I know it is sweet, because whatever passes near me puts out
its tongue to me; and yet you men have come here to talk with us, and
you say you do not know who I am. I want to tell you that if the Great
Spirit has chosen anyone to be the chief of this country, it is myself"
(Senate Report #283, quoted in Brown, *Bury My Heart at Wounded
Knee* 424).

Medicine Words

Folk remedies survive in how-to stories treating daily aches, pains, and
worse. Healing songs and herbal medicines carry knowledge of tending
wounds (one-third of the national pharmacopoeia derives from Native
panaceas, Virgil Vogel notes in *American Indian Medicine*). The psychic
disturbances of bad dreams, neurotic fears, raging paranoias, or collective psychoses (outsourcing grief that oversteps tribal boundaries) have
long been treated through the psychological tools of language to cleanse
wrong leanings. Freud called this the talk cure. "Grandfather!" Black
Elk prays to the Great Spirit at the end of his story on Harney peak, "all
things belong to you—the two-leggeds, the four-leggeds, the wings of
the air and all green things that live. You have set the powers of the four
quarters to cross each other. The good road and the road of difficulties
you have made to cross; and where they cross, the place is holy. Day in
and day out, forever, you are the life of things." To say so is to animate
the spirits and shadows. "To-day I send a voice for a people in despair."
To sing for help, for healing, for renewal is to petition power outside
tribal selves. "To the center of the world you have taken me and showed
the goodness and the beauty and the strangeness of the greening, the
only mother—and there the spirit shapes of things, as they should be,
you have shown to me and I have seen." And talk-cure with a medicine
person (animating anxiety) leads into the group therapy of healing tribal
discussions. "Hear me, not for myself, but for my people; I am old. Hear
me that they may once more go back into the sacred hoop and find the
good red road, the shielding tree!" (*Black Elk Speaks* 209).

GROWING WORDS

Humans grow things, gather animals and plants, talking to them, as the Hopi address their *corn* with the word for *children*. The Pima and Papago sing to the hunted deer; the Navajo sit still and call the game. Seasonal rites are ritualized in ceremonial words: clearing the irrigation ditches in March, tilling the earth and planting seeds in April, sprinkling and thinning the new plants in May, weeding and watering sprouts in June, tending buds tenderly in July, harvesting kernels in August, curing them in September, storing grains in October, and living on them through the lean winter.

The balance of sun and rain and snow is critical to these agrarian cycles. Tewa Pueblos sing to the Mother Earth and Father Sky (Herbert J. Spindon, *Songs of the Tewa* 94):

Then weave for us a garment of brightness;
May the warp be the white light of morning,
May the weft be the red light of evening,
May the fringes be the falling rain,
May the border be the standing rainbow.

Chants call moisture from the ancestral cotton-clouds, just as sunrise prayers align the sun's journey through the day with trails of pollen, sage, turquoise, and quartz. The Navajo sing the Night Chant (Washington Matthews, "The Night Chant," in *The Magic World* 62):

In beauty
    you shall be my representation
In beauty
    you shall be my song
In beauty
    you shall be my medicine
In beauty
    my holy medicine

SACRED WORDS

Words have powers to call upon greater blessings and prayers of thanks: for meals that restore the body, for courage to strengthen the heart's doings, for wisdom to nourish the mind's knowings, for grace to temper the spirit's acceptances. The Diné sing a Blessingway ceremony that titles Momaday's

Pulitzer-prize novel (Washington Matthews, *Navajo Myths, Prayers, and Songs* 54–55):

> House made of dawn,
> House made of evening light,
> House made of dark cloud,
> House made of male rain,
> House made of dark mist,
> House made of female rain,
> House made of pollen,
> House made of grasshoppers,
> Dark cloud is at the door.
> The trail out of it is dark cloud.
> The zigzag lightning stands high upon it.
> Male deity!
> Your offering I make.
> I have prepared a smoke for you.

The positive and negative charges—dark and light, cloud and mist, male and female, lightning and smoke—balance time and space through human imagining and voicing. *Mitak' oyasin*, as the Lakota say beginning or ending formal gatherings—"all my relatives." Words go out as protection and guidance for tribal travels along the good red roads. Travelers of the black road pray to return to right beginnings.

> Restore my feet for me,
> Restore my legs for me,
> Restore my body for me,
> Restore my mind for me,
> Restore my voice for me.

The singers ask perseverance, patience, will, stamina, skill, knowledge, or forgiveness in daily challenges to their courage and strength. With right breath and balance they move through a house made of dawn.

> Being as it used to be long ago, may I walk.
> May it be beautiful before me,
> May it be beautiful behind me,
> May it be beautiful below me,
> May it be beautiful above me,

May it be beautiful all around me.
In beauty it is finished.

RAISING WORDS

Minding children requires stories to focus and to calm childhood energies and adult anxieties. Children are taught chants and sayings to implant thoughts crucial to survival and good health, lullabies to quiet and put them to sleep, jokes to count heads and sort out the chaff. Northrop Frye in *The Anatomy of Criticism* argues modes of comic spring renewal that integrate a people, purge winter discontents, and refresh energies for summer. Laughter invigorates and strengthens the tribe for another solar round of romance, tragedy, irony, and comic renaissance. The Moccasin Telegraph, now a 'Skins Internet Trail, crackles with Indi'n humor. "You guys gonna stay long?" now-day Indians say Powhatan asked Jamestown pilgrims. "There goes the neighborhood."

How-to stories teach critical skills, right attitudes, group behavior, self-knowledge, spiritual guidance, improvisational resources, implied cautions, and the surety of evil as a pitfall among counterbalancing forces (avoiding wrong, observing shame, fearing stigma, abhorring ostracism tantamount to death). *Coyote was going along,* the old tales tell of his hilariously revealing thievery, stupidity, cupidity, unrestrained libido, and outright craven egoism, all comic violations of right tribal morality. And then there's always advice when things go wrong: trickster tales as anti-lessons in what *not* to do; animal fables of other-than-human guardians and helpers; heroic epics in how to accomplish impossible deeds; spirit stories about the unseen powers in things; god and goddess songs of benevolent overseers integral with sun, moon, tree, and stone.

WARRING WORDS

Soldiers
You fled.
Even the eagle dies.

—Lakota (Frances Densmore,
Teton Sioux Music 394)

War Stories and Fighting Songs tell how to survive battle; how to get out of a scrape when someone makes a mistake; how to hide and steal away from monsters and inimical forces; how to stand and fight with honor; how to defend the young, infirm, and old against aggression; how to be brave; how to touch the enemy and run away, as in Plains "counting coup"; how to surrender with dignity; how to kill when necessary; how to elegize the dead; how to die. "Let us see, let us see," the Pawnee warrior sings in *The Winged Serpent*, "Is this real, this life I am living?" (Daniel G. Brinton, *Essays of an Americanist* 292). Since war is the worst option (in extremity a necessary evil, some say, but still an evil), these stories and songs teach the people how to come home alive and live in peace. They counsel how to give up the warrior's life-and-death courage and return to a loving place among the people. The last defense of family, home, and land seems the only rationale for war, and even then negotiation leans to the prudent side of aggression. Stay home, the tested wisdoms say, and die at peace in old age. The ultimate Diné goal is *to age with grace and beauty* within the Southwest's four sacred mountain boundaries.

Mortal Words

There are tribal words about dying naturally, accepting mortality with grace and gratefulness, living in time-and-space for a good many years, and meeting death humbly and courageously, as the spirit goes on. To repeat Owl Woman's elegiac chant that surely bears repeating, *In the great night my heart will go out, / Toward me the darkness comes rattling, / In the great night my heart will go out.* Burial is ancestral rooting among the grandfather stones and grandmother hills, the Lakota say, lying down with the *Tunkáshila*. Grieving begs the hard necessary work of lamenting the loss, honoring transition to the other side. After Crazy Horse was killed in 1877, "I cried all night," Black Elk says, "and so did my father" (*Black Elk Speaks* 109). And a year later comes the *spirit release* ceremony, letting go of loss so the spirit can go about its business, and the living can go back to living. The afterlife is too big to know much about or to say with certainty, so best honor the dead and ask their blessing among the living. *Male rain, female rain,* the Southwest tribes pray, giving names to the spirits in all things: clouds over the Rio Grande represent Pueblo spirits of the departed, buried with cotton over their heads, coming back as life-giving rain and snow. The ancestors reappear in dreams and visions, bringing names, directions, strictures, and ongoing deeds to be done.

Grandparents live in the stones and trees. Animals give their names to honor humans. John Fire's great-grandfather spirit brought him the ancestral name of *Tahce Ushte*, or Lame Deer, in a vision pit. *Slow's* father heard a spirit bison muttering *Sitting Bull, Jumping Bull, Bull Among the Cows, Bull Standing Alone* as the Lakota four ages of man; then the hunter bestowed his lugubrious son with the first of these sacred names, *Tatanka Iyotanka* or "Bull Sitting." As a sash-wearing leader and powerful speaker-singer, his was a challenging name to live up to.

Ancestrally, a zoological repository of guardian powers watches over all, including the spirits of plants, animals, forces, and events essential to tribal life. And a name can choose to inhabit a person, the Cree say, just as a story finds its way to a speaker, or a song flows through a singer. Sing *with the heart of a bear*, the Lakota celebrate the bear's heart beating through human voices. Earth and sky, mother and father, "your children are we," the Pueblo chant.

Narrative and lyric define *homo sapiens* as tool-making animals sending their voices across the feared isolations of estrangement. Shared words empower humans to work together across differences. Traditional words ground people in history and place, rooted time and space. Tribal words make humans human. Native cultures are diversely made of words, the *word senders* say. Spoken, danced, and sung, their oral texts compose traditional literacy thousands of years ongoing. Writing down the sounds is a new word magic, as tribal writers emerge the ancestral guardians, contemporary gadflies, and advance guard of a transcultural, ongoing, sovereign America.

Writ in Stone

Rock art is a sort of pictographic writing which
constitutes humanity's largest and most significant
archive of its history for 40,000 years until the
advent of conventional modern ideographic and then
alphabetic writing.

> —Emmanuel Anati, "Valcamonica Rock Art:
> A New History for Europe."

Imagine: somewhere in the prehistoric distance a man
holds up in his hand a crude instrument—a brand,
perhaps, or something like a daub or a broom bearing
pigment—and fixes the wonderful image in his mind's
eye to a wall or rock. . . . all the stories of all the world
proceed from the moment in which he makes his mark.
All literatures issue from his hand.

> —N. Scott Momaday, *The Man Made of Words*

AGUA ES VIDA

West of my home along the Santa Fe River rises a forty-foot basalt cliff. A
million years ago the Jemez Mountains belched volcanic debris of magma,
granite, and tuff over northern New Mexico. Basalt lava flowed to the river
and stopped. Pueblo artifacts show that more than two thousand years ago
tribal ancestors made their homes tending fields in the Rio Grande Valley,
whereas ten to six thousand years earlier Paleo-Indians of the Pleistocene
Ice Ages (back twenty-three thousand years) hunted wooly mammoth,

giant bison, cameloids, and tapir, gathering wild seeds and plants. The Rio Grande is the second longest river in the United States, the world's most utilized riparian watercourse next to the Ganges for irrigated crops. *Agua es vida*, locals say with due respect: "water is life." The final 1608 leg of the Spanish King's Highway trailed the Santa Fe River near my house into the northern capital, a camino still called Agua Fria, "cool water."

Indians of La Bajada Mesa and Santa Fe Canyon trace back to 700 A.D. These past few years the Peña Blanca Project at Cochiti has uncovered pot-sherds; squash, corn, and bean storage cists; bones of butchered elk, deer, antelope, and rabbit; plus turkey, waterfowl, and two dog skeletons near human burials. Ironically, these Pueblo ancestors came to be known by the latter-day Navajo word *Anasazi*, or "old-enemy ones," corrected today by way of Hopi *Hisatsinom*, "Ancient People," to Ancestral Pueblos. Their ruins ghost the Southwest.

Eight hundred years ago, thousands of villages dotted the Four Corners area: Monument Valley of southern Utah deserts (John Ford *Stagecoach* country), to Canyon de Chelly of northern Arizona (Kit Carson's scorched-earth Navajo removal), to Mesa Verde cliff complexes of southwest Colorado (four corners of states), to the pueblos or "towns" of the Jemez Range in northwest New Mexico where I live. These ancestral peoples vanished by 1300 or so, abandoning the majority of their sites after a twenty-four-year drought, tree-ring samples show, including soil depletions, starvation, and probable social unrest. No one knows exactly where or why they went, since tribes north of the Rio Grande did not have alphabetic writing. Jared Diamond ponders the biospheric disappearance of Chaco in *Collapse: How Societies Choose to Fail or Succeed*, and in *Guns, Germs, and Steel,* as noted, explains why ancestral Natives didn't *need*, thus didn't develop alpha-betic writing as hunter-gatherers along a north-south hemispheric axis. By contrast, Mediterranean planters could hybridize seeds across an east-west trading climate zone that reached twenty thousand vertical feet in Iran and so develop forms of writing to commodify exchange goods. Modern literacy began as overseas agrarian bookkeeping.

Perhaps the missing Pueblo migrants moved in with existing peoples along the Southwest's rivers, some archaeologists think, or took to higher forests in search of water sources, or migrated westward. The Chaco tur-quoise capital, an empire sixty miles west of my home over Tetilla Peak and Cochiti Pueblo, also lay empty by 1300. Four-story structures built with 200,000 tree trunks dragged forty-three miles east from the Chuska Mountains fell permanently silent. Underground kivas went dark. Major roadways across the Southwest stood deserted.

And all that scholars *know* of these precolonial Southwestern peoples—all that they *wrote* about themselves—lies etched in the rocks. "Petroglyphs on rock outcrops along the San Jose River suggest that the Paleo-Indian ancestors of the Pueblos had already begun to make images of spiritual significance on the sandstone," Leslie Silko writes in *Yellow Woman and a Beauty of Spirit*. "Pueblo kivas have stylized abstract designs painted on the walls and altarpieces. The Pueblo people had long understood that certain man-made visual images were sacred and were necessary to Pueblo ceremony" (*YWBS* 175). Mostly facing southeast to village sites near water sources in springs, lakes, streams, or rivers, these rock carvings exist in the hundreds of thousands across the Southwest (among many fine books, see Polly Schaafsma's *Rock Art in New Mexico*, David Grant Noble's *Ancient Ruins of the Southwest*, and most recently Kurt F. Anscheutz et al., *"That Place People Talk About": The Petroglyph National Monument Ethnographic Landscape Report*).

Ancient iconic texts lead to contemporary Native *letters* or "literature." Alphabets, glyphs, or syllabaries trace back to early Mayan hieroglyphs before 600 B.C. in southern Mexico, or five thousand years to Sumerian cuneiform, the Mesopotamian beginnings of Western writing near Baghdad. So, too, Native American writings relate ancestrally to chiseled or "pecked" images in basalt cliffs along a Native fertile crescent. If scholars "read" stone glyphs as interwoven texts (Latin *texere* or "woven," as in textile and texture, so with Greek *hymnos*), cultural literacy includes images on ceramic bowls and baskets, painted pictographs and kiva murals, ongoing tribal myths and origin stories. Louise Erdrich envisions "a spiritual geography" meant "to provide teaching and dream guide to generations of Anishinaabeg" who contemplate pictographic texts inscribed in Lake of the Woods Minnesota rocks ("Rock Paintings," *Books and Islands in Ojibwe Country* 51):

> I am standing before the rock wall of Painted Rock Island
> and trying to read it like a book. I don't know the language,
> though. The painting spreads across a ten- or twelve-foot
> rectangle of smooth rock, and includes several spirit figures
> as well as diagrams of teachings. The deep light pulls the
> figures from the rock. They seem to glow from the inside,
> a vibrant golden red. . . . One is a horned human figure
> and the other a stylized spirit figure who Tobasonakwut
> calls, lovingly, the *Manoominikeshii*, or the wild rice spirit.

STONE POEMS

Anciently imaged stone texts led to a 1969 Pulitzer Prize novel, *House Made of Dawn* by N. Scott Momaday, set just west in the Jemez Mountains. Teaching at the University of Arizona, this Kiowa writer keeps a modern condo in Santa Fe close to his children and still frequents the family house near Jemez Pueblo where he grew up in the 1940s. "These things he told to his grandsons carefully, slowly and at length, because they were old and true, and they could be lost forever as easily as one generation is lost to the next, as easily as one old man might lose his voice, having spoken not enough or not at all. But his grandsons knew already; not the names or the strict position of the sun each day in relation to its house, but the larger motion and meaning of the great organic calendar itself, the emergency of dawn and dusk, summer and winter, the very cycle of the sun and of all the suns that were and were to come. And he knew they knew, and he took them with him to the fields and they cut open the earth and touched the corn and ate sweet melons in the sun" (*House Made of Dawn* 198). The solar agrarian calendar, cultural turnings generation to generation, complete a tribal circle.

Rock "art" of the ancestral past also informs the poetry of Simon Ortiz, an Acoma artist to the immediate south, who writes of poetic lineation as "woven stone" by way of his father's layered rock masonry in "A Story of How a Wall Stands" (*Going for the Rain*): "Underneath what looks like loose stone, / there is stone woven together." Ancient stonework aligns Leslie Silko's center-margined verse and riparian prose in the novel *Ceremony* set around Laguna Pueblo, sister village to Acoma. "He tasted the deep heartrock of the earth, where the water came from, and he thought maybe this wasn't the end after all" (*C* 46). The ancestral past colors Joy Harjo's lyrics, a Muskogee from Oklahoma who went through the Santa Fe Institute of American Indian Arts prep school and on to college at the University of New Mexico where she now teaches, after studying with Silko, marrying Ortiz, and circling the fifty states. "My cheek is flat against memory described by stone and lichen," Harjo says of petroglyphic earth-stories in *Secrets from the Center of the World* (48). The poet edges over the Rio Grande bajada rim west of Albuquerque among some 20,000 petroglyphs in *She Had Some Horses* (29):

cuchillo
    moon
        is a white horse thundering down
        over the edge
        of a raw red cliff

Petroglyphic icons shape the paintings of the late Harry Fonseca, California Maidu transplanted to the Land of Enchantment, now scoring his canvases with Native planes and aboriginal texts as *Stone Poems*. "Petroglyphs play a major role in our aesthetic, history, and keeping of intellect," the poet Elizabeth Woody forewords his 1996 Wheelwright Museum exhibit catalogue, *Harry Fonseca: Earth, Wind, and Fire* (8). "They are a means of telling a story, writing or describing an event, or are marks from some supernatural being with a specific intent." Hopi rock complexes layer the geometric paintings of Dan Namingha of Santa Fe and the chromatic *katsina* canvases of Mike Kabotie at Santa Fe's August Indian Market. Ancestral images influence the hip Taos musician Mirabel, a traditional and postmodern lyricist popular among young Rio Grande 'Skins. The old rock carvings move Allan Houser, Santa Fe Apache sculptor recently deceased, to monumental stone forms now featured in the National Museum of the American Indian on the Washington Mall (see McMaster and Trafzer's *Native Universe*). Petroglyphic mysteries inspire Sherwin Bitsui, Diné poet editing the Internet and print journal *RedInk*, to publish the surreal scree lyrics of *Shapeshift*, dense as spent uranium. "Apparition" asks of stone-carving ancestors:

> Strange, how they burrowed into the side of this rock.
> Strange . . . to think,
> they "belonged"
> and stepped through the flowering of a future apparent in
> the rearview mirror,
> visible from its orbit
> around a cluster of knives in the galaxy closest to
> the argument.

WATER-PLACE VILLAGE

Questions of iconic heritage rustle in the aspen around my house as I consider the shapes, sounds, contexts, and histories of Native American letters today—the works of over a thousand living Indian writers. Silko images Tayo's story-vision in *Ceremony*: "Everywhere he looked, he saw a world made of stories, the long ago, time immemorial stories, as old Grandma called them. It was a world alive, always changing and moving; and if you knew where to look, you could see it, sometimes almost imperceptible, like the motion of the stars across the sky" (C 95). The storied rocks and stars are rooted in ongoing tribal literacy.

What ceremonies, performed over hundreds if not thousands of years, still illumine the dreams and prayers and desires of contemporary Indian artists, as the San Juan Pueblo holds feast days with Turtle Dances at midwinter, or the Cochiti Pueblo celebrates Corn Dances in midsummer? Silko writes how icon evokes object as spirit calls shape into being—the old generative magic of images: "Pictographs and petroglyphs of constellations or elk or antelope draw their magic in part from the process wherein the focus of all prayer and concentration is upon the thing itself, which, in its turn, guides the hunter's hand. Connection with the spirit dimensions requires a figure or form that is all-inclusive" (*Yellow Woman and a Beauty of Spirit* 28–29).

As Plains tribes perform Sun Dances midyear, Iroquois and Algonkian peoples honor Green Corn Festivals at the beginning, or California Pomo and Wintu celebrate Strawberry Festival in spring and Acorn Festival in fall—grounded dance steps cadence Native lyrics and red-line contemporary narratives. Songs, embedded eidetically in Black Hills stones, resurface in "now-day Indi'n" verse, as my Lakota brother would say. Place-names, creation myths, how-to stories, and cautionary tales—engrained in granite, basalt, turquoise, tuff, crystal, obsidian, and sandstone striations—continue the lineations, the carved images and cut edges, of lyric narratives old as the rocks above the Rio Grande and Colorado River drainages. "And in the belly of this story / the rituals and the ceremony / are still growing" (*Ceremony* 2).

The village buried west of my house has no name (perhaps the lost Tziguma or "water-place" pueblo). As Santa Fe County blacktop #56 bends east, the unmortared stone foundations of a sunken pueblo mark a broken rectangle abrupting the pasturage around a whitewashed Penitente chapel. The Spaniards who made pilgrimage north from Mexico City in the seventeenth century, several thousand miles of El Camino Real to the "Holy Faith" citadel of Santa Fe, built their churches on Ancestral Pueblo ruins of some seventy Native settlements with thirty thousand peoples. It was a sign of conquest. Las Golondrinas Ranch just to the southeast, still farmed and worked as an historical site of local pride and tourist revenue, signaled the last stop on the trek north. The Tesuque Peak runoff surfaces in desert springs where I live at La Cieneguilla, or "little marsh"—precious snowmelt aquifer from the Sangre de Cristo Mountains to the east, southern tip of the Rockies. My well is 120 feet deep and the water pure as new snow. Giant cottonwoods guard the drainage into the village. Chile, bean, squash, corn, sunflower, and melon fields, plus fruit orchards of apple, peach, cherry, and plum show signs of continuous cultivation for some four hundred years now. Sunrise Springs, a Buddhist health spa in the wellspring of all this history, coexists with ongoing Hispanic cultures, migrant gringos, and ancestral spirits.

This adjacent Pueblo village has been ploughed over for safekeeping, the archaeologists say. The Natives fled in 1680, perhaps to Keres-speaking Laguna or the Tewa-Hopi first mesa Hano, after the Pueblo Revolt and the certain return of the Black Legend. Vengeful conquistadores cut off Acoma arms and feet to make a point about fealty, tribute, pagan gods, and forced acculturation. The Spanish gentry of the Baca Land Grant ruled the little Santa Fe Valley and La Bajada Mesa for three centuries under the King of Spain. Yet on horseback, the old Baca *patrón* herds longhorns to the Santa Fe River, here a creek from the city sewage plant.

Older voices backfill the valley. Four thousand petroglyphs from some fourteen hundred years look down on a five-mile river drainage. Bighorn sheep are scratched into the basalt, and ravens wheel over scampering roadrunners. Humpbacked Kokopellis gyre with flutes and epic phalluses. Sunbursts glaze toward the southeast, lightning snakes zigzag down lava rocks, spiders weave labyrinths into stones. Mounted Spaniards enter down the timeline, and eagles soar above it all. Tetilla Peak mounds behind the cliffs, El Camino Real snaking along the streambed at the base. Centuries-old wagon tracks are barely visible through the buffalo grass, rabbit brush, and chamisa. Cholla cactus lines the route north. Like the Dead Sea scrolls, Sapphic verse strips on mummy cartonage, the Rosetta Stone, or the Mayan Codices, the old texts must be read anew.

Desert light banks into every corner of my New Mexico adobe. The walls brace against fierce sun, high winds, desert aridity, and winter snows. Anything that wants to live through four seasons of penetrating cold and baking heat at seven thousand feet sinks thirsty taproots into the clay sandstone. Residents learn respectful humility, a deep-rooted resilience in the enduring humors of *koshare* clowns, Kokopellis, and crows. It takes time to make a home here.

Coyotes caucus by dark in the Jemez foothills. Stars over the Sangre de Cristo Mountains pebble the night with liquid crystals. Orion rises bigger than Paul Bunyan above the Galisteo basin to the south, where rock carvings at Comanche Gap record the passing of Tewa, Tiwa, Towa, and Keres Pueblo tribes, followed by Navajo, Apache, and Comanche wanderers, even Aztec and Mayan messengers from far south. Spanish settlers four hundred years back, Jewish exiles from Mexico City called *murenos* or *conversos*, rode here among the earliest cowboys. The old cemetery stones are etched with Stars of David among Catholic crosses.

Twelve crow-flight miles over the prairie ridge to the northeast, the oldest plaza in the country still holds commerce with the West. Santa Fe sits at the foot of Tesuque Mountain, a Pueblo sacred boundary peak. The town was named for the Spanish village near Granada where Queen Isabella and King Ferdinand defeated the Moors in 1492, then dealt with financing Cristoforo Colombo to the New World. Established a year after Jamestown, Santa Fe boasts the oldest church and public offices in the Union, the newest tinhorn frenzy and freshest westering of New Age pilgrims looking for holistic health, country kitsch, a kinder pace, and better art bargains. Southwest Indians in sidewalk lawn chairs spread blankets of turquoise, silver, pottery, and sand-pocked bread for tourists under the *portál* of the Palace of Governors, the first municipal building in the States. It was once commandeered by revolutionary Pueblos in 1680, later taken by Southern soldiers during the Civil War, driven back by Comanches and Unionists. A stone war memorial stands at the center of America's oldest Plaza:

> *To the Heros*
> *Who Have Fallen in the*
> *Various Battles with ——*
> *Indians in the Territory of New Mexico*
> *1866–7–8*

The original modifier of *Indians*, etched *Savage*, has been defaced in the past few years.

Edged and quartz-clear, shifting as quicksilver, the high desert light has attracted émigré artists like D. H. Lawrence, Ansel Adams, Willa Cather, Witter Bynner, and Georgia O'Keeffe for decades. The sky blues reach to the galaxies. Amber shafts of sunlight angle over the desert like stage lights. Storms belly in clusters—multiple cracks of lightning and mighty thunder to drench the Rio Grande drainage with precious downpour. My redbrick and tile floors flatten against the caliche desert, soaking up gnarled voices of soapweed and cholla cactus, sage and chamisa, tumbleweeds and saltbrush, cedar, piñon and juniper shrubs. Finches, bluebirds, juncos, jays, occasional tanagers and meadowlarks come by the bird feeder, as geese, cranes, and ducks make their seasonal migrations north and south along the rivers. The Sangre de Cristo Mountains edge half the northeastern horizon, Tesuque Peak snow-capped half the year at the top. The volcanic Ortiz peaks thrust up to the south across the flat desert plain falling away to Mexico. The Jemez

Range rolls off to the west with the world's largest extinct volcanic crater or caldera, Valle Grande, overlooking Los Alamos, matrix of global nuclear-weapons research.

South Corner Clowns

> The petroglyph area is where messages to the spirit world are communicated. It is here that our Pueblo ancestors "wrote" down the visions and experiences they felt. . . . We consider each of these petroglyphs to be a record of visions written here of some spiritual being, event or expressions attesting to and/or guarding a person's sacrifice or offering.
>
> —Governors of Cochiti, Jemez, Sandia, Santa Ana, and Zia Pueblos, *Albuquerque Journal*, 16 October 1996

Historians conjecture the daily lives of the precolonial Pueblos: how they survived hunting and planting, their creation stories and beast fables for going on, their rituals in cooking and preparing foods, their etiological tales as to why things were just so, their cautionary tales of what not to do. Life here through the hot and cold seasons, monsoons, droughts, and blizzards was not easy. If their households were managed around weaving and chopping, grinding and sorting, metates and storage bowls, scholars can only imagine their teaching stories and moral allegories on how to do these things well. Certainly they had families, clans, alliances, loyalties, and fears of unknown events and known enemies. What were the lullabies and love songs of their daily human contact, their marriage and burial ceremonies, their prayers and petitions, and how do these literacies survive in Pueblo life today? What were daily, monthly, yearly events in their health and history, and how did they sing of seasonal changes in their environment? What were their sustaining beliefs and daily faiths—spirits honored in their religious and ritual behavior, their dreams and hopes voiced as songs and stories?

All experts suppose of these Pueblo ancestors is carved into the rocks—facing southeast to the sunrise winter solstice, the *south corner time*. The logograms or imaged "word-pictures," whether numinous icons or ideational artifacts, can be glossed generically: an open hand of greeting (meaning both hello and sunrise in regional Keres, according to Franz Boas); animal or bird tracks (human migration signifiers); parrot, magpie, crow, hawk (winged messengers); deer, elk, sheep, squirrel, rabbit (nurturers); coyote, turkey, dog, wolf (sentinels); frog, fish, toad, serpent (underground scouts and rain bearers); bear, mountain lion, eagle, badger (protectors); dragonfly, ant, butterfly, spider (healers and teachers); and later horse effigies (Hispanic newcomers).

"What they have a word for, they have a thing for," Père Rasles noted in his Abenaki dictionary in the Northeast, as recorded by Thoreau in his *Indian Notebooks*. Images stand for "things"—the sun as a quadrant circle of cardinal points, the New Mexico state logo—and actions show things doing things. A squatting woman, for example, signifies birthing. An idea, as for Plato, is a *thing seen*, and abstractions are concretely imaged. An open hand, as noted, suggests "hello" or "sunrise." Images flower over the rocks: arrows and atlatls, bows and blankets, clouds and coitus, lightning and vortex, combat and corn, dancers and upside-down death, feathers and flutes, shamans and warriors, births and prayers, rattles and shields, spirals of time and four-corner solar circles, ithyphallic seed carriers with horns and flutes called Kokopelli after the Hopi fertility spirit, *kookopölö*. The Hopi *katsina* is modeled on the humped robber fly, some think, an aggressive insect predator that sucks the fluids of trapped prey and copulates incessantly. H. R. Voth collected a *Kokopell'Mana* in 1912, a Hopi *katsina* doll representing the Humpback Maid or fertility figure that chases men during certain ceremonies and simulates copulation. She and her humpback male partner are showered ceremonially with cornmeal by couples desiring children.

This last rock icon is the most lusty among the basalt petroglyphs: over a hundred humpbacked, flute-playing, penis-wielding procreators. Interpretations of origins range from traveling Aztec or Toltec *puchteca*, perhaps traders from central Mexico bringing pod corn, parrots, and macaws to Chaco; to a Water Sprinkler god fluting on a Cloud Blower, possibly a Pan or Orphic mediator between heaven and earth; to corn bringer and woman seducer and mischievous munchkin; to shapeshifter or hero with a thousand faces; to composite Magician, Pied Piper, Don Juan Trickster, and Johnny Cornseed negotiating cicada or locust swarms (Hopi flute-society patron), even assassin- or robber-fly agrarian *mishigas*; to a dancing, horned flutist personifying the procreative, integrative spirit of the Rio Grande Valley (see Ekkehart Malotki's *Kokopelli*).

Hopi flute-tooting *katsina*s play over springs for water, and the petroglyphic flute can serve as a smoke or "cloud blower" to bring rain, to melt snows with songs, to call sun-loving snakes and frogs, to draw water-loving insects. Courtship, seduction, shamanic ceremony, simple lyric—the flute is mankind's oldest musical instrument, as recorded in an 82,000-year-old flute made from a bear's thigh bone in a Slovenia Neanderthal cave (Dennis Slifer, *The Serpent and the Sacred Fire* 102). As with Kokopelli images, the seed traders also carried canes or crook-necked staffs, still in evidence among the Pueblo caciques today as bronze-capped Governor Canes from Spain, Mexico, New Mexico, and United States presidents beginning with Abraham Lincoln.

Imagine in the Kokopelli hump or burden basket seeds, songs, blankets, babies, caged macaws and parrots, buckskins and mocca-sins, rainbow and mist, spirits and piggyback partners, even a Hopi back-shield as moisture tablet to bring rain. Some medical researchers posit that living Kokopellis hundreds of years ago suffered a tubercular deformity of Pott's disease that produced spinal kyphosis or hump-back, clubfeet and misshapen legs, even a pre-Viagra priapism perma-nently engorging the penis (see Slifer and Duffield, *Kokopelli* 28–29; and Malotki, *Kokopelli* 25). The Puritan mind might recoil at the sight of erect penises pecked into the rocks, but posit a survivalist tribal cul-ture dependant on procreation, both the land's bounty and species regeneration. "In prehistoric art, pregnant women," Marija Gimbutas writes, "and excited men are not sex symbols in the twentieth-century sense. Our forebears were more philosophical; there was no element of obscenity in their art" (*The Language of the Goddess* 139). This fecund premise of ample breasts, open vulvas, and aroused phalli is ancient with tribal survival, back twenty-four thousand years to Venus of Willendorf, the earliest discovered fertility icon in the Western world, or further back some thirty thousand years to Paleolithic image magic of cave paintings in southern France. For tribal life the world over, infant mortality was life-threatening to the extended family clan, and death rates were critical to survival. Reproductive cycles were primary to population stability. "Prehistoric fertility symbols are symbols of potency, abundance, and multiplication, concerned with the perpetuation of life and the preserva-tion of life forces constantly threatened by death," Gimbutas continues. "Fertility symbols are seasonal, representing dying and awakening nature." To repeat, northern New Mexico is not a landscape or climate, an intermountain desert plain at seven thousand feet, for the weak-blooded. So given the primacy of procreative cycles, a high dependency on the natural environment for annual sustenance, the combined virility and fertility of the humanized land would dominate all concerns.

Ithyphallic "wife-hunter" Kokopellis may have been pecked in the rocks imaging the needed stranger's seed diversifying a gene pool, indeed deepening DNA through exogamy. Some historians argue that Mexican-Indian seed merchants were conflated with the natural image of the robber fly to depict phallic exaggerations in Kokopelli's humped back, flute proboscis, and horns. In any event *like produces like*, Pueblos say, and if the river valley is well seeded, the feminine body reproduces. Procreation is primary. The procreator sports horned animal virility and vitality—phallic extensions of the will and heart through the mind—not to mention fleet-of-foot hooves, generatively feral on the predatory high plain. This exaggerated phallocentric icon, dependent on feminine receptivity as mother earth's horizon line, suggests a mixing, indeed a melding of the danger and desire bound up in procreative sex as societal norm. Neo-feminists may warn that procreativity is an antiquated approach to gender and sexuality, but wedged between microbiologists and paleontologists, scientists are hard pressed to offer alternative readings. Sensuality across genders dominates fertility far back in human evolution, still driving the arts of survival, prosperity, and renewal from Hollywood to the White House.

The little man pipes the arts of seduction, a *come-hither* song on his flute, perhaps a *stick-around-baby* story. Richard Dawkins argues in *The Selfish Gene* that virile inseminators as tall dark strangers may be chosen by women as itinerate seed donors; or within the tribe, the cross-clan courtier will be selected after an engagement period of ample nesting and feeding, insuring the health and maturation of offspring who carry the surviving gene forward ("Battle of the Sexes" 149–58). All this to keep evolution, biologists say, evolving symbiogenetically to fuse ongoing life-forms. Today motels, galleries, kitsch stores, nightclubs, realtors, rafters, earrings, pendants, belt buckles, light fixtures, T-shirts, bike trails, and recorder societies all honor Kokopelli.

Consider a certain humor playing around the edges in all this. The comic exposure of an erect phallus might signal some laughing kind of pleasure principle that functions to renew the people and land, to cleanse the body of disease and death (as well as banish winter for the season), to tribalize the people as extended family (Northrop Frye's archetypal comic modes in *Anatomy of Criticism*). This spring renewal comes through necessary cultural and genetic openings, or pattern breaks—"laugh-hole" to "other-hole," Peter Blue Cloud says—for outside stimulation and renewal (Lincoln, *Indi'n Humor*). Traditional Southwestern weavings, quiltings, potteries, jewelries, and decorative-functional arts contain humbling pattern breaks for the spirits to enter and to exit, to breathe in and out, so matter and spirit can intermix at the perimeters of human endeavor. Maverick Kokopelli is possibly comic then—nature's phallic exaggerations are both imagined and periodically realized. The epic "size" of the erect penis is comically inflated and momentarily "real," conflating the fears and desires of copulation, empowering pregnancy and fostering healthy genetic issue, perhaps bringing a smile to the face of an old-time maiden.

However scholars consider these thrusting, flute-tooting, humpbacked and horned animal-men, their very presence throughout the valley (indeed Kokopellis of all persuasions, buggering each other or animals, for lack of basalt female receptors) says by their staying and proliferating power among ancestral rocks that viewers cannot ignore the priapic principle in human culture and ancestry, prehistorically or presently. Including all types of sexual persuasion, Timothy Taylor documents five thousand years of Eurasian interest in bestiality, homosexuality, prostitution, transvestism, transsexuality, hormone treatments, sadomasochism, contraception, racial breeding, acrobatic and competitive sex, and transcendental sex as a spiritual discipline (*The Prehistory of Sex: Four Million Years of Human Sexual Culture* 17). Where did Puritan inhibition go wrong?

HUMPBACKED FLUTE PLAYERS

The language of the wild rice harvest is intensely erotic
and often comically sexualized. If the stalk is floppy,
it is a poor erection. Too wet, it is a penis soaking in
its favorite place. Half hard, full, hairy, the metaphors
go on and on. Everything is sexual, the way of the
world is to be sexual, and it is good (although often
ridiculous). The great teacher of the Anishinaabeg,
whose intellectual prints are also on this rock, was a
being called Nanabozho, or Winabojo. He was wise,
he was clever, he was a sexual idiot, a glutton, full of
miscalculations and bravado. He gave medicines to
the Ojibwe, one of the primary being laughter.

—Louise Erdrich, "Rock Art,"
Books and Islands in Ojibwe Country

Archaeologists shy from reading ancient rock relics as *texts* for lack of cultural backup, neither historical document nor tribal authority to reassure them. Similar uncertainty dogs reading an Emily Dickinson poem, decoding a Sapphic ode, focusing on a Taoist fragment, or interpreting Biblical Apocrypha—say a Dead Sea Scroll by Miriam of Magdala. Some have trouble understanding a tax form. For that matter, viewers cannot be certain about a Klee canvas, a Calder mobile, a Rothko monochrome, or a Stravinsky symphony. Art is only *about* anything, to call on Heather McHugh's axiom of reading poetry, the way a cat is about a house. Certainly these petroglyphic images are eidetic images carved into Native stone, living figures of narrative action, perhaps even stories that survive centuries and still inform those who attend. Existing Pueblos look to these slate sites as mother villages. The ancestral etchings are outdoors, not indoors—etched into basalt, not printed on paper, long-lasting as the mountains themselves. They are immediate to the eye, edged to touch, concrete to reflect on as characters. As Ezra Pound notes in *ABC of Reading*, via Ernest Fenollosa on the stone-carved Chinese ideogram, *character* means cut or "engraved" in Greek, and so serves concretely chiseled poetic diction. These engraved characters convey information and ideas iconically, even elegantly image their messages directly to the uninformed mind's eye. They face the annual southeast return of light and warmth on December 21, every year since the first year at the *south corner* of time. Eighteen Pueblos up and down the Rio Grande Valley over 130 miles still celebrate, for over a thousand years now, this seasonal renewal with feast days and ceremonial dances and tribal chants and family celebrations and clan gatherings. Strangers are welcome. Everyone gets fed, bodily, socially, and spiritually. Some even find mates. A number have become writers.

So these stone etchings encrypt ecosystemic literature, a bestiary and biospheric garden of creatures and plants—leggéds and roots and wingéds and crawling things, sunrise to sunset, waxing and waning moonrise to moonset, night and day through all time—all under a 24-hour-daily, 28-day-monthly, 13-moon-yearly, all-seasons tribal text of natural cycles, as in Aztec calendars. Such images contain the spirits of place, as Keith Basso says of Apache place-names that particularize cultural myths and advisory tales where "wisdom sits in places." They tell the people why-they-are-who-they-are, the Cibecue Apache say; they "keep us straight." The rock icons are lasting testaments, stationary markers, solid life-forms of archaeological and geological time feeding into written literature. Ponder these shrines as living temple tablets surviving millennial changes. They are a sculpted literacy, requiring patient time to cut the images into stone, surviving all the catastrophes, even death. There is density and resistance in the edges and planes of their rock cuttings. The seasonal lights of day illumine figurative narratives by way of position and placement, apposition and clustering. Pueblos today say the grouped icons key stories that generate storytelling and singing, emergence celebrations, generative action figures, tribal motifs, biospheric interdependencies, seasonal shifts, spiritual reckonings, all in the native stones of a given shared place. These relational and figurative narratives read through crevasses and around corners in 360-degree associative patterns, not linear sequences, as in modern-art canvases and sculptures. Literally walking the cliff bases under the rocks to read the images, a viewer decodes these sculpted texts along the path of a story line.

ROCK WRITING

Among arched alcoves and long ledges of rock is
a wide sandstone wall on which are drawn large,
tapering anthropomorphic forms, colored in dark
red pigment. There on the geologic picture plane is
a procession of gods approaching inexorably from
the earth. They are informed with irresistible power;
they are beyond our understanding, masks of infinite
possibility. We do not know what they mean, but we
know that we are involved in their meaning. They
persist through time in the imagination, and we cannot
doubt that they are invested with the very essence of
language, the language of story and myth and primal
song. They are two thousand years old, more or less,
and they remark as closely as anything can the origin
of American literature.

—N. Scott Momaday,
The Man Made of Words

Noting that petroglyphs are called "rock writing" in Pueblo Tewa dialects today, Carol Patterson-Rudolph, inspired by LeVan Martineau's *The Rocks Begin to Speak*, has ventured to "read" these stone inscriptions as ceremonial narratives in *Petroglyphs & Pueblo Myths of the Rio Grande*. Above La Cienega she finds evidence of "The Jug Boy" myth from the Hopi-Tewa village of Hano, Tano migrants from the Galisteo

Basin in 1696 (recorded by Henry R. Voth, *Traditions of the Hopi*, in 1905; and Elsie Clews Parsons, *Tewa Tales*, in 1926). Clearly Pueblo story lines migrate from the Rio Grande Valley back and forth to the Hopi Mesas, beginning with Tewa migrations to Arizona around 1700, as artists travel between family clan villages still today. Consider the Jug Boy tale. A young maiden, too pure for the village boys, was mixing her mother's clay with her foot to make water jars when some impregnating mud spilled up her leg, and she gave birth to a round thing with protruding knobs, a little living water jar. The talking jar had no arms or legs or eyes, but he grew up and one day asked his grandfather to go winter rabbit hunting. He rolled against a rock, broke open, and hatched a full-grown, well-dressed boy who killed four rabbits and went back to the village with his grandfather. The Jug Boy then descended to another realm and found his true father and extended feminine family living in a spring, went back up to his dying mother bearing the news (with spring water perhaps), then returned down to the spring only to find her restored with his father, Water Snake Red. "That's the way that boy and his mother went to the spring to live there," concluded the Hopi narrator, a Tewa Bear clansman married at Sichumovi, speaking to Elsie Clews Parsons on First Mesa in 1923 (*Tewa Tales* xii), the year D. H. Lawrence settled north of Taos.

The La Cienega petroglyphs swirl in a descending S-curve: five flute-playing Kokopelli "wife hunters"; a horned (spiritual) woman birthing a round knobbed jar, repeated in copulating figures (zigzag lines of movement); a double-lobed water-jar issue; mountain lion (grandfather) and walking prints (signs of hunting and traveling); rock-broken and leaking double jar (a fortunate fall concretely imaged), coiling down a spring to a large-breasted bird (mother) and water serpent (father) with female-kin relatives. This sequence could be a drought migration myth. The boy (on an identity quest) discovers his "father" underground where the springs feed desert life, and returns again Orphically to tell his "mother," who dies, only to be reborn underground with the spring father Water Snake Red, aunts, sisters, and female cousins.

Gender questions rise from the storied images. Why the underground lost father found by a cross-cultural, illegitimate carrier-son? Why the matriarchal emphasis among the Pueblos to this day (reversing Anglo patriarchy) of mother rights, matrilineal clans, and women leaders? Breeding for futurity has always been essential to humans, particularly in stressed living environments. James Brooks documents how Southwestern "pagan Indians" from the seventeenth through the nineteenth centuries

were traded at a value of "two good horses and some trifles" for captive women from twelve to twenty years old, a sterile she-mule or poorer
horse with red-rag-garnished bridle for men (*Captives & Cousins:
Slavery, Kinship, and Community in the Southwest Borderlands* 63).
Bearing children, caring for tribal offspring, and carrying water-culture
as tribal futurity remain a matriarchal Pueblo cornerstone.

The runic panels read in a flow pattern from the top, across and back
again, down across the cliff face spiraling into the spring, all moving traditionally clock- or sunwise. The riparian images stream across, back,
over, and down the rock face in associative patterns, neither linear nor
through-line logical, but clustering in story arcs of linked narrative
actions or "panels." They seem designed to be regarded in different lights
from various angles, to be walked around and through and back over
seasonally, repeating the stories down through the ages, permanently
incised in temporal space. This outdoor fixed or set text has been readable and renewable for a thousand years or more, and still the Pueblos
make pilgrimages here to renew their ancestral songs and stories.

Characters generate narratives. Patterson-Rudolph finds that related
Keres creation stories of the sisters Uretsete and Naotsete, mothers of
Pueblos and non-Pueblo Navajos and Whites respectively, take place near
the Jug Boy among images of Turkey Man, Chaparral Cock, Serpent
Man, Crown Man, Magpie, Squirrel, White Dove, Coyote, and Spider.
These are interrelated twin-sister creation myths told and retold across
Keres traditions today (see her 1997 *On the Trail of Spider Woman:
Petroglyphs, Pictographs, and Myths of the Southwest*; and Paula Gunn
Allen's writings, especially *The Sacred Hoop* and *Spider Woman's
Granddaughters*). To the right of this second narrative panel, the rock
cryptologist discovers yet another creation story of Uretsete (Spider), and
the corn fetish Iariko, engendering or breeding myths of ongoing Pueblo
cultural values. And so on, for several miles of cliff carvings in the La
Cienega region.

Carol Patterson-Rudolph may not have the last word matching petroglyphic panels to migrant Keres myths, but she does show that the ancient
stories were and still are alive, marvelously suggestive up and down the
Rio Grande Valley, etched into the basalt cliffs above the Keres-speaking
villages of Cochiti, Santa Domino, San Felipe, Santa Ana, Acoma, Zia,
and Laguna Pueblos. What they are is there to see, as the Pueblo peoples
still journey there to talk with the stones. What the rock glyphs *mean*
is up for interpretive discussion among the Pueblo peoples and interested outsiders, as all lasting classic translations—the Vedas, the Bible,

Homeric epics, Dante's cantos, or Dickinson's fascicles—reawaken fresh responses. Leslie Silko begins *Ceremony* with a reworked Keres creation myth from her Laguna mother village. Ts'its'tsi'nake, or Thought-Woman, sits in her room thinking up reality, including her sisters Nau'ts'ity'i and I'tcts'its'i, and together they create this world and the four below. Spider Thought-Woman names things and they appear. She sits in her room thinking of the story Silko is telling.

Stone Prints

Petroglyphic narratives stand as mythic natural happenings, in this case animized or super-*natural* events in seasonal time. The reality and power of what-is-all-around Pueblo origins are figured as natural creatures, gods, devils, tricksters, spirits, climates, seasons, and human actors. Preponderant animal and plant shapes allegorize human dependency in the natural landscape of life narratives. Stories and songs intermix, as with spirit petitions and daily conversations, memories, and expectations. The La Cieneguilla Ancestral Pueblos were a living culture of real human beings at a time when Dante and Chaucer were encoding their own regional story-songs as literature—family quests, trysts and heartbreaks, clan crossings, daily food-and-shelter needs and fears, seasonal observances to petition natural spirits of place and time, muses and mythological advisories, the rocks and soil and foliage and streams and animals of a given place known as home or village.

"Today, the footprints of Hopi clans," writes Leigh J. Kuwanwisiwma, director of the Hopi Cultural Preservation Office, "are defined as ruins, sacred springs, burials, landscapes, migration passages, artifacts, petroglyphs, and trading routes and trails" (David Grant Noble's 2004 archaeological state-of-research collection, *In Search of Chaco* 44). Indeed, a site photograph on the following page, "Ancestral Pueblo petroglyphs in Chaco Canyon," suggests a variant of the Hopi-Tewa Jug Boy story: from the top, across and back and down and across in four pecked S-curving verse panels, trail five flute-playing Kokopellis (plus two waving ithyphallic figures); an added humpbacked flutist and two mothers birthing ovals (women and water); yet another horned Kokopelli and a crown-horned snaking figure (classic *Awanyu* or water deity) with an encircled abdomen (Jug Boy); several turkeys or roadrunners (path); a dog, two deer, and a mountain lion (protective grandfather); and an abstract rectangle with curling water lines at the corners (rain clouds) housing a water-mountain vortex, perhaps a sky-to-earth birth channel of moisture with a horizontal head and tail (personified Earth Mother?). The Chaco Canyon curvilinear flow of images is strikingly similar, almost a reduplication of the La Cienega Jug Boy panels in the Patterson-Rudolph study.

The story of Jug Boy seems archetypal as the odd child, the illegitimate stranger come home Pueblo style (see Jung, Kerenyi, and Hull on myths of the Divine Child). Reversely Oedipal, the misfit boy descends to find his father at a living spring, then Orphically returns to his dying mother, and descends again to find his parents reunited within a matrilineage of birthing promise. Clearly the rock-carved tale underscores the primacy of women and water, men as carriers and crossers (inverting patrilineal biases) at times of high-desert drought—perhaps the critical period of 1276–1300 when many Ancestral Pueblo villages relocated. The Santa Fe River from Tesuque Peak snowmelt would have run dry, and the bajada biosphere dried up, even died. It seems all too natural for a boy to explore valley villages to the southeast where springs were still fed by underground aquifers, as they are today in La Cienega and La Cieneguilla. The *springs* ensure the procreativity of land and people— hence the rebirth of the primal mother and her fertility all around, including Water Snake Red as the true father. These icons coalesce into meaningful stories still pertinent, the basalt cliffs as culture-bank repository of paradigms not to be forgotten. Scholars simply need to learn to read them freshly, as Pueblo cultures still do, and recognize their reemergence in today's Native literatures. The stone poems are renewed in Silko's *Ceremony* with Tayo's drought-pilgrimage home, in Tapahonso's rain-blessed desert poetry, in Momaday's essays on fluid literary origins, in Erdrich's water-drenched family sagas, in Welch's wasteland quests, and in Sarris's limpid "bi-autobiography" *Mabel MacKay: Weaving the Dream.* Sherwin Bitsui grew up herding sheep and contemplating the old stone images on cliff faces and in cloud patterns as *shapeshiftings.*

TALKING-LEAF TEXTS

We have lived upon this land from days beyond
history's records, far past any living memory, deep
into the time of legend. The story of my people and the

story of this place are one single story. No man can
think of us without thinking of this place.

—Taos Pueblo Elder, First Convocation of
American Indian Scholars, 1970

The people sang the stones whose glyphed images are ancestral to cultural ceremonies and talking-leaf texts. Under these carved cliff rocks must have taken place initiations, puberty rites, marriages, hunting and planting and gathering strategies, realities of sacrifice and loss, battle and defense modes, dramas of tribal life unfolding—birth to death to rebirth. The narrative motifs are ancient and universal, asking questions of how to live long and well among others: as the Diné say of the ultimate good, "to age with grace and beauty," or as the Pueblos speak of sacred reciprocity and interrelational harmony. Today the villages still gather around matriarchal clans in the Plaza or Middle of things to encourage their members, *Be as a man, Be as a woman!* (see Alfonso Ortiz, *The Tewa World*). This is the ultimate warrior, husband or wife, food-gatherer or hunter, shaman or healer, teacher or justice, acolyte or growing child. The kivas fill with creation stories and spirit songs. The clan mothers do not stop telling their how-to examples and cautionary tales. The hundreds of *kachina* spirits listen if the people speak and pray and sing and dance to them, the Pueblos believe, and the dead will return as rain clouds. Strangers and neighbors will come in peace and good will. Children will be born into the future.

As etched in the Rio Grande rocks from *time immemorial*, the people say in the Rio Grande Valley, the Deer Dancers at Tesuque on Christmas Day, the Porcingula devotees at Jemez in August, the Turtle Dancers at San Juan the day after Christmas, the Corn Dancers at Cochiti and Santa Domingo in July, the song keepers at San Ildefonso through the year honor seasonal dances and feasts and song-prayers that make the Pueblos who they are, and always have been. Newcomers do not radically change these patterns. All this is written in the stones that surround the villages. The inner images and structures of things are etched into time ongoing, the essential designs for all time.

But the moment I saw the brilliant, proud morning shine high
up over the deserts of Santa Fé, something stood still in my soul,
and I started to attend. There was a certain magnificence in the
high-up day, a certain eagle-like royalty. . . . In the magnificent
fierce morning of New Mexico one sprang awake, a new part of

the soul woke up suddenly, and the old world gave way to a new. (D. H. Lawrence, *Mornings in Mexico*)

Hetchetu alóh! the Lakota say back home in the old way: It is so indeed! *Speak Like Singing* explores how "now-day Indi'ns" still honor these grounded stories and songs, reinscribing anciently carved lines in living poetry and prose today.

Southwest Crossings

Luci Tapahonso and Leslie Silko

The Holy People left various drawings, primarily at
Diné Tah, so that the medicine people would have a
source of knowledge, and we would retain essential
songs, prayers, symbols, and stories. Changing
Woman now resides in the center of the Earth, and the
changing of seasons and the stages of our lives remind
us that indeed, she is our mother and that all comes to
life as she breathes.

—Luci Tapahonso, "The Radiant Curve,"
in *Native Universe*

Pueblo potters, the creators of petroglyphs and oral
narratives, never conceived of removing themselves
from the earth and sky. So long as the human
consciousness remains *within* the hills, canyons,
cliffs, and the plants, clouds, and sky. . . . Viewers
are as much a part of the landscape as the boulders
they stand on.

—Leslie Silko, "Interior and Exterior Landscapes,"
in *Yellow Woman and a Beauty of Spirit*

The rocks are speaking along the riparian mountains and desert val-
leys of the Southwest. The old stories and ancient songs still define the
People in Pueblo Feast Day ceremonies, in Navajo Blessingway hogans, in
Apache *Gans* dances, in Pima rain songs and Papago (Tohono O'odham)

salt pilgrimages, in Comanche hunting chants. From petroglyphs to kiva blessings, vision quests to Diné talk radio, Southwestern tribal peoples know who they are and where they come from. Writing down the traditions and modern improvisations, song-poem to talk-song, reminds Native Americans today how they came and continue to be.

Luci Tapahonso mixes poetry and prose in her writings, and her lines pulse as *narrative lyric*, while Leslie Silko, whose novel *Ceremony* fuses mythic verse lines with contemporary prose stories, moves toward *lyric narrative*. The differences are degrees of tonal pitch or rhythmic pace, eidetic density or local landscape, leaping luminosity or story arc. Tapahonso shapes her *row row* lines through syllable, syntax, image, and lineation, while Silko weaves her *run run* plots around character, landscape, time, and village, splicing Laguna creation tales and guardian figures, witches and goddesses into the prosaic historical mix. Tapahonso leans toward tensile flex in her lines, while Silko thickens the diction of dialogue and narrative plot. The lyricist sings *in* rhythmic dance steps, the narrator speaks *through* plotted character paths, as both writers cross genres in their Native Southwest.

LONG AGO THEY SAID

In her dreams, she was always there in New Mexico,
driving the winding roads to Taos, watching the
harvest dances at Laguna, or maybe selling hay and
watermelons with her brothers. In her dreams she
laughed, talking and joking easily in Navajo and
English. She woke herself up sometimes because she
had laughed aloud, or said, "Aye-e-e"—that
old familiar teasing expression.

—Luci Tapahonso,
"The Ground Is Always Damp"

The Navajo have a homestake in northwestern New Mexico, specifically the Gobernador and Largo Canyon drainages into the San Juan River valley, the Dinétah *Holy Land*. Diné origin stories of First Woman and First Man trace to Gobernador Knob in Largo Canyon, where the heroic Warrior Twins, Monster Slayer and Born-for-Water, were sired by the sun and birthed by the earth mother Changing Woman (Tapahonso, "The

Radiant Curve," in *Native Universe* 267–70). Tracing from Pueblo-Diné intermarriages, when Ancestral villagers fled the Spanish reconquest in the 1590s, pictographs and petroglyphs of the San Juan Valley and Chaco Canyon etch Diné history into basalt and sandstone cliffs: *ye'i* spiritual figures, shields, handprints, corn plants, cloud terraces, lightning, rainbows, birds, serpents, eagles, deer, coyotes, bison, horses, bats, moccasin and animal tracks, even the Humpback God or *Ghanaskidi* wearing sheep horns and carrying a staff or planting stick. Cousin to Kokopelli, his feathered backpack bears seeds and mist for planting. Cave star-ceilings date here from the eighteenth century, where the Diné origins of the Night Chant, Mountain Chant, and Beauty Way ceremonies are sketched and carved into the rocks. Dry sand paintings evolve from these ancestral stone texts, and wool weavings carry on the stonework traditions. Tapahonso writes in "The Ground Is Always Damp": "The New Mexico sky is clear and empty. It is a deep blue, almost turquoise, and Leona's family lives surrounded by the Carrizo Mountains in the west, Sleeping Ute Mountain in the north, the La Plata in the east and the Chuska mountain range to the southwest. They rely on the distance, the thin, clean air, and the mountains to alert them to rain, thunderstorms, dust storms, and intense heat. At various times, her brothers stand looking across the horizon to see what is in store. They can see fifty miles or more in each direction" (*Blue Horses Rush In* 49).

Born in 1953 at Shiprock, New Mexico, Luci Tapahonso grew up among eleven Bitter Water Clan siblings within Dinétah, traditionally schooled in *hooghan* keeping and sheepherding, weaving wool and planting corn, boiling coffee and roasting mutton, speaking Navajo and boarding-school English. She is among the most traditionally local, home-based, and matrifocal of the ten writers chosen for this study. Tapahonso's daughters step in and out of the poems; her subjects remain consistently a sense of family, home, and extended kin—who, and among whom, and where a person belongs. "My daughters and I communicated via cell phones, and voice and email," Tapahonso says in the inaugural Smithsonian *Native Universe*, "as we, and at times our husbands, prepared food for the First Laugh Dinner" (266). With local wit, compassionate and exact, she writes of earthen births, Native children, beloved siblings, uncles and aunts, parents and grandparents, lovers and husbands, rivals, cowboys, coyotes, sheep, dogs, and horses. Hers is a *gynecratic* grace, Paula Gunn Allen would say, a woman-empowered strength, coming from matrilineal tribal tradition. Tapahonso's grandmother broke wild broncos, according to one poem, and her former mother-in-law baked incomparable bread. The poet speaks often of tribal food—husked corn, deep-fat fry bread, mutton stew and tortillas, green chiles and sopapillas, blue corn mush, Spam, Diet Pepsi, Hills Brothers Coffee. She serves a hot brewed cup to her mother's brother, Tom Jim, noted as "a master at telling and performing stories with string" in *Blue Horses Rush In* (95). Uncle and niece talk things over in monosyllabic lines translated word-for-word from Navajo:

> I sit down again and he tells me
> some coffee has no kick but
> this one is the one.
> It does it good for me.

The Southwest animates her verse landscape—arroyos, buttes, mesas, washes, bajadas; mesquite, chamisa, sagebrush, cholla, greasewood, piñons, desert chaparral, cottonwoods, willows, and tamarack brush; peaks and intermountain plains, and the alluring Chuska and Lukachukai Mountains: "there is nothing quite like this to see." The Holy People spoke of singing, the poet recalls, as they walked eastward from Phoenix, and the land rose to meet them in the San Francisco Peaks near Flagstaff, "Holy Singing Mountain." In local names, naturally, lie details that inform and focus people's lives—that "stalk" people tribally, the Apache say, and keep them in line: Shiprock, Ganado, Keams Canyon, Red Rock; the Rio Grande, Chama, and San Juan rivers. Powwows, rodeos, raisin-eyed cowboys, dance competitions, "willie nelson and a can of beer," mirror sunglasses, blue jeans, pollen blessings for school daughters, sudden deaths, desert highways into the sky. Chinle and Albuquerque and Dulce and Gallup locate her poems among real events in Indian places today. The poet's voice sings quick, and quick to shift with a woman's sharp wit in nurture and teasing, gossip and prayer, hurt and care, discipline and midnight writing, sharp invective and dawn pollen blessings: "the good spirits in the gentle-bird morning." She loves to sing George Strait and Merle Haggard country-and-western tunes. Hers is the humor of a people who delight in going on adventures, assured of traditional home—a Navajo people who love and forgive and care for their own over vast journeys, wrenching acculturations, and odd accommodations that prove positive in the long view. Tapahonso writes of "REALLY HOT CHILI!!" on feast days with her first husband's Acoma people:

> Myself, I don't eat it straight.
> It's better mixed with beans or the kids' stew,

which is plain without chili.
They tease me about it but it's okay.

I'm Navajo: fry bread and mutton are my specialty.
Like my brother said I get along on sheep thrills.

Some Pueblos just don't understand.

This poet is happy to be alive, to be Navajo, to be woman, her humor finely edged and tempered with mother wit. *Wooshie, wooshie*, she explains of Old Salt Woman tickling White Shell Girl's chin in the beginnings: "(still a Diné way of making someone laugh). Then she put a grain of salt in the baby's mouth, and White Shell Girl laughed aloud— her bright laughter filling the hooghan. Such a radiant sound had never never been heard before. This moment became one of the most sacred acts of Diné life because the baby showed her thoughts were connected to feelings" ("The Radiant Curve" 269). This Navajo mother will not be abashed by her elemental delight in a good laugh, unquestioned love for children, her husband's work-day return, or her grandfather's quiet song at a dawn birth. In the matrilocal art of baking bread, she finds context for a poem about her mother-in-law, women being-and-belonging—not conflict, but accepted texture, culture-as-art. Tapahonso knows the feminist freedoms of her matriarchy, even tracing back through the Yellow Woman stories to heartbreak affairs. "Early Saturday, the appaloosa runs free near Moenkope," she sings in "She Says." Out of mainstream malaise or breakaway liberation, the poet is disarmingly up-front about the goodnesses all around her, above the historical losses and Native disasters. "I drink a lot coffee and / it sure does it for me." This sophisticated innocence and lyric naturalism make the poems singularly enjoyable, specially Navajo, and traditionally woman-centered.

Changing Woman's Daughters

When a rainbow appears after a cleansing rain, we
know that the Holy People have returned. When
they return, they marvel at the growth of new
spring plants, they revel in the laughter of children
splashing in the fresh puddles, and like us, they inhale

deeply of the sweet, clean air. We understand that a
rainbow sparkles with particles of dew, pollen, and
the blessings of the *Diyin Dine'é*. We exist within the
radiant curve of their care and wisdom.
—Tapahonso, "The Radiant Curve"

Tapahonso's first husband was from Acoma Pueblo, her second a
Cherokee academic. After an assistant professorship at the University of
New Mexico, where Tapahonso earned her degrees, then a stint at the
University of Kansas, this bilingual poet and prose artist now teaches at
the University of Arizona. The writer goes home to Shiprock as an elder.
"I am of my mother," she introduces herself traditionally in Diné, "born
for my father"—*spoken through* ongoing voices of four primary ancestral clans that she is *known by* back to Changing Woman. "Because
of them," the poet says, "I have been really fortunate to come to this
point." Not the art of one person, but the voices of tribal people *speak
her through*, as Linda Hogan will say.

Luci Tapahonso joined Joy Harjo in my UCLA contemporary
American poetry class, 22 February 2005. Sister allies from their first
marriages to Acoma men, their children and grandchildren are now
best friends. A sunrise double rainbow appeared over Los Angeles that
morning, and we were blessed with intertribal elders speaking of poetry
together. "I tell you my clans because we are never alone. There are
always relatives above, below, behind, and before. Words create beauty,
happiness, laughter, and calm," the Navajo poet told my students, "as
well as destruction or death, so be careful how you use them. We say in
Navajo that sacred begins at the tip of my tongue."

Song-stories surround the people, prayers and narratives and memories "make us up," she repeats; "we are here because people prayed for
us." So, too, everything comes from the earth, personified as Changing
Woman. "I am a child of Changing Woman, a holy person, a sacred being,
therefore I'm a holy person." Take care, Tapahonso advises, in what you
say and how you say things—many speak through each person. *That's
how I am known as a woman*, the Diné say traditionally. Navajo mother
of two daughters, Misty Dawn and Lori Tazbah Ortiz, this spirited grandmother has published five volumes of poetry: *One More Shiprock Night*
(1981); *Seasonal Woman* (1982, illustrated by the Navajo painter R. C.
Gorman and introduced by John Nichols); *A Breeze Swept Through* (1987,
with Klee-like drawings by the Flathead artist Jaune Quick-to-See Smith);
Sáanii Dahataal: The Women Are Singing (1993, cover by the Navajo

painter Emmi Whitehorse); and *Blue Horses Rush In* (1997). Tapahonso
told my UCLA students that she writes to *explore* and to *celebrate living*:
writing is "the way you come home"—smelling your sister's baking bread
or a good cup of coffee, simmering soup or blue cornmeal—entering your
mom's Shiprock house over a lifetime, the front porch "layered" in stories
and baby steps, gossip and laughter. Family is everything, kinship tribally
extended, the people one with the land and living surroundings, spirits to
springs. "It's knowin' they're fixin' something to eat and thinkin' about
you." As well as savory homecoming, writing gives a "place to feel comfort
and grief," reassured that all this is "part of the life cycle" and "there's a
way to get through it." The poet insisted that writing "enlarges my circle"
and "fills those spaces in our lives that can't . . . ," she said breaking off,
"like gettin' a good parkin' space."

The Diné are Athabascans from western Canada seven to nine centuries back, migrating and evolving over time. Their traveling tonal speech
has journeyed and changed too, not least in the eighteenth century of Pueblo
intermarriages, the nineteenth century of Hispanic accommodations, and
the twentieth century of English schooling acculturations. "We sat for
hours—talking, laughing, and sharing family memories and stories," the
returning poet writes in *Blue Horses Rush In*, conversations switching
"easily between Diné and English and, at times, a rhythmic blending of the
two" (ix). Tapahonso recalls an old storyteller in *The Women Are Singing*:
"We call him *Shúúh* because he is always ready to hear a story. After we
eat, we like to sit around the table and talk for hours and hours. That's
how we found out he knows how to talk that old Navajo—the kind we
hardly hear anymore. That language is ancient and some words we know
the feeling of, but not exactly what they mean" (59).

So, between petroglyph and the spoken word, old and new Diné
talk, code-switching to English and back, people know *the feeling* of
words, but not always *what they mean*. This writer intuits sense behind
sound, feeling things *in my bones*, as her grandmother knows that their
mother has died before her brother speaks. All this feeling for the earth
and stones, reading between the words, looking inside living texts, and
listening beneath sound layers in endless talking and cavernous silence,
a hand in daily bread and an eye to the horizon, the earth speaking
through dancing, walking, working feet. Tapahonso's Acoma mother-
in-law says of baking bread, "I just know by my hands, / just a little like
this is right, see?" Hoeing a field, the poet's mother tells her, "mother is
always ready with food, stories, and songs for the little ones." Nurturing
is the heart of Navajo culture.

Talking to a child

The various beings and Diyin Dine'é took part in
White Shell Girl's upbringing. They talked to her
constantly about all that happened and the nature
of her surroundings. She was taught songs and
prayers about every facet of daily life: cooking songs,
weaving songs, songs to keep animals healthy, songs
for fixing one's hair, hooghan songs, songs for birds
and other creatures, planting songs, and so on. There
are songs associated with most daily activities, and
so they remain meaningful. This is why parents are
encouraged to talk to their children; it helps to develop
the child's sense of identity, and shows how the child
is related to her ancestors. Parents are grateful when
someone says, "Your child is so well-behaved and
respectful; you must really talk to them." In "talking
to" a child, our traditional beliefs are passed on in a
respectful and spiritual way, much like White Shell
Girl was treated.

—Tapahonso, "The Radiant Curve"

Well-used words model parenting, the Navajo believe of extended family,
passing on values to the next generation continuously. In living well and
invoking blessings for others, the Diné show younger ones *how to be* by
being their best selves in a *house* made of dawn and evening light, blessed
with pollen and rain. "In the tradition of Changing Woman," Karen Ritts
Benally writes of "Thinking Good" among Navajo grandmothers, "the
ideal Navajo woman is simultaneously wife, mother, homemaker, teacher,
kin keeper, and preserver of tradition. For the Navajo, the ideal life is one
that is long and filled with *hozhó*; that is, with harmony, peace, happiness, and beauty" (*American Indian Grandmothers* 25). All this is bound
up in a single word, *hozhó*—as a speaker might say *good* in English, but
more interrelated with the sacred everyday all around. "*Hozhó* expresses
the intellectual concept of order," Gary Witherspoon explains, "the emotional state of happiness, the moral notion of good, the biological condition of health and well-being, and the aesthetic dimensions of balance,
harmony, and beauty" (*Language and Art in the Navajo Universe* 154).
Such goodness is an almost untranslatable expression, *hozhó*. The bilingual artist uses words less as ends in themselves, more for what they carry

and convey, just as syntax relays more in expressive sequence than syllable of any tongue.

> Yippee!
> Lori said when we sat down to eat.
> She knows where she comes from.

So the young *come from* a traditionally radiant, ceremonial home, foremost in the people's minds, modeled on the ancestral elders caring for them, as Changing Woman cared for the first human children. These are traditional maternal values, neither feminist-liberated nor politically correct by progressive mainstream standards, but essentially Diné over time. Mothers are advised to be kind, trusting, accepting, even in the face of betrayal or death. For the poet, this balance registers in a contained, elderly tone of voice—careful, discrete, syllabically concise, caring.

Luci Tapahonso's voiced English has a slightly broken, pointillist quality, where glottal-stop breath "talks" syllable-by-syllable in her second language. Hers is the voiced care of a soft-spoken person who chooses words thoughtfully. The title poem of *A Breeze Swept Through* commemorates her daughters' births. Dawn breeze, first breath, Grandpa's song, a mother's opening words, and all winds draw on what the Navajo call the soul, the "in-standing wind," breathing life through all creation. As republished from Washington Matthews, Diné origin myth holds that "It was the wind that gave them life. It is the wind that comes out of our mouths now that gives us life. When this ceases to flow we die. In the skin at the tips of our fingers we see the trail of the wind; it shows us where the wind blew when our ancestors were created" (John Bierhorst, *In the Trail of the Wind* 19). If sacred begins at the tip of the tongue, life lies in the fingertips, and all are connected through words of the wind well used. The poet advises her children to "Remember the Things They Told Us":

> When you were born and took your first breath, different colors
> and different kinds of wind entered through your fingertips
> and the whorl on top of your head. Within us, as we breathe,
> are the light breezes that cool a summer afternoon,
> within us the tumbling winds that precede rain,
> within us sheets of hard-thundering rain,
> within us dust-filled layers of wind that sweep in from
>   the mountains,

within us gentle night flutters that lull us to sleep.
To see this, blow on your hand now.
Each sound we make evokes the power of these winds
and we are, at once, gentle and powerful.

Language is the expression of knowledge, the Navajo believe, just as speech voices the outer form of thought, and wind is the external breath of the "in-standing wind" soul. Language does not intrude between speaker and listener, but minimally opens a cedar *hooghan* door to the people's lives, ceremonially woven together each day. As a child, young Tapahonso sat wrapped in Diné blankets, looking at the stars, listening. "Such summer evenings were filled with quiet voices, dogs barking far away, the fire crackling," she writes in *Blue Horses Rush In*, "and often we could hear the faint drums and songs of a ceremony somewhere in the distance" (99). So to "talk beautifully" without affectation is a Diné sign of cultural wealth, and the "combination of song, prayer, and poetry is a natural form of expression" (*The Women Are Singing* xi).

Tapahonso recalls returning from Kansas to her bilingual Shiprock upbringing in *The Women Are Singing*: "The songs the Yeibicheii sang, that the radio played, and that my mother hummed as she cooked are a part of our memories, of our names, and of our laughter. The stories I heard that weekend were not very different from the stories I heard as a child. They involved my family's memories, something that happened last week, and maybe news of high school friends. Sometimes they were told entirely in Navajo and other times in a mixture of Navajo and English" (x). Crossings are crucial, and code-switching linguistics aerate the shared seed grounds of cultures. Between languages, "words" are clearly what things *are called*. A Navajo personal computer is "talking metal," and a battery the "car's heart," as anatomy directs culture-crossing taxonomy (see Basso's "Linguistic Acculturation," in *Western Apache Language and Culture*). These translative images mark functional cross-listings, fusional dialects. They code-switch two-way traffic between cultures, reciprocal mixings of Indian and mainstream. These adaptions are not issues of losing sovereignty or sacrificing cultural integrity, but coevolving literacies—accepting others in a shared world, working things out together from local to global contexts. Not Red Stick wars, but radiant rainbows: all 'Skins are in this country together, despite what they *call* things on either side of the lingual chasms. Humans are similar beings, with separate inflections and dictions. Diverse tribes voice differing sounds for similar things, including common human problems.

Two sisters laugh about a husband's dalliance with "Ruthie" in a *la-di-da* poem about infidelity, comeuppance, and forgiveness, "*Yáadí Lá*":

> she fed the kids fried potatoes and spam and they watched TV.
> later her sister came over, she said, he's gone, huh?
>> *ma'ii' alt'aa dishíí*   honey, i won't do it again   *'aach' ééh*
>> *noo dah diil whod.*   (old coyote was probably saying
>> in vain: honey, i won't do it again.)
> they just laughed and drank diet pepsi at the kitchen table.

Sprinkled with an insider's Navajo teasing, the lines comically acknowledge the poet's own first tongue of intimate privacies and regional plots. Today's Diné go beyond in-joking to others listening in. The voices switch back and forth, poetically truncated, in a bicultural brand of adventurous Red English ("Joe Babe," Tapahonso explains in lecture, for acculturated boarding-school girls "who teased their hair, wore lots of mascara, and wore white go-go boots when that was the style"). The poem thus works in cross-tribal spoken dialect. "It does it good for me," Tapahonso's uncle says of Hills Brothers coffee, the Indian stimulant of preference. The effect is one of finely modulated, bicultural, cross-gender Indian humor. "I have grown strong in your laughter," the poet tells her daughter Lori, explaining that an infant's first laugh brings the extended kin together for a ceremony of feasting, passing the child around, tasting rock salt, and breaking bread as signs of lasting health and Diné belonging to one another.

A light trickster wit salts the verse, then—a woman's oblique, nurturing sense of survival, comic in the broadest sense. Children embody the future, a home sense to move with and from—a generational past with elders, land, tribal history, and communal culture, including recipes for preparing food, the most stable of all literacies. Most consistently, Tapahonso's poetry resonates to the tuning flute of her own lyric Navajo voice, filtering through a naturally visual imagination—careful, everyday, inventive selections from the common languages of both cultures in her life:

> he came home the next evening and handed her his paycheck
> signed. the kids brought in his sacks of clothes and sat
> back down to watch the flintstones. he sat at the table
> and said   i deserve everything you do to me.
>> you're just too good for me.
> . . . .

he sat awhile not saying anything then went out to get
some wood. she called her sister up saying:
      ma'ii nádzá!   want to go to town tomorrow?
      ayóo shibééso holó, hey! (coyote's back
      and I have money to blow now!)

Ordering breath, the narrative design of these verse lines is not so much an issue of metrics as it is the bilingual symmetry of speech, syntax, and visual space. A fluid pairing measures the everyday phrasings of tribal life, lyricized through a woman's point of view—mother, lover, girlfriend, wife, flirt, witness, confessor, poet-singer, and storyteller.

Tapahonso ends her fourth book with "that going home business." The Diné have been going on a long time, wandering and migrating, circling the Southwest like native gypsies, prisoners of war marched to Fort Sumner and back in the 1860s. Wherever they go, their spirits go with them. And so when the poet leaves Shiprock to see Paris in 1987, her grandmother says, "Remember who you are. You're from Oak Springs, and all your relatives are thinking about you and praying that you will come back safely. Do well on your trip, my little one" (*The Women Are Singing* 91). By absence and distance, by speaking and silence, this grand-daughter comes to know where she's from, who she is, why she's going and coming back home.

"I never missed Indians until I went abroad," Tapahonso marvels, sprinkling a corn-pollen blessing from the top of the Eiffel Tower (*The Women Are Singing* 92). She goes away to come back, learns to lose in order to have a good sense of place, listens (stops talking) to speak, and talks (stops worrying) to sing. In tune with Frost's respect for Yankee dialect, the poem is her fusional talk-story-song about Navajo life in the Dinétah Southwest. "This writing, then, is not 'mine,'" the poet says of grandparents and grandchildren in her work, "but a collection of many voices that range from centuries ago and continue into the future" (*The Women Are Singing* xii). From tiered calico skirts and bright velveteen shirts, Canyon de Chelly to Bosque Redondo, *Yeibicheii* songs to Navajo radio, traffic deaths to "jokes about cowboys, computer warriors, and stuff," Luci Tapahonso talk-sings her way lyrically home. "For many people in my situation, residing away from my homeland, writing is the means for returning, rejuvenation, and for restoring our spirits to the state of *hozhó*, or beauty, which is the basis of Navajo philosophy. It is a small part of the 'real thing,' and it is utilitarian, but as Navajo culture changes, we adapt accordingly" (*The Women Are Singing* xii).

SHAKE HANDS HELLO

Blue Horses Rush In slips in and out of prose and poetry with the ease of a bareback rider sliding on and off a sorrel mare. Galloping poem, sauntering story, cantering verse, ambling personal narrative—the rhythms are graceful and natural, Diné grounded, matrifocal as with most Southwestern cultures. *Yá'át'ééh diníi!* the people say, "Shake hands hello" ("The Radiant Curve" 271). Homecoming is the perennial event, extended kin the talk. "We meet relatives or friends almost everywhere, and conversations consist of jokes, stories, and intricate wordplay. Before we head home, we stop at the flea market for a roasted mutton sandwich and a cup of coffee" (*Blue Horses Rush In* xi). Parked beside the road, the family settles into a "talking mode" with a brother in a Ford pickup. "We know almost everyone who drives by," the returning poet says, and "our Navajo accents are still thick" (*BHRI* xii). Dedicated to her granddaughters and their great-grandparents, the future-of-the-past in *Blue Horses Rush In* draws from a Native language with sixteen verb tenses and 356,200 ways to say *go*, according to Gary Witherspoon in *Language and Art in the Navajo Universe* (21). Extended familial orality sets the textual touchstone—related kin talking, praying, and singing; old stories and gossip; family and clan matters. In relaxed lines of poetry and prose, Tapahonso takes the personal time and everyday tone to tell the stories and sing the songs deeply so they last.

The collection begins with a granddaughter-birthing verse for *She-Who-Brings-Happiness* that circles kitchen talk of quieting babies. The poet sings her own mother's Navajo lullaby and "Twinkle, Twinkle Little Star" for the July Christmas lights still up. These traditional and tribal songs tune the poems biculturally to a major harmonic of peace and joy. The second section counterpoints prose with the changes and challenges to clan goodwill—runaway children, fragmented families, trips to Europe and boot camp and college, a medicine man's *hooghan* for the reassurance of healing lyrics:

> *Because of the years I have lived, I am valued.*
> *Yes, I am pitied by the huge sky,*
> *the bright moon, and glittering stars.*
> *We consist of long, breathless songs of healing.*
> *We are made of prayers that have no end.*
>
> *I have seen the stars separate.*
> *And I am, I am.*

Prose matches her problems with explanatory details; poetry meets her fears with resonant song-lines. Four of Tapahonso's prose and poetry combinations accompany a Phoenix Arts exhibition defending thousand-year-old Hohokamki ruins from an expressway. She meets a medicine man in an art-center restaurant for coffee and hears a story about a story-teller's "old story" remade: "'The Holy People take care of themselves. They do. Just as they take care of us. I really like those old stories and I always feel good when someone wants to hear them. It's good when someone wants to understand what we know and what we believe in. That's the Indian way all over—to sit and tell stories together. Each tribe is the same but the stories different. It's a good thing, this storytelling'" (*Blue Horses Rush In* 24).

Along with fry bread and Diet Pepsi from a roadside Navajo vendor, "Notes for the Children" explains that *skirt* and *woman* are the same word "in the old way"; that children can nap, play, or eat on their mother's spread skirt as a tablecloth, blanket, or towel; that the round *hooghan* roof is like a woman's flared skirt because, as the old blessing song says, *Beauty extends from the woman*. Right side is female, left side male, Tapahonso explains in class. Female rain is soft, male rain driving, and the gender-bonding ideally fuses strength with nurturing compassion, as in sister culinary and verbal arts. Home cooking spices the stories and places them in family context, along with traveling objects of place—"an ice cooler full of mutton, frozen chile, and dry ice," her Diné luggage on a plane to Kansas.

Tapahonso writes natural words of honor and thanks to Changing Woman and the sacred peaks, both in Navajo and English ("This Is How They Were Placed for Us," *Blue Horses Rush In* 39):

> Because of her, we think and create.
> Because of her, we make songs.
> Because of her, the designs appear as we weave.
> Because of her, we tell stories and laugh.
> We believe in old values and new ideas.
> *Hayoolkáalgo Sisnaajiní bik'ehogo hózhónígo naashá.*

The poet's lyric stories draw a reader into character and plot, what's happening around Dinétah, as the poems immerse that reader in the lined music of her life. "It was music, after all, that saved me, I suppose. Songs on the radio, songs in restaurants and in stores; their rhythmic pleas and stories soothed me. They soothed the person I had become: the one he left

for someone else, the one he no longer loved" (*Blue Horses Rush In* 53).
A birthday poem answers the lovesick homing ache:

> Again, as a Diné
> woman, I face east on the porch and pray for Hózhó
>
> one more time. For today, allow me to share Hózhó.
> Some days, even after great coffee, I need to hear a song
> to reassure me that the distance from Dinétah is not a world
> away. I know the soft hills, plains, and wind are Diyin
> also. Yet I plan the next trip when we will say prayers
>
> in the dim driveway. As we drive, Kansas darkens. Prayers
> and memories protect us. In the tradition of Diné
> travel, we eat, laugh, refuel, sing.

And in the Navajo way, a title birth song, "Blue Horses Rush In," celebrates her granddaughter Chamisa's birth "amid a herd of horses, horses of different colors"—white, blue, yellow, and black for the balanced directions.

> Chamisa, Chamisa Bah. It is all this that you are.
> You will grow: laughing, crying,
> and we will celebrate each change you live.
>
> You will grow strong like the horses of your past.
> You will grow strong like the horses of your birth.

Voicing the world alive, this poet-storymaker writes Diné culture down for her children's children, just as the old ones carved and brushed their songs, stories, and lives into ancestral rocks.

Native singers, storytellers, and writers have always mixed modes. Half a century back in Acoma, Simon Ortiz wrote both poetry in *Going for the Rain* and *A Good Journey*, and prose in *Howbah Indians* and *Fightin'*. Most recently, he mixes genres in *Out There Somewhere* (Sun Tracks, 2002). Mesquakie Ray Young Bear combines surreal fictions and free verse in *Black Eagle Child* and *Winter of the Salamander*. Laguna Pueblo Paula Gunn Allen writes both novels and poems in *The Woman Who Owned the Shadows* and *Shadow Country*. The Paiute Adrian Louis crosses genres in *Blood Thirsty Savages* and *Vortex of Indian*

Fevers. Even Gerald Vizenor mixes lyric translations with trickster fictions, though to note exceptions, Native novelists like W. S. Penn and Greg Sarris sidestep verse, while poets like Barney Bush and Joy Harjo seem surest in narrative lyric. If Luci Tapahonso is a Navajo poet writing prose stories, her University of New Mexico college teacher Leslie Silko is a Laguna Pueblo novelist lineating poems in her storytelling. The crossings run fertile across the Southwest and all of Indian Country.

LAGUNA WOMAN STORYTELLER

People don't have anything if they "don't have the stories," the Prologue to *Ceremony* insists, and the storyteller keeps the moving life of the people in his belly. Leslie Silko's verse storyteller is the living character of Southwestern seasonal landscape—seeded by spring rains, nurtured by summer sun, life-giving in fall harvest, and stilled with winter snowfall. The Ohio poet James Wright wrote Silko of "hearing the landscape itself tell the story," calling *Ceremony* one of the best American novels he'd ever read (see Anne Wright, *The Delicacy and Strength of Lace* 3). Silko's sentences flow like high-desert waters, mountain snowmelt feeding down the New Mexico ravines in spring runoff, as it has for millennia, swelling creeks and pooling streams over summer fields of corn, beans, and squash, the legendary three sisters. The late summer and early fall monsoons flood into muddy rivers, all feeding concurrently with the San José Laguna Pueblo tributary into the second longest river of the land, the Rio Grande, emptying into Mexico and the Caribbean Gulf.

Ceremony's prose rhythms sweep into lyric currents, always in fluid motion from their local origins, searching terrain and gravity for the surest way down the mountains to the village fields and beyond. Silko's verse currents are organically true, her prose cadences lovely falls, her underground springs and deep cisterns life-sustaining. *Water, women, and words* trace back to petroglyphic Jug Boy across the Southwest: the sky-blessed, wind-swept landscape gives the mythic storyteller healing waters channeled to her readers through the spoken life of written words. High- and low-desert plants and animals, cerulean skies and curving horizons, stones and stars, histories and myths all flow together in a narrative physical as juniper, pungent as piñon, naturally landscaped as saltbrush, cholla, and chamisa. No writer, Native or otherwise, has matched the New Mexico local character of Silko's storytelling.

The narrative opens with the oldest story in the West, a war-shocked, dislocated Tayo searching his way back home, the *nostos* or Homeric homecoming. "He could feel it inside his skull—the tension of little threads being pulled and how it was with tangled things, things tied together, and as he tried to pull them apart and rewind them into their places, they snagged and tangled even more." This illegitimate "breed" also prototypes the divine child of ancient myth—a martyred Christ, stuttering Moses, or swollen-footed Oedipus who redefines communal life and evolving culture (see Jung, Kerenyi, and Hull's *Myth of the Divine Child*). Changes are organically constant. "Things which don't shift and grow are dead things," the makeshift medicine man Betonie tells a catatonic Tayo (*Ceremony* 126). Like the half-breed Hermes, son of Zeus and earth mother Maia, Tayo will serve both as culture bearer and messenger to and from the gods. And with the Warrior Twins and Creation Siblings of Ancestral Pueblo history, Tayo continues the renewal, rebalancing, and remaking of Laguna traditions.

The fragmenting time-space of the opening fifty pages splays from war-shocked dislocations and disassociations. Bastard Laguna breed, Tayo has fought in the Philippines and lost his cousin-brother Rocky, attempted to recover in a Los Angeles V.A. hospital, hallucinated dying and killing Japanese in the South Seas (triggered by voices of Manzanar detainees returning home at the L.A. Plaza train depot), and come back unheroically to a dubious Laguna welcome with Aunt Thelma and Old Grandma. Ethnocentrism, purity of Native blood, and conservative tradition block the breed's reentry. "I try to tell him to stay with our own kind," Aunt Thelma says of her brother Josiah going to the disreputable Mexican Night Swan's bed (*Ceremony* 92). Grandma simply pities and tries to comfort her troubled grandson, crying "A'moo'oh, a'moo'ohh" over and over again. Curses, guilts, losses, shames, deaths, imbalances—either no rain or too much rain—fracture Tayo's schizoid and dehydrated consciousness. There is no middle, only margin. Flashbacks and interrelated fragments of memory, pain, rage, shock, and confusion skitter like the centripetal swirl of the Jug Boy rock panels above the Rio Grande Valley. *He* and *she* float in and out as third-person indefinite referents, male/female divisions as first difference. No immediate names mark characters, only kinship and genetic terms: auntie or grandma or old man, uncle or brother, he or she, as in the distanced opening to Welch's *Winter in the Blood*.

So the narrative begins with a disorienting point of view, tribal gender the only visible marker. Commas, semicolons, colons, appositives, dependent clauses cadence whirling associations, a stream-of-consciousness flow in externalized interior monologue. "He wasn't sure where he was anymore, maybe back in the jungles again; he felt a sick sweat shiver over him like the shadow of the angel Auntie talked about. He fought to come to the surface, and he expected a rifle barrel to be shoved into his face when he opened his eyes. It was all worse than he had ever dreamed: to have drifted all those months in white smoke, only to wake up again in the prison camp. But he did not want to be invisible when he died, so he pulled himself loose, one last time" (*Ceremony* 17). The narrator filters Tayo's character through the disassociative voices of time-place-and-people decentered by war—American-English doctor, Spanish jukebox, Japanese speech in a train station, Keres medicine man back home, all floating in and out of a Native nightmare from which Tayo is trying to awake.

Mythically drawn verse lines center the confusion and density of the prose narrative—periodic insets of fresh breath, the old-time stories of hero twins, totems, witches, animal guardians, and astro-dramas to frame and decode contemporary chaos, as in the opening. In the belly of the story, the insert says, the ceremonies are still growing. Free verse spells the narrative density. Center-margined lines offer a homing search for belly, mother clan, tribal place, collective time, and communal peace in Tayo's quest, as mythic clarity and lyric concision trim the prosaic raggedness of a postwar Native plot. Harley, Pinkie, Emo, Leroy—Indian survivors looking for "a safe return" from war—end up bragging, drinking, and fighting each other in rat-hole bars just off the reservation, "defending the land they had already lost." A whiskey-brazen vet bewitched by killing, Emo speaks of Indians as objects of history, not subjects: "Us Indians deserve something better than this goddamn dried-up country around here. Blowing away, every day" (*Ceremony* 55).

A six-year drought of land, body, mind, and soul desiccates Laguna. Bar jives and rez riffs stud the dialogue with machismo, purple hearts, and stale beer—the street chaff of cheap shots, thoughtless angers, and bad jokes: "What we need is what they got. I'll take San Diego," Emo slurs the Anglo contagion of *mine* brought by surveys and quick claims. Greed justifies taking away the rights and properties of others, mistaking that people own the sacred mountain, rather than the reverse. "We fought their war for them," Emo says, rattling his little bag of Japanese teeth, "we don't got shit, do we?" Tayo simmers in the corner with his "spring water" Coors can of beer. "He was thirsty. Deep down, somewhere behind his belly, near his heart" (C 56). Tayo goes to the Men's Room and reflects as he looks "down at the stream of urine; it wasn't yellow but clear like water. He imagined then that if a man could bring the drought, he could also return the water, out of his own belly, out of his own body. He strained the muscles of his belly and forced it out" (C 56). And then the toilet bowl flows over—a purgative flooding, no auspicious beginning.

LET US TWO GO

The story circles, searching for a center, spiraling off in strands of stories like a chaotic spider web of word-images. Not so much a solid configuration or set text, the narrative draws the reader into a weave of frayed basketry. We see through a porous screen toward Southwest histories and hardships today: a nameless orphan under a bar table in Gallup, tribeless Helen Jean picked up for a joyless ride with abusive "bros," Harley and Pinkie, Leroy and Emo. These dry shells of stick-figure vets are up to no good, as though Edward Curtis's scrimmed Vanishing Americans were still vanishing.

In the center-margined insert Hummingbird says that three worlds below the plants are green and flowers blooming, and he goes there to eat. The mythic insets are not really lineated as verse units. Nor are they imaged concretely or edged in thick diction, as poetry would differentiate from less-sculpted prose riffs. The lineated columns layer more like a center-aligned bowl turning on a centrist axis. With more white space than the prose, the lines balance in midpoint symmetrically, layering down the page as free-verse story-flow. These insets retell old origin stories mostly, though some sketches spill from the contemporary plot (Emo's Anglo war "pussy" in San Diego). Still, compared with the swirling prose associations of Tayo's tormented mind, there is more space, more breath, more life and energy in the centering poetic lines, a gyroscopic myth-telling with folkloric dialogue.

The characters come in pairs, as customary in Pueblo thinking ("Let us two go," the Laguna people chant in *kurena* harvest songs for storing grain, Franz Boas records in *Keresan Texts* 299). The mythically named Tayo and his full-blood cousin-brother Augustine or "Rocky" serve as primary variants on the ancient Warrior Twins, one sacrificing for the other's cultural mission. Laura the scandalous mother and her proper sister "Auntie" Thelma: the Sister Twins who originate a given Pueblo matriarchy. Robert, Thelma's silent husband, and unmarried Josiah: brother-uncles in the matrifocal backdrop. Night Swan the cantina dancer and Ts'eh Montaña: the two Marys of legendary resurrection, mother-lover twin-sister goddesses essential to the hero's salvation and his culture's regeneration. Old Ku'oosh the antiquated medicine man and behind the inbred shadows, Old Grandma the blind matriarch. Betonie the mixed-blood healer, with his calendars of time and telephone books of place, flanked by the feral child *Shush*, half into the ancient cave world of guardian bears. Harley and Pinkie, bro buffoons; Leroy and Emo, bewitched killers.

These characters are not so much psychological complexes, via the modern novel, as figures in older origin myth, cautionary tale, or how-to story. They represent character nodes in a series of dramatic actions—global shifts in culture and consciousness, plot points in cultural and cosmic history unfolding. The character types allow readers to chart by way of kinship terms (grandmother and old man, mother and aunt, uncle and cousin, brother and sister, bro and babe) village relationships that recenter a culture in time and place, an all-my-relatives recycling that would heal a desacralized landscape. Silko's "people" resemble, then, generic character types—as the Pueblos prefer kinship terms like Auntie or Uncle to individual names like Leslie or Robert. So *Ceremony* moves forward through character arc and plot shift with kinship figures in a continuing tribal narrative, rather than idiosyncratic individuals pitted against each other—tracing back to petroglyphic panels before alphabetic "writing" and Paleolithic pictographs on sandstone escarpments.

STORY CARRIER

It took a long time to explain the fragility and intricacy
because no word exists alone, and the reason for
choosing each word had to be explained with a story
about why it must be said this certain way. . . . the
story behind each word must be told so there could be
no mistake in the meaning of what had been said; and
this demanded great patience and love.

—Ceremony

If words contain etymological stories as baskets hold seed grains, and all Pueblo tales come together in Grandmother Spider's woven web, then Tayo and his name-story are woven into an ongoing myth. Silko the novelist writes as a conduit or channel, such as a flute or medicine pipe, for stories between past and future. She crosses species, gender, and race to unify space-time in an ongoing story told through poetry and prose. As granddaughter of the first and final Mother, she receives and writes the words that readers hold in their hands: her stories as medicine, her belly moving in procreative tale, her lyric ceremonies a cure for today's crises by way of yesterday's song-stories. "You don't have anything / if you don't have the stories." Perhaps Tayo's core story is related to the Tewa-Hopi Jug Boy story carried back and forth from the Arizona mesas to basalt cliffs near Southwestern streams, lakes, and springs. In the beginning, Thought-Woman sits and thinks, "and whatever she thinks about / appears," Silko says in the center-margined invocation to *Ceremony*. She thinks of her twin sisters, as They create this world and four below, quadruple depths. As She names things, they appear, and the novelist tells the story She is thinking. Her web is centripetal, time an interweaving mythic thought, the village Middle or plaza a radial axis in the center of an earth bowl. Thought-Woman the creatrix is the ideal author thinking up the stories of modern lives, spinning Indian, Hispanic, Anglo, and others across the Southwest.

Spider Thought-Woman is the archetypal grandmother, personifying all ancestors as birthing mothers of mothers seeded by fathers. She weaves the world from inside the belly of history. As the body's center and time's still point, no less than the plaza Middle for the People, the storied belly centers the people matrilineally and androgynously—a deep ancestral cave, a curing and birthing womb, a storytelling and singing mouth, a listening ear and loving touch, a house and home, a tribal village. "Inside, his belly was smooth and soft, following the contours of the hills and holding the silence of the snow" (C 205). The story-center is etymologically and narratively deep, an ancient cave for water-bringing, sun-loving reptilian ancestors. This deep wellspring requires patience, care, and love to plumb, narrative time to cure contemporary ills. As readers sink into and beneath the words, they go below the surface of things, deep inside to the centers of mythic time carried through all *time immemorial* in tribal ceremonies. If the world sickens or dries up or dies, the stories internalize the imbalancing affliction (lying, shame, pettiness, racism, violence, poison, alcoholism, war), and characters must vomit up the bad story to cleanse themselves internally before they can be restored to natural balance and shared health.

She says the only cure for sickness is a good ceremony. And so the novel opens with a single image-word centered at the top of the page:

Sunrise.

Centered toward the bottom of the following page, the next word is

Tayo.

Franz Boas, godfather to Native American anthropology, notes that Hopi *Taiowa* is a *flute-playing* demigod of the sun. The Laguna *koshares* sing a sunbird song about the spirits migrating east from the Place of Emergence to live with the *kopishtaya* "angels" in the sun's house: "I came out / first early morning / *ya ayo* / there in the east / at sunrise the sun's house / the sun's (bird) / *TyOWI TyOWI* he sing*s* / *KAYO KAYO* he is singing" (*Keresan Texts* 292). A Southwestern variant of the bootlegged Tewa-Hopi water-woman-warrior myth—Jug Boy discovering self-identity, the true springs, and tribal lineage in a seasonal winter drought—Tayo's story parallels *Taiowa* fluting or *TyOWI* singing the sunrise of his pregnant mother who crossed the east river bridge naked into a dried-up Laguna. Tayo's journey retells a war-drought pilgrimage to find restorative water and healing women, no less than the Jug Boy petroglyphic panels of "wife-hunter" Kokopellis facing *south corner time*, the winter solstice in the Rio Grande Valley. As with the demigoddess Ts'eh, the feminine water myth (Keres *ts'ih* for water) migrates around the Southwest with the People.

First of all, Tayo is born the illegitimate, exogamous offspring of his Laguna mother Laura (laurel or eventual victory), impregnated by a stranger (non-Indian Kokopelli). Tayo's mother leaves and dies. Family shame and tribal gossip keep the orphan distinct from his "twin brother" Rocky, a full-blood inversely acculturated to White sports, schooling, and nationalistic war. So Tayo goes rabbit (Japanese) hunting (war down west to the East) with his Great White (Grand)father or Uncle Sam (mountain lion) in World War II, leaving Josiah his father surrogate in Laguna, but hallucinating his uncle's Asiatic features in the faces of executed Japanese soldiers. Superpatriot Rocky dies, his skull squashed like a (water)melon or water jug (perhaps the "kill-hole" of an Ancestral pot spirit *released* from use). The trauma is anticipated when Emo smashes an old man's field melons, and the violence is reactivated at the abandoned uranium mine as Tayo contemplates crushing Emo's skull with a screwdriver.

So the plot is archetypal: Tayo the breed bastard is tragically shattered and "reborn" through the loss of his Native brother Rocky, nicknamed for the stones of their origin, and in postwar shock the mixed-blood tries to go home to Laguna. Here Auntie Thelma (mother's sister) disapproves of his illegitimate presence, and Old Grandma (direct kinship line of mother's mother) tries to bring Tayo into the endogamous ancestral ceremonies by way of Old Ku'oosh. But like glyphic Jug Boy, the androgynous breed Tayo (conceived in Silko's first two drafts as a woman) must pool out centrifugally, not in. He is destined by birth and the stars to cross borders, not to hide behind blood at home. Story-carrier and gene-crosser, he strikes out as an intercultural traveler, a water-woman-hunter, a sun-and-rain balancer. The village women face off over ethnicity, the men shamed (husband Robert and bachelor brother Josiah), for Tayo is a mestizo, cross-bred between warring Red and White cultures, as Leslie Silko mixes her own Laguna, Mexican, and Anglo ancestry. All her stories, she says in a biographical note to *The Next World* (173), are about "what it is to grow up neither white nor fully traditional Indian."

Old Ku'oosh sends Tayo *down west* to a mixed-blood Navajo-Hispanic medicine man Betonie and his half-bear apprentice Shush, "bear" in Diné. On his way down to Gallup, Tayo finds himself recovering physically through a woman's body rhythmically moving under him during a drought-breaking rainstorm. Night Swan, a nurturing cantina dancer and mestizo lady of blue nights, tells him that his hazel ("Mexican") eyes, sign of mixed blood, bespeak the crossing story of his destiny. Earth brown and spring green renew a world blanched sick with racial war and winter drought. Mixed-blood, hazel-eyed others sacralize the story around him (old-time healer Desheeny and his Mexican bride, Betonie and Shush, Ts'eh Montaña, and Night Swan herself).

Sexually restored to his body (as Jug Boy breaks out of his clay mold), Tayo turns to his mestizo mentor Betonie as father figure, who tells him of the "transitions" taking place into the next (sixth) world by way of the signs (glyphs) of storied stars, speckled cattle, a woman and a mountain. Xenophobic crisis begs cross-cultural resolution. Navajo, Hispanic, Pueblo, and Anglo are estranged cousins, indeed cousin-brothers, coming together by way of the healing powers of mothering sister-lovers. The historical crisis is whether racial ethnocentrism or transitional pluralism will prevail: individual competition or tribal cooperation. Fusions prove the evolving rule of hybrid mixing. "You don't write off all white people," as Betonie warns Tayo, "just like you don't trust all Indians" (C 128).

Tayo goes back up to volcanic Mt. Taylor (migration up to the sky and back down with life-giving water stories), a mythic boundary marker for tribal peoples shared by intermarried tribes adjoining across the Southwest (Diné to the west, Ute to the north, Pueblo to the east, Apache to the south). He finds by way of the hunted mountain lion (protective grandfather replacing Uncle Josiah) a woman named Ts'eh Montaña, sensual guardian spirit of the Mt. Taylor snowpack, Keres *Tse-pi'ná* or "Woman-Veiled-in-Clouds." Ts'eh Montaña is a mother-lover surrogate whose name means "mountain-of-water." *Ts'ih* is water in Keres and Hopi, akin with the song of the water-bringer Dragonfly, *tsee, tsee, tsee* ("water" in several

Southwest tongues, as first noted among petroglyphs in 1893 by Garrick
Mallery in *Picture Writing of the American Indians*)

In the novel's inset verse, Silko narrates the mythomeme of Hummingbird and Fly helping Turkey Buzzard find tobacco medicine (as with
Kokopelli's "cloud-blower" flute) to aid Sun Man in stealing back rain
clouds trapped by the Gambler in the west. At the sandstone spring to
the south of Laguna, just before going to war and meeting Night Swan,
Tayo sprinkles the mountain waters with pollen, Old Grandma's ancestral
ritual, and watches a pregnant grandmother spider drink at the wellspring.
He remembers the old stories of Her outsmarting Gambler for return of
the rain clouds, and then the "rain-children" frogs come out and dreamer
dragonflies hover over the pool "all colors of blues." The dragonfly stories remind him of old Grandma's "long, ago, time immemorial stories,"
a world made up of living stories, changing, and moving. If he remembers how to look, he can see the stories moving across the sky like stars
(*C* 95). We are not far from the iconic, rock carved, women-water myths
of the Ancestral Pueblos along the Rio Grande Fertile Crescent. Dennis
Slifer documents the Dragonfly fertility dream-catcher and water-douser:
"the millennia-old petroglyphs where dragonflies perch on the shoulders
of horned, shamanic figures, along with other spirit helpers such as snakes
and birds" (*The Serpent and the Sacred Fire* 122).

HOME STONES

Consecrating the ceremonial song-stories and star glyphs from Old
Grandma and Night Swan, Tayo makes love with the water-mountain goddess Ts'eh, who goes by many tribal names: "He eased himself deeper within
her and felt the warmth close around him like river sand, softly giving way
under foot, then closing firmly around the ankle in cloudy warm water"
(*Ceremony* 181). Not aggressive entry, sex is rather a feminine opening and
easing within, as though sliding into a rebirthing river. "But he did not get
lost, and he smiled at her as she held his hips and pulled him closer." Postwar
Tayo did not exist in body or name, a paranoid schizophrenic whose violent
flashbacks blocked memory of his true past and mixed-blood identity. "He
let the motion carry him, and he could feel the momentum within, at first
almost imperceptible, gathering in his belly. When it came, it was the edge of
a steep riverbank crumbling under the downpour until suddenly it all broke
loose and collapsed into itself." The adjoining riverbank to another's body,
male seed releasing to female receptivity, Tayo's story begins in conception

and ends cyclically rebirthing in Laguna. Near the old cottonwood (water-seeking roots used to make kachina effigies) Tayo crosses the east river into the village at sunrise, the novel's focal center.

Restored sensually, rebalanced biospherically by gathering rain seed-plants, Tayo descends Ts'eh's mountain and goes home yet again to his maternal aunts and cousins (Jug Boy water-women at the springs) with reemergence story-signs for the kiva fathers. The daughters of Yellow Woman, the first mother (seen in Ts'eh's pollen-hazel eyes), are returning to the drought-stricken landscape (the desiccated two-mile lagoon of *Laguna*), working horticulturally to heal the spiritual sterility brought on by war and racial violence (mixed-blood veterans on mules "up-the-line" of Indian bars). Tayo comes home at sunrise, crossing the water-bridge east of Laguna as his mother originally carried him into the village. "There were blue-bellied clouds hanging low over the mountain peaks, and he could hear thunder faintly in the distance" (C 220). On the way, he finds life-spring signs and regenerative glyphs of the People crossing into the next world. The Paleolithic ancestral pictograph begins as a center-margined paragraph:

The she-elk was bigger than life, painted in pale lavender clay on the south face of sandstone, along the base of the cliff. Her great belly was swollen with new life as she leaped across the yellow sandrock, startled forever across the curve of cliff rock, ears flung back to catch a sound behind her. The priest who painted her each year always cried when they stood back from the cliff and saw her. "A'moo'ooh! A'moo'ooh! you are so beautiful! You carry all that life! A'moo'ooh! With you, the cliff comes alive." (C 230)

Through the mestizo help of Night Swan and Betonie, reborn in the Pueblo-Hispanic procreative spirit of Ts'eh Montaña, Tayo rediscovers his cross-tribal mothers and fathers, sisters and brothers, exogamous cousins all around him, as Jug Boy arrives at the maternal spring of his true father. And so the narrative spirals toward where it begins at dawn, facing sunrise in the fall equinox, crossing the water—coming home in the reader's hands as printed words bearing the old stories and songs carved into the stones, a panel glyph centered on the slate of the last page.

Sunrise,
accept this offering,
Sunrise.

Why begin and end with *Sunrise*? To close and open the hand, Boas says, fingertips touching the thumb then opening, is both a Keres sign of greeting and sunrise. *Shake hands hello,* the Navajo say. Just so in the ancestral petroglyphs facing southeast with their open hands, sun circles and spirals, water myths and culture bearers, ithyphallic Kokopellis, snakes, dragonflies, frogs, lizards, spiders, mountain lions, bears, turkeys, cloud-mountains, rainfall, birthing women, Twin Sister myths and Jug Boy stories. It's all there, carved into the rocks since *time immemorial*, the Pueblos repeat, all around today—songs and stories, ceremonies and narratives, poems and novels. Dark becomes light at sunrise, the solstices balanced in the horizon's equinox, just as hazel eyes fuse sky blue with earth brown and spring green. Sky comes to earth as mineral water, turquoise blending all these colors in medicine stones for the eyes (hence the old ones wear turquoise). Mestizos cross-fertilize gene pools (the dark stranger, the mysterious maiden); androgynes fuse male drive and female nesting (a woman writing a man's war recovery). The speckled cattle break the lie of owning or pure breeding any living organism, including the land. Fusions rule. The blind mule (old trading price for a man as captive cousin) is half burro, half horse. So, too, Betonie's hogan is half in and half out of the mother earth, Shush is part human and part bear. And just so, humans are spiritually inspired and sexually procreative, plots are ancient mythic quests, tribal folklore is true fiction. Silko packs traditional storytelling into a modern text no less than Tapahonso works through Diné culture to tonalize verse lines.

In Silko's *Ceremony*, poetry seeds into prose, the bear blues of the west fuse with the mountain-lion yellows of the north (Pueblo quadrants) to blend diagonally northwest on Mount Taylor into sandstone turquoise green-blues, piki-bread corn pollens, and sky-water rebirth—all by way of the circling star patterns, revolving seasons, balancing sun and rain, focused in the equinox sunrise returning to a true Laguna home. Sunrise is the ceremonial beginning of a new day. The light sphere rises out of the encircled horizon, as mother earth gives birth to her ball of light. A ceremonial prose-poem redefines Native literacy as cyclical storytelling, seasonal rebirth, Native re-naissance. This all works through Tayo's sunrise story, no less than the illegitimate petroglyphic Jug Boy finds his true lineage and tribal wellspring along the Santa Fe River of La Cieneguilla: " . . . he could see one big cottonwood tree, the only bright green in that valley. It was growing on the edge of the deepest arroyo, its web of roots exposed, held upright only by a single connecting root" (C 242).

LIKE BEGETS LIKE

The word "ceremony" comes from the Roman goddess of agriculture, Ceres, and refers to harvested grains or cereals for winter sustenance. A good ceremony is communal ritual practiced through physical space over time. Oldest cultural roots reenacted, the repetitions of seasonal cycles unify people and place. Ceremony as well could include totemic rituals and image magic to insure good hunting, as Arrow Boy hunts deer on Mt. Taylor for his sister Ts'eh. A healing ceremony could honor warriors going to or coming home from battle, as with Tayo's World War II buddies. A good ceremony could sanctify a wedding, cure witchery, heal a disease, fertilize a woman, bless a newborn, lament the dead. With prayer it could bless a home, a friend, a task, or a meal. All these ceremonies are ongoing today in the Pueblos. Ceremonies invoke the spirits for any number of reasons: to bring rain or to restore sunshine, to lower flood or to raise spring water, to call the game or to banish critters, to image the constellations or to sing up the sun. With the feasting dances up and down the Rio Grande Valley, ceremonies commemorate the seasons and their gifts: spring seeding, summer growth, fall harvest, winter rest and restoration. Annually Laguna ceremonies invoke renewal, from winter's south corner time at the winter solstice, as noted, to summer's north corner time at the summer solstice. Temperatures vary from a hundred degrees to zero; rainfall is less than fifteen inches, snowfall even less predictable—hence the need for ceremonies to insure a balance of all these forces of moisture and heat (the meteorological plot of the novel, balancing peace broken by climatic war, drought and flood). A new-year ceremony means starting over, a World Renewal, as with millennial ceremonies or astronomical observances, meteorite showers, eclipses, the eighteen-and-a-half-year Southwestern lunar cycle that concludes with time standing still (see the geologic calendar of the horizon's "light dagger" in Chaco Canyon caves petroglyphed with sun-and-moon dials). Tayo comes home at the autumnal equinox when things return to seasonal balance, when light and water return to the Laguna kivas for cultural storage and spiritual retooling.

All this ceremonial behavior ensures the natural ways of things, the right balance of communal energies—pairing and coupling and adjoining necessary to peace and prosperity in a demanding environment where enemies, witches, ghosts, evil spirits, and plain bad luck have just as much a place as tribal proprieties and the blessings of the good spirits and general goodwill of the people. *Like begets like*, as the Pueblos say: everything that is, is. Natural boundaries dissolve; borders disappear.

Honor the living organisms of an interrelated whole, ceremonial chants remind the people seasonally—humans and spirits, rocks and water, animals and plants, sun and moon and stars.

Stories have a rightful place as layered or hollowed-out cultural storages. Just as the people store things in baskets or bowls, granaries or housings, so are their homes architected in stories (up to four stories at Chaco and many other Ancestral Pueblos, the original apartment complexes of the hemisphere). So, too, does the land offer storage caves for creatures, grains, tools, weapons, and sentinels. Old men know story holes, caverns and pools of ancestral power, the deep centers of things. Animals, humans, even the winds have bellies, Josiah tells Tayo, as the spirits tell tales of ancient pilgrimages, vision quests, hero journeys, epic battles with gamblers and monsters, struggles with drought and flood, heat and cold, dearth and plenty. There is a centrist organics to all this, finding the due mean of not going against the natural way, accepting the way things are and always have been, according to the ancient stories.

A one-eyed witch misreads things: the imbalancing White lie of possession, for example, or the Native confusion of ethnocentric blood over mixed fusion. Ignoring the equinoxes, the people may weigh summer over winter, day over night, sun over rain. Mistaken racialism may pit white over dark skins in Anglo America, forgetting the exogamous global pooling of evolution. Some cultures put men above women, or vice versa; endogamous clans thin asymmetrically. Humans over gods, up against down, in not out, young rather than old, city above country, epic grandeur beyond common simplicity—all these forces continually need to realign and counterbalance. The people's ceremonies reenact stories to bridge spirit and body, to connect eye with ear through the heart-minded mouth—narrative lessons *about* living among the lyric moments of witness. With imitative magic (word-like-thing) people may image patterns that make sense and last memorably. Like begets like; witchery witches itself. The storyteller tells the people to heed the animal parables of Fly and Hummingbird, Turkey Buzzard and Coyote. Learn from the creation stories of witches inventing Whites. Take heart from the heroic fables of warrior twins, Enemy Slayer and Jug Boy, Corn Woman and Reed Woman, First Woman and First Man, soft mist and hard rain, crystal and turquoise, moon and sun. Note the Trickster jokes, the Coyote tales, the scandals and gossip of the spirits that comically model human pratfalls. Free the mestizo captives and cousins of historical people-stealing-and-selling times into the nineteenth century.

Silko honors the hybrid adoptions among Navajo and Pueblo villages, Apache and Comanche conflicts, Spanish and Anglo invasions, all fusing in Tayo's homecoming story, the good ceremony of storytelling. And as the Hopi petroglyphs above Third Mesa warn, by way of the Whirling Logs (ancient swastika) and Gourd of Ashes (atomic bomb)— the false "sunrise" of a 1945 daybreak nuclear explosion over White Sands, New Mexico, Old Grandma remembers, ushered in a dangerous time of transitions. Be aware, be warned, be careful, the old ones say— listen to the voices in the land. Tayo's decision *not* to attack the witching torture of Harley on barbed wire near the abandoned uranium mine, a positive-negative or Pueblo sign of restraint, is conflict-avoidant—a pacifist calculation *not* to return to madness and war. In the shadow of the nuclear false sunrise of 1945, the choice seems reasonable. Violence perpetuates itself.

Finally, *Ceremony* accepts the mixed blessings of sex and the sacred, Corn Mother and Water Sister, male rain and female rain, the procreative energies that exorcise poison and regenerate the living. "Sunrise," the novel begins and ends, "Sunrise." Greet the new day, the old stories say—welcome the stranger. Know this renewal of the daily equinox in midnight and noon, the rebirth of light from dark. With five-pointed stars in the knuckled branches and leaves shaped like hearts, the water-rooted cottonwood stands *kachina*-carved guardian over the San José River to the east of Laguna where Tayo reenters his homeland and heritage crying with relief that he finally sees the pattern of how all the stories come together as the story being told. There are no boundaries to anything, "only transition through all distances and time." The ear for a good story and the eye for patterns come from the living land where the river cottonwood at sunrise yellows like gold in fall sunlight. Mother, grandmother, sister, aunt, cousin, and lover become one. "He thought of her then; she had always loved him, she had never left him; she had always been there. He crossed the river at sunrise." (C 246, 255)

The river crossing will reappear at the end of *Love Medicine*, carrying words home through women and water, as written in the ancient stones. The seasons turn back into themselves, as all things return to their origins. Horizon space curves around the People, and time bends into the center of the tribal hoop.

Plains Ways

N. Scott Momaday

My father was a painter, and I watched him paint as
I was growing up. He belonged to that tradition of
Plains Indian art which proceeds from rock paintings
to hide paintings to ledgerbook drawings to modern
art, so called.

—N. Scott Momaday, Preface,
In the Presence of the Sun

Between Tapahonso's sacred *Dinétah* mountains to the northwest and
Silko's mythic Laguna valleys to the southwest, N. Scott Momaday carves
contemporary stories and classical verse out of Jemez Pueblo stones all the
way back to Kiowa Oklahoma origins. Cultural translation sets the text;
bicultural education layers the context for the artist-scholar's crossings.
Charles Simic in *Wonderful Words, Silent Truth* posits that "Translation
is the closest possible reading one can give a poem—a lover's reading"
(103). "Translation is also a type of shamanism. One reads words and sees
images inside somebody else's head. Then one speaks in tongues. In the
end, all poetry is translation of an uncertain and often absent original."

Jorge Luis Borges posits that there is no set text in any language originally, only classical translations over time (see Efraín Kristal, *Invisible
Work: Borges and Translation*). The collated Old and New Testaments
of the Bible, for example, approximate sacred words through Hebraic and
Greek transcription of tribal oral traditions, God's holy word never knowable to humans. Neither Moses nor Jesus wrote or critiqued Scripture.
Through translative history scholars encounter Latin and English renderings,

eventually hundreds of missionary biblical texts. No language, even the originating archaic ones, has cornered the market on divine inspiration or scribal exegesis. God's word is yet the Word *in translation*—and readers still search the texts for meaning, inspiration, and vision. The same can be said for the Tao Te Ching in China, the Upanishads in India, the Koran in the Middle East, Black Elk's Great Vision in the Dakotas, Navajo Beautyway in the Southwest, or the Iroquois Code of Handsome Lake in western upstate New York. Literate audiences read sacred and teaching texts translatively.

"To read is to translate," W. H. Auden takes literary crossings a step further in *The Dyer's Hand* (3). Poetry, specifically, is re-created from a prelingual source that ghosts or spirits phonemic writing signs, as melody precedes libretto. The cultural text may stir vatic or divine or daemonic origins, as in the "genius" of inspiration—even speaking in tongues, or sung *through* flamenco artists by the *duende*, or chanted as vocables in tribal ceremony. The "text" survives as a kind of holographic shadow in translation, and little more can be said about it authoritatively than it already says. Still, take hope in cross-literacy. When successful, the emergent text catalyzes translated thought as cultural language in social action ("words lead to deeds" for Saint Teresa) and may come close to recreating the original spark that set the words singing. According to Borges, lingual translation can never claim purity of origin or perfect carry-over as it comes alive freely in a derivative language. Better to accept regenerative rhythm and sparked inspiration in the *interpretive* tongue given than to worry about God's mouth to my ear.

And thus *all* poetry is translation, the Argentinean argues. All "texts" are renderings and recreations of the "genius" that inspired a poet in any language to sing out originally. The best poetic translations, as such, recognize their limitations while drawing or reconfiguring the muse through the language at hand. Add to this Walter Benjamin's task of the translator in *Illuminations*—a carrier language to *re-create* linguistic spark across tongues, plus bicultural reasons to reignite a metaphoric ember of another's inspiration crossing over. "It is the task of the translator," Benjamin says, "to release in his own language that pure language which is under the spell of another, to liberate the language imprisoned in a work in his re-creation of that work" (*Illuminations* 80). *Dis*-covering Native genius through a given tongue, then, sparking light from the fire within—translation is re-creative illumination, what John Miles Foley calls *reperformance* in *How to Read an Oral Poem*.

If male-based stories are of two kinds, Benjamin goes on to say in "The Storyteller"—those intoned by venturers who leave home (*The*

Seafarer or *The Odyssey* or guardian Vision Quests across the plains, for example), and those told by planters who stay home (say the Old Testament or the Confucian Analects or the Mayan Popol Vuh)—then talk-songs come from either traveling or homing tales as narrative lyric, found in the ancient Anglo-Saxon, Homeric, Siouian, Hebraic, Chinese, or Quiché oral literacies of tribal cultures not so removed from contemporary Native America. Nor need these singing texts ring foreign to modern ears. Adults still share the oral cultural delight of their childhoods, folkloric local knowledge, conversational interplay, humor, gossip, news, table talk, group discussion, folk song, hymn, prayer, anthem, and the thousand other ways spoken culture still informs contemporary lives. Oral poetry is very much globally alive today, as John Miles Foley records in *How to Read an Oral Poem*, beginning with Tibetan paper-singer, North American slam performer, South African praise-poet, back to the ancient Homeric bard. Oral poetry "works like language, only more so," Foley concludes: "Oral poetry is not a 'thing' but a process, not a set of discrete items but an interactive way of speaking. It uses a special language to support highly focused and economical communication, taking advantage of implications unique to that language" (*How to Read* 127). With literacy, readers access orally coded writing as talking leaves, an extension of daily narrative voices and nightly lyric aspirations.

Man-Made Passages

At Barrier Canyon, Utah, there are some twenty sites at which are preserved prehistoric rock art. One of these, known as the Great Gallery, is particularly arresting. Among arched alcoves and long ledges of rock is a wide sandstone wall on which are drawn large, tapering anthropomorphic forms, colored in dark red pigment. There on the geologic picture plane is a procession of gods approaching inexorably from the earth. They are informed with irresistible power; they are beyond our understanding, masks of infinite possibility. We do not know what they mean, but we know that we are involved in their meaning. They persist through time in the imagination, and we cannot doubt that they are invested with the very essence of

language, the language of story and myth and primal
song. They are two thousand years old, more or less,
and they remark as closely as anything can the origin
of American literature.

—N. Scott Momaday,
"The Native Voice in American Literature"

Navarre Scott Momaday grew up speaking English and Navajo in the
Pueblo Southwest, and at thirty-one he wrote down the "ways" of his
migratory ancestors. Momaday's paternal hunting ancestors crossed with
maternal agrarian Cherokees. Scott and Galyen Appalachian hill people
pioneered west as the Kiowas migrated from the Yellowstone headwaters
to "red earth" Oklahoma Indian Territory. No less than Silko before
the pregnant she-elk pictograph south of Laguna Pueblo, or Tapahonso
beneath Chaco Canyon petroglyphs of Corn Woman and Humpback
God, Momaday charts a chthonic "procession of gods" journeying to the
base of his grandmother Aho's Rainy Mountain cemetery stone.

The Way to Rainy Mountain opens with a running lower-page title,
a parental dedication, and a metered, end-rhymed poem. The continuous
title suggests rivering passages ancient as the Tao Te Ching. The classic
ideogram for the watercourse way reads *Stop-and-go-with-the-master*:
an elder's head leading an apprentice at a crossroad. Correspondingly,
the "way" to Rainy Mountain implies an ancient pilgrim story, step-by-
step ancestrally attending on-the-go, the tribal migration of a people still
evolving today. How am I Kiowa? the modern-day Native writer asks.
His way to the mountain is a family heritage lyrically cadenced, a cultural narrative flow he can't step twice into or out of.

An Indian with a Stanford Ph.D. in American Literature stands before
his father's mother's grave in 1965, asking how he is related in this red-
earth prairie of winding streams, rolling hills, and constant winds. Tell the
story, says the grandmother muse; write the talk down. Momaday begins
tracing his ancestral identity with the poem "Headwaters," a syllabically
intricate dedication to maternal life origins (*water-woman* cousin to the
Jug Boy petroglyphs). A *pre-script* oral literacy globally, John Foley says,
accounts for 94 percent of cultural history up to fourth millennium B.C.
Egyptian and Mesopotamian inscriptions (*How to Read* 219). Oral tradition to literacy, song-poetry to verse, Momaday's tribal genesis tracks cultural evolution through generative language.

This writer is a Native formalist, and "Headwaters" sets up as an
eight-syllable octet. The formal lines are end-rhymed *abab ccdd* in iambic

rhythms that first reverse, then regularize the meter across a medial caesura. The pattern seems formidably graphed until spoken aloud, when its
rhythms draw the reader into balancing 4 x 4 x 4 Alcaic cadences:

Noon in the *in*   ter *mountain plain*:
There is *scant tell*   ing *of* the *marsh*—
A *log, hol*low   and *weather-stained*,
An *in*-sect *at*   the *mouth*, and *moss*—

Yet *waters rise*   *against* the *roots*,
*Stand brim*ming *at*   the *stalks. What moves?*
What *moves* on *this*   ar*chaic force*
Was *wild* and *well*   ing *at* the *source*.

With the initial dactylic heave, "*Noon* in the," trochaically followed by
"*in*-ter *moun*tain *plain*," the step seems to falter, then smooth out in each
succeeding line: reverse feet in line 1, anapestic spondee in the second,
iambic spondaic rise and fall in the third, two regular iambic feet in lines
4 to 5 (where the *volta* tendons the octet across a stanza break), drilled
spondees in line 6, and regular iambic tetrameters in end-rhymed couplet
lines 7 and 8. With metric variations idiosyncratically subtle in each line,
the effect conveys an intricate organics, a sequencing artistry naturally
formal. The quadrant Alcaic design, aurally and visually, is watertight.
These lyrics close with *headwaters* as the "source" of tribal awareness in
on-flowing Kiowa ways.

Details speak—a Darwinian "scant telling" to be sure, but revealing
as archaeological evidence in a shard. Look and listen closely, the poetic
rhythms and syllabic cherts imply—too easy to find, the old lesson goes,
too easy to do. The poem flows from midday *in medias res*, a present-
tense Montana plateau between mountains (a "plain"-scape repose),
to the key aesthetics in "scant telling." Less is more; observation all.
Minimalist-surcharged as Dickinson and Tuckerman, Momaday honors
his literary models by way of Yvor Winters, under whom he wrote a dissertation on Tuckerman, as stated, and has long promised a book on
Dickinson. The light tapping of anapestic to spondaic feet patterns into
end-rhymed "marsh" beginnings. "What moves on this archaic force /
Was wild and welling at the source." No naked Edenic Tree of Life, no
pubescent Adam naming apples as Eve slips on the snakeskin—only a
fallen log, old as the waters of the firmament, prehuman and amoral,
lies "hollow" (an ancient passageway through evolutionary space-time,

empty of ego and callow innocence) and "weather-stained" (aged, seasoned, horizontally inviting human narrative rivering through history). The image is unobtrusively natural and eidetically suggestive, an old birth canal to the beginnings.

The end-line punctuations work at a scant pitch. Note the colon stop-and-go after "plain:" followed by the suspension of the dash after "marsh—" then half-suspended with the third-line comma after "stained," (rhyming back to "plain:") slowly falling toward the feeding "insect at the mouth," of the ancient culture-tree, "and moss—" (after the Dickinson arrest of the comma, cross-rhyming back to "marsh") and the first regular iambic line then smoothing the cadence. Every brush-stroke matters; details tell all. Marsh "mouth" is focal, the oral traditions of speech and song feeding the minute insect's needs, slant-rhymed with an alliterative flow into "moss." These are a people's evolutionary origins in the watercourse of time. Consistent with Darwinian biogenesis, new tribal beginnings emerge from headwaters, as oral lyric and narrative fuse into cultural literacy.

The volta of lines 4 to 5 smooths the passage of the *way* to a mountain-shaded *rainy*. As "waters rise," the river gathers against the "roots" of living things growing along the flow-line. Roots and rivers, earth and water, detail and movement—the waters "stand brimming" to the vertical "stalks" of pilgrim roots in motion, the poet walking the rhythmic path laid out by tribal migration. And the drilled off-rhyme with roots, end-stopped and framed in a triple spondee after *"stalks"*—*"What moves?"*—suspends the life-force query against the iambic urge to go on. The final couplet repeats the question in regular measure "on *this* arch*a*ic *force*" enjambed (without end-line break) to *"wild* and *well*ing" headwaters surging into the present. Sounding a natural "source" as the poet's wellspring cultural "force," the freely flowing aboriginal beginnings run through tribal memory always moving on.

The end couplet seals a pact evolving the tribal "way" of his grandmother's living traditions. Her stories are embodied in the stone toponym of rebirth, Rainy Mountain, as he retells and writes down her living tales and songs, told through her son, the author's father. Intricate flow is the rule. Why should the author write so discretely and formally? Because Aho's death threatens to end Kiowa identity for her grandson; indeed, without care the silencing of a tribal "way" to the present will die out mute, only a generation from extinction. The word-pilgrim rediscovers Kiowa culture striding through ancestral stories and lyric inflections that bring the old ones back to life.

Memory and imagination, the art and science of close observation and acute listening, hinge on the "scant telling" of tribal life known as personal being, ongoing. Homer and Lao Tsu, Virgil and Du Fu, Dante and Li Po, Chaucer and Wyatt (the author's progressive Stanford graduate curriculum) all wrote of traditional regeneration that this modernist Kiowa reawakens by his grandmother's grave. Tribal stories and songs remain alive at the headwaters of cultural time-space and genetically pool in a people's ongoing evolution. How to write ancestrally raises questions of voice (spoken, academic, artistic), research (oral history, library archives, field work), line drawing (paternal lines and planes), textual positioning (editorial judgment), structural pacing (crafted architecture), childhood memory (personal recall), artistic imagination (catalytic imagery), and individual-to-tribal reflection (maturing cultural identity). Many voices pool to tell this story.

Why spend critical time on formal questions of craft, accentual syllabic verse, when entering a prose narrative? "It took me a devil of a lot of time to get this poem into verse," W. B. Yeats, the Irish tribal bard, growled about chanting "The Lake Isle of Innisfree" over BBC radio, "and that is why I will not read it as though it were prose." Metrics are not muse, but they do ritually cadence Momaday's *way* to Rainy Mountain. Less sculpted than measured lineation, Momaday's prose is no less aurally crafted. "I'm writing this book with a pen," says Larry McMurtry, a Stanford peer, recovering from a heart attack, "unlike my twenty-two previous books, because I don't want the sentences to slip by so quickly that I don't notice them. They need to be the work of hand, eye, and ear" (*Reading Walter Benjamin at the Dairy Queen* 35). Indeed, from the handmade *Journey of Tai-me* as origin text to the academic, then commercial publications of *The Way to Rainy Mountain*, Momaday's literary work has encompassed artistic hand, painterly eye, and writerly ear (signed copy #80 *Journey of Tai-Me* is held in special collections at the University of California, Santa Barbara, where Momaday began teaching and made the rare book, as discussed in Lincoln, *Native American Renaissance*).

After the dedications and lyric framing, Momaday reinitiates the narrative with both a Prologue and an Introduction. This careful entry slows and informs passage, cadences and contextualizes attention, the way openings and introductions frame tribal ceremonial dances. Kiowa Plains people build up to a Sun Dance, rather than jumping in free form. A Jemez Pueblo ceremonial day starts after months of practice and preparation, prayers and instructions, dusk gathering of piñons and plumes, followed by dawn pollen and turquoise blessing; only then begin the all-day-long entrances and exits from the kivas, and the plaza dancings. The right tone must be established, the right notes struck, the grounds prepared and audience settled. Then the movement, pageantry, spirit, and reflection of the dance step and song activate the performing ceremonial *text* to register fully. The weather is no small matter, nor the respect of the audience.

And so Momaday begins again with the journey's beginnings, introducing his grandmother's voice through his father as a voice of the people: "'You know, everything had to begin. . . .'" Tribal narrative starts the Kiowa journey in Montana, traverses a Dakota plain past *Paha Sapa* or Black Hills, dropping down to the Wichita Mountains in Oklahoma, "going forth" with "a good idea of themselves." The people acquire the sacred *Tai-me* doll, ark and covenant of the tribe still today, and the horse, the "sacred dog" centaur of the revivified Plains cultures in the eighteenth and nineteenth centuries. All these local details root the journey in legend and history, "personal as well as cultural." How an individual relates to his people and their place-names in time gives voice to tribal evolution.

PLAINS ORIGINS

A single knoll rises out of the plain in Oklahoma, north and west of the Wichita Range. For my people, the Kiowas, it is an old landmark, and they gave it the name Rainy Mountain. The hardest weather in the world is there. Winter brings blizzards, hot tornadic winds arise in the spring, and in summer the prairie is an anvil's edge. The grass turns brittle and brown, and it cracks beneath your feet. There are green belts along the rivers and creeks, linear groves of hickory and pecan, willow and witch hazel. At a distance in July or August the steaming foliage seems almost to write in fire. Great green and yellow grasshoppers are everywhere in the tall grass, popping up like corn to sting the flesh, and tortoises crawl about on the red earth, going nowhere in the plenty of time. Loneliness is an aspect of the land. All things in the plain are isolated; there is no confusion of objects in the eye,

but *one* hill or *one* tree or *one* man. To look upon
that landscape in the early morning, with the sun at
your back is to lose the sense of proportion. Your
imagination comes to life, and this, you think, is
where Creation was begun.

         —N. Scott Momaday

Consider the first paragraph of the Introduction as an ancestral tuning
fork. Scott Momaday's voice stands distinct from Aho's limpid storytelling through her son Alfred, even further from the descriptive discourse of social scientists, the first and second voices of each section.
The poet's cadences cluster around blank verse as a working pattern for
walking through cultural history: "A *single knoll* rises *out* of the *plain*
in Oklahoma, *north* and *west* of the *Wich*ita *range.*" The 6–4 division
through the comma rides loosely on iambics, as the next five sentences
bear out.

    Rainy Mountain rises out of the prairie a geological epic, a sin-
gular "knoll" called a mountain gathering life-giving rain on the Great
American Desert. The flat surfaces of common things flare this plain
style across *Oklahoma*, a Choctaw "red earth" horizon to measure and
check rising impulses. As Wallace Stegner portrays the Saskatchewan
plains in *Wolf Willow,* a man represents an upright, challenging question
mark against big sky and broad expanse; courage and humility are converse prairie virtues. All this space tests the imagination to particularize
and to focus. So with Choctaw *Oklahoma*, Native place-names striate
aboriginal mystery into homesteaded English. Uninterrupted plains space
requires sun-reckoning as well—north (wintry) and west (sundown) of
another tribally given namesake, the *Wich*ita Range. Indians, pioneers,
cowboys, and oil men reckoned by the sun and ranged this heartland
flyway for centuries, Texas to North Dakota, leaving their ancestral
marks and telling place-names.

    "For my people, the Kiowas," the tribal Sooner makes his claim, the
landmark "knoll" is ancient; they named it Rainy Mountain as an earth-
to-sky cistern on the prairie desert. So who is he by way of "my people"?
What landscape lies in the blood? this young Kiowa writes toward Native
realization; what mixed histories and tongues give voice to a bicultural
writer? An historical stranger resides within—no stable dictionary pro-
nunciation of *Ki*-o-wa, *Kee*-o-way, Kee-o-wa, Kee-o-*way*, or Kya*ways*,
(a softened form of Comanche *Gwaigu* for "differing halves")—the

name perhaps mutating from the older Kiowa-Tanoan *Kwuda* or *Tepda*, "coming out." A mixed verbal identity evolves from many tongues and histories filtering through outsider tribal voices. Strangeness elicits crossing wonder, outsider curiosity.

Name indicates location, and age is venerable. Geology and meteorology draw from deeply sacred, common meaning. "Rainy" is a homey tag for the imaged mountain, a life-landmark on the dry plain of migratory history. Humans are born, the stories agree, into tribal names and landmarks within a Native setting, beginning early on with "red earth" Adam (the Semitic root *dm* = "red" in *Adam* or "man" fused in *adama*, meaning "dust of ground" [Genesis 2: 7]). There may be no deeper ferrous soil in America than the cinnamon fields and sorrel cutbanks of southwest Oklahoma where the streams run blood amber—homeland to dozens of "Removed" *Red* peoples. Not so much giving, humans receive namesakes, homegrown or removed, acknowledging the original names in things. In the tribal sense all are *named by* the Garden, desert or woodland, coastal or in-land mountain. And so with the "red earth" *Oklahoma* peoples.

In normative iambic pentameter, Momaday claims the oldest seasonal brag: "The *hardest weather in the world* is *there*." Climate may be humanity's most generic gossip, and it certainly caches the information necessary to negotiate landscape through time: wintry blizzards, spring tornados, "and in *sum*mer the *prairie is* an *anvil's edge*." The author's signature pentameter formally brackets a frontal voweling cadence *(uh eh ih a eh)*, as both variety and particularity distinguish local modulations of weather, temperature, and human activity. Change and continuity mark the solar ceremonies of place. To know a place is to know its changes—not one characteristic, but the many timed variations in a given setting. "My grandfather, trying to survive on the frontier," Larry McMurtry says of the Texas Panhandle at the southern Kiowa rim, "needed to remember where water holes were and what weather signs meant" (*Reading Walter Benjamin* 35).

The prairie "anvil's edge" strikes a workingman's image old as Hephaestus, the game-leg blacksmith oddly chosen by Aphrodite, goddess of love. The iron image seems radical as horseshoes and railway tracks to the plains, a metallurgy revolutionary to the cultural mix of homesteaders and Kiowa centaurs—and yet the earthen alchemy of historical change serves as perfect meeting for prairie wilderness and the metal-edged migration of plows, spades, and iron wheels. The Kiowas treat "at the forest's edge" of pilgrim exchanges, here at the anvil prairie's edge, a westering image of fiery metamorphosis.

The "green belts" lining the rivers and "cracking" grass, alliteratively "brittle and brown" underfoot, detail vegetation essential to sustaining prairie life. The pasturage feeds buffalo and cattle. Hickory and pecan nuts sustain foraging humans. Willow provides aspirin tea and sacred tobacco (Lakota *kinnickkinnick*, for example, from the inner bark of red willow). Witch hazel renders an antiseptic astringent. Grasshoppers and tortoises slow time to the singular isolation of upright life against the horizontal plains. "This, you think," the writer turns to his reader now placed in time, "is where Creation was begun." A primal imagining is shared with all: in the beginning was—a story of beginnings.

An orator's tone modulates the Introduction, one for public speaking and tribal persuasion, based on the affective power of the word. This is the voice of a man speaking, in command of storytelling, expecting to be heard (at the University of New Mexico Momaday majored in public speaking and planned to be a lawyer, changing his plans at the University of Virginia when he heard William Faulkner read in 1957). The sentences are deep-voweled and rounded—the harmony, resonance, cadence, and balance of Navajo *hozhó*. His dialectics are reader-collaborative, trusting in an audience listening. The speaker trusts his art and audience, adapting the tone of father and grandmother speaking to her grandson, *you know*, implying tribally [we]-the-people are imaginatively reciprocal. And the translative connection projects across cultures, as with Black Elk's "word-sender" who arcs his "word-arrows" across time and space.

The handmade prototype *The Journey of Tai-me* seems to be spoken by Aho and her matriarchal peers, Keahdinekeah and one-eyed Ko-sahn (see three generations of Mammedaty matriarchs in the family cover photo to *The Names*). The more tailored University of New Mexico Press commercial edition is prefaced, introduced, and afterworded by the author, bracketed in poems to Aho, glossed with redacted social science, personalized through historical reflections on migratory landscape, and illustrated by the artist's father, Alfred Momaday. The tribal narrative—a collective Kiowa voice of myth, folklore, and legend—is free of individual or documentary history. Aho (Florence Mammedaty on her tombstone next to John Mammedaty in Rainy Mountain Cemetery) told these tales to her own son, Al Momaday, who in turn retold them to young Scott, who visits her grave in 1965 to reactivate the tribal tellings. The tone is personal without being idiosyncratic. The storyteller could be male or female, ancient or contemporary—inclusive of all tribal folklore and Kiowa myth, as in the best of oral traditions that inform modern

Native storytelling and prose fiction, Silko to Erdrich, Welty to Hogan, McMurtry to Sarris. In the reissued, redesigned 2001 edition, Momaday invokes all the inherited voices of his people's storytellings, saying that the "first voice is the voice of my father, the ancestral voice, and the voice of the Kiowa oral tradition." No copyright, no ownership—tribal anonymity grants collective telling, everyone at once character, speaker, and listener in the oral traditions defining Kiowa being, past and present.

The telling involves a call-and-response dialogic with an common tribal heritage, recognizing one's own kin. A painter's visual landscape works through eidetic detail and aural signs in place-names, the specific sound-signs in the names of things—"flax and buckwheat," a dung beetle, sidewinder, or scissortail that are what their names say. A two-step cadence rhythmically phrases all this in iambic measure and rhyme, the relaxed pentameter gait of the Euro-American blank-verse spine, Chaucer through Heaney. The author keys on conjunctive pairing—*and, or, but, yet, still*—moving one way, turning, then going another in tandem. All pairing in balanced kinship, the aesthetics prove receptive and reciprocal, a hearing voice listening to itself and to the natural world, the ancestors, and chosen others for telling cues through relatively unbroken space and vast silence. It is an emotive voice, inspired, fearful, respectful. As Aho would say of something wonderfully strange, *zeidlbei*, or personably to her grandson through her own son, "and oh! you know."

Matriarch of personal and tribal beginnings, Aho is a knowable Great Mother, an elder Eve among the living. She saw the beginnings, the changes, the passages onward to her grandson's day. She saw the infant Scott taken to the House of the Bear, *Mato Tipi* among the Lakota, and named by Pohd-lokh the arrow-maker *Tsoai-talee* or Rock-Tree-Boy after the origin story of the seven star-sisters chased up a sacred tree by their brother-turned-into-a-bear. At night the Kiowa look to kinswomen in the sky, she says. The eternal gender disputes, incest prohibitions, civilized and wild instincts interface in earthly chases as starry signs of Ursa Major, the Great Bear—all in the dialectic of a people named for differing sides, *Gaigwu*.

DREAM WHEEL NAMES

This is the Wheel of Dreams
Which is carried on their voices.
By means of which their voices turn

And center upon being.
It encircles the First World,
This powerful wheel.
They shape their songs upon the wheel
And spin the names of the earth and sky,
The aboriginal names.

        "Carriers of the Dream Wheel"

Concisely cadenced verse etches these storied origins in time. Momaday's "Carriers of the Dream Wheel," title poem for the Harper & Row 1975 initial gathering of contemporary Native poets, calls the tribal voices: "Come, come, / Let us tell the old stories, / Let us sing the sacred songs." Stories and songs cross back and forth across time, heft and age measured by the tare and texture of language, "old men, or men / Who are old in their voices." The *text* is verbally "woven," as in its Latin origin *textus* of textile and texture, Barre Toelken reminds readers in *The Anguish of Snails* (57). And this ongoing verbal tradition circles the camps of old-timers and contemporary writers. The *vers libre* of a spoken, freely lyrical voice spins a tribal "Wheel of Dreams," the sacred hoop of the four winds, bearing history and ancestral ceremony forward. These traditions are renewed by the "aboriginal names" still coming forth and circling through cultures from the origins of time.

Age makes these spoken and sung words sacred, ongoing. Holy is the spirit of things remembered, what binds tribal peoples through time and space, as though a sacred potter's wheel, powerful shield, Sun Dance circle, and the horizon itself were spinning "the names of earth and sky" eternally above human cycles of continuance and renewal. Indeed, the earth's curvature is a visible arc, sunrise to sunset in the southwest Oklahoma plain. Aho's fading legends are critical to her grandson's regenerating song-poems and tale-tellings, his born-again sense of evolving tribal definitions—no less than her redefining emergence with the people through a hollow mountain log down onto the high plains and out into a century of life-altering crossings.

Momaday's artistic transition channels singing and storytelling into written lyric and narrative. His is a revolution in tribal literacy no less radical than Homer's Grecian epics or Lao Tsu's Chinese ideograms 2,600 years ago. When the voices of a Native tongue begin to speak in talk-marks, or the dance rhythms and lyric tones course through crafted verse lines, culture alchemizes from *singing stones* into *talking leaves*. Literacy crosses traditions for posterity, as Sequoyah fashioned an eighty-six-character syllabary for translating the Bible into Cherokee, or Momaday's own Cherokee mother Natachee, as discussed in *The Names*, educated herself at Haskell Institute to be an Indian school teacher. Ceremonial dancing becomes metered step—traditional Native dance, say the Kiowa Gourd Dance, as poetic melody concretely imaged, phonetically measured, graphically suspended in time and space.

> They are old men, or men
> Who are old in their voices,
> And they carry the wheel among the camps,
> Saying: Come, come,
> Let us tell the old stories,
> Let us sing the sacred songs.

Momaday remembers his grandmother cooking meat in an iron skillet, beading at the south window, walking with a cane, praying naked by the bedside, her hair a long black shawl. The young writer clearly loves the ancient beauty and storied wisdom of elder women, Kau-au-ointy and Keahdinekeah to Aho and Ko-sahn. Aho is a dark Madonna muse (see her younger photograph in *The Names*), sensuous in her natural aging—"mother-of-us-all," as the Pueblos say.

The crowded house is still, now that Aho is dead. The "endless wake of some final word" echoes through an empty home grown smaller. A cricket on the handrail (a Tuckerman totem) fills "the moon like a fossil." Near loss is framed by distantly waning and waxing unity, the "whole and eternal" perspective of regenerative cycles. Yet grief ages toward elegiac acceptance and going on, the natural landscape and emergent life reassure this young writer. Tribal voices come back to tell Aho's stories, as a warm wind rises up purling "like the longing within," to translate and to carry the cultures onward.

And so this Kiowa grandson rises the next morning at dawn and follows the "dirt road to Rainy Mountain." The measure lopes in six- and seven-beat cadences, shortening to a normative five. Each of seven sentences in the final paragraph ends varying the interjective vowel *ah* (mount*ah*in, *ah*ir, sh*ah*dows, l*ah*nd, gr*ah*ve, n*ah*mes, *ah*way). The grasshoppers hop and the birds sing, the grass shines and a scissortail *hies* "above the land," a slightly archaic, lyric diction altogether fitting in this celebrative elegy. The final prose rises up in pure rhythmic dance (here lineated metrically 3/5/3/5/6):

> *There*, *where* it *ought* to *be*,
> at the *end* of a *long* and *legendary way*,

was my *grand*mother's *grave.*
Here and *there* on the *dark stones* were ancestral *names.*
*Look*ing *back once,* I *saw* the *moun*tain and *came a*way.

Ancestral names send the wayfarer out on the good red road of renewal.
At Aho's tribal journey's end, this grandson goes to his grandmother's
grave to begin the Kiowa "way" again. After the initiatory travel-talk of
oral telling and singing tribal chants, the book opens further passages
into Kiowa culture—a journey through history to the present, tribal ways
evolving toward being Indian in contemporary America. The restorative
glance back into Aho's life turns this young writer forward to his own
journey through the set texts of *The Way to Rainy Mountain.*

AGE WITH GRACE AND BEAUTY

I imagine the time of our meeting
There among the forms of the earth at Abiquiu,
And other times that followed from the one—
As easy conjugation of stories,
And late luncheons of wine and cheese.
All around there were beautiful objects,
Clean and precise in their beauty, like bone.

Momaday's poem for the aged, blind Georgia O'Keeffe, "Forms of the
Earth at Abiquiú," feeds prose narrative into the occasional lyric. Their
first meeting came in 1972 among the flesh-colored striations of Abiquiú
earth and sky, an incantatory place-name of Ancestral Pueblo history not
far from Jemez Springs, New Mexico, where the Momaday house still
stands. In 1747 the Spanish settled *Abiquiú* Pueblo ruin abandoned in
the 1500s, Tewa *Pay shoo boo-oo* corrupted Hispanically to "timber end
town" of San Juan Pueblo. The Tewa then said of the Spanish appropriation, *abay* or "chokecherry" end, hence *abay shoo* or Abiquiú (Pierce,
New Mexico Placenames).

The artistic friendship between painter and writer was marked by
stories, late luncheons, bones and stones "clean and precise in their
beauty." The stark desert objects—which O'Keeffe chose to paint as
though dead objects could flower and bear flesh through clean vision and
simple brush stroke—rest naturally as toponyms defining north-central
New Mexico: Ojo Caliente, Tierra Amarilla, Chama, Questa, Española,

Pilar, Tres Piedres, all in the river watershed that has gathered living Pueblo cultures since time immemorial—Tesuque, Pojoaque, Nambé, San Ildefonso, Santa Clara, San Juan, Taos, Picuris. And there in the "flat winter light," the blind matriarch could see with her fingertips the beauty of a small brown stone:

> At once, accordingly you knew,
> As you knew the forms of the earth at Abiquiú:
> That time involves them and they bear away,
> Beautiful, various, remote,
> In failing light, and the coming of cold.

An artist sees and feels earth forms in the stones of Abiquiú land-scape—the sweeping bajadas and sandstone escarpments, volcanic swells and granite scree, basalt petroglyphs, porous adobe, riverbed caliche, and red earth flushed with ocher and strawflower mud. The words appear mysteriously and slip away. "And anywhere / Is a street into the night," the poet recalls, "Deliverance and delight— / And evenly it will pass / Like this image on the glass." Memorably, musically, free verse cadences these imagings, cool and delicate as snowmelt. As with Aho's tales, age reminds the living of their tenuous and fragile touch, together with the beauty of lasting forms—Plato's good through Sequoya's alphabet. This poem narrates character as scene and lyricizes the landscape of artistic exchange, the passing of gifts from one artist to another. The writer's small brown stone passes hand to artist's hand.

Coming Out

"Yes, I thought, now I see the earth as it really is," Momaday opens *The Way to Rainy Mountain*; "never again will I see things as I saw them yesterday or the day before." Momaday's prose releases information through a centrifugal flow. It offers and explains tribal history in speaking details—three-part, *en face* sections of folk tale, social science, and personal observation over twenty-four cycles (after sales of over 200,000 copies by 2001, the University of New Mexico Press redesigned separate fonts for each voice). The artist observes the high plains: "At first there is no discrimination in the eye, nothing but the land itself, whole and impenetrable. But then smallest things begin to stand out of the depths—herds and rivers and groves—and each of these has perfect being in terms of distance and of silence and of age" (17). Distance tracks landscape, silence traces sound, age tells human history. The artist's eye modulates and interprets tribal identity as passage through land, language, and time.

By contrast with outgoing prosaic sweep, Momaday's verse incises data in centripetal swirls as though he were scoring icons in basalt. "These figures *moving in* my *rhyme*," as earlier cited, "*Who are* they? Death* and *death's dog, Time.*" Rhythm cadences perception, as normative iambic tetrameter gives way to a trochaic answering heave. The couplet end-rhymes with a triple spondee of initial dentals that rivet mortality to a death end-stop, the unruly dog at humanity's heels.

Aho takes her own time getting where she wants to go through her grandson's retellings. She knows where that place is—the beginnings of time onward. "You know," she tells her progeny in the familiarity of personal kinship and common knowledge, "everything had to begin, and this is how it was" (*WRM* 16). There is direct and casual intimacy in speaking *through* her offspring, an assumed knowing of shared heritage. All my relatives, all in the family. These are our beginnings, she instructs her son to tell his son. This is how it was for us, our nature, how we came to be, and so it is. The people emerged "one by one" as collective individuals (Plains variant on Pueblo pairing), following *each other* along the way (both individually free and united in difference) through a "hollow log." This ancient tree of life falls open to a new world, horizontally inviting passage.

Aho's grandmotherly teachings come intimately from inside the tribe: the reader sees what she has heard told from childhood, then tells her own son to tell his. A select people's stories pass on generation to generation, the inheritor Aho's grandson and his children's children. The redacted social science of James Mooney's *Calendar History of the Kiowas*, Elsie Clews Parsons's *Kiowa Tales*, or Mildred Mayhall's *The Kiowas* comes from outsider observation, dispassionate data collected by non-tribal observers. The reader stands outside looking in, as the stranger at the tipi crease watches the arrow maker and his wife. Momaday's own personal observations, childhood memories, and lyric interjections lie between tribal inclusion and mainstream education. These are the classical *-emic* and *-etic* divisions drawn by anthropologists between phonemic meaning (inside a culture looking out), and phonetic description (outside the culture looking in). The reader sees through the artist's educated eyes what Aho saw imaginatively and ethnically, what scholars describe scientifically, what Al Momaday illustrates in pen and ink: a landscape beyond comprehension, a heroic people evolving, a history of epic wonder and tragic loss and continued redefinition.

So Aho's is a migration story retold in the twentieth century, an emergence myth seasoned with the humility of age, rather than aspiring Edenic innocence. A pregnant woman got stuck, the people say, and that's why Kiowas are so few. This could prove comic in the larger sense of the word, a fortunate fall with future promise. Or in the short run it seems sacrificial, perhaps a reminder of the childbearing on the move, the losses of life along the way. As in many emergence images warning and celebrating ancient hardships, the tribal signifier works both ways.

Aho's son Alfred narrates through a common voice of reassurance and acceptance, simply speaking, trust that is casually conjunctive: "and this is how . . . and that is why . . . they looked all around and saw the world." The coupling conjunction "and" conjoins traveling ancestors, while "but not all" differentiates their turns in history and explains their particular circumstances, today and yesterday. Theirs are tribal stories of beginnings, first things, old truths, deep origins—the natural miracles that italicize a people's definition and ongoing sense of who they are.

In the second *en face* paragraph, historical record describes a people so others will know them with an outsider's detailed objectivity. "They called themselves *Kwuda* and later *Tepda*, both of which mean 'coming out,'" Momaday writes as a student of Indian history. The distant perspective is critical to a descriptive science of knowing what things mean in translation: reading the details, interpreting data that fills in context. This information may be known inside implicitly, assumed by a people who do not consciously voice it, but missing to an outsider. Explanatory detail is consciously non-lyric in attempting to clarify otherness. "And later still they took the name *Gaigwu*, a name which can be taken to indicate something of which the two halves differ from each other in appearance" (*WRM* 17). Not we but "they," the scholar observes, and their evolving, dialogic naming unravels through doubly dependent clauses, Latinate syntax, and a passive verb construction, "which can be taken," acknowledging alterity. Plains sign language allowed Indians like the Comanche to speak of Kiowa others without words—holding the shaking palm cupped to the side of the head, perhaps to indicate the Kiowa as a people with differing minds, even humorously rattle-brained to other tribes. This is not a personal but a public voice of intercultural relativism (other-minded peoples as neighborly others), dispassionate historicism where supposed facts, not personal belief or family loyalty, determine knowing what needs to be known. Such a flattened voice can call for neutral report and balanced reasoning. In this way *object*ivity partners with *subject*ivity—non-ethnic, non-insider information grounds intimate story and personal witness.

Finally the writer, as experiential pilgrim and lyrical visionary, steps into the tribal name *Kiowa* that originated as *coming out*: "I remember coming out upon the northern Great Plains in the late spring." His is an individual reenactment of a collective tribal myth. Personal vision renews the continued story of a people's definition: not just as-they-view-us, *you see*, but how I know who-we-are. The individual journey retraces history as a mythic passage of renewal. Spring sunrise marks the rebirth of Kiowa ways, and the landscape freshly seasons his senses. Near detail and distant perspective call for the names of things to connect personal observations through time and space. Distance, silence, and age layer proportion, balance, and perspective into the lyric narrative. Part joins whole. Tribal singular "I" fuses into they-as-we, "you know," and the defining communal moment envisions tribal past as present. "Yes, I thought, now I see the earth as it really is." A lyric instant in time becomes visionary for all time—narratively brought down to earth, wild-flowering in the landscape, at home in the vast space of human and ecological history.

Collaborative Art

Earth and I gave you turquoise
    when you walked singing
We lived laughing in my house
    and told old stories
You grew ill when the owl cried
We will meet on Black Mountain

I will bring corn for planting
    and we will make fire
Children will come to your breast
    You will heal my heart
I speak your name many times
The wild cane remembers you

My young brother's house is filled
    I go there to sing
We have not spoken of you
    but our songs are sad
When Moon Woman goes to you
I will follow her white way

Tonight they dance near Chinle
    by the seven elms
There your loom whispered beauty
    They will eat mutton
and drink coffee till morning
You and I will not be there
I saw a crow by Red Rock
    standing on one leg
It was the black of your hair
    The years are heavy
I will ride the swiftest horse
You will hear the drumming hooves.

Consider Momaday's earliest published poem, "Earth and I Gave You Turquoise," as narrative example of a personal lyric vision. Prosaic details carry metaphoric weight in an elegy for a lost lover. Animate Earth makes turquoise for human use. The lapidary artist adds his art to natural craft, connecting himself and his beloved through storied stonework. Art is collaborative and conjunctive, a tribal, sacred reciprocation. "We lived laughing in my house / and told old stories." Earth resonates, stones speak, words conjoin, lovers walk singing. The syllabic count 7/5/7/5 is naturally exacting. The unpunctuated metrics shift delicately from trochaic heave, to balancing anapestic spondee, to triple spondaic reversal in the third line, to voweling reversal in the fourth: "*Earth* and *I* gave you *turquoise* / when *you walked sing*ing / *We lived laugh*ing in *my house* / and *told old sto*ries." Stress patterns shift rhythmically:

$$X - X - - X -$$
$$- X X X -$$
$$X X X - - X X$$
$$- X X X -$$

Sickness interrupts line 5, and the following line promises reunion: "*You grew ill* when the *owl cried* / *We* will *meet* on *Black Moun*tain."

$$X X X - - X X$$
$$X - X - X X -$$

The plot is lyrically cadenced in the first stanza, embedded in natural detail: artistic connection, talk-song, joyful union, ancient way, past omen, future promise. Black Mountain marks a sacred Navajo place in Arizona, and the owl cries as a warning. Momaday grew up speaking Diné as a second tongue that he eventually taught at UC Berkeley. Navajo is a tonal language with glottal stops, accented by bilingual speakers, hence the carefully pointillist metrics. The stanza's English-speaking aesthetics are regional and tribal, no less than Tapahonso's local dialect, the diction and rhythms expressly Red English—or as the Navajo say, "Joe Babe," imported from boarding school (see cartoonist and songwriter Vincent Craig's Navajo radio KTNN hit song "Rita," discussed in Lincoln, *Indi'n Humor*).

The conjunctive *and* implies extended kinship throughout the cosmos. Just so, gerunds (*-ing* verbal nouns) or participles (to participate in the action adverbially or adjectivally) allow noun-things and verb-motions to work through each other (walk singing, live laughing). Objects come alive (planting corn, cane remembering); actions become physical things (standing crow, drumming hooves). The specifics of tribal place and shared culture cross, domestic corn to wild cane, mutton to coffee, Black Mountain to Moon Woman to Red Rock. The poet speaks of future procreation between lovers, artistic seed and sensual heat producing the corn-children that will feed at her breast and heal his heart. He chants her name, lamenting, and the native world of "wild cane remembers you." This poem seems a present-tense, personal version of the Aho elegy—heart loss answered by spirited language, a brother's house for singing tribally, but by taboo, not speaking her name. The Beautyway path on the moonlit water will carry the song-poet spiritually home to his beloved: "When Moon Woman goes to you / I will follow her white way."

Conversational stresses give Native dignity to natural grieving. The spondees throughout the poem ("*you walked sing*ing, / *We lived laugh*ing *in* my *house* / and *told* old *stor*ies") slow and break up the easy iambic rhythms and syllabic metrics. Pattern varies from stanza to stanza through a five-part narrative drama carried in steadying syllabics, shifting metric feet, and visionary searching. The song-poem moves through the impasse of death toward spiritual reunion (if not literal), idealistic (if not realistic), a belief surely imaginative. The courage to keep going steps ever so carefully on a syllabic-metric form that cadences and balances the shifting time sense of personal and public grieving.

In each stanza, the concluding seven-syllable couplet brings hope and futurity to balance the grievance. "Tonight they dance near Chinle," the speaker says of a Navajo place-name near Canyon de Chelly. This is the historic site where Kit Carson burned the peach trees; shot the ponies, goats, and sheep; and herded the Diné in captivity hundreds of miles on the Long Walk to Fort Sumner, New Mexico. And in Chinle, by the sacredly numbered seven elms (earth number four and sky number three), the beloved's loom once "whispered beauty," still embraced. In distinctively tribal ways his family "will eat mutton / and drink coffee till morning," but "you and I will not be there." The conjunction binds through respective pronouns of other and self, "you and I." The beloved's procreative absence figures in an elegiac omen, a trickster crow standing on one leg by "Red Rock." This solo balancing recalls "the black of your hair," a natural image that locally says all. Time is passing in the heavy years, but this man's heart rides heroically forward, his passion to be heard in the "drumming hooves." His is a declaration of love in the face of death—a challenge to loss reaffirming tribal intimacy and connective loyalty, a love that will go on declaring itself alive. Momaday wrote no better narrative lyric.

CHILD OF EARTH AND SUN

"The twins lived for a long time, and they were greatly honored among the Kiowas," Aho, says in *The Way to Rainy Mountain*. Aho's storytelling through her son is complemented by her grandson's extra-ethnic research—filling in the missing details and explanations of a tribal history shattered by cultural explosion, change, and conflict. In turn, the insider-outsider dialogue is counterbalanced by personal experience and lyric recall. Aho's people tell of the baby left in a tree who grows into the wife of the sun. She bears a child and disobeys her husband by digging up a sky bush, then looking back regressively and returning to earth; but the sun's wife dies on the way (analogue to the primal mother stuck in a hollow log) from a magic ring hurled by her jealous husband. Their earth-sky child lands back among nature's grandparents, spider and snake. One mirrors two when the child, against Grandmother Spider's advice, throws up the ring, splitting him into his twin. The doubling theme reappears in all the storytelling voices and narrative facets. The two brothers go adventuring in a giant's cave and are saved from the smoke by remembering their grandmother's magical words, "above my eyes." Then they kill Grandfather Snake, and one disappears into the water as a submerged twin or tribal alter ego, always a shadow self just beyond the known tribal perimeter, an echo to every spoken voice.

There seems a "fortunate fall" at work in these boyhood teaching stories, the happy culpability of *felix culpa*, a nativist trope embedded in

American culture by way of tribal creation stories and Milton's *Paradise Lost* (ubiquitous with the Bible in nineteenth-century parlors). Humans are hard-wired to test rules, perhaps, learning by trial and error. Fortunately a second set of verbal rules comes into play through magical incantation when the going gets tough. The earth-mother disobeys her solar husband regressively, but her child lives to pass on the gaming ring and how-to story by speaking to the world-at-large, whether it be under the cave giant's smoke; the tornadic horse-fish rushing over; the protective *Tai-me* doll spirit-feathered and deer-footed; an enemy at the tent flap; a totemic guardian underwater or underground; a food pack of antelope, deer, or buffalo; a carrying centaur; or a lost brother. Talk is survival. Everything speaks.

As the sun and moon dance in tandem, waxing and waning through quarrels, sometimes eclipsing one another and "dying," so do children play, break rules, and learn by consequences the lessons of life, death, and survival. This is how they grow up. Unity is broken by experiential searching, and reunified through right words and re-righting reason. "They are not afraid of *Man-ka-ih*," the Kiowa say of the storm-spirit, "for it understands their language" (*WRM* 48). And her grandson adds his faith in talk. "By means of words can a man deal with the world on equal terms" (33).

Humans can speak with their world on personal and tribal terms. Song and story carry the power of origins, a world equally conversant. "Speak your name": the arrow maker shields his family with the Kiowa language (*WRM* 46). After no response, the mute stranger-enemy is killed by a tooth-edged arrow straight to his heart. Words conversely separate friend from foe, a familial tongue that joins or divides *us* from *them*. It is no small matter that Aho's second husband was Podh-lokh, the arrow maker, giving young Scott the tribal name *Tsoi-talee* or Rock-Tree Boy after *Mato Tipi* or the "House of the Bear" (the title of Momaday's most recent book, a table conversation between Yahweh and Set, the mythic Kiowa "bear" and protagonist's name in the novel *The Ancient Child*).

Given animal guardians and godly powers, earthly creatures and spirits of creation, ravages of history and ragged dog of time, humans have sacred, daily recourse to the powers of language as connection, prayer, defense, and recovery of a world lost without verbalization. So, too, the tribal imagination can story a locomotive on dividing tracks that destroyed the buffalo herds as a steel-horned bull derailed by sacred arrows. Aho's son can speak of a hunter blinded by the wind for his early recklessness, only to be abandoned by his lying wife and forced to graze like the animal he hunts, then retribalized by proving his worth, as his wife exhibits her disloyalty in lying further about his death. Bad people are known by their misuse of words. Doubly proven bad mates are thrown away, as bad men are ostracized when they threaten tribal well-being.

In any case the lives of women were hard among the Kiowa, this grand-son confirms of his grandmother's grandmother Kau-au-ointy, buried near Aho in the Baptist Rainy Mountain Cemetery too, a blue-eyed Mexican captive (freed when she could speak the tribal language) who worked her way out of indenture to own many cattle. The lives of all Kiowa were hard, the stories show, and the seven-foot warrior Kotsatoah wrestling down a buffalo is dwarfed by the storytelling grandmother whose Kiowa name, reversely accented as *A-hó*, means "thanks" (Parsons, *Kiowa Tales* 133; see Lincoln, *Native American Renaissance* note 43, page 267).

East of Aho's house, a beautiful woman is buried in a beaded dress with ceremonial moccasins that touch the earth. And here the sun rises out of the plain daily. At least "once in his life," Momaday ends the tales, a man ought to concentrate on the "remembered earth"—touch and listen to it. Feel and hear the creatures and the wind at noon, dawn, and dusk. See it from angles of wonder and colors of delight. Dwell on it in the deep heart's eye. The earth remembered is the place that takes place in all family tellings. It is the remembered earth as story imprinted trib-ally in the blood, "red earth" *Oklahoma*. Tribes re-member the people with words of common and ongoing origins. So, too, time, place, and sound-cum-silence carry the language of tribal bearing, going on going in the final verse lines:

> The early sun, red as a hunter's moon,
> Runs in the plain. The mountain burns and shines;
> And silence is the long approach of noon
> Upon the shadow that your name defines—
> And death this cold, black density of stone.

The collection closes with a formal Epilogue, again noting 1833 as Year of the Falling Stars, when the ancestral sisters in the Great Bear fell back down to earth. Al Momaday illustrates this Kiowa his-tory when everything began to change. A century and a half later, Aho and Mammedaty are dead, their grandson left with shards of memory, legend, hearsay, and fragmented history. Can the writer now remember well enough to carry the spiraling dream wheel onward?

The hundred-year-old Ko-sahn, one-eyed witness to Aho's time, remembers in her own childhood a hundred-year-old woman bringing the sand for the Sun Dance and chanting in blank verse, "As *old* as I *am*, I *still* have the *fee*ling of *play*" (*WRM* 88). This tribal delight is carried in a singing voice over two centuries. It is no less the sacred play of language, the feel for story and the pitch for song.

The final elegy, "Rainy Mountain Cemetery," invokes Aho by the sun's shadow cast on an engraved stone, a speaking petroglyph. The unheard name reappears in the elegiac absence of her being, the living presence of her voice. The wake of Aho's name is measured by two five-line stanzas of perfectly rhymed iambic pentameter. As noted, the name Florence Mammedaty, not Aho, inscribes the umber granite in Rainy Mountain Cemetery. Blessed are the listeners when voices fall silent. "And *death* this *cold, black den*sity of *stone.*"

The shadow of Aho's fading name is cast by the sun's light; her grandson journeys home to bear the storytelling presence of his ancestors. Aho's blood calls through the descendant word-sender. Hers is an ancestral voice to rise up and set out at dawn, as in the beginnings, the *headwaters* of tribal evolution. Tell the stories anew, the people chant; sing the songs today. The past and future of tribal people turn on this ancestral presence living in words.

EIGHT

Winter Naming

James Welch*

Before us lay
the smooth stones of our ancestors
—James Welch,
"Thanksgiving at Snake Butte"

Across Native and Euro-American cultures stretch precedents for tribal fusions of lyric and narrative in evolving Western forms. Dante scupted local Tuscan dialect to write *La Vita Nuova* in sonnets with prose commentaries. Joyce scribbled *Chamber Music* beside *The Dubliners*; Melville chiseled *Drum Taps* after *Moby Dick*. Lawrence penciled the American *New Poems* along with *Mornings in Mexico* under a Taos piñon. Williams redefined American free verse in the variable foot and wrote a novel about his wife, *White Mule*. Formal ambidexterity is not true for all. Charles Dickens, Joseph Conrad, or Cormac McCarthy would not be caught *in flagrante* writing verse. With hard-wired lyric density Wallace Stevens, Robert Frost, or John Ashbury might balk at prose fiction, and Virginia Woolf is a poet despite the fictive mask. Native writers are no less cross-genred or complexly talented or culturally filigreed. "The oral tradition of the American Indian is intrinsically poetic in certain, obvious ways," thinks novelist-painter-essayist-poet N. Scott Momaday. "I believe that a good many Indian writers rely upon a kind of poetic expression out of

---

* An earlier version of the James Welch chapter was published in *American Indian Culture and Research Journal* 29, no. 3 (2005), and some of the Louise Erdrich poetry section in *North Dakota Quarterly* 72, no. 3 (Summer 2005).

necessity, a necessary homage to the native tradition, and they have every right and reason to do so. It is much harder, I suspect, for an Indian to write a novel than to write a poem" (Bruchac, *Survival This Way* 181).

HARD AND CLEAR ABOUT WHAT HURTS

Native writers answer and often counter one another, tribe to locale, temperament to taste. N. Scott Momaday writes as a classicist—fusional classics across cultures—Native and Euro-American models of the best that masters have thought and written, sung and spoken down through global time and tradition. "But in America there is something else," Momaday says in appreciation of Jorge Luis Borges, "a continuum of language that goes back thousands of years before the printing press— back to the times of origin—an indigenous expression, an utterance that proceeds from the very intelligence of the soil: the oral tradition" ("A Divine Blindness," *Man Made of Words* 84–85). "Oral poetry is a crucial cog in the revolving wheel of culture," John Miles Foley argues, "a verbal support system for social activity and identification, a partner to effective cultural citizenship. . . . oral poems can cure disease, or weave a fractured community back together, or record family history, as well as celebrate historical heritage or ethnic pride. Oral poetry is a socially embedded, functional brand of verbal art. Not *Ars gratia artis* ('Art for the sake of art') but *Ars gratia vivendi* ('Art for the sake of living')" (*How to Read* 189).

Momaday the *man made of words* walks in a sacred manner, as Black Elk would have it, with a good people in a good land. The Southwestern artist believes in ancient *hozhó* or good form—symmetry, style, dignity, respect—the balance of four winds and directions at all times in all places. He reveres age and tradition. "I would like to have heard the voices of those ancients who crossed the Bering Bridge to the North American continent thirty thousand years ago" (*MMW* 85). He deals in Kiowa *legend* (Latin "meet to be read," as the saints' lives in the twelfth century) and *mythos* (Greek "true story" as the archaic beliefs of others). Momaday sees culture as personal history and would rise to the pride of the past. He thinks in tribally conjunctive pairings, a community of relatives, extending kinship to all beings, reciprocating with the sacred and daily spirits of all things. This Kiowa *word sender* would recover, or better evolve and carry over the Old Ways into modern times—at times nostalgically, at others heroically and realistically. Momaday grandfathers a Native American renaissance, a tribal way to Rainy Mountain, inheriting his grandmother's childhood stories and songs.

> *Who hath divided a watercourse for the overflowing of waters,*
> *or a way for the lightning of thunder;*
> *To cause it to rain on the earth, where no man is;*
> *on the wilderness, wherein there is no man;*
> *To satisfy the desolate and waste ground;*
> *and to cause the bud of the tender herb to spring forth?*
> —Whirlwind Voice, Book of Job 38: 25–27

Only a couple of years after Momaday, James Welch enters American literature as an Indian postmodernist, a fractured classicist of the West, collating fragments. Reading the likes of Peruvian mestizo Cesar Vallejo and early Modernists from Pound to Roethke, including decreationists such as Ray Carver through Richard Hugo's tutelage at the University of Montana in the sixties, Welch translates the nightmarish reality of a postwar Native Fall and a post-holocaustal Wasteland into contemporary Blackfeet truth-telling. He writes "hard and clear about what hurts," to reapply Hemingway's formula to the daily lives of modern-day Indians. Welch's work is not heroic, legendary, or mythic: he tells of the true West, working cowboys and real Indians, hardscrabble survival and off-rez scrapes.

Welch's kinships are sadly warped, the sacred hoop broken. As evident in his titles and names (or lack of), there is a misnaming asymmetry of human, animal, and natural life-forms—"cock-eyed" as the deer see things, the hermit grandfather says in *Winter in the Blood*. A pale horse named Bird dies freeing a cow stuck in the mud, bawling for lost sons and brothers. The "airplane man" buys a blue car called Falcon for a no-name narrator, delivering him fugitive to Canada. Mother Teresa sacrifices a prophetic duck named Amos for Thanksgiving dinner. Father John First Raise falls dead-drunk in the blue-white winter ditch, where brother Moses was killed by a drunk motorist a decade before. A distempered, unsaintly Teresa farms the leftover homestead with a newly wed, rickety breed husband, Lame Bull.

The novel registers imbalance in the four winds and seasons, a hard rain falling from the northwest, "to satisfy the desolate and waste ground," as Job's Whirlwind says. Subzero numbness sears a late-summer winter of delayed tremens and battle-fatigue depression. The novel's antihero is as distant from himself as a "hawk from the moon," turning winter-count icons upside-down, Momaday's cricket askew against the framing moon. Welch's art is an eccentric anti-style of nameless, faceless, sodden mirages against a toneless horizon—generic old lady, runaway lover, dead dad, lost brother, caustic mother, parodic stepfather, and madcap Anglo airplane man who took a little something not belonging to him. The old images of pilgrim up against Indian—cannibal, barbarian, *Wilden*, libidinist, pagan, warrior, heathen, feathered *salvage*, lawless hostile, ageless *Abergeny*—tip cartoonishly *virtual* in this surreal fiction (the "real" real or supra-reality of things, so André Breton defined *surrealism* in French modernist poetry). This story will take some parsing at the outset.

Written in Blood

Hath the rain a father?
  or who hath begotten the dew?
Out of whose womb came the ice?
  and the hoary frost of heaven, who hath gendered it?
The waters are hid as with a stone,
  and the face of the deep is frozen.

—Whirlwind Voice, Book of Job 38: 28–30

To have something "in the blood" means a person is born with it—maybe a good or a bad thing. A born loser is not good. To have romance in the blood—a born lover, for example—can be fetching, or if the person is odious, not so. Reality in the blood might be better, if one has the Native heart and guts to stomach betrayal, loss, or outright tragedy. Blood is blood, and families are thick with it—thicker than wine, they say—especially Native families. Most know that bad blood is trouble; eugenicists argue the purity of true blood. And in the old-time Indian world, now colonized hierarchically, a pecking order falls from full-blood (real Indian), to mixed-blood (bi-tribal Indian), to half-breed (half-Indian), to bloodless White Man (not-Indian).

Winter words? Welch is no stranger to the Western canon. "Now is the winter of our discontent," carps Shakespeare's Richard III, fomenting civil strife in trochaically reversed blank verse. "Winter kept us warm," the torpid maiden Marie laments in Eliot's *The Waste Land* three centuries later in London. From discord to distemper, dead winter gets a bad literary rap.

Winter is its own native reality, the word itself cognate with the Proto-Indo-European (PIE) root for *water*. Mediterranean winter meant fertile rains, a godsend to Eliot's hollow men gathered on the tumid river's banks. So, too, the whiteness of winter is dyadically charged: light itself, innocence, and idiosyncratic albinism; inversely dead bones, sterility, absence. To an Indian, this inversion points a pale bony finger at the White Man as invader, destroyer, prevaricator, and jailer. Yet in Blackfeet mythology, "Old Man" the Sun, *Na'pi*, is known as "dawn-light-color man," associated with the sallow or yellow-white newborn bison. These tribal icons, native ironies, and modern laments are peckishly buried throughout *Winter in the Blood*.

A reader questions just what James Welch means, writing a Native novel available to Americans at large, by "winter" in the blood—dubious curse, blessing, or mixed bloods of both Native culture and American invasion? The uncertainty rattles an ironic disquiet about mixes of White and Indian, promise and betrayal, vision and bitterness. *Winter in the Blood* extends this ethnic division to good-and-bad blood between men and women, realist continuity and romantic tension, even issues of intimacy and distance between writer and reader. "Bones should never tell a story to a bad beginner," the novel opens with the torn-off scrap of a title poem to Welch's first book, *Riding the Earthboy 40* (1971). The reader is in a tilting blood feud with titles alone.

The verbal noun "Riding," *to ride* and *a ride*, teeters between pure action and portable stasis. One mode is verbal energy, the other a noun that begs the question of acting or acted on, given the unbalancing ride, a debatable instability. This *riding* seems a condition played out or upon (*give me a ride*), or perhaps it is an unsteady perch on the back of something skittishly moving out west (*they took him for a ride*). These and other disquietings unsteady entry into *Riding the Earthboy 40*, whose outtake as poetic shard introduces *Winter in the Blood*. Passive or active (straddling the difference with the motion-sick rider)—to stay up on this thing moving, whatever it is, or wants to be, this book of poems or stories, *it's hard.* . . .

Earthboy? Boy of the earth, a reader assumes, even child of nature in the popular Western lexicon—born of the fertile elements. Earth suggests agrarian nurturing, rather than the cowboy struggle with its unruly synonym "dirt." Perhaps native Earthboy is akin to "red earth" boy, as in the Semitic etymology of the word *Adam*, not to mention Choctaw "red earth" *Oklahoma* already discussed with Momaday's Kiowa homeland, or Pomo meaning "red dirt," discussed later with Greg Sarris profiling

Mabel McKay. Red for ancestral blood, then; red for passion and violence; red for heat, anger, and action; red for Indian, as Linda Hogan introduces *The Book of Medicines*. It's truly a day-glow misnomer, Red Indian (for Iroquois face-paint, it is said), but that's what Welch deals with—images and their relation to reality, words and implications, the romance of truth and vice versa. And his fictive earth seems falling and cloddishly fallen, "dirty." The torn-off piece of a poem questions "those foolish claims that he was better than dirt."

Boy, that is, Western cowboy or young Huck running off to the territories, seems paradigmatic of the New World frontier, but does this runaway trope apply to nomadic Red Americans? Are these men delinquent Indian cow*boys*, Native Earthboys, or "dirty" *salvages*, as the Puritans complained of people who bathed daily in streams, rather than took the weekly or even monthly Plymouth ablutions? Natives held aromatic flowers to their noses to blunt the stench. "*Earth*boy *calls* me *from* my *dream*," the fragment closes in trochaic tetrameter off-rhymed, "*Dirt* is *where* the *dreams* must *end*."

What about the numerals 4 and 0, as in Earthboy 40? Four is a sacred-earth designation in the Native world—a stable, grounding number ("rational") in most numerical systems of thinking: four winds, four roads, four cardinal points, an x/y quadrant axis, and the twice bisected or squared circle. But to couple 4 with 0, the naught of numbers, spells trouble in a quarter section of dirt. Balance four with the zero black hole of nothing? When Emily Dickinson notes the startle of a garden snake as "Zero at the Bone," she cuts to a leukemic fear of emptiness, even a colorless void of dis-ease at the Edenic heart of matters that terrify Westerners. Call it white absence or abyss, anxiety or ennui, obsession or depression, any zero at the bone is dead-center unsettling.

SQUARING THE LAND GRAB

Maybe there's a cartographic tack to this erratic craft of "Riding the Earthboy 40." Consider geographers and map makers drawing and quartering the New World—property squaring of riparian watersheds and ragged mountains and broken coasts and endless rolling prairies and desert plains. George Washington, the first war president, was a surveyor who was party to the initial federal treaty with Iroquois warriors, "Of utmost good faith . . ." (Northwest Ordinance, 13 July 1787, Statutes at Large 1:51–53). His thirteen colonies ran right over America's surveyed allies in a few years, forging west through the Alleghenies and into the Ohio River Valley frontier. Picture national heroes like Daniel Boone or Davy Crockett, Native resisters like Tecumseh or Black Hawk. Over a century or so of frontier wars, surveyors forged straight lines across the country, made right angles out of slopes and curves, staked the plains for fence posts, and checkered rectangular grids across pooling lakes and wandering rivers. Quick-claimers and Sooners and homesteaders boxed the lots and squared America for ownership and equity resale, then banked the venture real-estate profits. Americans have a national industry, perhaps a leading economic factor, founded on stolen, squared, and resold Indian land.

And so the Natives, in Welch's case buffalo-hunting, semi-nomadic Blackfeet, were conquered, boxed in, and fenced on POW camps called "reservations" by 1883—"land set aside for Indians, surrounded by thieves," General William T. Sherman said (Nabokov, *Native American Testimony* 189). By 1887 the Dawes Allotment Act subdivided 140 million acres "in severalty." Which meant that any acreage left *over*, when every Indian head of household got 160 squared-off acres, was given *free* to migrant Whites. Civil War soldiers were paid off in Indian land by a bankrupt Union. What Indians weren't using, Anglo-Americans reasoned, they didn't need, and soon enough Whites got 640 acres after the 1898 Curtis Act. Tribes got salvage lots at best, usually the land that could not be farmed, logged, mined, or otherwise re-engineered, hence "waste" land.

Between allotment and reservation relocation, gerrymandered land rip-offs and outright thievery, some 87 million acres of Indian lands disappeared overnight, or shifted ownership, as "settlers" saw the swap. Natives saw homesteaders *un*settling Georgian valleys of loam, gold, and civilization; Ohio bottomlands; Red River Dakota farmlands; Kansas pasturage; Washington forests; Oregon fisheries; California orchards; and Arizona riverbeds. Any acreage still Indian was soon chopped and quartered into still smaller parcels of inheritance, down to forty-acre quarter sections of land (the White man likes fractions, Indians say). Forty acres and a mule were offered to two-thirds-a-Black-man escaping slavery for free-holding citizenship in the West. Not given citizenship until 1924, Indians were dumped on their squared-off reservations and forgotten (until Indian Gaming, that is—witness a city plat of Palm Springs checkerboarded with the Morongo Nation). Most know the general outline and gist of the country's frontier platting. A poet distills lyric crystals; a novelist rubs noses in the prosaic dirt.

DIRTY REALISM

Admired by James Welch, Simon Ortiz, Adrian Louis, Ray Young Bear, Greg Sarris, Sherman Alexie, and Sherwin Bitsui, among others, Raymond Carver's grainy lyricism disrupted grammar and manners (cultural form) to reveal an unharnessed rhythmic pulse down in the shared language. Saint Teresa held that "words lead to deeds," Tess Gallagher reminded her late husband when he marveled how Chekhov's prose, once lineated, showed poetic luminosity. Carver copied passages of Chekhov to be interspersed with his own poetry in a final volume, *A New Path to the Waterfall* (1989), published posthumously. He wanted Homer's song-story fused with Frost's story-song, and he found the crossing in Chekhov. "Ray had so collapsed the distance between his language and thought," Gallagher prefaces *A New Path to the Waterfall*, "that the resulting transparency of method allowed distinctions between genres to dissolve without violence or a feeling of trespass" (*NPW* xxi). *Will You Please Be Quiet, Please?* Carver titles his short stories, perfectly echoing the librarian's voice, speech dictating and undermining the poetics of grammar—the directive entreaty of proprietary silence for reading in common spaces. A verbal preposition circles *What We Talk About When We Talk About Love*, and a dangling preposition originates *Where I'm Calling From*. No less than Homeric remixings of cross-regional dialects, Carver brackets his late poetry in old-time chiasmus, *Where Water Comes Together with Other Water*. Native writers get this colloquial, inventive play with American speech. Indeed, no less than Frost or Welty, they draw from daily talk to shape their own tribal lexicons of Red English (see Anthony Mattina's *The Golden Woman*, as discussed in Lincoln, *Indi'n Humor*).

What does postmodernist *dirty realism* have to do with Native literacy, and James Welch in particular? At his death, Ray Carver was called the "American Chekhov." His "transparency of method" allowed readers to see *through* the aesthetic medium—the writer's tools invisible, the technique embedded—as close as language comes to common being. This is something like the verbal experience of experience, the unaffected embodiment of consciousness in language. Consider an experiential narrative or poetic method erasing itself: Native plain-style writers like Silko, Tapahonso, Hogan, or Sarris skein oral traditions through technical transparency and artistic backlighting. "The story given as poem could unwind without having to pretend to intensities of phrasing or language that might have impeded the force of the story itself," Gallagher explains the artless art of Carver's song-story, "yet the story could pull at the attention of the reader in another way for having been conceived as poetry" (*NPW* xxi). Thick line slims to tensile strength, luminous image begs shadow, leaping rhythms glister. The classics of all times reify and crystallize common idioms. Talk in *The Odyssey*, as Michael Schmidt argues in *The First Poets*, courses gossipy-rich with street-smart dialects (*FP* 40–41). The best companion for reading oral poetry, John Miles Foley offers a critical maxim, is an unpublished dictionary (*How to Read* 184). So the story-poem moves cross-generically with the quickened pace of limpid diction drawn from daily speech; narrative overrides the lyric slowing of lingual focus and depth.

No faults, only sins

Students of Carver by way of Welch, Sarris, or Hogan write plain-style prose or free-verse poetry. Silko's Native (con)texts draw populist origins from tribal storytelling and ceremonial chant. Not art for art's sake, Tapahonso insists, but lyric lucidity crossed with narrative pace. The result is a transparent reality in language, artistically convincing, formlessly rich and tonally deep, cadenced with the rhythms of common speech. Reversely torqued, Erdrich's poem-stories pull the reader deeper into character and plot by way of lyric conception in storied execution. Narrative in motion, Momaday's lyric action echoes through metaphor. Not that the language is effortless or without shape: words are stripped to essential detail, diction, image, rhythm, and pacing of real life lived without formal distraction, as Momaday writes in "Simile":

> What did we say to each other
> that now we are as the deer
> who walk in single file with heads high
> with ears forward
> with eyes watchful
> with hooves always placed on firm ground
> in whose limbs there is latent flight

The illumination is all, the gist of things in motion, the impact of the experience as *lived* writing, essential to classic literatures. An artist "so simple he has no faults, only sins," Yeats asked in *Responsibilities*. Shakespeare stripped dramatic poetry to heath, wit, and bones in *King Lear*, and Hemingway spoke of writing clearly the hard truth of what hurts by *In Our Time*. James Welch dips his pen in frontier caustic to write *Winter in the Blood*, and Joy Harjo pivots from off-rez acid rock to chant *She Had Some Horses*. The models of leaping, luminously detailed lines are universal. The hundred-year-old late poet laureate Stanley Kunitz confesses, "I never tire of bird-song and sky and weather. I want to write poems that are natural, luminous, deep, spare. I dream of an art so transparent that you can look through and see the world" ("Table Talk," *Paris Review*, no. 83 [Spring 1982]).

The impulse for unaffected truth-telling leads to the epic style of the realist commoner, tribally *one of us*, says Genesis or *Gilgamesh*—Everyman as town crier, singer, storyteller, elegizer, praiser, or gadfly. Sherman Alexie wants to be a poet of the people, storyteller homing in *The Odyssey*, Dante flexing Tuscan into national literacy. Consider lyric narrative of the high plains: Louise Erdrich stewing up *Love Medicine* in North Dakota, James Welch wringing Montana sweat and tears from *Winter in the Blood*. Still there are rules, forms, and caveats: no art that impedes insight, no experience unessential, no false reality clouding perception of the world we live in, as language shapes and gives form to common experience. "The swift and natural observation of a man as he is shaped by life," Yeats said of Odysseus ("Why the Blind Man in Ancient Times Was Made a Poet" 153). Some do this better than others. All words are not art, and all art is not tribal tryst to lived experience, as witnessed in Sherwin Bitsui's crossword mazes. Carver was drawn to Czeslaw Milosz's lines in "Ars Poetica" (*New Path to the Waterfall* xxix):

> I have always aspired to a more spacious form
> That would be free from the claims of poetry or prose
> And would let us understand each other without exposing
> The author or reader to sublime agonies.

A Book of Luminous Things, the Polish-American poet Milosz later prefaced his international anthology of verse translated into English. "My proposition consists in presenting poems, whether contemporary or a thousand years old, that are, with few exceptions, short, clear, readable and, to use a compromised term, realist, that is, loyal toward reality and attempting to describe it as concisely as possible. Thus they undermine the widely held opinion that poetry is a misty domain eluding understanding" (*BLT* xxv).

Ceremonial culture may be foregrounded or backgrounded in Native American texts, tribal to mixed-blood writer, country to city spokesperson, but each makes the Native voice and vision a horizon reference.

James Welch adds in Bruchac's *Survival This Way*, "Kind of growing up around the reservations, I just kept my eyes open and my ears open, listened to a lot of stories. You might say my senses were really brought alive by that culture. I learned more about it than I really knew. It was only after I began writing about it that I realized what I had learned. I knew quite a bit, in certain ways, about the Blackfeet and Gros Ventre ways of life, even though I wasn't raised in a traditional way" (*STW* 314–15). With four out of five Native peoples living off-reservation now—many going through mainstream schooling, retribalizing to traditional ways back home, often writing about reacculturation—Native American literature charts a passage of leaving and returning home once more, beyond removal and dispossession. Welch postscripts the mix: "I feel that I'm always writing from the same world in the poems and the novels" (*STW* 317).

A Bell for Sinners

Welch starts his novel with the broken chert of a poem. "Earthboy: so simple his name / should ring a bell for sinners," the reader finds from lines lost in transition. Earthboy farmed the land sky "with words." Written in staggering iambic trimeters, but metric feet all the same—scoured diction, lyric minimalism, stubborn logic, taciturn imagery—these cut, mean lines startle to Christian curses, bad jokes, racial slurs, fallen metaphors, and elegiac shards that deride the Earthboy name. "I ride / romantic to those words": the poet canters into his fiction with a end-stopping, anti-sentimental realism as the ground sense essential for renewal, and if it ever has a chance, modest romance based on dark comic promise. The reader is back to Blackfeet Adam and Eve, *Na'pi* and *Kipi'taki* in the old creation stories (see Grinnell, *Blackfeet Lodge Tales*). Old Man Sun and Old Woman Moon gamble creation in a tragicomic dialogue of promise and limit, fancy and fact, innocence and irony, romance and realism—the ways people fool themselves, together and apart, and the ways they try to fix it, but can't, discussed more in detail as things go along.

To catch the lyric tenor of Blackfeet storytelling written down, here is the opening narrative voice of *Winter in the Blood*:

> In the tall weeds of the borrow pit, I took a leak and watched the sorrel mare, her colt beside her, walk through burnt grass to the

shady side of the log-and-mud cabin. It was called the Earthboy
place, although no one by that name (or any other) had lived in
it for twenty years. The roof had fallen in and the mud between
the logs had fallen out in chunks, leaving a bare gray skeleton,
home only to mice and insects. Tumbleweeds, stark as bone,
rocked in a hot wind against the wet wall.

On the hill behind the cabin, a rectangle of barbed wire held
the graves of all the Earthboys, except for a daughter who had
married a man from Lodgepole. She could be anywhere, but the
Earthboys were gone.

The fence hummed in the sun behind my back as I climbed
up to the highway. My right eye was swollen up, but I couldn't
remember how or why, just the white man, loose with his wife
and buying drinks, his raging tongue a flame above the music
and my eyes. She was wild, from Rocky Boy. He was white. He
swore at his money, at her breasts, at my hair.

Coming home was not easy anymore. It was never a cinch,
but it had become a torture. My throat ached, my bad knee
ached and my head ached in the even heat. (*WIB* 1–2)

"*In* the *tall weeds* of the *bor*row *pit*," the nameless man confesses roughly
in measured verse, "I *took* a *leak* and *watched* the *sor*rel *mare*, / her *colt*
be*side* her, / *walk* through *burnt grass* to the *sha*dy *side* of the *log*-and-
*mud cab*in." The weeds have gone feral for some time. No Name Indian
straddles the unwanted wilds of a "borrow pit" where highway engineers
stole dirt to crown a white-striped, blacktop highway across aboriginal
land, ironically an echo of Dante's *Inferno* which opens, "Mid-way in
my life I fell off the straight path into the dark wood." He may have seen
taller grass, this Red cowboy, but urinates where he must. Scatological
evacuation purges the narrative throughout—John First Raise pissing
the boy's name in the snow and Yellow Calf recalling him as "a young
squirt"; his off-color stepfather guffawing purgatively and falling drunk
off his chair; teenagers masturbating in filling-station toilets and old men
spitting; one-night relieving stands in hotels and trailers; a thin tourist
girl vomiting in the weeds by the road; Bird the horse farting catharti-
cally in the recognition scene; and the narrator finally laughing out loud
epiphanically about ancestral winter in his blood—a nasty joker playing
a bad joke on all. So this Indian man tends to his business unceremoni-
ously in a ditch where the earth has been dredged, an absence of stolen
land ghosted by the Earthboy homestead. This opening scene serves the

vernacular with a twist, the homely poetry of "leaky" working men (women might not say it this way)—toxic elimination in bodily functions made public—first-person candor, creative desecration, small-time scandal, and dirty realism all in one opening sentence. No Name is a dispassionate observer of mother-child kinships, mare and colt, later cow and calf in his brother's death and the final mud rescue when Bird dies, finally mother-daughter and father-son lineage.

The "burnt grass" bespeaks a seared desert needing rain, a Native wasteland. The "shady side" or shelter refuge of a "log-and-mud" box cabin, not a circular tipi, recalls Black Elk's remark that the white men pen up their own in boxes, even the grass. Rather than Momaday's "they called themselves" naming of the Kiowa, the narrator says, "It was called the Earthboy place, although no one by that name (or any other) had lived in it for twenty years." Casually enough, the subjunctive Indian-White tagging suggests that a secondary language is only attached to things—not the Native thing itself, but what it's loosely called in English.

The chthonic name Earthboy may be archaic. Mother Earth has fallen on hard times in this story. A corrosive, reverse-field irony jerks the syntax, "although," as realistic check to romantic looking-back. The fact soon emerges that brother Mose (monosyllabically contracted prophet of Exodus) died on the spot as road-kill in this borrow pit twenty years ago, when the Earthboy house was deserted (dubious witness to the milk-and-honey Promised Land, God's burning bush and stuttering Ten Commandments). Is No Name then a latter-day Indian Aaron who speaks for his speech-defective brother Moses? And here ten years back, John First Raise, an ironic Baptist-Redeemer precursor, froze to death coming home blind drunk ("just a *blue-white lump* in the *end*less *skit*tering *white*ness," as etched nine chapters later in iconic blank verse; *WIB* 19).

The Earthboy roof has fallen in, the mud fallen out (inversional patterns) in a low comedy of dereliction and neglect. This is the death rattle of tradition, the tribal bones of the matter. The abandoned house registers the singsong collapse of a "bare grey skeleton," home to varmints and vermin. The tumbling homelessness of the West hollows out the bare necessities in striding hexameter, Homer's six-beat verse line impacted with four spondees: "*Tumbleweeds, stark as bone, rocked in a hot wind against the west wall*." Anglo boxes resurface in the "rectangle of barbed wire" fencing the Earthboys buried in a barbed coffin. That military wire kept Indians on reservations and cattle from straying, as ranchers "won" the Wild West and still overrun it (to this day, millions of reservation acres leased on the cheap to White cattlemen).

One daughter escaped to Lodgepole and married out, so she can't pass on the Earthboy name, anticipating runaway Agnes (whose name means "chaste") with the stolen rifle and razor, a siren Cree virgin (teen Algonquin Pocahontas out west). Agnes shows up late in a bar, wearing a green mermaid dress and white graduation flats. The narrator advises this dusky Eve to "learn shorthand" as the "essential" language of survival, a coded essentialism that rules the novel's fenced range. Be brief, be blunt, confessional instructs, be gone. "She could be anywhere," No Name opines, "but the Earthboys were gone." Anywhere, nowhere, Native claims are unlocatable, accountability incalculable, kinship lost, families scattered, names erased. The king's prodigal son is "coming home," an ironic *nostos* crossed with lamentable Hamlet fable, to a generic mother, a rocking old lady, and the absence of "the girl who was thought to be my wife." Grandmother never does get a name, as with the narrator himself who hasn't earned one. Nor does the foggy airplane man, who doesn't recall one, or the old man in straw hat and green gabardines facedown dead in oatmeal at mid-story (see Van Gogh's 1888 "Portrait of a Peasant," in the artist's own words "a poor old peasant, whose features bear a strong resemblance to Father, only he is coarser, bordering on a caricature").

Local resident talk internally rhymes in torqued blank verse and broken trimeter: "The *fence hummed in* the *sun* be*hind* my *back* / as *I* climbed *up* to the *highway*." These prose metrics catch the ear by surprise in fallen places. And then the story mode switches to plot, action, and character definition: with a swollen eye from a bar brawl, a wounded knee from long ago beside his dying brother, the nameless Native foggily recalls an Indian girl from Rocky Boy, her white husband, swearing, and probably a skin-color fight—but none of that counts, he says, along with his homecoming. "For that matter none of them counted; not one meant anything to me."

Distance is his psychic razor through cursed country or "burnt prairie," rancid green Milk River, sagebrush and cottonwood, "the dry, cracked gumbo flats." This is the spondaic beat of a beaten-down man and land, the sun-pounded dirt of "a distance as deep as it was empty." No boundaries, horizontal or vertical—emptiness out west dwarfs a man. The opening chapter ends in a dry pocket of white space: "My throat ached with a terrible thirst." The famished Fisher Prince will plead for rain the rest of the story.

Perhaps this stumblebum stagger is meant as an ironic figure of vision quest or fallen delirium tremens, or some of both. Visionary aloneness has morphed into a conquered Indian sense of alienation. The numbed, catatonic, travel-shocked pilgrim may not make it back on his secular trek home. He goes everywhere dry-drunk, cotton-mouthed, breast-famished, and mother-rejected. "I *drank* a *long suck*ing *bellyful* of *wat*er *at* the *tap*," the lost son says, temporarily home. And here the story rests momentarily. It never goes anywhere very swiftly, or in a straight line, and nothing much happens dramatically, except to say that No Name discovers his true grandfather—his mother's father—in a story that defines the ancestral past as fallen present (but contrary to Momaday's way home, no paternal ancestry revealed, John First Raise the last unrisen Indian). Shadowing Momaday in Rainy Mountain Cemetery, No Name passes the Earthboy plot and finally puts his grandmother to rest, no small spiritual matter ending a surreal tale.

SYNTAX OF SURVIVAL

Winter in the Blood began in a poem after James Welch had written verse for seven years, his prose taking on poetic rhythm and density. "One of the things I found when I was trying to balance poetry and prose," James Welch (at home in Montana, 12 July 2000) said to Kathryn Shanley, "was that my prose was very jumbled up, very thick, and my poetry was kind of losing the lyric quality and losing its elasticity. So I was not satisfied with the language in either one. That's why I had to drop poetry and concentrate on the fiction" (*Paradoxa* 36).

In light of Welch's crossing over to the novel, what can fiction do that poetry doesn't? Lyric poetry tries to say *what is*, presenting language as its own ceremonial chant and dance, from Pueblo Grant Entry, to Plains Sun Dance, to Momaday's "Carriers of the Dream Wheel"—"Let us sing the sacred songs." It seems that narrative prose extrapolates the story and details of *why* what is *is*—and *how* it is—the who, what, when, and where of characters and actions in given places and times, working from and through character arc, plot points, and essential problems—"Let us tell the old stories." Dickens's caricatures in *Our Mutual Friend* give character to London, Erdrich's Argus eccentrics in *The Beet Queen* colloquialize North Dakota, Twain's Hannibal locals in *Huckleberry Finn* thicken Mississippi River time and place in regional narratives. Variations and exceptions riddle these distinctions, to be sure, but essentially poetry is defined within line lengths (determined by lyrical metrics of some kind, even free verse) and takes its origin from song and dance—hence the ability to chant the lines musically, a primary tie to oral ceremonial traditions. From Aristotle's *Poetics* to C. M. Bowra's *Primitive Song*, Andrew Welsh's *Roots of Lyric* to David Lodge's *Consciousness and the Novel*, critics have debated oral literary origins, print innovations, and lyric, dramatic, and narrative genres. Cut to a Native set of benchmarks. Put simply by the Navajo, if a medicine man can't dance, don't waste time or money. Bilingual Lakota insist that Sitting Bull's meadowlark cadence can be *sung* in translation. The Cree say that a good story keeps a person alive when times are hard. Tribally, a story that can't be remembered is probably not well told.

The mechanics are basic. Prose narrative talks its way to the ends of stories. Prose readers want something to happen and the results to show a change that matters—a character transformation in Dickens's *Great Expectations*, a plot resolution in Erdrich's *Tracks*, a spiritual victory in Momaday's *The Ancient Child*. Verse chants its own vision without explanation or resolution; the dancer dances. Fiction would describe in detail what goes into making and executing and understanding the human, environmental, and mystery-based elements of a plot, as with Silko's *Almanac of the Dead* or Welch's *The Death of Jim Loney*. Dramatic timing here, or structural arc (temporal and spatial plot points, as in drama and film) paces chapters of the constructed whole.

Time and space are incidental to the gyroscopic spin of a poem. Poetry frames the ecstatic instance, the perception suspended, unparaphrasable. "I am an angle of geese in the winter sky," Momaday chants his name-song, "I am the hunger of a young wolf." Image quickens the pitch; rhythm courses the lyric pace. Each syllable draws the poem through itself into a ghostly light standing behind luminous tableaux, the translative shadow behind ink on the page. This backlight correlates with a white space of silence around the text, literally the relative blankness of the page compared with prose narrative. "If I told you the deer was a hide / of light," Linda Hogan says, "you wouldn't believe it" ("Skin," in *The Book of Medicines* 32).

Foregrounding event rather than backgrounding character, prose fills the page and takes its own lined time and space to unravel a story through people, place, history, culture, event, and the *viva voce* passage of time itself. From Tolstoy's *War and Peace* through Erdrich's *The Master Butchers Singing Club*, a reader gets to know characters and the character of place. Tell me why, the psychological-fiction reader asks of plot (poetry asks to be overheard)—the prosaic motivation and inner workings of a character among many others acting in tandem. Virginia Woolf calls this "tunneling" a character; a psychological novelist goes into and through personality to lifelong details in dramatic backfill and causation. As with Louise Erdrich's eleven interlocking fictions, "tunneling" creates the back story of a front-running plot. The third dimension deepens a flat stage into full-rounded character action, whereas poetry embeds such dramatic action in metaphor and rhythmic diction. In dramatic narrative as noted, something happens between the gun on the wall and the gunshot. Some logic of persuasion, some spicy explanation fills in and around the plot expectation and timed explosion. Extended plot brackets in the generic story arc: the angry man and the naked corpse, the sad child and the runaway father, the baby born and the dying grandmother, the gaffe and the fight, the kiss and the knife, the border incident and the nationalistic war. Plot depends on watching what happens, cause-and-effect listening for clues, hearing a speaker out. Characters speak and are spoken about by other characters, and narrators speak for them. The reader never stops listening for, or guessing, or filtering details.

It seems that poems speak for themselves. Welch chants, "The children of Speakthunder / Are never wrong and I am rhythm to strong medicine." Poetry contracts time, prose expands it. "You don't know about me without you have read a book by the name of *The Adventures of Tom Sawyer*," Huck Finn opens his story; "but that ain't no matter." Poems pull readers in, stories propel readers along, and some do both. "I / the song / I walk here," the Modoc sing, as cited. The reader of a poem dives in and dances with words, parsing the sound of sense. A prose audience reaches through the narrative to implied character and catalyzed action. "To say the name," as the Cree tell tales, "is to begin the story."

Crossing from poetry into prose, *Winter in the Blood* is both lyrically rhythmic and narratively conversational, varying diction from imagist concision and metric density to cowboy and barroom talk. The story is told through the Plains dramatic monologue of a Montana Indian in a medium and tongue called Western, even frontier demotic. The narration is certainly farmhand and wrangler working-class. As with the opening verse fragment, lyric thickens the narrative texture. The compressed diction is hard-bitten, tangible, leathery—like Native pemmican from lean wild meats, dried and pressed to last through a hard winter. The monosyllables are concentrated, the images stripped of decoration, the rhythms tendoned. Here is an essential common tongue with unflinching honesty, candid and close to the bone, in a tradition crossing Ray Carver with trickster tales, Ernest Hemingway with antiheroic narratives, T. S. Eliot with elegiac tribal laments.

Poetry speaks privately *in tongues*, as it were, to break through the assumptions of language and human endeavor, to insist on irreducible mystery at the core of things. "These songs are not meant to be understood, you understand," John Berryman chants in *The Dream Songs*, "They are only meant to terrify & comfort. / Lilac was found in his hand." Prose brings the reader back to earth, describing and discussing shared things among others. "What's up?" June asks in the opening scene of *Love Medicine*. "Where's the party?" Sing and dance it out, the poem asks; see and talk it through, prose says. Sometimes a writer as narrative lyricist, a singer of tales—Homer to Virgil to Dante—does it all, as in Joy Harjo or Luci Tapahonso. Listen to the lyric compression and narrative cant in a lyric outrider to Welch's prose narrative, "Surviving," a winter-blood tale dramatically inscripted and shamanically encoded as verse (second poem in the 1971 World Publishing first edition of *Riding the Earthboy 40*). Up close, a reader begins to understand what's going on inside the lines, unpacking them carefully, or not at all.

Surviving

The day-long cold hard rain drove
like sun through all the cedar sky
we had that late fall. We huddled
close as cows before the bellied stove.
Told stories. Blackbird cleared his mind,
thought of things he'd left behind, spoke:

"Oftentimes, when sun was easy in my bones,
I dreamed of ways to make this land."
We envied eagles easy in their range.
"That thin girl, old cook's kid, stripped naked
for a coke or two and cooked her special stew
round back of the mess tent Sundays."
Sparrows skittered through the black brush.

That night the moon slipped a notch, hung
black for just a second, just long enough
for wet black things to sneak away our cache
of meat. To stay alive this way, it's hard. . . .

No poem opens so spondaically driven. "The *day-long cold hard rain drove* / like *sun*." Six drilled accents, the first hyphenated for double stress ("day-long"), radically slow the *run run* of narrative progress to a broken-step pace. The dentals toll through voweled a's and o's—*a-o, o-ah, a-o*—lowing back and forth as empty cavities. There's an unsettling sense the line might not make it to the first break, then the line falls across the metric drop with an illogical and cracking iambic simile "like sun." *Rain* / like *sun* will be a hard rain all around, since sun is everywhere insistent and nowhere soft on a hot, late summer Montana day.

Out west, working men and women ask how something is made and how it functions. This begs dressing the critter down to nouns, pronouns, verbs, articles, adjectives, adverbs, conjunctions, prepositions—and that least considered, most primal unit of measure, the interjection, which linguists say signaled the beginning of speech some two million years back, Stephen Pinker writes in *The Language Instinct,* before syntax began to cluster syllables in cadences or grammatical phrases a million years ago and the human brain mass quadrupled. Let's parse the syntactic ligatures of "Surviving" in prose parts of speech to see how its components work and what it does—the shorthand "essentials," as No Name says to Agnes.

Prosaic tare thickens Welch's poetry toward narrative lyricism. First the everyday nouns: *rain, sun, sky, fall, cows, stove, stories, mind, bones, land, range, girl, kid, coke, stew, tent, Sundays, brush, night, moon, notch, second, things, meat.* These are real nouns a reader can bite into and test like old coins—the common noun-things of Western experience, two dozen crowded into the poem with simple off-rhyming diction (to be exact, 108 monosyllables to 20 disyllables and a single tri-syllable, no less an actor's dream-speak than "To be or not to be—that is the question"). Down the avian ladder high to low, eagles to sparrows suggest winged spirits. In the name "Blackbird" a winged noun becomes a human-animal totem, generically a trickster spirit. Blackbird is dark, testing, daring, dangerous. In "Christmas Comes to Moccasin Flat," the figure reappears as Charlie Blackbird stabbing fire far from bar and church. Animate presences flit through things, as guardian spirits flash the metaphoric potential in all beings, objects, and conditions. Though common, everything means something further, every object goes totemically deeper than first thought, as with wind and moon, elk and badger, quartz and cedar.

So common becomes uncommon, first and finally considered: rain is not just "rain," but spring promise, inversely so in the "fall" ending of the novel. Elements frame the day. Sun shines, sky beckons, fall falls, cows feed, stove warms. Noun-things narrow down in the West: range ranges, girl thins, kid cooks. And in human cultural terms, stories tell, minds mind, bones last, land gives (inversely speaking, "making" the land incests Mother Earth). Coke, stew, tent, and Sundays flag the non-Indian elements in this narrative, as brush, night, and moon return the story to the natural spiritual world. Notch, second, things, and meat leave a consonant-haunted sense of ending that doesn't end—the need at any cost is to survive, as in the last line. Converse to these endless endings, spring, food, warmth, tribal history, and generosity would naturally feed body and soul, from the most common daily necessity of rain, sun, stew, and stove, to the cultural sustenance of stories and land, to the spiritual cruces of the vision quest—sun's day, moon's night, the creationist province of Old Man Na'pi and Old Woman Kipi'taki. This lyric density is not easy to unpack. Fictional prose proves more thematically accessible, as Welch's novel challenges tribal values with father-loss, brother-grief, misogynist suspicion, and petty chauvinist crimes. Yet both poetry and prose register a human testimonial that would purge the native confessor in his fallen state out west.

Pronouns are minimal in "Surviving" and tribally referential: *we* (twice), *his, my, I, her, our.* There is no *they* or *theirs, he* or *she, him* or *them, us, you,* or *yours.* This is a very tight campfire—some say a story that should not go outside the tribal circle.

Verbs embody physicalized motions in concrete actions: *drove, huddled, skittered, envied, slipped, sneak. Told, cleared, left, spoke, dreamed, stripped,* and *cooked* offer the gritty monosyllables of personal actions. A reader can feel these tonalized gestures as movement, the verb-as-the-motion of people and particular things. Significantly there are only two weak or *linking* verbs, "was" and "it's"—no-verbs, as it were, since linking verbs are positional markers. A past casual loss and slackening verbal tension show up in "sun was easy." It's a relaxing memory that betrays Blackbird, a false dream before Adam's curse with the cook's kid.

The infinitive "to stay alive" says all, and the contracted linking verb "it's" leads to a final admission of difficulty, anguish, vulnerability. "To stay alive this way, it's hard. . . ." The line's inverted syntax twists grammar, while the simple linking verb contracts to an idiomatic monosyllable: it-as-Id or "other," the most of what *it is,* nothing going anywhere, just hanging on, foreshortened. So, too, "it's" calls back eleven lines to "he'd," a contracted masculine pronoun in past possessive—things "he'd" rather forget, or leave behind in the black sack of guilt and self-loathing. *Surviving* leaves the speaker with an endless confessional, "it's hard. . . ."

The construction "to stay alive this way" echoes the infinitive "to make this land" in line 8, but from "dreamed of ways to make" through "to stay alive this way," how long is this hard living infinitively viable? Will the story go from mythic origins *in medias res* to personal salvation and tribal reacceptance? Will it lead through the Native Holocaust to a genocidal Final Solution—Revelations and the Second Coming of what rough critter slouching where? A final ellipsis suspends the imploding point: a hard rain falling before winter snow, hard times to get through, hard edges on all things. A darkening ellipsis mutes loss and regret, the abuses and sins of omission, the coming silence.

The physical pointers of articles (Latin *artus*, meaning "to join"), that is, directives of action (where to look for a noun)—*the, that, this, a*—scatter minimally, beginning with "all the cedar sky" pointing to the animate adjective *cedar*. In this encrypted text, adjectives shape-change as metaphors of things—spare, sparse, real, densely imagist. To press the issue, the phrase "cedar sky" is not so much an image as the blooded nature of the sky, surreally, wood in a sunset as *thing*. Consider cedar as a dream wood the world over, a red-brown or flesh-and-blood-colored arboreal "meat" wood that serves as ceremonial incense for Native Americans (sweat lodge, house blessing, sacred objects, even the lowly #2 *Blackfeet* lead pencil once ubiquitous for scoring tests and voter ballots). But this is an apocalyptic sky at sunset in late fall. The surreal "cedar sky" carries both the physics and psychic colorings of "things" blooded in the sensate world. And it is expressly "late fall" where timing is essential, the slippage of seasonal light and heat dangerous, the coming winter darkly lethal. The poem is running out of time the moment it begins.

The "bellied stove" works as a male-protuberant Homeric epithet set terribly against the "thin girl" or "cook's kid." "Out back of" the men-feeding "mess tent Sundays" (of all missionized days in a Sun Dance culture), the kid stoops and "cooks her special stew." Lonely men around a campfire dream of "ways to make" a resistant feral land unfit for White farming, and they unspeakably *make* a girl-child. And so in the "black brush," an alliterative dark thicket, "wet black things" steal away "our cache of meat."

The spondaic fecundity of this wet darkness, inchoate and blindly terrifying, creates a condition where men don't see, but hear and feel awfully. *Toward me the darkness comes rattling*, Owl Woman chants. These dissonant "wet black" ad-jectives (Latin *adjicere*, "to-throw-to") are parts of speech of another color—colors of night, as Momaday writes, de-creating language and reality: "A young girl awoke one night and looked out into the moonlit meadow. There appeared to be a tree; but it was only an appearance; there was a shape made of smoke; but it was only an appearance; there was a tree" (*In the Presence of the Sun* 29).

There is only one verbal modifier among the bone-clean verbs. "*Oftentimes*," the lone trisyllable among 129 words, stands as a colloquial adverb, a turgid dactyl ("finger") offset with a comma. *Once upon a time* begins traditional stories, or as Native tales open, *Long time ago, the old ones tell. . . .* This *Oftentimes* entry into the poem slows Blackbird's confession, as though he were hesitant to speak, nervously clearing his throat through white space. It's too often, too "easy" that a false Montana sun slackens his bones; the agrarian dream becomes wasteland delusion for a hunting Indian.

The only other possible ad-verb in the poem is an enjambed adjective, "hung / black for just a second," where a gaping line break gaps the spondaic accent line to line. It's as close as adverbial outriding comes to color the verse (not black-ly, but "hung / black"), more a verbal action or extension than a tincture. Think of this "black" as the true stain of bad verbal action extended, all the way to the infinitely echoic ellipsis at the end. Such "black" is an adverbial condition of absence, an ad-verb of a lost verb ghosting the entire poem. It's terribly true, if in no way a pleasing picture, this bad Indian testimonial—a lament, a moan, a confessional necessary to survive desecration and starvation and anti-visionary humbling. *Tunkáshila, onshimala ye, wani gta,* the Lakota sing in visionary ceremony, piercing and breaking free during Sun Dance: "Grandfather, have pity on me, I want to live."

There are few conjunctions, misappropriately, but for a terribly disjunctive coupling, "stripped naked / for a coke *or* two *and* cooked her special stew." For one "or two" sodas, sadly, a thin kid stripped "and cooked" her virginity "round back of the mess tent Sundays." Blackbird's *cri de coeur* comes from a solo cow*boy* fear of the heinous thing that needy men, isolate and alone, have done to their young in dreams of *making* the land. There is no tribal pairing or parental connection, no amorous *ar*m or locating *ar*ticle or fertile *ar*ticulation (recall PIE root *ar-* means "to connect"), only a desperate and indefensible coupling that disconnects gender and generation. So, too, "and cooked her special stew" desecrates by way of coarse metaphor, a bad "liking" or anti-image to dislike—shamefully disconnecting in child abuse (recall Pocahontas, Sacagawea, or La Malinche as teen concubines of invaders). So the poem goes bad—some fear lower than a Native poet ought to go, lower than a man would ever stoop if he were really a man.

Prepositions function in pre-positions as extensions of verbal actions: drove *through*, huddled *before*, thought *of*, dreamed *of*, stripped *for*, skittered *through*, sneaked *away*. The prepositions get progressively more ghostly and disconnective, as the verbs grow more dangerous. Nouns cloud and slip off to "things" wet and black that lurk and steal, but can't be seen or known, a shadowy sexual darkening. There are no prepositional "phrases" or tripping cadences as such—in the dark sentimentally, down by the river, of the night—only verbal thrusts *through* and *of*, *for* and *away*. These prepositions in motion extend and unsettle events as adverbial disconnectives, things and actions hopelessly estranged. The effect is to shrink prepositional slackness back into concrete nouns against physical verbs of action—the syntactic and stylistic impacting of cut diction, tense grammar, imploding imagery, and taut rhythms that the poem rides on and through.

WET, BLACK THINGS

All this leads to "poetic" likenesses that readers don't much like, but must hear. These dislikings tell a story as cautionary tale, an anti-trickster history whose poetic display grounds out in personal suffering, narrative penitence, and petitioned grace. Think of the poem as testifying negatively. The initial simile "rain / like sun" offers a torqued likeness that is arresting, strange, disturbingly real in the Montana seasons of intense summer heat and driving fall rain and coming winter freeze. The surreal image of a "cedar sky" gives the reader a noun-in-space axed from the forest, uprooted from any sense of healing incense or dream vision. The homely metaphor of "bellied stove" touches a warming noun with a swollen tag lifted out of Homeric epic, perhaps grafted from Pound's opening canto, Odysseus' ship with "bellying canvas" (Homer's "bellied sails" of black Greek war ships). And the totemic man "Blackbird" figures shamanically as a winged spirit grounded in disgust, failure, and self-recrimination, tormented with personal castigation and confessional guilt. In the old days Blackfeet shamans who failed were killed. The "special stew" rustled up with a cook's kid "behind the mess tent Sundays," a last cowboy supper, is a bad likeness of Charlie's crime.

The final symbol, the "moon hung / black" and "slipped a notch" in the cedar sky, hangs dissonant. Lunar witchery drops with a catch in the speaker's throat. Welch's spondaic "wet black things" recall Pound's "wet, black bough" of petaled faces in a 1913 Paris Metro station just before the outbreak of the Great War—Hemingway's "lost generation" in wasteland aftershock. As with modernist lyric, there is interjective tension everywhere in Welch's poem through synapse, disconnection, fear, startle, and the final imagist burst of "wet black things" stealing the men's winter cache of meat away. *Aiee, a-ho!* Perhaps the men's lunar grief is a distant echo of the 1883–84 Winter of Starvation that frames the back story of Welch's novel, all the way back to Blackfeet origin stories: the rain-driven sun Na'pi to the notch-slipping moon Kipi'taki recalls the creation story of Old Man and Old Woman in Grinnell's *Blackfeet Lodge Tales*, gambling life and death with a floating buffalo chip and losing their first-born daughter to a sinking stone. The lunar-slippery moon is anciently feminine ("Moon is speaking / woman to the ancient fire. Always woman," the poet grieves "In My Lifetime"). And "wet, black things" may be dangerously fecund succubi of the lunar night, sensual spirits, sexual daemons. Old Woman could be avenging the desecration of her girl-child. Native father and mother lose another issue, "old cook's kid," to the incestuous Sunday stew of predatory lust—famished men without decency with their own tribal offspring.

The range of diction in the poem does not rise above common speech. Talk is weirdly "real," convincing as the chatter of ordinary horror too daily witnessed on reservations and off. Iambic lyric speech, trimeter to hexameter, recalls the natural talk of Frost's dark poems like "Design" or "Acquainted with the Night." Less oracular, Welch's imaging goes inward without affecting tone or forcing subject, as with Garcia Lorca's concept of "deep song" in his first collection, *The Gypsy Ballads*—the scorched flamenco throat seared with "tears of narcissus and ice" (Lorca, *In Search of the Duende* 37). This is searching song-poetry, never decorative but arrestingly physicalized, disturbingly true.

The poem's structural change of pace, as the diction shifts gears and descends, moves from a density of natural poetic detail in "cedar sky," to the demotic image of the cook's kid stripping and stewing for the men, to the dangerous night tricks played on their guilt by slipping lunar spirits, to the shamanic disturbance of "wet black things," to the anti-styled statement of fact on a contemporary reservation afflicted with poverty, despair, shock, and self-abuse. "To stay alive this way, it's hard. . . ." As Robert Lowell's "Epilogue" opined at the poet's lowest moment of self-realization, "Why not say what happened?" The final ellipsis admits of humility, mortality, limits of speech, and the courage to voice powerlessness.

It is a start.

Welch's narrative lyric is bled true as tales get: "Told stories." The diction is cleansed of loose detail, false connectives: "Blackbird cleared his mind, / thought of things he'd left behind, spoke:" and everywhere stop-enjambed, "special stew / round back." Line breaks shatter normative syntax: "hard rain drove / like sun" and "stripped naked / for a coke or two" and "hung / black" and "cache / of meat." The structural effect of the six- then seven- and four-line stanzas replicates a crazy-quilt, ragged-edged sonnet that spatters over the volta in the thirteenth line when the poem sneaks into the third stanza of ghosted consequence, breaking decency and form. First a trimeter line with three spondees, then iambic quatrameter loosening and lengthening the second line, then a trimeter pulling back with two spondees divided by a full stop, down to the horizon line of iambic pentameter, solo-rhymed. The lines stumble, lurch, fall away, adumbrate, jam, enjamb, and barely *survive* the weight of scansion as a true poem searching for the sense of its sound in elusively shamanic measure.

In the fifth line, alliterative spondees thickly back up the tetrameters with identical rhymes and echoic vowels ("Told stories. Blackbird cleared"), slipping into the rolling pentameter of the sixth line. There's more or less a regular 5/4/5 pattern in lines 7, 8, and 9, until the terrible revelation in line 10—a triple spondaic impacting of Blackbird's confession, "That *thin girl*, old *cook's kid*, *stripped naked*," replicating the jammed-together rhythms in the opening line. The 5/3 line pattern then repeats, followed by two four-beat lines with heavy alliterative spondees, easing into the final three lines of irregular iambic pentameter, the base-spine of the poem. This is stumbling measure to stagger on, slipping feet to stay up—a stumblebum meter that hardly holds form as it falls. Its suspect freedom recalls the collapsing blank verse of T. S. Eliot's "The Love Song of J. Alfred Prufrock."

Metric drag resists end-rhyme. The scheme unravels a/b/c, then makes a weak attempt to square things rhyming *drove* with *stove*, but then jumps to *mind* and attempts a poor back-vowel rhyme with *spoke*, less certainly with *bones*, then gives up kinning the end of lines—but for an echoic *mind* with *land*, *brush* with *cache* (a solid off-rhyme). There are twelve isolate phonemes in seventeen ends-of-lines, a record dislocation of rhyme scheme concealing the art hidden within—compressed and smuggled into the lines in surreptitious ways that allow the whole to sound naturally gathered, even idiomatic. This is Native art in the face of charges that poetry is too crafted, too well made perhaps for reality—not for working Americans to waste time on.

Conversely, everywhere within lines come hidden rhymes. *Long*, *rain*, *sun*, *mind*, and *behind* cluster assonantly, as *day*, *cold*, *drove*, *cedar*, *had*, *huddled*, *told*, *Blackbird*, *mind*, and *behind* are consonant through their voweled dentals, all in the first six lines. Phrases like *special stew*, *cook's kid*, and *sparrow skittered* alliteratively press the diction inward. *Huddled* with *Blackbird*, *mind* with *behind* seem decently embedded rhymes, the nervous crowding even more jammed in smack rhymes like *that night*, *close as cows*, and *told stories*, with fetching hints of slant rhymes in *brush*, *notch*, *black*, *second*, *cache*, and *meat*.

Yet the final line's ending "hard . . ." rhymes with nothing at all—a voweling consonant with the Proto-Indo-European root *ar-* as ironic dis-"connective" of art, arm, arc, etc. In the Euro-American beginning (*arch*) was the defining word, *En archei en ho logos*, but where is the connection now? *Hard* is stuck on its own at the end, trailing *hung* four lines up, repeated from first to last line as metronomic toll, "hard rain" to "it's hard . . . ," but tied into nothing specific. *Hard* has no kinship, no assonance anywhere (some "h" and "d" overtone with had, huddled, or behind, but "hard" is essentially stranded).

This hard-driven poem "Surviving" stands alone and lonely as the Indian cowboy's orphan lament. The estranged workingman admits frustrated desire, shameful lust, and poverty-driven grief. Cold and hunger, false hope and lasting despair, broken narrative and shattered dream, sham comfort and kinship disconnect—all the Native tenets of tribe are defiled, indeed *de*-rided on Earthboy 40 in this wretched trickster lyric. "To stay alive this way, it's hard. . . ." Notwithstanding history or holocaust, the poet laments, Indians are doing these things to Indians: men to minors, Earthboy de-ridden into the dirt. This may be the most terrible lyric ever told about Native Americans. It takes the reader back to a novel radical in "dirty realism"—poetry darkly radiant with truth, prose thick with hurt, humor, and heart.

CUSSED KIN

choose amazed to ride you down with hunger.
—"In My First Hard Springtime"

A poem that tells a disturbing tale, an opening chapter rife with poetic grit: where does the reader go from here? Mother Teresa, the story's unsaintly martyr, serves as acerbic foil to the narrator's bruised innocence and callow aches. His stepfather, Lame Bull, looms a fool to filial kinship. No

Name Indian "never expected much" from Teresa's "clear bitter look, not without humor," and he "never got it"(*Winter in the Blood* 134)—an edgy mother *not* with *no* humor, so to speak, minimal laughter in her nominal humor. It's doubly twisted, twice ironically maternal—the negated negative as a motherly absence proves a dangerous intimacy, just close enough to be distant, as writer to reader at times.

The rocking old lady holds the key to No Name's past and future, but this smoking sphinx isn't talking. "One winter evening as we sat at the foot of her rocker" (two decades back when brother Mose was still alive) "she revealed a life we never knew, this woman who was our own kin" (*WIB* 34). She has traces of grandmother ancestry in her eyes, "black like a spider's belly," her hands "small and black as a magpie's feet," but granny rocks under three army-issue blankets and a star quilt. Small details tell all in a novel where lint on a comb, collar dandruff, nostril hair, lip mole, or a fly drowning in spilled wine spatter the narrative. A star quilt is an ancestral blanket from birth to death on the high plains, a visionary icon of hope and guidance, a four-color balancing, spiritual and worldly pattern for life. The three army blankets bespeak military conquest and POW camp, bad commodities and broken treaties, the ignominy of a colonized people and their ongoing despair and poverty. Such is a condition too often today on the rez, especially among the old nameless ones who look back into the traditional past. This ignominy is a far cry from Momaday's grandmothers telling tribal history. Grandfathers are haunted by historical nightmares in shamanic magic gone sour.

Buried thirty-three pages into the 1971 first edition of *Riding the Earthboy 40*, "Magic Fox" opens the reissued 1976 Harper & Row collection, reissued again in 2004 by Penguin. It is a fairly simple, stripped iambic poem, almost free verse, about nightmare and reality—until a reader factors in the realization that old Indian warriors snoring the green leaves down is about all that's left of tradition and history. Imagine Homer, Sophocles, and Tiresias locked up in a Turkish hospice on Lesbos. Sappho is a taunting blonde dancing like morning birds of dawn, dragging the nightmare of grief down around the snoring relics of warrior times past—the 1833 Year of the Falling Stars, when meteorites and smallpox began to decimate the Native West. Anything but simple, "Truth became a nightmare to their fox," too foxy for Trickster's antics. Horses turned to fish, or "strung / like fish" on wired simile, or worst of all, "fish like fish / hung naked in the wind?" There are times when people can't believe what they see—when reality terrifies credence into disbelief, and witnesses conjure things as shadows of themselves.

Everything is metaphor, horrifically, reality echoically mocking itself. "And this: fish not fish but stars / That fell into their dreams." When the heavens fall, and earth is no longer earthly, shamans fail and truth defies poetic likeness: falling stars, fish-strung horses, nightmare images. No metaphor fits or grounds truth. Magic decreates reality dangerously, and the metastasized dream of the real seems too unstable to trust.

Just such happened to the insurgent Blackfeet when they went out to hunt bison in the fall of 1883, seeking their winter cache of meat, and came home empty-handed. Government-hired sharpshooters had slaughtered two million of the western herd, and the bison stragglers refused to migrate north across the Union Pacific tracks. Soldiers herded the famished warriors onto unarable reservations and ordered them to become Bible-toting, flannel-suited potato farmers. A quarter of twenty thousand Blackfeet died in that "winter of starvation," the beginning of the end of their way of life. Ten years later in the 1890s, the frontier was declared officially closed, Indians reserved. The national parks began reserving what was left of the West, including wild flora and fauna. The Great American Desert was white-washed with quick claims, homesteaded, plowed, fenced, and gun-powdered into Manifest Destiny under White Man's Burden. Civilize the savages—or barring culture, slaughter them.

In that 1883 Winter of Starvation, Yellow Calf, the blind hermit-seer still alive in the 1960s, saved Standing Bear's ostracized young widow by staying behind and hunting deer, rather than removing to the new reservation with the others. Eighty-some years later, this unknown grandfather to No Name carries wintry resolve, manly courage, and stoic wisdom in his blood. His is an unheralded heritage, a heroism lost on "fools" of the present—but for the "silent laughter" of one who knows, who needs not explain saving the nameless old rocking lady back home, No Name's mute grandmother. Who will tell the unstoried past when no one is left to listen? No Name remembers as a boy, "When the old lady had related this story, many years ago, her eyes were not flat and filmy; they were black like a spider's belly and the small black hands drew triumphant pictures in the air" (*WIB* 36).

If winter in the blood is nascent ancestral history, positively speaking, the negative rez side remains torpor and amnesia, tribal despair and cultural depression at large. Prisoners of war are after time prisoners of failed memory, bloodless detainees, ghosts of a shattered past walking around numbly, or catatonically rocking. The old forgotten ones withdraw into blindness, poverty, dull regret, and the simplicity of few possessions, language at its essentials. Every holocaust leaves a shattered legacy to the remnant survivors, a tragic/low-comic/survival Blackfeet revelation for No Name. He teases the blind old hermit Yellow Calf (*WIB* 67):

> "Come on, tell me. What have you got in those pants?"
>
> "Wouldn't you like to know . . ." With that, his mouth dropped open another inch but no sound came out.
>
> "I'll bet you have a woman around here. I know how you old buzzards operate."
>
> His shoulders continued to shake, then he started coughing. He coughed and shook, holding his cup away from the cot, until the spasm of mirth or whatever it was had passed.
>
> He stood and walked to the stove. When he reached for my cup, his hand struck my wrist. His fingers were slick, papery, like the belly of a rattlesnake. He poured to within half an inch of the cup's lip, to the tip of the finger he had placed inside.
>
> "How is it you say you are only half dead, Yellow Calf, yet you move like a ghost. How can I be sure you aren't all the way dead and are only playing games?"

No Name's ancestral secret hovers in tribal images and silent innuendos (too easy to find, one might think it too easy to do): Grandmother Spider's hands and Grandfather Snake's fingers, the spent lexicon of traditional song-poetry, the disregarded old stories. But these old stone faces aren't talking to postmodern Indians.

STUMBLE-BUM

Clues to the iconic ambiguity of old-time wisdom appear in Welch's poems, outriders to his fiction as narrative lyrics. "Her husband was a fool," the narrator says in "Grandma's Man." He laughed at seductive lies as he "passed stumble-bum down the Sunday street." And in the century-old race over eroded hills, the poetic myths that children need to grow alive are forgotten with "Blackfeet, Blood and Piegan Hunters." Drinking warriors string together tall tales of white buffalo, medicine cures, lovely wars, and white massacres. Dancing for pennies, they vanish as spectators look back to faint tracks, "our song strong enough for headstrong hunters / who look ahead to one more kill."

The lyrics of "Thanksgiving at Snake Butte" come with 1621 reminders of old betrayals, mutely etched stone icons of even more ancient slippage ("the cold moon tugging at the crude figures / in this, the season of their loss"). Christmas comes to Moccasin Flat with reappearances of Old Man and Old Woman, blind Yellow Calf and the granny rocker. The quatrains drill home the blood lessons of winter in insistent off-rhymes and urgently repetitive spondees. *"Christmas comes like this: Wise men / unhurried, candles bought on credit (poor price / for calves), warriors face down in wine sleep. / Winds cheat to pull heat from smoke."* Far from church and bar, distant from "Surviving," Charlie Blackbird "stabs his fire with flint" and dreams of wise men among wine-drunk warriors. Drunks drink antifreeze "for love / or need," and fallen chiefs eat snow while elk cavort in the mountains. Medicine Woman smokes twist tobacco in her clay pipe and names the blizzards by spitting at the five o'clock news, the weather as predictable as time's nameless clock face. The "news" has replaced storytelling, public television standing in for myth. Still, children need stories to live by. Medicine Woman tries to explain the solstice mystery of winter in the blood: Christ as the re-arisen Ghost Dance warrior or *make-live* savior, men back rich with "meat and song," a starry sign in the eastern sky, quick rebirth. Government commodified, they all wait, as Indians have for centuries. "Blackbird feeds his fire. Outside, a quick 30 below." Far below "Zero at the Bone," colder than Emily's snake in the garden— "so cold no fire can ever warm me"—the reality of poetry and a desperate hunger take the inebriate top of Charlie's head off. All the wise lyricists agree: that's the only way to know winter blood or deep song, true need or honest humility, fire or ice, the end of the world or the beginning.

ENDLESS SKITTERING WHITENESS

If I read a book [and] it makes my whole body so
cold no fire ever can warm me, I know *that* is poetry.
If I feel physically as if the top of my head were taken
off, I know *that* is poetry. These are the only way
I know it. Is there any other way?

—Emily Dickinson to
Thomas Higginson, 1870

In terms of song-poetry and talk-prose, what did the ancients know and old ones do that moderns don't? Painfully silenced today, the ancestors knew heroism and honor, martyrdom and sacrifice, life-giving story and song, Welch intuits: at least No Name Indian's blind grandfather Yellow Calf knew days before White devastation. The ancients knew to speak their names, sing and dance their ceremonies, as in Welch's third novel, *Fools Crow*. Chief Joseph to Gertrude Bonin, Black Elk to Buffalo Bird Woman, they knew to pray to their gods, call their spirits, and tell their stories one generation to the next, lest their culture be lost to memory. Elders knew the four winds and seasons, changes to plant and hunt, times to go out and come home, moments to praise the dead and circle the living. All this to survive. They gave their lives down to the present generation of retribalizing descendants—who may know this, or not.

Dead brother Mose knew that drunk drivers and rez horsemen come to a bad end. "There was no headstone, no name, no dates" (*Winter in the Blood* 143). In his sunken grave under a Styrofoam cross, dead-drunk father John knew where to kick a baler awake, but didn't know his way home through snow-banked borrow pits. "Was it a shoe sticking up, or a hand, or just a blue-white lump in the endless skittering whiteness?" (*WIB* 19). The old man in green gabardines and Van Gogh straw hat can only say "Heh, heh" to the *Field and Stream* mystery of fish in the river before expiring facedown in his oatmeal. Grandma says only one word twice, "Ai, ai," asking for radio music, then stonewalls history to her orange-coffin burial. A slapstick parody of Hamlet's fatherless quandary, No Name's stepfather muffs the closing eulogy: "Here lies a simple woman . . . who never gave anybody any crap . . ." (*WIB* 175–76).

Blind Yellow Calf knows all, but says nothing—only that "hunger sharpens your eye" and the deer sense by the moon that the world is "cock-eyed." He knows to keep things essential, including explanations. He knew his grandson when he was just a "little squirt," when father John stood "peeing what he said was my name in the snow" (*WIB* 161), when childhood times were different. Now, the distance in Yellow Calf's eyes is permanent. He lives alone. As with the sole Yana survivor Ishi farther west at about the same time, Yellow Calf's family died off, one by one—except for Teresa, his illegitimate daughter, and her rocking mother, child widow before she herself became a mother. Yellow Calf knows what his people did to survive; how they outlived the removals, slanders, and betrayals; why they now isolate themselves in cataracted silence. He knows winter in a man's bones, the always changing seasons, by the way ancestral blood makes him laugh silently. He knows ironic persistence no less than old Bird the cow pony senses the sheer irony of it all, the mean quirks of destiny, the way survival turns on deep, dark humor in the humus of all things, including scatology. The bathroom graffiti in the American Legion Club scrawls the low patriarchal gaffe, *What are you looking up here for? The joke's in your hand (WIB* 92). The Malta barmaid, who knows her father when he doesn't know her, reversing No Name's predicament, knows the rules of social engagement and the novel's bottom line: "you don't joke with them unless you mean business" (*WIB* 50).

Bird's fart punctuates No Name's insight into family history, a vision through the snow-white blindness of his grandfather. "I began to laugh, at first quietly, with neither bitterness nor humor. It was the laughter of one who understands a moment in his life, of one who has been let in on the secret through luck and circumstance. 'You . . . you're the one'" (*WIB* 158). Indeed, Yellow Calf's the one who saved Teresa's rocking mother and withdrew in order not to disgrace their name. Grandfather and grandson wordlessly share "this secret in the presence of ghosts, in wind that called forth the muttering tepees, the blowing snow, the white air of the horses' nostrils" (*WIB* 159). The litany of White offenses is thick: butchering Long Knives, hapless game-and-fish idiots, storytelling anglers, love-starved suits, airplane man on the run, self-righteous off-rez missionary, pathetic Michigan tourists, one-night stands with the M-girls (barmaid from Malta, Malvina, Marlene). No Name pursues the mermaid Cree *virgin* Agnes ("chaste" in name only), who got away with his rifle and razor but might one day be his wife (the coupling anagram MMMA). Indians are the butt of this long bad joke, the Creator a trickster, an isolato, or a confidence man on the lam.

No Name now knows the source of familial naming, the tribal genetics of his own life-story, if nothing else, before a blind old man standing in for Na'pi the sun father, Old Man himself. "The answer had come to me as if by instinct, sitting on the pump platform, watching his silent laughter, as though it was his blood in my veins that had told me" (*WIB* 160). And so the story ends with the deaths of the spotted cow, the pale horse, and the rocking grandmother. No Name finds the cosmic joke and winter/water fertility in a "driving rain" trying to rescue an old cow stuck in the mud. He cries laconically to his horse Bird and mother Teresa, "Slack up, you sonofabitch! Your mother dead, your father—you don't even know, what do you think of that? A joke, can't you see? Lame Bull! The biggest joke—can't you see that he's a joke, a joker playing a joke on you? Were you taken for a ride? Just like the rest of us, this country, all of us taken for a ride. Slack up, slack up! This greedy stupid country—" (*WIB* 169).

With no brother left, fatherless, unwedded, No Name goes back to the beginning, warily riding the Earthboy 40, hanging on for dear life.

The novel's Epilogue seems both curse and blessing, a throwaway heritage, either good medicine or bad, never simple. No Name Indian ends things, "I threw the pouch into the grave" (*WIB* 176). Grandmother will need her tobacco for the spirit journey that Aho dreams on the way to Rainy Mountain. Running past wintry graves, laughing darkly in his blood, the mute poet rises from the dead in "In My Lifetime" and looks "for signs that say a man could love his fate, / that winter in the blood is one sad thing." He runs "these woman hills" and translates wind "to mean a kind of life, the children of Speakthunder / are never wrong and I am rhythm to strong medicine."

Welch's winter breath is neither Navajo "in-standing wind" nor Lakota "breath in the pipe," but he speaks with old-time thunder, and his arresting rhythms heal with tribal candor and dark Red humor. His lyric courage to measure the terms of reservation life "hard and clear," his narrative edge to tell the truth of contemporary Native reality *talk like singing*. No one writes more honestly of modern Indian life.

Narrative
Dakota Poet

Louise Erdrich

Here I am, where I ought to be.

A writer must have a place where he or she feels this, a place to love and be irritated with. One must experience the local blights, hear the proverbs, endure the radio commercials. Through the close study of a place, its people and character, its crops, products, paranoias, dialects and failures, we come closer to our own reality.

—Louise Erdrich,
"A Writer's Sense of Place"

As with many Native American novelists, N. Scott Momaday through Sherman Alexie, Louise Erdrich began as a poet. Her verse seems more character-as-plot than Momaday's modernist lyrics or Welch's chiseled metrics. Her poetic settings trail the breakdown lanes of North Dakota from Dairy Queen to deep woods, even more prosaically than Silko's riparian arroyos or Hogan's home-bound verse, still mythic and modern from spotlit northern clearings just outside the forest's edge. Erdrich's diction turns on prosaic building, as in Pula Gunn Allen or the younger Alexie, but hers is more a thickening texture using rhythm to cadence lines. She does not employ the pointillist precision of Momaday's syllabics, or the torqued slowing of Welch's variable blank verse, but more a narrative lyric that leads through plot dramatically, from a given character or setting toward an insight or outcome. Her metaphors layer naturally with daily rural life-forms, less italicizing than tonalizing—turtle, cow, deer, mustang (horse and car), crane, or geese. Her poetic tools—heightened diction, rhythmic tension, imagistic mystery, cadenced memory—all work in service of the verse-story as character-and-place on-the-go.

Erdrich's craft follows a Native voice in true rhythm from a tribal site, ancient roots still active, a poetry that differs from Western set text and fixed form. Native lines are not so much *made* in the Greek sense of *poietes*, as they are *shaped by* local origins-in-process, voice-crafted tools rising out of ongoing ceremonial traditions and homemade tribal literacies. This Native or "born" origin does not rule out art, but reorients the word in its working beginnings—already discussed, art as the "arm" (PIE *ar-*) of continuous tribal location and interspecies connection. Think of the armature or girder of common ties to a natural world interconnected with other living beings and spirits. As in Celtic Ireland or Mende Africa, this tribal art also includes the strange and distorted, the unimagined and ostracized, the immigrant and alien (see Ruth Finnigan's *Oral Poetry* and Isidore Okpewho's *African Oral Literature*). Erdrich's local-to-global poetics key on the stranger within. As A. Irving Hallowell documented in *Culture and Experience*, "Other-than-Human Persons" inform the animate naturalism of Chippewa landscape, spirit and matter morphing across species—a given stone, tree, plant, bear, or bird answering a healer's call. The poet-novelist includes *all of us* in a hybrid fusion of old and new worlds. Through Chippewa recurrent myth and German-American ancestral patriarchy, Louise Erdrich connects Native shaman with town butcher, introduces wanderer to local farmer. She correlates ancient wars with contemporary acculturations. *Our* is the poet's favored word, both Native and American, wedding wild stories with healing songs.

METIS MIXINGS

No less than Welch, Erdrich's narrative poetry sisters her lyric prose, as though the verse outtakes came directly from the novels. *Jacklight* was published the same year, 1984, as *Love Medicine*. Each resonating with the other, poetic prose crosses into prose poetry. So, too, her cultures have mixed German-American and pan-tribal Chippewa-French complexes (especially in Metis or "mixed" Euro-Indian North

Dakota, where Natives and immigrants intermarried more seamlessly than among New England British, Hudson River Dutch, or Southwest Spanish colonists). Clichés of noble savage, dusky maiden, and ruthless pioneer give way to the reality of mestizo, literate, Indian-White collaboration through the century. Mixed-blood Native models are legendary. Recall Will Rogers's all-American humor or D'Arcy McNickle's pan-hemispheric historical scope. Note Jim Thorpe's Olympic athleticism or Reuben Snake's cross-tribal diplomacy. More recently, remember Alfonso Ortiz's intercultural social science or Wilma Mankiller's relocated tribal sovereignty from the Carolinas to Oklahoma. Religions have crossed broadly, too, specifically for Erdrich Roman Catholic myths and Native American tribal beliefs. Finally, this off-reservation poet from Wahpetan, North Dakota, backpacked tribal American legends and kinship systems to the Ivy League—Dartmouth College (originally an Indian school) and Johns Hopkins University—where she honed and hybridized Western literary tools. Erdrich is no subaltern to Western literacy, the Great Books canon, Euro-American fiction, or theoretical criticism. A fusion of oral tradition and textual literacy doubly empowers her to write America down, as the people read and talk out their lives with each other locally.

In "Where I Ought to Be," Erdrich speaks of regional details bringing locals home, "a place to love and be irritated with" over time—seasonal blights and radio stations, bad weather and poor crops, finicky rivers and dusty back roads. "I grew up in a small North Dakota town, on land that once belonged to the Wahpeton-Sisseton Sioux but had long since been leased out and sold to non-Indian farmers." Yet émigrés still resist the groundings of homing. Why has Mayflower Van Lines, she asks of "nomadic" migrant lives, become a national trucking icon? Native-borns always seem to go away where the jobs go. If humans are carried nine months beneath a mother's heart, Erdrich asks, what Native home are they born into, where are their ancestors, and why do they leave their origins, then try to return? "Location, whether it is to abandon it or draw it sharply, is where we start." In this sense, Erdrich's first writings are all about returning to the heart of the country's heart—literally the geographic center of North America near Rolla, North Dakota, where Lawrence Welk or Sacagawea began, just south of Turtle Mountain Reservation on the Canadian border. "Here I am, where I ought to be": Erdrich appropriates the words of Isak Dinesen, the Danish émigré Karen Blixen who wrote *Out of Africa*. Uprooted, how do people regain this Native sense of people and place?

Stone Spirits

On a great gray sweep of boulder, high above
Obabikon channel, a rock painting gives instructions
to the spirit on how to travel from this life into the
next life. Such a journey takes four days and is filled
with difficulties. For that reason, loved ones provide
the spirit with food, spirit dishes, and encouragement
in the form of prayers and songs. We climb to the
painting with tobacco and leave handfuls by the first
painting, a line with four straight, sweeping branches,
and the second painting, which is of a *mikinaak*, or
turtle.

—Louise Erdrich, "Rock Paintings,"
Books and Islands in Ojibwe Country

America is an immigrant new land with old ghosts—the Native cultures
dispossessed, nearly wiped out by 1900. Genocidal statistics in the New
World defy comprehension. The "Discovery" liquidated most of 40 to
60 million tribal peoples. They did not vanish, but are now four-and-a-
half million strong in the United States, doubling their counted numbers
in the last half-decade. Since the late 1960s, a reversal has been in the
making—a Native American resurgence among tens of millions in the
Western Hemisphere. Traditionally proud cultures are recovering from
slaughter and desuetude with vital stories of reemergence and renascent
song-lines. New World émigrés would do well to listen, since survival
may turn on lessons learned from Native endurance and tribal wisdom.

One woman's voice rises above some thousand or more professional
Indian writers in the country, her lyric pitch grounded in narrative grist.
Louise Erdrich has published eleven novels, three children's books, two
works of nonfiction essays, and three books of poetry, most recently
Original Fire: Selected and New Poems (HarperCollins 2003). Sampling
her verse of twenty years, *Original Fire* debuts a long poem on sleepless
pilgrim questing and ends with the alchemic fires of loss and renewal.
The gathering is mostly a selected retrospective of Erdrich's first two collections, with new poems since her husband's death and the birth of her
fourth daughter Kiizhikok, or Rita.

In these scattering new lines are thematic rebirthing sites and an
elm-rooted phoenix nest. Eight verse stations chart the poet's recovery:
birthing agon ("Our bed is the wrecked blue island of time and love"),

early loss ("a rose of spikes"), *natural grief* ("let the blue snow cover you"), *after desolation* ("the flies of sorrow to eat"), *lifelong search* ("the snow bleeds white around the base of Sweetgrass"), *natural acceptance* ("tree of forgiveness"), *temporal renewal* ("Air, fire, golden earth"), and *metamorphic endurance* (animate ancestral stones that bless, talk, and cure in "The Sweat Lodge": "When we break ourselves open—, that is when we begin to heal"). This woman writes to not be alone, to talk beyond time, always to go on in "Advice to Myself": "Accept new forms of life / and talk to the dead." Her earth is molten with grief that ignites her will to live at the end of "The Seven Sleepers": "Shadow of my need, shadow of hunger, / shadow infinite and made of gesture, / my god, my leaf, / graceful, ravenous, moving in endless circles / as the sweet seeds hang waxen yellow in the maple."

MOTHER OF GOD

> And even now, as I am writing in my study, and as
> I am looking at photographs I took of the [rock]
> paintings, I am afflicted with a confusing nostalgia.
> It is a place that has gripped me. I feel a growing
> love. Partly, it is that I know it through my baby and
> through her namesake, but I also had ancestors who
> lived here generations ago.
>
> —Louise Erdrich, "Rock Paintings,"
> *Books and Islands in Ojibwe Country*

When *Love Medicine* begins, a dislocated June Kashpaw walks herself through a spring blizzard home to a motherly haven: "The snow fell deeper that Easter than it had in forty years, but June walked over it like water and came home" (*LM* 6). Christ fasted forty days in the desert, the disciples report, and walked on water. June Kashpaw, or JK, comes home with the life-giving, resurrective powers of *water*: as Linda Hogan cites in poems and essays, cell source for all organisms, 70 percent of the human body, father's semen, mother's milk, amniotic fluids, baptism and cleansing, anointing and sterilizing, life spring and eternal rest in streams and oceans, the restorative spirit tears from the sky. And cyclical change filters tribal continuity: you cannot step twice into the same river, Heraclitus says, for all things are always flowing on—cycling from sky, to earth, to organic growth and back again. Erdrich tells interviewers that water is the tonal medium of *Love Medicine*.

In March 2004, NASA found proof of water at one time on Mars, further possibility of life elsewhere in creation, and since then Saturn's moon Enceladus has revealed icy geysers (*Science*, 10 March 2006). "It's this elusive, magical mystery molecule," says James Gavin, lead scientist for Mars exploration. Water is a molecule carrier used to bootleg other molecules, a "bipolar" electron setup that bonds and releases. As hydrogen bonds with oxygen, they partner electron-pair-over-electron in a molecular quadrille. These stick-and-release molecules flow freely and dissolve most everything, a matrix to mix all matter. Vapor, solid, or liquid, water transports things, metamorphoses with other molecules, and remains essential to life. Combining with carbon, H_2O scaffolds all organisms—hence it is an archetypal native element the world over.

To accent the key opening line, "The *snow* fell *deep*er that *Easter* than it *had* for *forty years*, / but *June walked* over it *like water* and *came home*" (line break suggested, as with metrically accented passages throughout). Rolling and reverse iambics in an unrhymed couplet cadence June's lyric ascent over death and fix the novel's crucial plot point, a Native American rebirthing. The vowels moan home—rising and falling from low to high front and back of the mouth again (*oo ah o uhr ih ai ah uhr ae a o*). "Came home" again, the Native *nostos* or return: Indians will not be defeated, but will rise once more, talk on, keep on going on, despite all odds. The reverse slant rhymes, opening to closing—*snow, forty, over, home*—cross-stitch the couplet acoustically, everything naturally knitted together, no formal closure. The lines thicken with metaphoric grist, suggesting a feminine savior tested by wintry disaster and saved in spring promise, walking home eternally over the flood. This verse prose tells a story of the human spirit transcending death. June is a born-again feminist "make-live" (Lakota Ghost Dance *wanékia*) martyr-heroine.

Melodic cadences weave Erdrich's chapter endings together in lyric refrains where the prose won't sit still or slough off. When a war-crazed Lyman comes home from Vietnam and drowns his red convertible in the Red River, reverse trochaic hexameters surge over the chapter ending like cries of migrating geese. The final paragraph of "The Red Convertible" sets up in iambic hexameters giving run to blank verse: "I *walk back* to the *car, turn* on the *high beams*, and *drive* it *up* the *bank*. / I *put* it in *first gear* and *then* I *take* my *foot off* the / I *get out, close* the *door*, and *watch* it *plow soft*ly into the *wa*ter. / The *headlights* reach *in* as they *go* *down, search*ing, *still light*ed / *ev*en *af*ter the *wa*ter *swirls* over the *back end.* / I *wait.* The *wires short out.* It is *all fin*ally *dark.* / And *then* there is *on*ly the *wa*ter, the *sound* of it / *go*ing and *run*ning and *go*ing and *run*ning and *run*ning." The terrible trochaic voweling of the first pentameter line, "*ev*en *af*ter the *wa*ter *swirls* ov*er* the *back end*," churns Henry's lapping watery death with spondaic finality. Even the "*back end*" is done for. The haunting mechanistic image of headlights going under searches futilely, the trochaic pentameter waters repeatedly, indifferently, "*go*ing and *run*ning and *go*ing and *run*ning and *run*ning." This is the hard narrative *run run*, as Jorie Graham says, of lyric rise-and-fall terror. Many of the stories search desperately for the drowned in the flooded dark of reservation waters, a nightmare vision, Indians lost and tumbling under the rivering floods of time. Always, water is the source of death and life. Nector cannot sink himself in the lake, but according to Ojibwe belief, Henry Jr.'s Red River drowning ghosts the place forever, as suicide is the unpardonable Roman Catholic sin.

Retold through Native eyes, *Paradise Lost* hangs in the wings of this novel, especially with an Adamic Nector Kashpaw and his runaway Eve, Marie Lazarre, concluding "Wild Geese" in pure verse narrative: "*This is how* I *take* Marie's *hand.* / *This* is *how* I *hold* her *wound*ed *hand* in *my hand.* / She *nev*er *looks* at *me.* / I *don't think* she *dares let* me *see* her *face.* We *sit* al*one.* / The *sun falls down* the *side* of the *world* and the *hill* goes *dark.* / Her *hand* grows *thick* and *fev*ered, *heavy in* my *own,* / and I *don't want her,* but I *want her,* and I *can*not *let* her *go.*" These are the *true* common lives of sainted Indians, their low heroic sufferings and lifelong romances—festered wounds, stigmatic confusions, stubborn refusals to give in or up—the defiance of the desperate, the heroics of the first, the lost, the helpless, but not hopeless Natives of America. Still-living soft laughter marks tricksters who survive, or as Nector says of his "rail-tough and pale as birch" teen bride Marie, "the kind of tree that doubles back and springs up, whips singing" (*Love Medicine* 59). Nor does the writing lie down, but keeps surging back and forward sensuously, with Homeric hexameters rippling to the chapter's end. It is the first and the last sunset on earth, the Fall and ensuing fortune of a Native Adam fatefully coupled with First Woman Eve. The insistent iambic rhythms loop and tangle, cross and crisscross and hold in mythic finality: wedded for life, despite the odds, beyond personal choosing, gladly and godly so. Nector and Marie will engender rich stories.

Two-thirds of the way into the novel, Marie draws her beloved wandering Nector, always the romantic errant, across her waxed kitchen floor back into their marriage, all with a stigmatic trick of a fork wound inflicted by the deranged nun Sister Leopolda (who turns out later in *Tracks* to be her illicit and crazed mother, Pauline Puyat). Marie forgives her stray husband at the end of "Flesh and Blood": "I *put* my *hand* through *what scared* him. I *held* it *out* there *for* him. / And when he *took* it with *all* the *strength* of his *arms, I pulled him in*" (*LM* 129). Half a life later, the stigmatic grace of selfless love transcends marital, even maternal infidelity, as Marie hovers over her rival Lulu, a mother tendering "good tears" to a blinded and reborn daughter "took in" the Old Peoples' Home. Imaginative realism edges all this—from the very language in its iambic sheen, to mythically deep characterization, to deft dramatic plotting, to the rich Native and American themes merging naturally as streams flowing into a wooded lake.

Finally, Lipsha brings the Firebird spirit of his sacrificed mother, June Kashpaw, home to the rez, as he delivers his legendary outlaw father, Gerry Nanapush, to a reborn life across the Canadian border, and the novel closes: "*I'd heard* that *this riv*er *was* the *last* of an *anc*ient ocean, / miles *deep*, that *once* had *cov*ered the Dakotas and *solved all* our *prob*lems. / *It* was *easy* to *still* imagine *us* be*neath* / them *vast* un*rea*sonable *waves*, but the *truth is* we *live* on *dry land*. / I *got* in*side*. The *mor*ning was *clear*. A *good road led on*. / So there was *noth*ing to *do* but *cross* the *wa*ter, and *bring* her *home*." The vowels lean forward, the iambic cadences settle in for the hexameter ride, the images reach deep into crossing-the-water and good-road mythic homecoming. The open-voweled, double spondees seal comic futurity in Dante's sense of promise after a long journey down and up through circles of pain and suffering: "A *good road led on*." All the plot points and mythic resonances cant together in this doubly spondaic, homing resolution. If prose carries the *run run* of getting somewhere expeditiously, and the *row row* of poetry flows leaping and luminous (more like dancing than walking), then Louise Erdrich crosses prairie-stride with high step, horizontal forward thrust with vertical spiraling burst. Her poetic fusions have a narrative physics all their own. As Albertine says of June Kashpaw, the martyred aunt-muse early in *Love Medicine*, her "long legs" keep dancing across the aurora borealis lighting up the winter night sky, "her laugh an ace" (*LM* 35). Narrative iambics cadence lyric drum-steps across the high plains.

Cultural collision and artistic collusion layer Erdrich's prose lyrically. There is no small law of exclusionary middle, neither racial essentialism nor elitist formalism. Hers is a crossing rule with natural selection of the best of both sides. Gregor Mendel pioneered fusional genetics with red-and-white petunia combinations (crossbred pink flowers turned out the strongest). Erdrich's cultural fractures bridge opposites; her ethnic challenges shape heroic border crossings. Interspaces determine plot. And the liminal places-between, what Sherwin Bitsui calls *inbetween* moments, generate opposites that call for meetings *at the forest's edge*. Trickster elbows out hero, as improvisator edges over formalist, making room for more imaginative, more positive tribal realism. *They* become *we* in a paradigm shift fusing Native with American. They are not over, the crossings, and it has never been easy, but the times are changing and peoples coming together.

At the Forest's Edge Again

"We have come to the edge of the woods, / out of brown grass where we slept." Erdrich sees today as a time of fusions. Open her first volume *Jacklight* to the lead poem. A spotlight "fist" has drawn hunters and wild beings to the forest's edge, where four centuries ago newcomers and Natives first made treaties in felled clearings. This artificial "jack"-light—a portable glare for spell-blinding, then sniping animals at night—unnaturally divides the human tribe. Terribly alone now, each being, animal or human, edges forward to gun-barrel "raw steel," to leather stink of "mink oil," to "sour barley" tongues. Women smell their abusers' "breath steaming behind the jacklight" and their "minds like silver hammers / cocked back." We readers see, feel, and sense through the wild forest eyes, blinded creatures and threatened spirits of the dark—untamed in their stirrings, wantonly targeted as kill for machined malice. Classical past is mythically present, Christ's sacrifice near in "crushed dogwood," Eve a fallen sister to "bruised apples." Roman Catholic or Chippewa, the stories tell America how Native peoples are and why they got to the forest's edge, a complex mixing of beliefs as cross-blood heritage.

After calling across the clearing, the poem reverses the chase and turns back to the forest. "It is their turn," a Native voice says of the men, "to follow us"—into the lightless depths of the New World wilderness and back to original being—echoes of Faulkner and Frost, ceremonial hunts and elegiac chants, peace of minds broken and dark promises to keep. Taking their first steps, men relearn here what is gained in losing themselves in the chartless and sensuous woods, "not knowing / how deep the woods are and lightless. / How deep the woods are." And so it is time. A Native rebirth, a great turning homeward, comes upon the cultural landscape.

Clear homing grace lies in Louise Erdrich's poetry and prose. Entering the mixed-blood lights and poetic darknesses of *Jacklight*, the reader faces the nature of an anciently inhabited New World, contemporary now with the glare of steel. *If they* still can hear, homeless hunters switch off their spotlights, put down their rifles, and follow Native women back into the re-sensualized forest of mystery and passion, a belonging long prayed, too long abused.

So a newly hybrid culture is springing out of Native lands—fusions of ancient tribal groundings and revolutionary freedoms. The fusions come in uneasy mix, to be sure—odd placements, personal frustrations, and brilliant crossings. The common denominator is local insight. Personal differences and regional dialects shape the voiced arc of Erdrich's lines, no less than the intrinsic Jersey groundings of William Carlos Williams, the discrete feminine insights of Emily Dickinson, the delayed plain-style discoveries of Elizabeth Bishop across continents. The tare and texture of everyday talk fleshes the Native poet's medium, rather than form imposed on language (fixed rhyme, iconic image, or parsed meter). Linda Hogan, the Chickasaw elementalist, and Linda Gregg, the archaeological minimalist, seem mixed-blood, migrant sisters. Blessed are the listeners "when no one is left to speak," Hogan whispers, and Gregg adds, "We Manage Most When We Manage Small." These women divine naturalistically. The free-verse pitch of Native grace tunes Erdrich's horizon note among diversely democratic peoples. War-torn tribal histories texture her burden, calling, and spiritual regeneration.

Americans are dispossessed of Native Eden, cultural historians argue, yet an indigenous spark smolders in fallen primal dreams. Indeed, mixed light-and-shadow fuse Erdrich's message—both the imagined Native light humans are genuinely born with, and the jack-lit artifice whereby men stalk others. The healing logic is catholic, common to all: a light spirit and an earth body divide humans between this life and another. The torch of the old days, the dying ember of the spirit's commonplace, still lights the marginalized heritage of tribal descendants, despite jacklights in the garden. "He spoke like singing," Nicholas Black Elk said of the "all-colors of light" spirit in his Great Vision, bridging the losses and promises of a new century and the last. Anciently, the caring resolution of native and made, natural and artificial comes with *enlightenment* as moonlight on the water, to repeat what Dogen Kigen said long ago in another land—the moon does not get wet, the water is not broken. As native readers all, Americans can see the magic effect of light on the world, but never touch or hold it. And so with *Jacklight*, readers "come to the edge of the woods" for enlightened healing, for imaginative fusion, for Native rebirth.

YET WHY NOT SAY WHAT HAPPENED?

"What's happening?" are June's first words. "Where's the party?" Who and where, she asks, what's up? Lyric leap crosses with narrative run, as all the stories in *Love Medicine* constellate around the opening character as epilogue. June carries her hotel porcelain doorknob to the Ladies' Room for security. This thing means things—phallic protective self-control, sad inanimate exhaustion, on-the-road home security. That and Andy's blue bar Easter eggs and Angel Wings accompany June to her death and resurrection: "The *snow* fell *deep*er that *Eas*ter than it *had* in *forty years*, but *June walked ov*er it like *wa*ter and *came home*." Lengthening iambic hexameter, the old Homeric traveling foot, followed by reversely enjambed spondees—three in four feet, seven stumbling accents in all, and a homecoming finality that cannot be contested, even by death. *The highest good is like water*, Lao Tsu says (*Tao Te Ching* #8), and this novel flows and pools through the Turtle Mountain streams and sloughs with the subtly decreative and regenerative powers of water. *It flows in places men reject. In dwelling, be close to the land. In speech, be true. In ruling, be just. In action, watch the timing. No fight: no blame.*

June walks over lethal waters that drown Henry Jr. in the Red River, the border Lipsha recrosses finally to carry his mother home. Lying with cousin Lipsha in spring wheat, Albertine knows that June's leggy, fluid, two-stepping laughter is "her ace" among the stars. Across the northern lights, June bounces back like Nector rising from the lake bottom in a comically failed suicide. She rides over Gordie's slippery highway glare just as Marie draws her love-sodden husband across a waxed kitchen floor. June's purifying water passage leads to the redemptive "good tears" that Marie puts into Lulu's cataract-dimmed eyes. Lipsha finally crosses the border river waters to "bring her home," all the lost mothers back with the cast-off orphans, Kiowa Sky Twins to Laguna Tayo to Blackfeet No Name Indian to petroglyphic Pueblo Jug Boy, come to their rightful people and place. Things finally come together.

Love Medicine is much about *things*—cars, geese, bars, floor wax, potatoes, salt and sugar jars, butter, motels, knives, rivers, jelly beans, beer cans, Lucky Charms cereal, crimped cards. It's really about the things that define people's actions as errant kin, wayward nuns, mixed-blood families, going away and coming back home—twisted rosary, wrong keys, smashed pies, dandelion forks, frozen turkey hearts from the Red Owl Store. It's mostly *about love*—from sex sickness, to playful flirting, to deep intimacy, to friendship and betrayal, to lifelong rivalry, commitment, and compassion—*as medicine*, the remedy for the sickness love gives you, down to the children and "took-ins" born in and out of love, the tribal future.

Welch's Malta barmaid says of men, "You don't joke with them unless you mean business." To mean business, joking may well involve play across gender for keeps, and all the attendant humors found around loving *homo ludens*, as Johan Huizinga outlines joking: a free play-sphere where things are contested and acted out, rewards are at stake, odds and winners and losers gambled, rules accepted and up for revision, time-space relieved, bonding wits and guts as the tools of "permitted disrespect" defining community, Mary Douglas says of tribal teasing ("The Social Control of Cognition"). Jokes are hooks of engagement and self-gain, the nub as come-on to deeper things, foreplay, interplay, play-for-keeps. *Winter in the Blood* means business facing despair and death with edged Indian humor. Its ironies draw readers into and through a grainy realization to comic judgment, sympathy, connection, and provisional acceptance of rez and off-rez life. Welch carves a dark comic realism out of Indian cultural history, a sad Red humor that snags the reader on the truth of things Indian and otherwise.

The tone of *Love Medicine* is not so desperate or darkly decentered. A woman's compassionate play tempers the hardness of male despair, softens the edges of a man's irony. June wants to know what's happening, where's the party—she's hungry, road-weary, lonely, game to play for keeps, and loses her life skidding out of Andy's pickup into a spring blizzard. Here, June gains the novel's laurel as familial muse. Two-stepping through the stars, "her laugh an ace," June is loved by her niece, looking up from a spring wheat field through the aurora borealis, or northern night rainbow. Erdrich finesses survival, even celebration and delight in lasting *character* here. A favorite aunt's mothering life spirit courses through all the stories, an adoptive love for took-ins all, a birthing and nurturing and blessing humor. Sex is a complex dance in these stories—procreative play—beginning with the epic comic sadness of June in Andy's pickup; then the fortuitous fall of Marie and Nector on the convent hill; the backseat buttery heat between Lulu and Nector at mid-novel; the compassionate sorrow of Albertine's affair with Henry Jr. as *Mr. And Mrs. Howdy Doody* in the motel; the offstage romantic losses between June and Gerry (resulting in the novel's comic hero Lipsha getting born); and the tragic marriage between June and Gordie, himself love child of the opening fall down the hill. By the end, Nector and Lulu are still trying to get it on in a senior laundry basket.

If love is a medicine, much as the homeopathic healer believes poison antidote is the right dose of selfsame poison (to cure the ailment through its own chemistry)—love confers the illness that it would cure, both a sickness and a tonic for the sick. As the novel and its characters grow up, flirting moves through foreplay, to the sensual madness of body heat and procreative juices, to lifelong romance and disillusion, and with luck learning again to love through marriage, child-birthing, raising and putting up with, enduring, surviving it all. This is what people *call* love, but is it medicinal? Love would bond, and hold, and barring perfection reconnect human beings over time and place. It's the tangled complex, the positive-negative poles of the oldest tales and earliest jokes back to First Man and First Woman. "You know, everything had to begin," Aho tells her grandson about the way to Rainy Mountain, "and this is how is was. . . ." Everything turns on the right approach, the right touch, the right word. Erdrich's oscillating and unstabilizing triangle, the old *ménage à trois*, replaces the balancing and pairing earth numbers two and four, the mythic *we-two-go* resonance of genesis before the fall. Still this is a tribal story, the triangulated mixed-bloods say. Three times three sets of characters tumble out over half a century of present-tense love triangles, mythic as Adam, Eve, and Lilleth, or Orpheus, Eurydice, and Dis, or Jesus, Mary, and Joseph. These Greco-Roman-Christian sky triads are not unfamiliar to a quiescent Roman Catholic.

Love Medicine appeals to a broad audience. Most of Erdrich's writings are offbeat love stories and fallen lyrics, a peculiar and arresting mix of canonical literacy—such fictional favorites as Charles Dickens, Eudora Welty, Emily and Charlotte Bronte, William Faulkner, and Ray Carver—fused with Native feminine verse lines by Joy Harjo, Roberta Hill, Linda Hogan, or Leslie Silko, coupled with distant Chippewa trickster and creation myths. "This is not to say that *Love Medicine* is Indian or is not," David Treuer argues in "Smartberries" most recently, "just that it is 'Indian' in a more modern sense than has been assumed by most scholars" (*American Indian Culture and Research Journal* [2005]: 33).

With narrative voice and dramatic timing, Erdrich's poetry crosses tribal heritage into national literacy. The first section of *Jacklight* is titled "Runaways," the horizon-cursed refugees of a receding Native frontier—an abused sister curled under the park cottonwoods; Uncle Raymond Twobears "knocking the Blue Ribbons down"; boarding-school truants in long green dresses; John Wayne's "horizon of teeth" over the local drive-in; the man who drank Vitalis and Sterno "in the woods coughing feathers"; the rodeo-circuit prostitute Francine talking alone in her Tarsus hotel room; the stripper in the pink Mustang hissing, "*I don't sell for nothing less*," as she paints her nipples silver.

All these *characters*, more or less cousin misfits of Carver, Harjo, and kin trickster debris, are caught in lives tediously, desperately rep-etitious. "I've been through here before," Francine says. The known is a haunting shadow of itself. As in the final poem of the section, a nod toward James Wright and Simon Ortiz, James Welch and her own June Kashpaw in *Love Medicine*, Erdrich's characters are all "walking in the breakdown lane" to the side of highway traffic. "They pound, pound and bawl, / until the road closes over them farther on."

Specific to an off-road threshold of beginnings, the opening poem, "A Love Medicine," steadies uneasily in unrhymed trimeter. Everyday details and North Dakota place-names (her hometown) pocket these lines: "Still it is raining lightly / in Wahpeton. The pickup trucks / sizzle beneath the blue neon / bug traps of the dairy bar." Off-lyric static introduces a sec-ular sister. Saintless Theresa, in a green halter and glittering chains at her throat, wades into the flooding Red River Valley night—a balladic valley, once Chippewa homeland, overrun with Dodge trucks and Dairy Queens. Theresa "steps against the fistwork of a man," as forest spirits were rav-aged by a jacklighted "fist," and falls in wet grass to his booted grin. Love medicine for Natives is perilous, the poem suspended on a note of frontier misogyny, no less than Sylvia Plath down west, or Carolyn Forché in a country between us: "*Sister, there is nothing / I would not do.*"

"Family Reunion" lengthens the line to blank verse. Raymond Twobears drives home "up the backroads, hardly cowpaths and hub-deep in mud." Uncle Ray is "crocked," man-smelling of "hair tonic, ashes, alcohol," and the incested girl-speaker mutters, "We've been through this before." The poem is rife with local talk, the tongue-of-working-Native-place, true west. "Them's Indian dogs, Ray says, lookit how they know me." Ray fishes a yard-long snapping turtle out of the Indian-named Lake Metagoshe and blows off its head with a cherry bomb, then curls up around a bad heart to "sleep his own head off" as the turtle drags its shell into a marsh. Turtle and uncle become one headless Indian *totem*, a bad-dreamed "fellow clansman," until the last catholic line graces their fall: "And the angels come / lowering their slings and litters." Peopled and placed as a record of mixed-blood times, how-ever sodden or terrible or sad, "Family Reunion" is a real story-poem of local people, tribal legacy to émigré struggle. These lyric narratives make Native Americans a storied people of Turtle Island, ongoing.

In blank-verse near-rhymes, "Indian Boarding School: The Runaways" records an acculturational tragedy of kidnapping assaults on Native ways. "Home's the place we head for in our sleep," the poem opens sleep-talking, later off-rhyming "scars" and "lost" and "place they cross" in voweling trochees and iambs. "Boxcars stumbling north in dreams / don't wait for us." The runaways catch them on the run, the rails shooting across their faces, "old lacerations that we love." These relocated children ride the rails home to Turtle Mountain Reservation, the mythically named island of refuge Uncle Ray slogged toward, "remembering / delicate old injuries, the spine of names and leaves." Again, the breakaway last line rises over broken homilies of Native displacement. As in *Love Medicine*'s chapter endings, lyric grace saves these runaways from prosaic limbo.

Women are haunted through the poems by rough-cut men. "It's the region's hard winters," Francine says in her bed-for-rent hotel room, "snowed in with the snow / half the year." The truck drivers blink their lights *"How much"* to the lady in the pink Mustang. The wilds of sex and despair, drugs and desperation snare these lost working Americans in surreal roughage, *"Until the last / coin is rubbed for luck and spent."* And so they go on running, surviving on next to nothing, sinning and grinning and sorrowing along the back roads of America, walking in the gravel breakdown lanes "between the cut swaths and the road to Fargo," wanting to lie down finally "in standing wheat or standing water."

(MOSTLY) TRUE GRIT

Erdrich's fictional spin comes in part from cartoon and fable, no less than Dickens's character idiosyncrasies and Welty's plot twists. These are the virtual or fictively unreal caricatures of human failings and mythic "dreamstuff," Lulu says, of human musings. Creation myths to television soap operas, the plots give new tweaks to old paradigms, the classics to pop culture. Ojibwe Nanabozho to "As the World Turns," hers is a quirky, parabolic realism in our time, as Hemingway called his war tales of men, women, and wilderness. More westerly here in the Dakotas, a kind of alternate womanist realism to Hemingway or Jim Harrison, Erdrich's stories prove cartoonishly true, domestically conflicted back home, as though Ripley's Believe It or Not! were crossed with a hodgepodge of contemporary anthropology around Indians and the miscegenated family, Winnebago Wakdjunkaga to *Desperate Housewives*. Grounding her narratives in a tribal base, Erdrich draws on the storytelling inventiveness of Dickens and Faulkner, the real low-life situations of Welty and Carver, the eccentric truths of master tellers of tales the world over, Aho to Talking God, Pushkin to Günter Grass. Think of fusing Momaday's lyric with Welch's surreal humor and Silko's mythic realism, then tossing it all across the Great Plains.

No less than Silko, her sources lie in gossip, swirling through the opening-chapter wake in kitchen chatter and banter, what people say about others when they talk stink and still love them. She's fond of secrets—the hidden truths, privacies, and mysteries of human character all collating around Lipsha's illegitimate lineage. Erdrich deals in fantasies, the alternative wishes of Lulu's dreaming and Marie's cleaning and Nector's fooling around. She hears rumors of her characters in their stories, the suspected shadows and scandals that riddle communities. It all stays in the family, relative to all. She tells tales about *our* people, how *we* know each other as others in common, *our* tales. The plot layers characters' lives with half truths and white lies, the false stories that people tell and tally, the bad mouth that corrects and threatens extended families with slander. So, too, Erdrich trades on dreams, the subconscious desires, the alternative realities of the extended reality—what humans can't have, or fear, or desire beyond the realities of given or fixed lives.

Her stories, like the interweavings of Grandmother Spider from the Great Plains to the Southwest, stitch private givens into public mysteries with webs of understanding and suspicion that interlace Native community. Rez storytellers listen to what people say about themselves and others to weave a narrative of place and time around a six-by-twelve-mile patch of Indian land called Turtle Mountain Reservation. And these stories make up a novel when Erdrich sets them in motion as voices and plots that interconnect through a common plains setting. *Love Medicine* then presents a three-generation saga, a cross-family historical "tissue" of human time passing, and passing on generation to generation as loose tribal chronicle (eleven interacting novels of this mixing to date). Erdrich mixes the horizontal *run run* of narrative, the get-up-and-go arc of plot, with the vertical leaping of lyric in a poetic prose whose rhythms and dictions rise up off the page, especially at the ends of chapters. Images blaze out at times, illuminating scene and character. Her style is a voice—better stylized or idiomatic voices that captivate the tuned ear and tested eye. Erdrich's may be the best of tribal storytelling gone literate. She speaks of Ojibwemowin as her surviving Native language wedded to the land, waters, forest, and plains, a tongue originating with the animals and stones whose place-names and spirit songs were revealed in dreams. The pictographs speak with a "glow from within the rocks" (*Books and Islands in Ojibwe Country* 83).

RAGTAG LOCALS

The second section of *Jacklight*, "Hunters," drops lyrically into the high Dakota prairie. The wild woods are feminine, and earthly love a womanized craze. Free of jacklighting, the dark forest beds men down in free verse, bringing them home from the body's loneliness to a lover who may be a conjugal muse, illicit mistress, or mother death. No longer wearing a man's touches but the woods as clothing, she lowers her "headdress of bent sticks" and straps on "a breastplate of clawed, roped bark," then fits broad sugar maple leaves to her hands "like mittens of blood."

Naturally echoing diction settles like leaves of womanly grace or deadly love over male hurt lying down in a slashed tree grave: "I cover you, as I always did; / this time you do not leave." Wild terror and raw survivalist hope rule here—innate sensual intimacy to mend the hurts between genders or sear the wounds, to bridge the chasms between peoples or bury them forever, to fuse culture and nature or just be done with things. Not knowing the outcome is key to the lyric searching through voice and image.

"Husband, by the light of our bones we are going," the second poem, "The Levelers," elegizes a weary necromance in today's falling world. "Beneath our own hands our bodies are leveling." The light touch of Bishop, a small Sapphic urgency—man and wife, Old Man and First Woman, lie down beneath the slowly turning, seasonal earth. The weight of life and loving keeps revolving in the train wheels of the next poem: "Here is the light I was born with, love," the poem "Train" ends, "Here is the bleak radiance that levels the world." These lines shoulder the earthly burdens of a mother's soul, forever settling.

The poems are spoken as quirky dramatic monologues, the odd voices of Native land and people, here and abroad. Mary Rowlandson tells her version of "Captivity," then caged animals call through their bars, *"Run with me."* Mad Charles VI, "The King of Owls," prates medieval French in four-beat quatrains. Shaded with an Andrew Wyeth landscape, "Painting of a White Gate and Sky" hangs vacant over a prairie woman in North Dakota, her "heart of gray snow," her "wrists chained" and "stomach locked up," emptiness tapping "sorrow's code / in its cage of bone." Eve despairs in a ravaged land, Sylvia Plath rages at womanly dispossession, Elizabeth Bishop salts a barren tongue, and Emily Dickinson's slanted images strike an hour of lead in feminist fallout. "There is no one to see grief unloading like train cars." Only a northern-plains poet—say Willa Cather, Mari Sandoz, Bobbi Hill, or Linda Hogan—could write a line like this. "You sister," the poem tremors, "You heart of gray snow" in the remorse of sodality across races, plains, and tongues.

The section ends with a crystalline love song, "Night Sky," bylined "Lunar eclipse, for Michael," the poet's night-sweat, suicidal husband. An earth-laden lyricist is stranded in this New Land with half-a-dozen tribal children, the losses of old tales, late birthing promises, always a gap between the stars and human stories. The couple lies alone "with the ragged breath of our children / coming and going in the old wool blankets." In "bear heft, shag, and acorn fat" of wild courage, man and wife search each other out, lost Arcturus of the night sky tracked by his bear-sow, hanging unresolved in a canvas-page "stripped and shining / to ride through crossed firs." The lines scatter in free-verse fragments across the black night sky, no pattern fixed, no assumption unquestioned.

LOVE QUARKS AND DREAM FRACTALS

Oddness tells all in Erdrich's love stories of family medicine, marked finally by the "fucked" arrhythmic heartbeat, Gerry Nanapush says, a lucky family skip that keeps his illegitimate son Lipsha out of the military. Margin marks Indian mainstream here, difference proves the rule, eccentric stretches the norm. Playful quirks sketch character, from June's come-hither entry into the bar and Andy's offer to peel her as he shells a blue-dyed Easter egg, to crimped poker cards for Mom's insurance-scam Firebird at the other end. The "touch" in this, as Lipsha calls his born-again healing feel, fires and backfires, as with the frozen Red Owl turkey hearts that choke Nector. Character backbone bends and snaps back, as with Marie's "whipsinging" birch resilience on the hill. "I've had better," this marked maiden snaps, and years later Marie must pull her errant lover and lifelong husband across the dangerous shine of a waxed kitchen floor through the nun's stigmata in her hand. Saint Marie of the Burnt Back and Scalded Butt has earned domestic grace. And, too, the novel's insistent gullibility endears and endures, a steeled kind of motherly, indeed fatherly innocence that resides in Nector's sweet tooth, Marie's sainted goodness, Lulu's free love, and Lipsha's boyish loyalty. Sexuality burns and bonds these characters with love medicines of all kinds, rival jealousy to forgiving sympathy, tribal unraveling to family rejoining, sibling rancor to took-in compassion, war trauma to sexual transgression. And in the end a card crimp makes a "perfect" royal family, a high-heart flush that frees Dad and brings Mom home across the waters of the tragic, romantic opening.

Given the alternate perspectives of Marie and Nector into their fortunate fall down the hill (Chippewa Jack and Franco Jill tumbling into wedlock), love is early on characterized as personal belief and luck, a fated point of view, a tribal medicine: how people see themselves in relation to others seeing themselves and others. Consider Sister Leopolda's not-so-repressed incestuous desires and sadistic claims on a fourteen-year-old racial "passer" brat, her own daughter. Follow Nector "in love" with Lulu while inseminating Marie (he claims without really knowing) as she opens and pulls him into her life plan. So plot here is a sensual, comic entanglement with others, family and otherwise, connecting and collaborating, cussing and discussing and cohabiting, or not. Old Man and Old Woman are nearly children holding up under mortal weight, callowly bearing their own and going on, taking in adopted orphans and crossing blood lines and intermixing six families, French and Scandinavian, Chippewa and Cree, German and English thrown in around the edges. It's called *Metis* up there, the Gallic-Indian "mixes" that draw a lot of other ethnic bloodlines across rez borders into extended tribal family. Everybody's related, or soon will be.

For a moment, think of mixing the blood of sun and moon, male and female. Moon Woman oversees the province of family and relatives, a took-in reciprocity of lineage mix-blooded through the domestic sainthood of Marie Lazarre, a poor-white sort of Indian (not so much Indian that matters, she passes off her crossed blood, what Cooper's Natty Bumppo in *The Leatherstocking Tales* calls a "cross" or cross-blood burden to carry across the frontier border). Saint Marie marries Nector Kashpaw, the brother who sells the geese that his *real* Indian bro Eli shoots. Sweet Nector acculturatively passes into poor property owner, tribal chairman, Hollywood stereotype, and archetypal romantic fool with a fatal addiction to Milky Way sweets, including mother's milk. Traditionally mothers nurture children, as men go to work to survive, and Mother Marie adopts June, her dead sister's orphan, and later June's illegitimate son, Lipsha. Nector wanders away to fame and fortune and his own Hollywoodish folly. Growing things, adaptations, keeping house and home define Marie's character. Nector wanders around supposedly working, getting into various kinds of trouble disrobing and all, straying. His granddaughter Albertine, a "dirty-blond" Scandinavian Indian with a mannish moniker, crosses the reservation border to find working love, first as a runaway teenager in a Twin Cities motel, then as a "Patient abuse" nurse, finally in later novels as a doctor of (love) medicine. Lulu guards the dreams, feelings, and heat of love, while a bad-apple, cross-generational son like King plots to buy the blue Firebird with his dead mother's life insurance. King calculates with goal-oriented male logic, planning, scheming, and taking, including the usurpation Cain-style of his half-brother's birthright. Lipsha, a girlish boy with long eyelashes and a woman's healing and cheating "touch," rises as the prince of sensitivity, empathy, and his grandmothers' "good tears" (not to mention card chicanery), restoring love vision in the old folks home. Distant cousin to Silko's Tayo, Lipsha is the androgynous healer and peacemaker and final comic hero, just as Henry Jr. is the wounded Native warrior come home lethally armored and suicidal, his defenses all turned against himself drowning in the Red River (internalized colonial oppression). Gender may be curse or blessing, confusion or liberation.

If the arts are a domain of women, especially tribal language and social talk, kitchen gossip at a wake or motherly storytelling as understanding character, then men boss the silence of the workroom, the business of market strategy most wildly parodied in Nector's foolish infamy, and Sapphically satirized in Sister Leopolda's denatured sexual politics at the Sacred Heart Convent (her wrong-shoe, weird ways begin after rape and murder in the third novel, *Tracks*, Erdrich's first-written manuscript). Sexes cross over too, as do ethnicities (see the closet gay uncle Wally Pfeff all the way over in *The Beet Queen*, or the cross-dressing feminist priest Father Damien in *The Last Report of Miracles at Little No Horse*). Women keep peace whenever possible, with family spirits and religious observances and the homeless martyrdom of heroines like June, a Christ figure of a woman with the initials JK. Men go to war, at home and abroad and back home again. Gerry Nanapush plays a now-day Nanabozho and political prisoner (based on Leonard Peltier, the Chippewa fall guy for two FBI deaths in 1975 at Wounded Knee) and trickster outlaw who finds his true son Lipsha in the end. Gordie wars within and drinks himself into oblivion. King deals cards for Lucky Charms and loses the blue Firebird to his spurned half-brother. Finally, women like Lulu (or her dark medicine mother Fleur in later fictions) seem prickly independents, free-love radicals queried by society, perhaps entrusted by nature with sentiment, spite, self-purgation, procreation, and secret sorrow. Men, both as defending soldiers and dying love addicts, act from irony, rage, internal and external destruction, self-parody, or despair. Mix this with crossing ethnicity and twisting gender in a novel about love medicine, the cause and effect of comic human survival and modern Indian endurance.

BUTCHER-SHOP OUTTAKES

The third section of *Jacklight*, "The Butcher's Wife," is dedicated to Erdrich's grandmother Mary Korll, German immigrant beached under North Dakota downpours. "Granddaughter of a pair of butchers," the author as a child worked in their shop (*Books and Islands* 117). The paternal surname reverts with a slight vowel slide and consonant shift to Mary Kröger. By now it is clear that the poems are peopled and land-scaped locally and diversely, Old World to New, as Erdrich's fictions are lyricized and dreamscaped, all imaginatively candid about her places of origin, her tribal lines both Euro-American and Native American. From her second, *The Beet Queen*, to her second-latest novel, *The Painted Drum*, the fabulist shoulders the twentieth-century immigrant saga of her surname. *The Master Butchers Singing Club* features a World War I German sniper who migrates to North Dakota and raises his sons, who as World War II American soldiers go back to Europe to kill Germans.

Mary Kröger's husband Otto "could lift a grown man by the belt with his teeth" and died "pounding his chest with no last word for anyone." Brute elegy and émigré truth edge these hard lines: "Who else would give the butcher roses but his wife?" The unhoused curse of a new land, not all ours, locks Otto's fate in blank verse crying for another round of drinks until "the whole damn world reels toward winter drunk." Otto's death sends Mary to gin to overcome the "reek of oxblood" and slaughter memories. "Mallet or bullet they lunge toward their darkness," she says with sympathy for crazed and half-cracked creatures, including the widow Step-and-a-Half Waleski. That "pull from the left" keeps tugging at the widow's balance: "Something queer happens when the heart is delivered."

Characteristically, an oddball last line hangs twisting, begging, and defying translation—the deep heart's passionate mystery, unsettlingly wild near Native woods. "*Mary, you do not belong here at all*," the boiled, meatless bones rattle with migrant uneasiness in a strange new land, and still the unsheltered immigrant longs to come home in the dead of war "deep in this strange earth / we want to call ours." Unspoken prairie knowings root the souls of working people—a blank verse enduring displacement, tough as the land, surviving everything. Families complete their lives blazing through ordinary days, "and through our waking selves / they reach, to touch our true and sleeping speech."

Euro-Americans ask where they come from, émigrés all, still migrant. Again Mary puts in a good word for Step-and-a-Half Waleski, rag-and-bone-shop stranger in unsettled plains, "Scavenger, bone picker" living off the alleys. Even less than Williams's mixed-blood Elsie in the suburbs or Stevens's cold hooker in "The Emperor of Ice Cream"—maybe half-sister to Jim Welch's ragged Agnes in *Winter in the Blood*, or shirttail cousin to Leslie Silko's runaway Emma Jean in *Ceremony*—these lost, hybrid prairie souls hang on and try to "fit / each oddment to each to resemble a life." Cracked Leonard mentally commits "redeeming adulteries" all over town and no one cares, as Mary breaks into wild rhyme, the artificial witchings of syllable and sex. She's the worse for wear, doubly true, too many times fallen, "a man might misconstrue / my conduct, for a lack of innocence."

Rudy J. V. Jacklitch dies repeating Mary's name, the curses of "great, thick men" driving her to the grave "by the light of whiskey." These are eccentrically real characters, as in Breughel, Welch, Carver, or Welty—men heavy with earth and "thick blood pudding," women driven by heart-spirit and "terrible blind grief." Strange tongues from old lands mix with frontier-plains English, *echt* (true) and *Blüt* (blood), "bitch" and "butcher": "*Mary willst du, meine Kleine, noch wieder.*" Just one more time, little one, the man-child pleads.

After three years of grieving, Mary casts her "hood of dogskin / away, and my shirt of nettles" and returns widowed to the forest of her own being, married to the dark firs in death's release, drinking "without fear or desire, / this odd fire." Speech cradles this woman's salvation, the mother wit's soul in all of us. A forest of liberating phonemes wildly brings her loss, her release, her damnation and rescue through "these stunned, loosened verbs." The hissing, shifting wind allows her to "speak in tongues." The deeper forests of being are untranslatable lyrics—the prayers and curses, the sighs and howls, the longing songs of others in a stunned new land.

Dreaming Stuff

A Western male author might not title his novel *Love Medicine*. Certainly *House Made of Dawn*, perhaps *Fools Crow* or *The Ancient Child*, but not a narrative ribboned with love as medicine. In this homey Redbook title, Erdrich combines a Native American renaissance (after long endurance) with feminist liberation. She fuses tribal rebirth with a woman's nurturing sexuality and comic trickster graces. Love softens the edges of human pain; mothering rescues the lost, abandoned, or bastard child. Forgiveness and understanding keep people together, for the most part, family focusing human priority. Love then is the reality of human interaction, intimacy the glue, romance the bonding "dream stuff." And the seductive come-hither of play, the coy intrigue of courting, hooks the reader—engaged, amused, intrigued, and tolerant of six first-person participant narratives: from Albertine's mixed-blood homecoming for Aunt June's wake, to Marie's sainted motherhood that begins with snagging her man, to Nector's role as Adamic father and sensual fool, to Lyman's shirttail cousinhood (more prominent in the outtakes reattached to the New and Expanded 1993 edition), to Lipsha's took-in healings, to Lulu's lifelong place as the other woman (the Magdalene to Mother Mary, whose husband strays into affairs out of wedlock or in). The interwoven distances of eight third-person points of view blend intimacy with authorial omniscience. The author shifts inside, outside, and through the three interlocking generations of stories of comic epic romance across half a century or more of tribal history—an expanded, updated way to Turtle Mountain, all as collective family stories about love's mixed medicines.

What kinds of Indians live in this fictive place of love concoctions? All kinds, and all mixed up as Metis or mixed-bloods. Nobody's anything pure, except maybe Lynnette the "full-blood" Norwegian (she claims), who regretfully marries the bad-blood King. The Nanapush twins, Eli and Nector, seem stand-ins for forest instinct and clear-cut education, old and new Indians, dark and light skins. Eli figures as the other brother, underwater in Momaday's Kiowa stories and elegized in Welch's novel, who carries the old ways, while Nector forges the acculturated Indian-White new path. Most everyone is marginal and mixed: Marie Lazarre passes for White as a French-Cree from low-life drunks, while fecund Lulu (nickname for Louise) Lamartine procreates with all skins for eight truly mixed-blooded sons, plus Bonita her Mexican-sired daughter. Albertine's father is Swede Johnson, and Lipsha at first doesn't even know his blood parents, though they turn out to be the legendary outlaw warrior Gerry Nanapush (fathered by Old Medicine Man Pillager with Lulu offstage) and the redeemer-womanist-martyr June Kashpaw.

So if Lipsha is "took in" by grandparents Marie Lazarre and Nector Kashpaw, he's an adopted blood-kin twice claimed, who unites the other clan lineages of Pillager-Lamartine-Nanapush-and-Morrissey. It all traces back maternally to grandmothers like loving Marie or lovelorn Lulu who faces down the tribal council with a parcel of threatened paternity suits. Indian pride is defined by June's pugnacity ("I don't care," she defies her adoptive auntie Marie) and Gerry's wiliness (in prison for breaking out). There are moments of high comic Indianness in Nector's prayers shouted in church to a God going deaf, "HAIL MARIE FULL OF GRACE!" and Marie's snap-back damnation of sadistic Sister (mother) Leopolda, "Bitch of Jesus Christ! Kneel and beg! Lick the floor!" (*Love Medicine* 53). Indians sadly share Gordie's alcoholic rage over the dead deer confused with his lost wife, and Henry Jr.'s chortling war-sick suicide. The strong ones survive, the lucky ones laugh, the smart ones stay low, the few cussed ones don't count much in the end, even if nominally related.

Names tell all in three generational sets of creation adaptation myths as modern fiction: Marie the Kitchen Saint as Mother Mary, a living Eve in feminine realism; Nector the sweet-toothed romantic and softened male model of modern comic Indianness; Lulu the original seductress, Lilleth to Mary Magdalene, mother as dark stranger and the other lover beyond the norms (a Native feminist rewrite of Hebraic, Greek, and collective Western Penelope and patient Griselda myths). Missing from the opening wake melee, the second generation lines up even more problematic, squeezing a road-warrior woman between two hunted and haunted men: Gordie of the Gordian knot twisted in disconnected parts and "opposite-thinking" or *tipikochiyetim* contraries, as the Cree say, conceived between convent hilltop and reservation sloughs (see "Trickster's Bones," in Lincoln, *Native American Renaissance* 128); June, the spring-blizzard promise of premature birth, a feminine savior, martyr, and dancing spirit (signifying the tragicomedy of survival through sacrifice); Gerry, trickster outlaw and epic lover-father (something of a cartoon mythic hero, political activist, and high-plains warrior). The third generation over fifty years places a mannish woman between a womanish boy and his lowlife half-brother: Lipsha the divine child as took-in orphan with the feminist healer's "touch," an androgyny of crossings in his mixed-up bloodlines; can-do cousin Albertine, the border adventurer and boundary hopper of gender, race, and sovereign nation; King, the false royalty of nominal kinship, the ugly Indian brother as a Nativist choke on ethnocentrism ("You don't trust all Indians," recall Betonie saying in Silko's *Ceremony* [128], "just like you don't write off all White men").

Marie has the stubborn patience, indeed the maternal grace, to keep the family together with spit polish and true grit. Home is her fixed heart point, a centripetal locus for blood and breed adoptions. Nector plays the

Noble Savage as good fool, a kind of Adamic clown caught between two women, *true* and home love. Lulu portrays the centrifugal tart as sugar baby, *femme fatale*, or "lulu" as dream-stuff gambler who teaches her grandson "the touch" to crimp cards and win his true inheritance from an unworthy brother. Gordie seems tragically obsessed with the failure of love, more poison than medicine, as with the alcohol addiction that doubles into his schizoid reality. June rises above all things as the long-legged spirit dancer who laughs and loves in the face of death, ascending to the comic northern lights. Gerry plays her larger-than-life true lover, trickster on the run, absent husband-father trying to come home. Lipsha serves as the coalescing tribal storyteller, both erratic healer and comic hero. He is a survivor, indeed a winner, whose heroic river passage and peaceful homecoming is summed up in one line, crimping a royal flush or "perfect family": "Belonging was a matter of deciding to" (*LM* 255). Albertine adds the stabilizing voice and horizon note to her cousin's journey home, a progressive kinship passer leaving and returning to the rez imbroglio as medicine practitioner with true grit and a loving heal-er's tools. Lyman witnesses his half-brother's drowning in the Red River, lucks out with the crazy Tomahawk Factory, and lucks in with a casino, reinscribed outtakes to the novel. King drops in and out as the bad seed, braggart, liar, and cheat, a wife abuser unloved by his own breed son Howard who would turn him in to the police. He's a reality check on Native racial sentiment.

TRUE STORIES MORE OR LESS

"Myths," the last section in *Jacklight*, means true stories. "I Was Sleeping Where the Black Oaks Move" opens the fourth part with an elegiac ca-dence from Whitman's *Leaves of Grass* ("When Lilacs Last in the Door-yard Bloomed"), leading into "The Strange People," antelope women (Erdrich's sixth novel) drinking coffee till dawn with a jacklight hunter: "asleep in clean grasses, / I dream of the one who could really wound me." The Lefavor girls ripen with harvesting, their bodies breaking open as the snow begins falling "past all the limits we could have known." Startling moments of sense bring closure in each poem, as with the prose chapter endings—rain that breaks the love drought in "Three Sisters" who walk out at dawn and catch "the first, fast drops on our tongues." Despite all the pulling down, the characters keep looking up. For Erdrich's maternal grandmother, the Chippewa Mary Gourneau, "Whooping

Cranes" elegizes a foundling love-child ascending among the breast arks of migrating sky birds, their beaks "swords that barred the gate. / And the sky closed after them."

Crossing over to verse-prose fabliaux, *Jacklight* grounds and loosens poetic tare with modern trickster tales about Old Man Potchikoo. This warty potato man wanders the world and hooks up with a wooden cigarette statue named Josette. Potchikoo breaks wind during Holy Mass and makes love to a slough, only to rise in mock ascension and to conceive mud-marsh daughters, finally weighing him down into the earth. What next? The wilderness Windigo even merits verse, followed by a Native memory of buffalo runs, "The Red Sleep of Beasts," leading into the final lines titled from the poet's motherland, "Turtle Mountain Reservation," dedicated to her maternal grandfather, Pat Gourneau, a tribal chief. The main family characters return: heron low over the marsh, the heart an old compass to the four directions, the runaway poet come home. Sister Theresa rises through the double-hollyhock dust, and Grandpa speaks Indian to himself "between spoonfuls of canned soup." Drunken Uncle Ray dreams of a fabled beast near Cannonball, twenty nuns falling through the sky. The boys come on to Theresa in the local dives—The Blazer, The Tomahawk, The White Roach Bar— and Grandpa leans into the bingo game, then hitchhikes home from the Mission, warbling good-bye to his driver, Ira Comes Last. Grandpa walks through "the soft explosions of cattail" and seeds scattering on still water, "all the time that there is in his hands." Here lies the poet's tribute to her genetic origins, her tribal calling, "Hands of earth, of this clay / I'm also made from."

FICTIVE KIDS IN THE MIX

Momaday defines his lineage through his father's mother, Aho. Black Elk traces his spiritual heritage through Tunkáshila, "grandfathers of grandfathers and grandmothers of grandmothers." No Name finds his family history through his mother's father, Yellow Calf. These familial stories and visions all seem bound up with ancestral history. Lipsha's stories among all the others turn toward contemporary history. The mixtures are already so crossed that nobody really knows who belongs to whom in extended families that all belong to each other. As he ties all the family lines together, Lipsha legitimizes the illegitimate orphan "took-in" as one-of-us. He finds his dad through a tossed-off veteran's empty bottle of Old Granddad, his mother through a lulu of a story that could "make or break" him, his other grandmother warns. The plots all wind up as a contemporary tribal call to bring Mom and Dad home, never "free," always a hitch in the get-along, but home here is a matter of deciding to belong. "There was nothing to do but cross the water and bring her home" (*Love Medicine* 272). The novel ends at the liminal borders of countries, cultures, ethnicities, clans, genders, personal definitions, and acceptances. Father freed to another country, mother spirit at rest with her son, going on laughing and playing and defying the odds—the uprooted, relocated, orphaned cultures of Native and immigrant America come home through their special mixed-blood grandchildren, Lipsha and Albertine.

Mother of half a dozen plus, Erdrich conceives characters through raising children and writing novels; she traces family ties and imagines lives going on, generation to generation. She knows her characters intimately, birth to death, the way a mother knows her issue and nurtures her took-ins. The novelist senses their growth as a plot that develops through place, a character arc that sprouts and ages through time. She has the maternal empathy to imagine others as fully independent selves related by blood and upbringing. She knows the patience to wait, to observe, to listen, to learn from her offspring. There are no norms, only "characters," and no small characters, only relative parts.

How do children change the character of a story? "I always begin my work," Luci Tapahonso says in public lecture, "no matter what I'm doing, with something for my children" (UCLA, 22 February 2005). Linda Hogan dedicates poetry and memoir to her adopted daughters, most recently *The Woman Who Watches Over the World*. James Welch writes through adult pain, sensing childhood in flashbacks of arrested development. "My name's not sport," Malvina's trailer-trash son sneers at No Name. Erdrich writes out of less cruelty and indifference, softened violence and spite. Hers is a protective and nurturing tone, a forgiving eye to future developments. She trades on the consequence of actions, the promise of grace. Erdrich seems a parenting female author, whereas Welch and Momaday serve as chronicling male witnesses, less father figures than male protagonists in their own stories and verse.

Details key everything, particularly in *Love Medicine* with the daily foods people consume. See the novel as a mother's nurturing attention to her children eating, a working woman's palate. Characters in *Winter in the Blood* survive minimally on chicken-fried steak and boilermakers, Fritos and *vin rosé*, whereas the runaway June sucks "pine sap" to survive the woods in *Love Medicine*. June and Andy peel blue Easter eggs and chug Angel Wing slingers in a bar. At the wake, smashed crab-apple and Juneberry pies scatter from the reservation sloughs. Gordie binges on Schlitz beer, the can warped as a tin woman's hips in his grip. Nector eats too many Milky Way candy bars, a diabetic romantic fool who goes under the deep waters of mortality with a fishing-bobber grin. A pregnant Dot pops absinthe jelly beans. Lulu makes love with Nector, all smeary with pantry butter, in the backseat of her Custom Nash Rambler. Marie peels three hundred pounds of potatoes, waiting for her husband to come home from Lulu's burned-down house. Lipsha mortally feeds his grandfather frozen turkey hearts. Howard eats Lucky Charms for breakfast, the pink sugar lumps appropriated as gambling chips by his father King and Lipsha, playing for their mother's blue Firebird.

Car names say much about an American romance with migration, mobility, and frontier conflict (Pontiac, Cherokee, Winnebago, Thunderbird down to the Apache, Kiowa, Comanche, and Black Hawk military helicopters in Desert Storms): Albertine's battered black *Mustang* (appropriately a Metis breed of wildly homebred horse blood); Henry Jr.'s red *Oldsmobile* (the old mobility of patriarchy in question, one father a car suicide on the railroad tracks, the other an itinerate encyclopedia salesman adrift in the Twin Cities); Lulu's tan Nash *Rambler* (the butter queen of the road); and June's blue *Firebird* (the Nile mother phoenix reborn from her ashes, divine sign of the returning Aztec sun king Quetzalcoatl).

In a cousin state to Montana, Indian humor finally saves these North Dakota characters from the despair of winter in their blood. Erdrich calls it "survival humor" in a taped interview with Kay Bonetti (American Audio Prose Library, 1986). Marie laughs at the devil in Sister Leopolda, and at herself waxed into a domestic corner. Drowning in the Red River, Henry spits in the face of his swirling executioner. Nector grins at a deaf Christian God the Father, going under the runoff waters. Erdrich seems to have a feminist humor to make the most of what is, to *under*stand things from the bottom up, as Joyce would have it through Poldy and Molly Bloom in *Ulysses*, another tribal novel of dispossession and native continuance through comic resilience.

Compared with Welch's dark rez irony, Erdrich's humor is more compassion than discipline, more forgiveness than justice, more acceptance than purgation. She loves the unlovable in one's own kin, even the lowly King Jr., hardly a prince. She tolerates the unregenerate in a character like Gordie. She confronts the threat to family and homestead as Lulu stares down the tribal council wanting to appropriate her land. Erdrich evinces a distinctly Cree-Chippewa "opposite-thinking" humor, where surprise always serves to wake up the reader, where people think by inversions, where a reader imagines freshly the way things might be by way of what is given—family to clan and tribe, story to myth and history, livelihood to calling and culture, chance to destiny and fate.

CATHOLIC GRACE?

That is why I stand by your great plaster lips
waiting for your voice to unfold from its dark slot.
—"The Sacraments"

Baptism of Desire (1989), Erdrich's second book of poetry five years later, exorcises the catechistic fantasies and sensual nightmares of a Dakotas Metis girlhood. As with Anne Sexton, Bobbi Hill, or Adrienne Rich, Erdrich hexes her lines domestically. Bewitchingly, she would liberate housewives shackled through the patriarchal years of westering America. With due measure of Medusa's liberationist laughter (a global feminist dash of Hélène Cixous and Julia Kristeva), a burst of American Indian Movement brashness and Women of Indian Nations courage, Erdrich turns Roman Catholic myth back on itself in dark whimsy and bemused candor. Less ironic, but no less fusional three centuries ago, Samson Occom, the Mohegan minister and founder of Brothertown, preached the Apostles across the waters in England and raised money for founding Dartmouth College, where Erdrich went to school. Father north and later in upstate New York, Handsome Lake conquered demon rum and revived an Iroquois vision of the White Roots of Peace that survives today. Out west in the Dakotas of her childhood, Nicholas Black Elk served as both Sun Dance *heyoka* and Catholic catechist among his Lakota people, from the nineteenth century halfway into the twentieth. Vine Deloria Sr. was the first Lakota Episcopalian priest in the Dakotas, and his son Vine Jr. went to seminary before joining the Marines and going on to law school. Spirits are not ethnocentric. Whatever works, works—in selective adaptation, tough-love purgation, or surviving tension.

Baptism of Desire seems less tautly lineated and broadly crafted than *Jacklight*, more focused on Christian feminine scars and girlish liberation from the hamstrung flatlands. "My Catholic training touched me intellectually and symbolically," Erdrich admits twenty years later in *Books and Islands*, "but apparently never engaged my heart" (85). With wild exorcist humor and woolly poetic texture, her first-person poem-stories twist in passionate frustration to break out of working-class North Dakota tedium. Think of this gathering as the Metis liberation of blue-collar women dead center in the country, their in-house trial and spiritual triumph in the millennial twentieth century.

Acknowledging her late husband Michael, "the flame and the source," and citing first appearances in major poetry journals, *Paris Review* to *Partisan Review*, *Poetry* to *Prairie Schooner*, the collection opens quoting "The Cloud of Unknowing" by an anonymous fourteenth-century mystic: "but still go on longing after him whom you love. . . . in this cloud, in this darkness." So religious and personal love fuse through a longing darkly, the negative capability of inspired unknowing a poet's source of vatic utterance and personal salvation. From Turgenev, Erdrich notes the mythic longing for "that other, unknown something" beyond "First Love," which frightens and fascinates romantics in the unknowable darkness, "an unfamiliar, beautiful, but menacing face." This uprooted love-ghost could be what Freud saw as the *unheimlich* or estranged soul of the Western psyche, literally "not-at-home" and longing-to-be. Erdrich reverses the migrant curse in a Native woman's passion to find the way home, to belong somewhere, to love herself and get along with her life.

Part One begins with "Fooling God." Not far from Dickinson's off-Calvinist come-hither with religious orthodoxy, the poem plays trickster heresy to decenter a Roman Catholic patriarchy. In anaphoric riddling, the speaker works "tireless as rust and bold as roots" to unhinge her Maker. She would be "strange as pity" and terribly haired to tease Him home. A bewitching love insinuates itself into the creation by contraries. "I must insert myself into the bark of his apple trees, / and cleave the bones of his cows." Small and forgotten, irascible and riddling, this girl persona fears and fusses her obsessional love for God, though she will not be among the kneeling and fainting devotees, but hiding out, the ever-errant, never-supplicant true lover and prodigal lyricist.

The poet invokes "Saint Clare" from a Pocket Dictionary of Saints, an unholy soliloquist who tells her life of denial and absolute poverty under Saint Francis. Baptized in the fires of desire, her trials feed on menstrual temptation and the grace of hunger. This sister's poetic life poises upon "Immaculate Conception" of the fourth poem, but with a licentious twist in the Virgin Mary's dramatic monologue where her candle taper is dipped in her own blood and "being rests in the bowl of my hips." The "nails are forged" and the "tree thickens."

"The Savior" is born with the fire next time, an incendiary Messiah smoldering in the recreant embers of Native America:

> I want no shelter, I deny
> the whole configuration.
> I hate the weight of earth.
> I hate the sound of water.
> Ash to ash, you say, but I know different.
> I will not stop burning.

This Son of God soliloquy verges on heresy, only to be followed by an anti-Christ out of Ted Hughes's darkly witted collection *Crow*, modeled on tribal trickster myths and ethnographic transcriptions dog-eared by his wife Sylvia Plath (see "Crow on the Beach," in *Winter Pollen*). "Christ's Twin" falls into the world as lordly afterbirth. "He understood the prayers that rose / in every language, for he had split the human tongue." The disobedient Crow-Savior shadows the stone sealing his godly Brother's tomb. This all-too-American hero and frontier con morphs into "Orozco's Christ," the Latin American–Aztec Avenger in the Darmouth murals where she studied as an undergraduate. An anti-American terrorist, Jesus strides home with revolutionary fervor and anti-imperial rage.

> Who rolls the stone from the entrance over his mother,
> who pulls her veil out from under it,
> who ties the stained cloth around his hips
> and starts out,
> walking toward Damascus, toward Beirut,
> where they are gathering in his name.

In a land of plenty and mindless freedom, readers are reminded of a Native holocaust waged west in God's good name, a rough beast at Tenochtitlán and the Little Big Horn, a Middle East crusade ongoing. A renegade warrior band hides out underground, still resisting.

Sex is ever revolutionary. The beloved prostitute "Mary Magdalene" drives boys mad, "my face a dustpan, / my body stiff as a new broom," to even the domestic score with abusive patriarchs: "It is the old way that girls / get even with their fathers— / by wrecking their bodies on other men." Meanwhile, cat-eyed, pre-Christian witches resurrect Old Testament jealousies and unforgiving curses: "the very old angels, the first ones, / in whose eyes burned the great showers of the damned." Recalling early Greek, Scandinavian, or African tribal deities, these unpredictable mother gods punish and wreck, as well as grace us—not Yeats's "pale Galilean," but the émigré sphinx slouching into Bethlehem, Baghdad, Beirut, or Boston with pitiless hunger. And so "The Sacraments" run rich in sensual taboos and Sun Dance offerings to fickle spirits. Starved nuns shudder over plaster-lipped effigies of Christ. "I was meant to have your tongue in my mouth." Their ecstasies flute to a God of abject poverty. "I open my mouth and I speak / though it is only a thin sound, a leaf / scraping on a leaf." The opening section ends with Christ's troubled birth at the winter solstice, "the systole, the blackness of heaven," a feminist revenge of Welch's "Christmas Comes to Moccasin Flat."

This is heavy-witted ritual, a dark condolence of starved souls, if sacrament at all. With secular relief out of *Jacklight*, the next section brings back the butcher's wife, Mary Kröger, maternal prototype for fiction in *The Master Butchers Singing Club*. Rudy J. V. Jacklitch returns from his truck wreck to haunt Mary, and her dead husband Otto lights red votive candles for Mary's empty womb. "God, who in your pity made a child / to slaughter on a tree, why don't you just / fix the damn thing and be done with it?" Our Mary talks back to God in blank-verse candor and working Christian icons. Hers is a German-American, nononsense, butcher's-wife's life, "—a stone, a knife, / ten years, and the slow patience of steel." Mary bluntly mouths a heartland prayer for redemption on an unforgiving prairie, where "Poor Clare" gets knocked up by "carnie men" and throws her infant down a well. A woman's cry for grace echoes from Chaucer through Eliot and Plath: "April was the thickest month for birth."

Part Three, the five-part poem "Hydra," was written from two to four in the morning, the notes say, out of pregnant insomnia. It coquettishly de-creates the Dakotas going back to Wahpeton on Halloween, embracing the high school band leader and flinging the telemarketeer on "the moon-dark couch." Searching for strange phonemes in a deadsea boredom, the poet comes across the Gnostic *mot juste*, "abraxas," containing Greek numerals adding up to 365. Perhaps necromantic language offers a way out of her insomniac flatlands, incessantly rhyming: *abraxas, caduceus, rocks, scrolls, taxes, Nazareth, wax, oxen, otherwise, azimuth*. "Again, the child is whipped toward the place of skulls." This othering literacy pulls dark, acrostic rhyming from the tongues of lingual others. And so the poet-mother unchristens herself nightly in mock penitence, an estranging passion at the dark crystal heart of poetry: "I release myself cell by cell, / from the pieties, the small town / monks of platitudes, the crystal of Christ Tortured / sold on Shoppers Cable Network." Dakota expatriate undoes her middle-class girdles with maverick confessional: "I unlink the scarves, I smash / the gold-filled chain, the bracelet / of tiny commemorative charms, / the ski-boot, the pom-pom, the silver typewriter." Among all the other recreant mistresses of modern verse—Dickinson through Plath, Bishop and Stein, on to Joy Harjo and Sharon Olds—Erdrich takes Satan to her bosom as the "sideways" sidling serpent, old-time Ouroboros, "Snake of hard hours, you are my poetry."

Section Four loosens the verse lines again with Potchikoo's prosaic afterlife, traipsing past Anglo heaven through an unmarked Indian paradise, into a hell of catalogues dragged by the damned endlessly around a Sears Roebuck warehouse. Potchikoo remates with Josette to "pitch whoopee" yet once more à la Nector and Lulu, only to fry his member and remake it with wax; suffers more disgrace from a spiteful lover; gets confused with his evil twin; and finally is exorcised, forgiven, and cremated by Josette. She saves his ashes "in her purse" for some ongoing tall tale to pass the time, to tell all in future days, no less than Lulu's love medicine.

A last section gives birth to the book's release, both an end to pregnant weariness and a return to the base of ordinary things. Mother of three Lakota adoptees and three more mixed-blood children with Michael Dorris—now her seventh child Rita at forty-seven, as mentioned, with the Ojibwa linguist Tobasonakwut ("a one-man spiritual ER" and traditional healer, as detailed in *Books and Islands in Ojibwe Country* 23)—Erdrich earns the artistic rights to write of childbearing and homemaking. See, for example, *The Bluejay's Dance* on the first maternal year after giving birth, plus her three children's books. "My body is a golden armor around my unborn child's body": the poet wakes "wild for everything" in her ninth month. Hers is release from the Roman Catholic wreckage of Edenic passion, "the crushing weight / of church" and God crossing like the Hindenburg, her marriage bed "the wrecked blue island of time and love." And then comes the small, whole, free-verse poem "Birth": "When they were wild / When they were not yet human / When they could have been anything, / I was on the other side ready with milk to lure them, / And their father, too, each name a net in his hands." From W. B. Yeats reworking the Greek myth of infants honey-drugged into this world in "Among School Children," to Louise Glück fearful of harvesting souls from trees in "All Hallows," this birth-catch carries all the magic and terror a parent feels when bringing new life into a crossed world. No émigré or Native mother ever felt less sensually skittish or rapturously apprehensive about childbearing.

Postpartum lines still find "Sunflowers" in a field of conjugal dreams rimmed with needy children as glowing clocks turned to the burning sun. Humans are spirits trapped from birth in the body's flesh, the writer-mother imagines, plagued by domestic weariness and fatigue—Plath's heavy body, Sexton's maternal anxiety, Silko's desert runaways—yet in Native America an overriding mother's care holds out for the small, still, poetic, parenting detail. The work and sacrifice of mothering, child care and domestic chores are no small matters to Indian women poets—Linda Hogan with her two adopted Lakota daughters, Paula Gunn Allen with her three mixed-blood Pueblo children, Bobbi Hill Whiteman with her Cheyenne-adopted and Iroquois-born brood, Luci Tapahonso (from a family of eleven siblings) with her Navajo-Pueblo-Cherokee passel of kids, Joy Harjo on-the-road with her mixed Cherokee-Acoma-Muskogee clutch. With no apologies to mainstream liberation, these mothers are now grandmothers; the elder voices of the grand matriarchies of Native America—traditionally some 93 percent of the tribes—go on going on.

Back to the last poem: a Dakota plains daughter tries to escape child-hood fears by crawling into the storm cellar (perhaps a spill from Plath's deadly *Bell Jar*), her six siblings and parents knocking about upstairs: "it was as if I could escape only by abandoning everything." She uses school to get away from plains tedium, the dry flats of frontier horizons, only to be haunted in New England by the "raw need" and dark-night sensu-alism of "Owls," harbingers of ill, messengers of death (Ojibwa *Kokoko*, Erdrich notes). So the poet gathers up her motherly courage and steals out of bed in the middle of the night, "The Ritual" home-tending as old as women's caretaking of family and culture for two hundred years in an old New England house: "She has arranged her body / with the child inside / to guard her sleeping husband with its light."

The midnight realism of motherhood staggers the poet downstairs to her children—dawn hours of kitchen anxiety, mouths to feed, souls to calm, hearts to tender, more breaking details: "In the hour of the wolf, the hour of the horn, / the claw, the lead pipe, and the oiled barrel of roulette." Her salvation comes in whispering "every living word she knows" and going back to sleep, returning to the ordinary bone-zero that gives origin to wild poetic flights. This domestic humor, this non-poetry of everyday family gets a mother up again to go on—from a baptism of desire to a consecration of mortal fear and endurance through rebirthing courage, with an imaginative belief in the whole ball of waxen gods and our good needs for each other.

Baptism of Desire ends on receding footsteps and homespun lines awakening to an ordinary day, sunlight fanning across the ceiling.

POETIC CROSSINGS, PROSE MIXINGS

Not without contraries, this writer is of our time, for all times. She reads *Tristram Shandy* on an Ojibwe landing, Mallard Island, haunted by her ancestral past and the ghost of a "white Indian" of the Great Lakes, Ernest Oberholtzer (*Books and Islands*). "Perhaps, I think, the air of Tinkertoy idealism here has something to do with the confluence of fascinations that occurs when Germans and Ojibwe people mix. This place reminds me quite a bit of my own family" (103). No less than James Joyce leaving Irish parochialism for the Continent, Elizabeth Bishop abandoning Puritan New England for Brazil, or Richard Wright rejecting Harlem culture wars for Paris, Louise Erdrich left the small-town Dakotas for an East Coast education in the arts, only to circle back to Turtle Mountain in her fiction and verse. So, too, N. Scott Momaday scripted his Kiowa heritage at Stanford with Yvor Winters, as mentioned earlier. Simon Ortiz brought Acoma, and Joy Harjo her Oklahoma Creek origins to the Iowa Writers' Workshop. Bobbi Hill and James Welch carried Oneida and Blackfeet rhythms to the University of Montana to work with Richard Hugo. Greg Sarris graduated from UCLA and Stanford with a doctorate in Modern Thought and Literature and held a distinguished chair in American Literature at Loyola University in Los Angeles, now another endowed chair from his own Coastal Miwok tribe at Sonoma State University.

Fusions run throughout. Indian-White crossings, pioneering gender liberation without cutting free of the median family, sexual freedom and domestic nesting, religious wars and mothering salvation, forest wilderness and farmed clearing, Native and émigré—Erdrich's imaginative landscapes are courageous and original, unflinching, deeply passionate and common sensically grounded. A writer never truly leaves what she is born with, only brings the mileage and lens of an artistic life to bear on her Native origins, wherever she lands. Through the necromancy of language—narrative *run run* to leaping poetic luminosity—a poet-novelist gathers the reader into her own imagined being and rebirths other lives, too, in the daily renaissance of enlightened attentions. The old ones here and abroad asked no less of their storytellers and singers, tribally and culturally.

This woman draws readers back into the Native forests of creative unknowing. Hers is a visionary realism where poetic words sensually and sacredly save Americans from overlooking ordinary things, where narrative is knowing the people and place in-common. Today this maternal bibliophile runs a Minneapolis bookstore, Birchbark Books, in order to surround herself with crafted words. "So that I will never be alone," she ends *Books and Islands in Ojibwe Country* (141). All the Jacks of Christ and spring Junes of a torched Eden, all the lost warriors and dispossessed women, might gather among the spines and leaves for one more chance to give thanks, still treating interculturally at the forest's edge of wild freedoms in a New World. Louise Erdrich is fictionally run-running ahead, poetically rising on the talk-arts of Native crossings.

TEN

Singing Verse,
Talking Prose

Joy Harjo and Greg Sarris

It was in song that I first found poetry, or it found
me, alone at the breaking of dawn under the huge elm
sheltering my childhood house, within range of the
radio, of my mother's voice. I used to think that the
elm, too, was poetry, as it expressed the seasonal shifts
and rooted us.

—Joy Harjo, *Ploughshares* (Winter 2004–05)

"I propose a different structure," Joy Harjo protests the Euro-American
trinity as hierarchical spirit over flesh. "It's not original but what I've
learned from being around tribal peoples, and in my own wanderings"
(*The Spiral of Memory* 127). Hers is a pan-tribal, earthly vision in process, on-the-road around the country, tribally interconnected. "The
shape is a spiral in which all beings resonate," a spiral that forms an
open circle, moving outward and inward simultaneously, taking in
and giving out. "The bear is one version of human and vice versa," so
Momaday can *be* a Southwest bear, as he imagines, or Welch a hawk-
eyed visionary searching Montana, or Hogan identify with Western raptors, or Erdrich play a Dakota trickster Lulu. "The human is not above
the bear, nor is Adam naming the bear." Greek *Arctus*, Latin *Ursus*,
Spanish *Oso*, Lakota *Mato*, or Kiowa *Set* offer diverse morphemes to
suggest that a bear is still a bear by any other tongue, and best known

by ancient names—*Old Man, Grandfather, Wise One, Courage Maker, Healer, Orpheus, Odysseus, Beowulf.*

"Male and female are equal, useful forces—," Harjo levels the field, "there's no illusion of domination." Such a radically traditional concept is worth considering tribally. No man without woman, no son without mother, no daughter without father, and why should one silence the other? "We move together," human forces in motion no less than What-moves-moves, Lakota *Takuskanskan*, the prime mover that moves all that moves through things. "Transformation is really about understanding the shape and condition of another with compassion, not about overtaking." Empathic othering, not taking over—extended kinship as a gathering of all family, no less than kin, more than kind—spiraling connections across differences. This resonating spiral could be a tribal story of evolutionary symbiogenesis. "God, then, is a relative, and lives at the root of molecular structure in all life, humans, animals, plant life, minerals as well as in the essence of the sun" (*The Spiral of Memory* 127).

Two energy sources drive nuclear physics. Solar fission shoots an electron at the molecular nucleus and explodes the mass, dispersing vast friction. Particles fire everywhere in chain-reactive fallout, the light of a million million suns hurled outward centrifugally. Conversely, liquid fusion shrinks and collapses molecules centripetally into each other by splicing electron shells. Scientists say that sound blasts can create solar bursts of light with star intensity, as molecules fuse through "sono-luminosity." In March 2004 chemists completed laboratory experiments where a cup of hydrogen-rich acetone molecules was squeezed, shrunk, and fused by intense sonar bursts to emit a solar-spot of energy the temperature of the sun. This is now called "sono-fusion" (a refinement of nuclear cold fusion) and may be the answer to the world's energy needs. The fuel supply is unlimited, there is no destructive shattering, little radioactive fallout.

High-intensity sound serves to solar heat, that is, to illuminate leaping verse lines—"the Soul *at the White Heat*," Dickinson has it. Consider phonemes compressing lyric matter in sono-fusional bursts of luminous fire—*the blazing out*, as Lowell said of Roethke's work. Wordsworth glimpsed this starburst as "spots of time," a poetic heat Mallarmé called the "flash of intellect." Shamans speak so of the spirits: the *yuwipi* lightning streaks among Lakota all-night healings, or Beautyway reflections of moonlit water among the Navajo. Spiritual powers refract sunlight, reflect moon gaze, or focus lightning. Zuni fire priests seek out lightning scars on the sacred mountain, as Peter Nabokov details across Native America in *Where The Lightning Strikes*. Joyce used the liturgical term *epiphany*, Hopkins spoke of poetic *instress*, and Dickinson experienced ecstatic terror through "a certain Slant of light" that obliquely illumined her Amherst bedchamber. Sound < Light is the lyric equation. In poetry, what humans *hear leaping* is what they *see luminous*. From that poetic illumination comes intense cultural energy, a sono-fusional verse reaction that charges the tribal world without poisoning it. *Tunkashila / onshimala ye / wani gta*, Lakota Sun Dancers stare into the sun and sing to break free of suffering. "Grandfather / have pity on me / I want to live." The poet does not so much change the world or construct what humans see, William Carlos Williams and Linda Hogan insist, as give the reader new eyes to see the world's truth, life, and promise. A new poem, a new world.

BLUE LIGHTNING

> An oral poem is not composed *for* but *in* performance.
> . . . Our oral poet is composer. Our singer of tales is a
> composer of tales. Singer, performer, composer, and poet
> are one under different aspects *but at the same time*.
> —Albert B. Lord, *The Singer of Tales*

Joy Harjo is a Native woman liberated—a restless intelligence, a roving imagination eager to see the world, the whole interconnecting network of languages, cultures, ethnicities, and histories. She is curious about differences, revolutionary in her androgynous passions, self-correcting in her fears, fierce in her angers over injustice. She is not a local-knowledge essentialist or Red-on-Red exclusionist, but a pan-tribal androgyne, a fusional crosser. Hers are traveling-woman poems, talk-songs of abandoned sisters who find themselves alive and born again in an Albuquerque Sunday sunrise, with her Navajo friend Goodluck listening to Baptist hymns on the truck radio. Who see themselves in Anchorage through an Athabascan grandmother homeless on the street. Who identify amorously with a Latin American cleaning woman in Los Angeles. Who give birth with a Navajo mother in Gallup. Who hang from the thirteenth-floor hotel window desperately in Chicago. Who ride with Noni Daylight through Albuquerque late at night with a lap pistol.

The blues whisper and shadow every corner of Harjo's tribally feminist America. *Been down so long it looks like up to me*, New Orleans singers say. The voices in her poems are colloquial low tones, the common tongues in uncommon mixes, trying to speak quietly and often to herself about fear and loss. As Louis Armstrong trumpeted at Carnegie Hall in 1947, *What did I do to be so black and blue?* Voices not so much confessional as slightly conspiratorial—searching for words and understandings, never too certain, edging along the borders of knowing. *He's got a way with women*, the lost-lover blues go, *and he just got away with mine*. Steering between daydream and prayer, this song-poetry is a murmuring, a questioning, a lyric gathering of impressions. *Nobody knows you when you're down and out*, Bessie Smith sang, trying to name the nameless feelings of anxiety and ecstasy, disillusion and desire, terror and passion.

SHADOW EDGES

"Call It Fear," the opening poem of *She Had Some Horses* suggests, but what could it be? Give the darkness within the darkness a name, say Id or repressed "other" of a muted Latin tongue—the disappeared voices of women singing, a call-and-response among silenced voices. "Learn how to speak," she told my UCLA contemporary poetry students when visiting with Luci Tapahonso, 22 February 2005. "Learn grace. Learn how to sing. You need to listen." Listen when no one can speak, cry out to a world indifferent, resist torpor and conformity. "We all come in with gifts. Go back in here," she said pointing inward, "to that place of breath."

Call It Fear

There is this edge where shadows
and bones of some of us walk
                      backwards.
Talk backwards. There is this edge
call it an ocean of fear of the dark. Or
name it with other songs. Under our ribs
our hearts are bloody stars. Shine on
shine on, and horses in their galloping flight
strike the curve of ribs.
                Heartbeat
and breathe back sharply. Breathe
                   backwards.

There is this edge within me
        I saw it once
an August Sunday morning when the heat hadn't
left this earth. And Goodluck
sat sleeping next to me in the truck.
We had never broken through the edge of the
singing at four a.m.
        We had only wanted to talk, to hear
any other voice to stay alive with.
        And there was this edge—
not the drop of sandy rock cliff
bones of volcanic earth into
        Albuquerque.
Not that,
        but a string of shadow horses kicking
and pulling me out of my belly,
        not into the Rio Grande but into the music
barely coming through
        Sunday church singing
from the radio. Battery worn-down but the voices
talking backwards.

The poem opens with colloquial grounding, "There is this," and edges toward a fractured "edge where shadows." The line break drops away from shadows surviving death, "and bones." The indefinite casting for detail, "There is this," echoes other uncertain opening poetic lines. "There's a certain Slant of light," Dickinson ponders winter afternoons— or more assertively, Frost concludes of "Mending Walls" at the outset, "Something there is that doesn't love a wall." On the edge of collapse, Harjo's line is about to fall, the cut edges of a voice in danger, risking a poem: "edge where" is still imprecise, folk-talky, searching for footing in "shadows." The line hangs on a collapsing trochaic foot, "*sha*dows," then falls iambically, "and *bones*," linking spirits with things. A skeleton is reversely preceded by its ghostly afterimage, "of some of us," the double remove—not all of us, the few survivors. The duplicate preposition slows the pace even more from the drop of enjambed fragments, reducing the faltering stretch of the line to "walk." Then comes the terrible drop to the trochaic heave "*back*wards" as a dangling fragment, a line all to itself, reversing it all. In converse order, reverse foot, the contrary poet leaps into coyote dark.

"Talk backwards," she speaks in tongues, and then tries again: "There is this edge," a second go at defining it, "call it an ocean of fear of the dark." The oceanic darkness within the darkness of measureless fear, with the full-stop tag "Or," the line surges on and breaks over itself into "name it with other songs." Common songs of sorrow, songs of betrayal, songs of confusion, songs of loss. "Under our ribs," the line tries to go on defining things, then again breaks syntactically across free-verse metrics, "our hearts are bloody stars." After so much tentative searching for the right words, this image flares off the page, a spondaic syncopation that heaves against convention: not guiding stars or crooning harvest moons that "Shine on / shine on," but the line bucks with "horses in their galloping flight"—horses within the breast that "strike the curve of ribs" like a wild hunger bone-sprung to bust out.

"Heartbeat," an enjambing half-line to itself, falls ungrammatically to "and breathe back sharply" from that broken rib. "Breathe" again falls across the line break "backwards" in a spondaic reverse heave against common sense. Think of Lorca's "deep song," gypsy "tears of narcissus and ice." Heartbeat to breath, this is an opposite-thinking blues warrior, a contrary at heart who walks, talks, and breathes backwards. And so she tries a third time, "There is this edge within me," now claiming the break within as a defining line. "I saw it once," the poet says, catching narrative stride of an August Sunday sunrise with Navajo buddy Goodluck in a truck on the bajada west of Albuquerque. Two powwowing Indians could not break through the "edge of the / singing" by early morning, wanting only to talk, "to hear / any other voice to stay alive with." The prepositional extension, against all grammarians who say no to a dangling connective, gives Harjo the dialogic courage to reassert a fourth time, past tense in mid-line dangling, "And there was this edge—." Not a basalt drop "into / Albuquerque. / Not that," she says, no, "but a string of shadow horses kicking," the bone ghosts now sunfishing and crowhopping birth inside her belly. The horses do not disappear underwater into the Rio Grande, "but into the music." The contrary realigns her life forces, the "Sunday church singing" of other needy song-poets on the dawn radio, worn-down as battered old batteries, "but the voices / talking backwards." Speaking in *reversed* choral tongues, always an extending "but," never entirely alone, the voices sing of angels and demons, horses and humans, a cultural and spiritual chant common as a pickup-truck radio at sunrise calling fear what it is. She survives fear by chanting through her open wounds, tearing through her scars, reaching deeply into her vaginal birthing tracts to re-create a voice from all the maternal voices ever on the edge of suicide and coming back for one more singing sunrise.

What kind of fractured lyric text is this compared with linear prose narrative? The story is not told in line-item fashion, but disjunctively, selectively by way of modulated diction, cadenced phrasing, catastrophic line breaks and onrushing enjambments. The images are uncommon as "shadows" of "bones," common as the (missing harvest) "moon," or startling as "bloody stars" in broken hearts. The range of diction is truly democratic. White space everywhere opens the lines and words to breath, to echo, to thought about what's being said, and just as critically not said. How can anyone name the unnameable fear? Only by working through it, remembering death and rebirth. The poem moves toward the edge of knowing, crosses back, talks backwards (the gibberish of shamanic searching), receives the vision of horses galloping in flight, catches breath, and remembers: a moment of dawning peace, an insight talking all night with a good-luck friend in a truck overlooking Albuquerque. Shadow horses rebirth a woman through radio church hymns "talking backwards."

No explanation, all demonstration. The reader is not told but shown the data—the crisis, not the analysis—and working through voices to deeper voices and shadows of reality that prove more deconstructively real than loss and fear. The reader must listen, meditate, and work for engagement, breaking through each word, falling line by line and sometimes within lines to the thickenings below, all with a faith that the descent will lead to insight, hopefully purgation, certainly cleansing of the wound by letting it sing out. "A song sung while understanding each word—the way Billie Holiday or Bessie Smith did it," Charles Simic says in *Wonderful Words, Silent Truth* (86). Blues lyrics work this way—timbre, tone, pitch, key, texture, rhythm of voice—feeling into and through the pained words, sliding on and off the notes, more than collating the story being sung. Yes, there's a storyline of a kind, a character arc of sorts, but the listener intuits the resolution of plot point and character development "talking backwards," such as it is, rather than having the package boxed, wrapped, and bowed with dedicatory gratuities. The poem is as difficult to feel and to ferret out as the personal journey through fear itself. The poet asks no less of her reader.

SURVIVING ALL

These are song-stories of survival from "those who were never meant / to survive," a dramatic retelling and reenactment of history from the 3 percent survivors' point of view, "the fantastic and terrible story of all of our survival." Her duplicative preposition "of" tells the story of the story of all. Far north in homeless Anchorage, far south in Latina Los Angeles, far east in suicidal Chicago, far down in powwow Albuquerque, far over in birthing Gallup or drinking McCartys, far under in DeSoto's New Orleans, far into horse-neighing Jemez—no matter how far away or down under, remember the ancestral ways that bring the people here: "Remember all is in motion, is growing, is you. / Remember language comes from this. / Remember the dance language is, that life is. / Remember." The current poetics are jagged and knife-like—broken bottle edges spilling blood and milk, staggering variable foot—shattered and reimagined tribal unities.

> This is how I cut myself open
> —with a half pint of whiskey, then
>   there's enough dream to fall through

The deep-song, blues music will not let her stop or betray herself:

>   I am free to be sung to:
> I am free to sing. This woman
> can cross any line.

And so she has horses to sing.

Women had horses too, *some* horses in the old days. They were heroic riders, both in the past and nearly lost to the matriarchal past, as male stereotypes flooded the frontier. Their warrior myths remember a heroic age of androgynous centaurs, both mares and stallions (see, for example, John Ewers's *The Horse in Blackfeet Culture*). Momaday reminds today's Indian that his great-great grandmother, the blue-eyed Mexican captive Kau-kau-ointy, rose to Kiowa power with a great herd of cattle and horses. Welch writes of a widowed virgin, her husband's horse sacrificed and eaten by others, surviving ostracism and the Blackfeet Winter of Starvation. Silko gallops away to the goddess mountain with Yellow Woman in her essays and fiction. Native women know strength and power, even break-neck speed, and they know travel to distant places, the mobility engendered by the four-hooved carriers that were called sacred or super dog, Lakota *sunka wakan*. Tribal women today know sensual passion, fertility, and virility, as they understand by blood the natural wild energies that produce children. And they know the powers to move, to change, the powers of transformation that Black Elk sees in the humanly interchangeable grandfather-stallions of the four winds. Harjo chants their powers and sodality. Hers is an androgynous icon, the male-female strength-sensitivity of all living beings, from the horse sense that grounds human animal selves, to horse whisperers, to the equestrian stirrup that changed Europe and the Americas, to the legendary martyr Crazy Horse or Lakota *Sunka Witko*, to the Four Horses of the Apocalypse. And in the New World, the *musteño* or mustang was bred from Spanish mares, no less than mestizo, Metis, breed, or mixed-blood crossed one tribe with another. "Pure mustang, Ma'm," the mixed-blood Lakota Frank Hopkins assures the blue-blood English lady of his stallion's breeding in the 2004 Disney docudrama by the "painted" horse's name, *Hidalgo* ("son of something," that is, of lesser rank, *hijo de algo*).

The Buckskin Curtain has always had mixed-blood feminine openings, from Pocahontas to Sacagawea, La Malinche to Ramona, Winona La Duke to Wilma Mankiller. As the Kokopelli petroglyphs illustrate and Silko writes of Laguna Yellow Woman, women choose from genetic donors and cross-cultures with maternal grace and power, no less than men, perhaps more fluidly. She had some horses from the shattered classical Native past:

She had horses who were bodies of sand.
She had horses who were maps drawn of blood.
She had horses who were skins of ocean water.
She had horses who were the blue air of sky.

She had post-modern horses:
She had horses with eyes of trains.
She had horses with full, brown thighs.
She had horses who laughed too much.
She had horses who threw rocks at glass houses.
She had horses who licked razor blades.

She had horses of romance:
She had horses who waltzed nightly on the moon.

She had contemporary horses:
She had horses who liked Creek Stomp Dance songs.
She had horses who cried in their beer.

She had word horses:
She had horses who called themselves, "horse."
She had horses who had no names.
She had horses who had books of names.

She had horses of mystery and fear:
She had horses who whispered in the dark, who were afraid to speak.

She had horses of sensual desperation:
She had horses who tried to save her, who climbed in her
Bed at night and prayed as they raped her.

She had whole horses:
She had some horses she loved.
She had some horses she hated.

They were the same horses.

These lost and recovered, indeed reimagined and reified androgynous horses figure as transformative guardians of modern Native American poetry, from Black Elk's vision of the grandfather stallions through Frank Mitchell's Navajo horse songs. Indeed, she has some horse songs to sing.

Fear is generative for this feminine centaur, *quickening* the poet, as James Wright said. A woman's supposed powerlessness is here empowered, fear spoken and exorcised, loved and given back to the dark. *In medio noctis vim suam lux exerit,* Van Gogh wrote in the margins of a Rembrandt etching; "In the middle of the night light spreads its power" (Borafoux, *Van Gogh* 32). In the bottom of the night, Roethke sang, the poet's eye begins to see. And chant Harjo does through the night light, oral to written texts, dancing and cantering across the Americas with her saxophone and bands, *Poetic Justice* to the reconstituted *Native Joy for Real* today. "Poetry and music," she said in my UCLA class, "they belong together."

Surely Harjo's poetry disrupts convention and assumption, breaks connections, interrupts patterns, shakes up a reader or listener. Poems do not come from books, she insists. They are written anywhere and everywhere (bus stops, plane rides, taxis, park benches, café napkins, academic offices, sacred mountains, massacre sites, vision quests, daydreams, nightmares, fantasies, muses). "Poetry you can write with pencil," she says, "on the back of a grocery bag." Poems come from the spirits, if people are lucky. A woman knows they're present, the poet claims, when she feels it. "The poet was sorcerer and seer before he became 'artist,'" Albert Lord insists in *The Singer of Tales*. "His structures were not abstract art, or art for its own sake. The roots of oral traditional narrative are not artistic but religious in the broadest sense"

(67). When Joy Harjo teaches or performs poems, she *does* dance-song, she does not dissect them. Her sources are internal and spiritual, cultural and historical, not just from workshop talk or craft sessions, but in tribal "Prayer" common as daily breath.

> We see you, see ourselves and know
> That we must take the utmost care
> And kindness in all things.
> Breathe in, knowing we are made of
> All this, and breathe, knowing
> We are truly blessed because we
> Were born, and die soon within a
> True circle of motion,
> Like eagle rounding out the morning
> Inside us.
> We pray that it will be done
> In beauty.
> In beauty.

SONGS FOR ALL THAT

> I never knew nothing but the spirit.
> You have to know me to know what I'm talking about.
> —Mabel McKay

Introducing Joy Harjo's reissued *She Had Some Horses* in 1997, Greg Sarris quotes Mabel McKay on curing chants, the relation of medicine prayer to song-poetry: "I have songs, songs that speak to the disease. It is living, the disease; so I have to know it, work with it, before I cast it out. I have songs for all that" (3). And in song-poems, Joy Harjo gives fear back to itself, intoning her many-colored horses, openly chanting away losses. Harjo is animated by lyric, Sarris driven by narrative. The contrast helps to define postmodernist Native genres, song-poetry to talk-story.

Native cultures seek to heal a five-hundred-year-old wound from first contact with the invaders: tell the story the way it is, Mabel would say, get to know our talk to know us. From Queen Isabella's commissioned lieutenant Cristoforo Colombo ("Christ-bearer") enslaving the Tainos in the 1490s and pandemically decimating four million Caribbean Natives in a matter of decades; to the Spanish Conquest of Mexico by Cortez through his Aztec concubine La Malinche in the 1520s; to Johns Smith and Rolfe seducing young Pocahontas and beachheading the British in Jamestown, Virginia, in 1607; to Jacatequa dueling Aaron Burr in Georgia, and Sacagawea leading Lewis and Clark across the Northwest in the early nineteenth century—women play an integral part, trying to buffer their families and keep tribes together as they face insuperable odds.

In 1542 Cabrillo sailed into San Pedro Harbor, as Angelenos know Long Beach, California, and saw the inversion-layer smoke of five thousand Gabrielinos or *Tongva* Natives camped along the Los Angeles River basin. So Cabrillo named the place *Bahia de los Fumos*, or Bay of Smokes. Over 10 percent of the Native population of what became the United States lived along the California seacoast, and 15 percent lives there today—the largest state concentration of Native America in the country (687,400 as of 1 July 2004, according to the national census of 4.4 million; *Indian Country Today*, 23 November 2005). The Spanish Golden Age hyperextended its empire by way of El Camino Real (King's Highway) through California and the Southwest, where the Black Legend missionized and enslaved Natives to adobe the way for colonization. Father Junipero Serra, sainted in modern-day church history, oversaw the indenturing of mission-building Indians in a diasporic invasion. By the end of the nineteenth century, émigré Californians had slaughtered nearly all of the Native population.

The United States forged west with the Louisiana Purchase early that century, then took the Hispanic Southwest, including California, by force of the 1848 Treaty of Guadalupe Hidalgo. Gold was discovered the next year at Sutter's Mill near Placerville, California. The Gold Rush unleashed a horde of mining-crazed prospectors who "shot Indians like rabbits" (one survivor observed), engineered gigantic land swindles, chopped down forests to build cities, indentured Asian and Latin American labor to build railroads and high-rise cities, and cross-tied a gun-barrel Far West diplomacy to the Golden Bear killing fields. Los Angeles, or simply *Los*, bragged the highest nineteenth-century murder rate in the country.

Ishi was born among the central California Yahi near Mt. Lassen in 1862, a year before Black Elk on the plains—in the middle of the Civil War raging back east, a genocidal Indian slaughter raging out west. Over the next fifty years, four thousand of Ishi's Yana people were exterminated. *Ishi*—"a man," since no Yana speaker was left to introduce him to strangers—hid alone in a cave, the "Bear's Hiding Place," for the last twenty years. Wearing a scrap of covered-wagon canvas, the last starving Yana stumbled into an Oroville slaughter yard in September 1911, after his mother, sister, and all the elders in his cave had died. Newcomers thought the "Digger" Indians of California had vanished. Spring runoff in northern California still uncovers skeleton villages—entire corpse populations—reeking of what the locals call "stench flesh."

Born in 1907 in north-central California, Mabel McKay was four years old when her neighbor Ishi surrendered in the Oroville slaughter yard. Her story bridges the Indian-killing of the old days with the revived medicine ways of recovering tribal cultures. Her amanuensis was a UCLA student in the 1970s, Greg Sarris, a junior-college transfer football player. Twenty years later a colleague, Sarris wrote Mabel's life story in the next-door Rolfe Hall office just before Mabel died on 31 May 1993. *Mabel McKay: Weaving the Dream* was published the following year by the University of California Press in their Portraits of American Genius Series.

COUSIN PROFESSOR COMING HOME

Spirit show me everything.
Each basket has Dream . . .
I have rules for that . . .
—Mabel McKay

Prose foregrounds a story. Mabel McKay and Greg Sarris collaborate in the telling, or "bi-autobiography," as Sarris argues dialogically through intertwined life stories. The dual biography cants across six hundred as-told-through life stories of mostly Native men (more than four out of five authored by Anglos), so the text requires historical context (see *Keeping Slug Woman Alive*, Sarris's published 1991 Stanford dissertation in the doctoral Modern Thought and Literature program).

This section considers how Mabel McKay represents California Natives, and why Greg Sarris was given—or better, challenged to earn— the authority to write the book. If Joy Harjo's poetry spirals out to pan-tribal, even non-Indian cultures, Greg Sarris's prose brings all tribes spiraling back into a mixed-blood family graduation that portends Native empowerment from Mabel's songs, baskets, dreams, and stories to the most advanced academic degrees and positions, the most coveted literary reviews and awards, the highest circles of California economic politics in the New Tribal Gaming proceeds from Casino Indians. Sarris advanced quickly to full professor at UCLA, was then chaired at Loyola Marymount University, and is now chaired at Sonoma State University near his upbringing places and tribal bedrock. Five times he has been elected tribal chairperson of the Gratton Band of Coastal Miwoks, through the 1990s and into the twenty-first century—"Cousin Professor," his relatives dub him, or affectionately "Junior Junior" by Granny cousin Marguerite in East L.A., recently deceased—Sarris as teacher, critic, editor, translator, biographer, short-story craftsman, novelist, and acclaimed filmmaker.

Sarris lives talk-story, a true *character* "engraved" in California culture. His life-as-story stages the critical moment in history to act with the best tools and training possible—to write, to teach, to lead, as the Greeks spoke of the "heroic moment," to seize the day. He became a UCLA full professor in record time, publishing a record number of books (five in six years, including the Robert Redford–coproduced, five-hour HBO teleplay *Grand Avenue*). Sarris learned how to succeed surviving the street wars, the culture wars, the gender wars, the legitimacy wars. He learned survival skills in college athletics, specifically as a recruited defensive secondary for the Bruin football team that beat the Stanford Indians in the 1978 Rose Bowl. He learned to carry his weight as a body builder and English professor, a creative writer and cultural critic. He learned mind-war *poison* at an early age along the Grand Avenue back streets of Santa Rosa. He saw cultural disease as a teenager with crime and drugs, then as a young adult with racial slurs, demotic curses, and ritual hexings. He faced down bad medicine as an academic against knee-jerk dismissals of ethnic margins by the Moral Majority and provincial jealousies from party-line colleagues. As a hypoglycemic scriptwriter, Sarris learned to avoid sugar and fats, alcohol and drugs, cigarettes and Hollywood hype. He learned all this the hard way, the old fashioned way, on his own and by watching others, their successes and failures. Greg Sarris learned to model himself the best way he could with some help from *took-in* family and friends, chiefly his adoptive grandmother Mabel McKay, "a mother who cared enough to tell you stories" (*Mabel McKay* 49).

Sarris is a master minimalist storyteller, and this section focuses on his narrative writing. Consider a pivotal scene in the Woodland Happy Steak of the Central Valley:

> "No, Mabel, I mean for your book. When did the Dream start?"
> She laughed and wiped her mouth with the napkin. "It didn't have no start. It goes on."

"But I mean the Dream. Not the spirit."

"Same thing. Well, it said to me when I was little, 'I put these things to you, and you have to sort them out.' It wasn't always a good thing. It's many. Then it's saying, 'You have to learn many bad things so you know what to do when the time comes . . .' That's why people say I'm poison. I don't know. How can I be poison?"

"Maybe we should start with the baskets. That's what people know you best for."

"Well, same thing. Spirit show me everything. Each basket has Dream . . . I have rules for that . . ."

I got up and filled my plate again at the all-you-can-eat-counter. Later, when she was sipping hot coffee, she said, "You're kinda funny person. You try to do things white way. On account you're mixed up. You don't know who you are yet. But you're part of my Dream. One day you'll find out."

"What's wrong with me?"

She laughed and pulled out a cigarette from her purse. "That's cute. 'What's wrong with me?' Nothing. How can anything be wrong with you? You're young and healthy."

So what was the point? I paid the bill and we left. (*MM* 31)

Post-dissertation and cubicled at UCLA through a torrential 1993 winter, drafting the Mabel story, Sarris learned how to write by listening through memory, as his mentor admonished—to the ways people speak (not write); to how he himself thinks and talks (academic to street-smart); to things left unspoken (where and who are the lost cultures today); to the "ever-lasting" Spirits behind all this (no *art*, Mabel insisted, only the *Dream* can teach prayer baskets or give healing songs). Remembering imaginatively is critical, as with Momaday's Aho or Silko's Old Ku'oosh. Start in a reader-response position, as Sarris teaches in the classroom, with the ideas critical to the writing: what will readers come to see and know and remember about California Indians? A reader-friendly intimacy seems crucial to trusting the narrative, never too cooked, never too frontal. Positioning here is critical, the writer-reader's relationship to the text. So the Spirits tell Mabel of Albert's medicine coming through her, "the songs growing in your throat . . ."

"Doctors can do many things. Already you can do special things. Look at your baskets. Each one is a miracle. And the songs growing in your throat . . ."

"What's he want?"

"He knows you have songs. He has spirit power. He knows about you. He wants to help you, give you some of his songs. Those ladies are his helpers. They're his singers." (*MM* 43)

If song-poems begin as a spirit in the throat, how can anyone tell Mabel's story? The woman talks in circles, Sarris grouses to himself, or backtracks, or doesn't tell him anything substantive at all, like names, dates, cultural details, or insider information. For that matter, her stone-walling tacitly suggests, how do humans come to know anybody or anything worthwhile? Do people know anything significant to tell anybody? What do people remember to pass on?

The Dreamer's strategy is to avoid textual or authorial interference whenever possible, literally to keep words out of the story's way. So Sarris begins the book with Mabel's epigraph—more of her words in one space than anywhere else in the story:

> *I was born in Nice, Lake County, California. 1907, January 12. My mother, Daisy Hansen. My father, Yanta Boone. Grandma raised me. Her name, Sarah Taylor. I followed everywhere with her. I marry once in Sulphur Bank. Second time I marry Charlie McKay. We live in Lake County, then Ukiah, then Santa Rosa. I weave baskets, and show them different places. Have son, Marshall. Now grandkids, too. My tribe, Pomo.*

People don't speak in complete sentences, especially not bilingual speakers whose mixed grammars and lexicons seldom mesh neatly. Fragments, bits of information, pointillist data, nods and winks and sighs, and a richly honed and mellowed irony edge Mabel's multivocal monologue. *There, how's that? That's how I can tell my life for the white people's way. Is that what you want?* Well, not exactly, the reader demurs with Sarris—scrap the white people's way—we're just getting warmed up to cross over to tribal ways. Who are you, really? her scribe asks. *It's many*—Mabel overrides his question—a multiplicity of history, people, place, spirit, and thing. *It's more, my life. It's not only the one thing. It's many.*

Right away a reader notes the caution not to simplify, not to reduce Indians to icons or stereotypes. Never shrink a life into names and dates, missing parents and failed marriages, empty baskets and failed adoptions. The key is voice, the Spirit speaking through idioms and inflections.

Memorable speech is taken from storytelling arts of prose narration. As with lyric, word choice and cadenced silence cross, but the gaps are narrowed. Listen for the spaces around things, the white noises, the quiet between people and their chatter. Silence defends a culture or person against misreading.

Listen, Child

> You have to listen. You have to know me to
> know what I'm talking about.
> —Mabel McKay

What she's talking *about* will never be said directly, only indirectly. The scribe must search for the missing words and know he will never solve the mystery, only stitch a narrative through the dream basketry that weaves Mabel's life. And the reader must listen too, feel the words spoken, parse the prose rhythms—ask questions and draw connections where Mabel leaves one to overhear and to learn for oneself, just as Sarris must do.

"The scene was typical," the narrative opens in a Stanford University auditorium with Mabel indirectly lecturing on medicine baskets. What do you hear and remember, she teases the students, do you have any insights? The opening sentence is the atypical "typical" setup. The audience is academic, still they dangle questions before the honorary Ivy League Sucking Doctor. So the key themes are laid down in the first few pages: Dream, Spirit, medicine, basketry, lineage, where people come from, who they are, how they talk, coy secrecy and slant humor.

How will Sarris tell her story? "Do it so *you* remember," Mabel tells Greg when elsewhere the tape recorder breaks in the field. Watch and listen. Record her interacting with others. Quote her directly.

"What do you do for poison oak?" a student asks.
"Calamine lotion," she says deadpan. (*MM* 1)

Mabel's no-talk is direct evidence of her evasively engaging humor, Natively embedded wisdom. The audience must think for itself. "It's no such a thing art. It's spirit," she insists on her training. "I only follow my Dream. That's how I learn." Imagine a Stanford audience practicing that formula in civil engineering or constitutional law.

She prays to plants for herbal medicine, but whether plants talk to each other, she can't say. "Why should I be listening?" The abbreviated one-liner is a strategy of tacit truth-telling, not to mention reticent contact. No wonder the indirection, given the history of ecological appropriation and forced acculturation, federal assimilation and religious hypocrisy that pockmarks her history with California non-Indians.

What You Learn

You have to learn many bad things
so you know what to do when the time comes . . .
—Mabel McKay

The muse is never verbose, Native or otherwise, seldom speaking in "our" tongue. Skeptics see the disruptive spirit as possessed, demon rather than Greek *daemon* or visionary "genius." Nevertheless Tiresias riddled Oedipus, who blindly outsmarting the advice, fell down on three legs. T. S. Eliot's Thunder says *Da* in the Sanskrit wasteland voices of God, where lyric acolytes shape meaning out of need: *give, sympathize, and control*. Pomo-Wintu spirit-granny all the coastal way out west, Mabel could be reticent daughter to Momaday's Kiowa grandmother Aho, wise niece to Welch's Blackfoot Old Lady, offstage sister to Erdrich's dark twin Eli in the Ojibwe woodlands, adoptive mother to Harjo's Muskogee missing father. Mabel is the slant voice that hides easy access to any tribal story (some things you don't talk about, the old ones chide). Her words are cryptically encoded in common sayings. *Ravens are widows*, as the elder Apache say to Basso. Mabel's ways only obliquely reference a reader's curiosity. *White man is a carrion beetle.*

Crypted script is incisively American. Recall Emerson's epigrams, or Abe Lincoln's Gettysburg Address written on the back of an envelope, riding a train to the blood-stained battlefield. Geronimo spoke to the point, and Cochise said in surrender, "I speak straight and do not wish to deceive or be deceived" (A. N. Ellis, "Reflections of an Interview with Cochise," in Nabokov, *Native American Testimony* 177). Through all these male speeches, the women stood smiling with tearful eyes. At times they might laugh stoically, courageously, silently to themselves.

Native women have been left to care for home and children, to defend the heartland against the final onslaught when the shooting stops and the culture-soul-and-land-stealing begins. Mabel takes Greg to the old Wintu graveyard, past the ancient oak above the creek, past the No Trespassing sign on the barbed-wire fence, past the mattress springs and junked refrigerator and cow manure to her grandmother Sarah's unmarked burial site:

> I looked at the expanse of packed ground.
> "Well, where is Sarah's grave? There's no marker anywhere."
> "Hmm. I don't remember. Somewhere in there, though."
> I jumped out and looked around. There wasn't anything to see really. A warm breeze blew, and I could hear the low-running creek below. A lone cow bellowed in the distance.
> "I can't see anything," I said, getting into the car.
> "Oh," Mabel said, as if I had just mentioned what I had eaten for breakfast.
> I looked out at the empty ground. "So this is where it ended for Grandma Sarah Taylor," I said.
> Then all at once, Mabel burst into laughter. Not her light chuckle, but loud raucous laughing. She was looking at me sideways. I wondered what I had said or done that was so funny. How was she going to make fun of me this time? Then I heard it.
> "No," she said, barely able to contain her laughter. "Grandma didn't end here. She didn't die here. She's just buried here. Who ever heard of a person dying in a cemetery? Well, I guess they could. It's a good idea, anyway. Is that what you learn in the school?"
> "No," I answered. (*MM* 33)

No, people don't die in cemeteries—Sarris gets the point—they die when others forget them. Mabel was abandoned by her mother Daisy and deadbeat father Hanta Boone. No less than her scribe, she was "took-in" as an orphan by her grandmother Sarah Taylor. Childless, Mabel adopted her sister's son Marshall, and was in turn adopted across Pomo tribal boundaries by Essie Parrish as a Dreamer Religion sister. The *adoptive* tribal signifier red-lines life stories from Momaday and Welch through Erdrich and Hogan: family becomes what a child makes of it, an active not a passive identity. Just so, tribal belonging is deciding to act on lineage and history and need. An orphaned, abandoned Indianness—junked cemetery plots to racial dismissals of darker-skinned "diggers"—re-roots its Native self in a homeland base, a cultural history, a sense of ancestry and posterity, a spiritual calling thousands of years ancestral. Mabel seeks to weave the people back into the tribal Dream through Native basketry and hands-on medicine and local stories—coil the lifelines together, weave the connective patterns, feather the nest anew for flight, beauty, and song in the people's lives. Look at the hand weaving a coiled basket on the title page, or go see one of her exquisite feather baskets in the Smithsonian, or San Francisco's de Young Fine Arts Museum entrance. Universally, Mabel's story suggests that people find themselves as relatives in one another's story, all humans interrelated, back to First Man and First Woman.

People learn these things by listening to others tell their stories—or not, as the case may be—then watching and making up the story truly. *You have to listen*, the old one says, *to know me*. Listen actively, participate in the storytelling, as in call-and-response oral traditions. No proscenium, no pit. All are interactive and participant in the retelling of tribal lore and legend. Mabel's story is less lyric leaping (though the songs are crucial) than narrative *under*standing, getting down into the ethnic grounding and spiritual core of tribally related being.

Sarris learns to catch Mabel's character in her diminutive bearing, her dark coloring, her dyed and coiffed hair, her flower-print mauve dress, her modish shoes, spectacled eyes, and pursed mouth. The things around Mabel characterize her specifically: Benson and Hedges cigarettes, K-Mart medicine bag, feather basketry with rules, cannery apples, patent-leather purse, plastic African-violet corsage. Her quietness and waiting and mumbling *Hmmm* and *Oh* and *Oh my* give Greg indirections to read her nonverbally. A deeper listening goes on: tricky rules to living, critical interweavings of lives, generations, hopes, bitterness, and dreams. This is an act of narrative listening, imagining through acute hearing—seeing the story unfold through fleshed-out characters, catching their voices, reconstructing setting and scene to tell their stories (requiring for Sarris, the Stanford doctoral student, several years of California Indian research in archives and libraries, documented in *Keeping Slug Woman Alive*).

Despite the hard scholarly digging, the text is not fancy. In Mabel's worldview *you don't make up nothing*. As Linda Hogan says, it *dreams you through*. The Dream informs everything, spirit voices from childhood, intuition and improvisation in the arts of living—watching and waiting and listening for clues to how things are and how to do things. "See how it turns out," the spirits tell Mabel. Learn by observing, listening, thinking, modeling. Join in the story, stranger; the world does not explain itself. Interpret what you hear, and judge for yourself.

What will you say about me? Mabel challenges her young writer. Better let characters themselves tell the story, since the story tells her, rather than the other way around. Sarris discovers his and her voice in the telling, an out-line as it were *in* the circling narrative. Her story becomes his story, and all stories are interwoven by the Dream behind everything (text, as cited, *textus* or "woven"). A religious conviction, a faith pure and simple, keeps Mabel going and empowers her to weave baskets collected by the Smithsonian, to heal others up and down California, to dance the Charleston and can apples in Sebastopol, to clean a San Francisco brothel and set up a booth at the county fair. She's willing to meet the Pope at Happy Steak if he wants to come all this way to talk.

Mabel is the moral touchstone of Native scant telling. Her voice sets the gently laconic tone, her pitch *Hmmm* and her rhythm *Oh* or *Oh my*. People actually talk this way—not proper, but real—syllables true to life. A real-life, life-giving, life-sustaining dialogue with this world or the next. Less syntax and grammar than candor, to-the-point monosyllables. No art, all Spirit. Know me, she repeats; tell my story.

Talk's cheap in the free seats. Preverbal knowing is instinctual wisdom. A child crawls and walks before knowing the words, breathes without thinking, opens its eyes and suckles without being told how or why. Native wisdom and natural ways are not sentimentally regressive, as more urbane critics might charge, but primally astute, catching on, Natively acute. For sure, people waste a lot of time making time talking, especially academics. After all, what's important to humans, things or each other? Keep what you know to yourself, the old ones whisper, until the right time, the right audience, the right need to know—then tell the true life story. Like fruit, judgment ages in time to maturity.

And what do elder Natives know that the younger lack? *Age with grace and beauty*, the Navajo say of the highest human good. Keep quiet and pay attention, Mabel says. Old people know time-tested intelligence to avoid the wrong choices, hence their cautionary tales to the young of blind alleys, quick fixes, long shots, and misleading shortcuts. Learn from the mistakes of those going before. Old ones have perspective: the bifocal view of what works over time, a sense of priority and proportion about what matters most, the big picture of life, death, and the living in between. Old people have empathy for the lives of others, the virtue of knowing many human beings, the pain of losing more than their share, still surviving all the falls. They have the patience to wait, to think, to feel things. They know the time it takes to know anything. Elders learn humility in the face of mortality, the afterlife of a splintered ego, the many losses and gains, the powers greater than self.

Old ones gather the collective historical experience of many others gone before them, as with Aho and Ko-sahn in *The Way to Rainy Mountain*. All those ancestors collate into one ongoing story with each life telling itself. Their wisdom is seasoned, ripened, ready to be passed on as the cultural fiber of what nurtures people and lasts tribally. Grandchildren embody promise to them, the future incarnate, animate, ongoing. Perhaps most importantly, age understands critical timing: how and when to do something. It's not just what a person knows, but how someone knows and uses that knowledge in process—as Lulu knows in *Love Medicine*, when to show your cards, or hold or fold them. Where to open a hand or to close or to stand pat. The old Na'pi-Kipi'taki wisdom of Yellow Calf in *Winter in the Blood* respects withholding until the right moment, the mortal edge of honesty, the candor of facing and for the moment surviving neglect or catastrophic death.

Age knows the time needed to tell real stories. Storytellers know the need for someone to pay attention. "She [Mabel] talked about listening," Sarris says in *News from Native California* 1988, "the way she talked about knowing and following rules" ("Conversations with Mabel McKay" 4). Or as Sarris quotes Essie Parrish, her Pomo sister in the Bole Maru roundhouse and healing ceremonies: "Don't just take these things I am talking about and put them away. Don't drop them here and there like old clothes. Search yourselves, in your lives, for the meaning" ("Conversations" 6). And old ones truly have mother wit. They laugh for the right reasons. In the seams of mortality they know things. They know not to, they know why and why not, as far as possible—and then the elders trust and pray for guidance from the Spirits. The same holds collectively true for older or cooler cultures, as Marshall McLuhan would say, cultures that have lasted over time from Asia to Native America. By all estimates, the Pomo-Wintu peoples have been stable in north-central California for seven thousand years. They may know things that more recent émigrés miss.

> "Books can't tell *you* everything," Mabel scolds. "*You* can't learn about it just from a book."
>
> "I know," Sarris protests. "But people won't know about this. It will all be forgotten. No one will be around to tell them."
>
> "Yes, because people don't listen." ("Conversations" 3)

Know me

A world of white people and strangers.
New world that was no world.

—Sarris, *Mabel McKay: Weaving the Dream*

Poetry draws readers into the paint, prose to the picture. Narrative words here serve as transparencies readers see through—not a medium, or stated message even, so much as passing messenger, that is, a voice that tells the story and does not intrude between reader and character. The story does the talking, the seeing and hearing. For Mabel the Dream is all, silently narrating, the unspeakable truth that the Spirits work through—not words over-voicing dreams so much as incandescent images that convey thought immediately. Old-time basket patterns are dreamed naturally: *deer-teeth, crow-foot, bat-wing*. Mabel's diction is minimal, the rhythms elemental, no artifice or distracting metaphor, no metric cadencing that calls attention to the poetic feet, at least not noticeably. "The scene was typical." Mabel on an ordinary college day turns the tables on academic certainty, inscrutably reversing the field. Don't so much *tell* about her telling, Sarris learns to trust indirect presentation—watch how she *does* the scene. Mabel withholds direct answers to get people thinking. Indeed, poetry never explains itself but elicits response, so there may be a deeper lyric link with Pomo narrative.

Sarris writes in generally unraveling prose sequences, moderately sayable sentences that unwind naturally—a narrator caught up in telling story as discovering character through plot, even if Mabel defies plot linearity. The narrative pulls up short when a point is to be made, as in Mabel's opening statement, *You have to know me to know what I'm talking about.* Sarris is often at a loss to say anything conclusive. "What Dreamer? What spiritual person? What Lolsel? What people?. . . . A world of white people and strangers. New world that was no world. Why, then, this child in a place that was not home?" (*MM* 22). The orphan question, indeed a tribal dislocation question, haunts the entire story. The narrator himself doesn't "know *who* or *what* I was"—Mexican, Indian, or Black perhaps. His illegitimate father is listed on the Sebastopol birth certificate as "unknown non-White," and his mother, dead from mismatched blood after giving birth, is buried under a lying horseshoe in a pauper's grave. She was falsely eulogized by her blue-blood mother as fallen from a horse (*MM* 47). Well, Sarris later tells his uncle, here's the horse.

Talk's easy, as most people know. Sarris must earn the story, feed the basket of rules, live honestly by the spirit, in order for the Dream culture to continue with healers and dancers moving, rattles and clappers going, behind it all Mabel lowing, "Ooooh, oooh, oooh." The Dream music is unscripted—no text, no precepts, no tablets, no teachings. These lyrics are not parsable so much as they give spirit to interjective prayers. The Dream dreams people all together, and in telling about each other people discover collective stories. Watch and learn, keep powers and poisons to yourself, use them when needed, and only then. All script is translation, Borges says—from preliterate silent spirits, to speaking in second-language tongues and writing things down.

The theme, then, seems to be the Estranged Bastard Coming Home. "Get in here," Essie's daughter Violet says to Greg inside her trailer, "and quit acting like a stranger" (*MM* 138). Where and who people *come from* is key, why they may be "took-in" a saving grace. Sarris's illegitimate lineage to Tom Smith and Richard Taylor ("roads going everywhere, even to the moon," *MM* 16) means that all are finally related, all spirited, all healers of the tribal ongoing. As the "took-in" Lipsha says in *Love Medicine*, "Belonging was a matter of deciding to," no less than Momaday's blue-eyed Mexican captive great-great-grandmother Kau-au-ointy rose to cattle-and-horse-herding power among the Kiowa. Remember that Mabel herself was abandoned by her Wintu mother Daisy, raised by her grandmother Sarah Taylor, and adopted across tribal/lingual lines by her Pomo sister Essie Parrish, making her a co-leader in the deep-rooted Bole Maru, an underground chapter of the Ghost Dance resistance to White encroachment.

Sarris learns quickly that he cannot legitimize a story or lineage through artistic language, book talk, or academic filler. The Spirits choose the words, the rules show, so writer stay out of the way. Tell a people's story, storyteller, not so much a biography. All is collaborative. Humans are made up by the Dream. Words and stories don't "make" art, but *connect* with the Spirits, as in the PIE root *ar*. The Dream finds people when they're ready to listen. Careful, listener, bad spirits are out there too, along with false teachers, seducers, sorcerers, ethnocentrics, abusers, exploiters. Let lyric narrative be that which convinces a reader, draws a listener into the character and principles at stake—daily integrity, personal honesty, earned kinship, spirit dreaming, attentive living, laughing in the face of devastating odds, and surviving—persisting at all cost.

Mabel and Essie dig sedge roots by a stream near a cemetery, one day to be inundated by dammed waters, a scene that sets all the scenes.

Listen to the traditional pentameter and hexameter rhythms, seamlessly interwoven, that course through the narrative to cadence and score the moment (my metric lineation):

> *That afternoon* they *drove east down* the *moun*tain /
> to *dig sedge a*long *Dry Creek.* / The *creek* was *low,*
> and the *sandy soil* was *still moist* from the *spring rains.* /
> They *found* a *patch* of *ground* where the *digging would*
> be *good,* / where the *fibrous sedge roots grew straight* and
> *long un*der the *sand.* / They *sat down* with their *handpicks*
> and *garden trowels* and be*gan work*ing. / They *worked* a
> *long time, dig*ging and *cut*ting, *piling* / *wet soggy roots*
> on *newspap*ers and *gunnysacks.* / *When* they *took* a *break,*
> sitting *back* and *drink*ing / *warm cof*fee in *plastic cups*
> from the *tops* of their *ther*mos *bottles,* / Essie *told a*bout
> her *Dream.*
>
> "They're *going* to *build* a *dam here one day soon.* /
> *Where* we're *sit*ting will be *hund*reds of *feet un*der *wa*ter. /
> This *last good sedge-pick*ing *place* will *be* no *more.*"
>
> *Mabel knew* to be*lieve Essie, just* as she *knew* to
> be*lieve* / what *Essie* had *said a*bout her *own end* on *earth,*
> a*bout lock*ing / the *roundhouse.* But *sitting there* in that
> *afternoon spring sun,* / Mabel *felt* some*thing time*less,
> *end*less, *something* fa*mil*iar and for*ev*er / *a*bout *dig*ging
> *roots by* the *wa*ter with a*nother wo*man.
>
> (*MM* 111–12)

We know the horrible truth of urban devastation across a natural watercourse. Yet beyond tragic loss, women gather tribal medicine roots to heal the people—a river of history diverted by invasive technology, a pure wellspring of tribal headwaters that are no more. The sedge medicine roots will be drowned, and there will be an epidemic of drugs and drinking and intercultural poisons. What scholars call "internalized oppression" will inundate postcolonial Native peoples, especially the men. Still, the rhythmic sodality holds "timeless, endless," and there is "something familiar and forever" that Dreams the story of two elder women gathering medicine roots by the water on a warm spring afternoon. No dates here; this is "forever" time, as Mabel says from the start, innately ceremonial and natural. And the iambic-hearted sisters dig medicine roots in the face of the imminent and ongoing holocaust of their people's ways. Women persist. Trust the Dream, the Spirit, the ancestral ceremonies, the story encourages, as natural watercourse ways to live well together. There is no other way in the face of all that has happened and will come to pass. Trust.

A Scott Patterson photograph of Mabel collecting sedge during the construction of the Warm Springs Dam on Dry Creek in Sonoma Country, 1978, made the California newspapers and fronted *News from Native California* in 1988—inside, more Mabel photographs and a Sarris conversation. In the dam protest, Mabel is photographed before a massive yellow Euclid earthmover, half the size of its front tire. Mabel looks straight on, hair dyed and coiffed, glasses level, mouth slightly down-turned in something of a smile. Her shoulders are squared, feet firmly grounded. Behind her leaf-print paisley blouse, the number 8–536 is stenciled on the dozer fender. Sarris weaves this historic portrait into his biographical narrative, underscoring the primal sedge-digging scene: "The photo appeared everywhere, in calendars, on museum walls, splashed on leaflets announcing American Indian and environmentalist meetings and events. The picture made a statement, and Mabel was glad of it. But that day at Dry Creek, amid the noise of busy people and hovering helicopters, she thought of Essie, of the quiet time she and Essie sat digging sedge on that warm afternoon in spring" (*MM* 126–27). Two adoptive sisters by time's deep-rooted medicine waters carry "something familiar and forever," a shared timelessness. This sodality is a convincing touch of feminine sentiment through the story.

STORY BASKETS

Roads going everywhere, even to the moon.
—Sarris, *Mabel McKay: Weaving the Dream*

Mabel teaches through character modeling. Setting an example helps her adopted scribe learn their people's story, no less than Aho teaches her grandson Scott through Kiowa legend, or Lulu shows Lipsha how to crimp a card: a granny healer, a go-and-see way of doing things. This is old-time thinking where the young learn by listening, looking, and parsing things. From Lao Tsu's simplicity, Homer's directness, Christ's candor, or Grampa Tom Smith prophesying, protecting, and healing the Pomo, look for the right advice, how to go about things to do. Mabel's "basket has rules," and Greg must find and figure them out. Too easy to tell, too easy to do.

The scientific premise here, let alone moral issue, insists that nature has implicit rules. God does not show His hand or play bones with the universe. Humans evolve from nature's ways and must keep those ways natural. Don't go against nature's flow. Respect the elders as you respect tribal history. Humble yourself and seek the wisdom of the ancients, the way found in going. *Caminante, no hay camino / Se hace camino al andar*: the Mexican poet Antonio Machado left his own tomb epitaph. "Walker, there is no way, / You make the way by walking." Be careful. Be considerate. Be respectful. Be thoughtful. Behave, there's a long red road going on.

Mabel's baskets are the icons of her life-teachings. Keeping things for future need, baskets store *stores* ("stories" as chapter floors for *telling* storage). The rounded container is not so much crafted object as functional space within. Basketry implies gathering, grouping, containing more than one "thing," hence the variety and natural orders of nature. And so, storytelling is tribal basketry. The finest Pomo woven sedge basket, beautifully useful, would hold water and cook food.

The Pomo still make coiled basketry with spherical designs—a "line" that turns back and over on itself in patterned circularity, conical repetition with a difference—always a pattern break called *dau, ham,* or *hwa,* Alfred Kroeber notes, or the basket maker fears going blind (Heizer, *The California Indians*). The baskets are handmade from natural materials: root, bark, and branch decorated with bird feathers. These baskets could tell stories and sing, as implied in their picturing names: *turtle-neck, quail-plume, sunfish-rib, killdeer-eyebrow, goose-excrement, grasshopper-elbow.* Storytelling as basketry became a way to harvest the ancestral past for posterity's future. Fertile Crescent tribes 12,000 years ago settled in Nile Valley places where they could bury their dead and store their grain to survive winter, as documented in Lewis Mumford's *The City in History*. Paleo-Indians were well established by this time all over the Western Hemisphere.

Storytelling is ancient basketry. Moses was found in a bulrush basket. The stuttering prophet listened to the burning bush and received the petroglyphic Ten Commandments, parted the Red Sea and stood on Mount Pisgah over the Promised Land. Carriers of the dream wheel begin as mother cradlers. *A tisket, a tasket, a green and yellow basket*—nursery rhyme and rhythm allow children to remember when they lay coiled in carriers close to their mothers. As natural basketry, a bird's nest is the perfect cupped or *breasted* home for raising young ones. Women have long carried their work in burden baskets, water baskets,

cooking baskets, bread baskets, green-grocer baskets, laundry baskets—
even bags, bookbags, and satchels today, no less than Mabel's K-Mart
plastic shopping bag of medicines and ubiquitous patent-leather purse—
protecting, transporting, clothing, feeding, paying for, and cleaning up
after kith and kin.

Mabel's Pomo baskets are woven from natural stalks, barks, and fibers—
centrifugal coil basketry from sedge root, willow rod, and redbud bark,
often decorated with mallard, meadowlark, or robin feathers. Completing
itself as a basket rim, this centrifugal pattern centripetally returns spring
strawberries and autumn acorns to the people gathering them ceremoni-
ously. And the small, eraser-head, prayer-basket rulebook that Mabel pins
on Greg—his tribal diploma—condenses her teachings in a guardian icon
powerful as bear or eagle, prescient as hawk or lynx, solid as stone or rooted
tree. Recall the diminutive Aho, and *ahó* or "thanks" in Kiowa. Mabel's
Dream of the Great Spirits for all—a grandmother's basket for all times in
life closely pinned to him—silently reminds Sarris of the maternal ways that
will keep him well and healthy, writing down tribal stories. More than professor, filmmaker, or Gratton Band of Miwok-Pomo tribal chair building a
casino, this is his narrative role in the present history of California Indians.
In some good sense, writing a book weaves a prayer basket. As evolving cultural basketry, the book opens to stored, that is *storied* food, art, history,
morality, spirit, and medicine. People know how to *do* these arts of survival
with the right words ancestrally passed down.

Baskets are maternal carriers and open containers within, just as
a woman's body is bearer, cavity, or protector. Food is gathered, water
transported, infants cradled, medicine carried, the future stored in nests,
stones, sun, moon, stars, solar and lunar cycles, as imaged in Momaday's
Carriers of the Dream Wheel, or Silko's mythic verse insets, or Black
Elk's discussion of Native circles. A prayer basket can be imagined, Spirit
given, a spatial poem dreamed from nature's tools. *Weaving the dream*
comes from instinct and observation, watching others make their weavings, stories, and songs. No verbiage intrudes between the Dreamer's
instinct and chanting the basketry (weaving and singing often overlap
tribally): see to do, listen to speak, hear to sing-dance. The weaver-storier
is apprenticed in trial-and-error craft, modeling individual basketry and
dream narrative with respect for time and tradition gone before.

The Pomo have "baskets of songs for everything" (Sarris, Santa Fe
Bread Loaf talk, 25 June 2003). The best songs and stories mark the richest
members: songs for making acorn mush, sex songs, healing songs, tired
songs, thirsty songs, tree songs, animal songs, protection songs that are

traded, bought, and sold. The keeper has to feed and water a song, just as the basket's rules must be talked to and honored. No singer without a listener, no storyteller without an audience: these traditions are the cultural cache of tribal living, the relating pine pitch.

Stanford Graduation weaves everyone together. It's not just an academic affair, but a *powwow*, as in the old Algonkian meaning of the word—everybody coming together "to make medicine" as extended tribal family. Sarris knows "all the gutter snipe, the lost Indians," Essie's daughter Violet parochially scolds him outside the Ukiah Foster's Freeze. "Greg, I don't know how you know *those* people" (*MM* 57). Half of him isn't white, he knows, and the other half isn't talking. Spirit story collates them all at the end:

> Friends were there. Faculty. And family. Lots of family. Jews.
> Catholics. Filipinos. Mexicans. Indians. Violet. Anita and
> her children. Violet's middle sister, Vivien, and her children.
> Marshall and his family. Grandpa Hilario and his niece Amparo
> and her children and their children. My Indian grandmother's
> sister's daughter, Marguerite, and her daughter, Velia, and her
> daughter and son from Los Angeles. Mary and her brother
> Vance and his family, her sister Joan and her family, and her
> brother Jack's family. Mary's son, my brother Steve. Howard
> Hartman. On and on. Abundant food. Congratulations. I gave a
> brief talk. Something about family and how we were all related.
> I said I thought my mother, Bunny, and my father, Emilio, would
> be proud. So would Mabel. She had always been there along the
> way for me. I missed her. (*MM* 160)

Each name, family connection, racial and ethnic division, relation is cited as a distinct unit of prayer and thanks—a dedicatory tribute as extended-kin roll call back to Achilles' shield in Homer. There's something of the Roman Catholic blessing and gratitude, a rosary touching of each bead in the woven necklace, tribally acknowledging *All My Relatives*. The anaphoric listing also points with respect to the elders and those who *helped out*, as the rez saying has it back home—a pointillist catalogue of nonheroic helpers who make up life and accomplishments. *I am related*, Greg Sarris can finally say, stepping forth, a true graduation ceremony (Latin *gradus*, a step). The individual finds his family tribe, the stranger returns as a *special friend*, the Pomo say, through adoptions. The homeless street kid of unknown origins—a punk, a tough, a hoodlum at times—comes home as "Cousin Professor" to milk and cookies with his adoptive granny healers and their kin. Defenses drop ("Put your hands down," *MM* 167). Borders prove porous, boundaries permeable, orphans adoptable, most everyone lovable. Genders can be crossed, race and culture miscegenated with integrity—in the Sarris case ("unknown non-white" father) poverty bridges into Tidewater blue blood, politics pluralize as tribal interconnections. A free and democratic American promise still-in-process, it's equality and coming together worth waiting for, worth writing about.

Mabel's story is where Greg Sarris got his true start. The short stories in *Grand Avenue* fictionally extend Mabel McKay's life story and milieu with outtakes into the Santa Rosa community. The novel *Watermelon Nights* backfills Mabel's life and circles her time generationally, with a Sarris-surrogate Johnny Severe telling the first section in the recent past and present, a Mabel-sister Elba Gonzales narrating the second part early in the past century, and an acculturated niece figure of the 1950s, Mrs. Iris Pettyjohn, speaking the third. The illegitimacies of racism, homophobia, xenophobia, class warfare, high art, low brow, and talking stink come clean in these stories. "Why call they me bastard?" Shakespeare's Edmund pleads his case, "nature has no bastards" (*King Lear*).

The issues boil down to the orphan bastard coming home to family and friends—a tribal belonging and cultural, indeed historical, challenge. The illegitimate *divine child*—as Keryenyi, Hall, and Jung have written—comes to society strangely, the outsider a leader (Christ, Mohammed, Buddha, Krishna as illegitimates). In some respects people are all outside the tribe, orphans to a chosen family inside cultural walls (Heathcliff or Hester or Huck Finn), until they find their adoptive stories in the histories of others. History includes a composite retelling of each other's lives, a mutual narrating of one another. Culture involves experiential dialogue, Bakhtin argues; no speaker is alone—always an implied audience, an other self to talk to. No child is unrelated. *All my relatives* exist somewhere, an extended kinship for all the tribes. No blood runs purely exclusive of other blood, regardless of skin color, pedigree, or social caste (unlike decaffeinated coffee or skim milk, blood is not half-blood when diluted or mixed). No culture stands isolated from any other. Kin should marry out, not in, as the Kokopelli icons suggest healthy mix as hybrid fusion. Captives and cousins, all sluice into other cultures at the mix-and-match margins of exogamy (endogamy threatens lethal inbreeding).

The question seems to be how people remain culturally unified while evolving and hybridizing. Culture, like water, turns to poison when static. Remaining tribally legitimate is not a matter of form, but evolving genetic fusions, bearing the DNA codes of the past and cultural values changing into the future. And in some sense, as with languages back to Eden and Babylon, dispersion works back to fusion. English is now spoken by four-fifths of the world, for better or worse. The loss of Native languages—down to perhaps fifty in the country, functionally speaking—alarms cultural survivalists who feel that culture is speech; yet Americans still evolve multilingually and cross-culturally, as in most of Europe and much of the world.

The Spirits willing, one day there might be a global reconciliation on issues of peace and justice, democratic distribution of resources and food, communal care through medicine and social assistance, shareable translations of song and story into poetry and prose. The tribal heart holds out for peaceable union. People maintain their ongoing cultural sense of self in telling locally specific stories: Who humans are as families and extended kin. Where people come from in the landscape of time. What happened to the ancestors. How what happens to everyone is happening. Why what's happening to the children matters. When people find themselves telling the stories of others.

> "Why did you do it for me?" Greg asks Mabel at the end of her narrative life. "Why'd you do so much for me? Why me?"
> She looks at him straight on. "Because you kept coming back." (*MM* 165)

Mabel McKay's amanuensis addressed the San Francisco Jewish Community Center, 15 May 2005, on "Culture and Memory: What Has Been Lost? What Can Be Recovered?"

> I have identified my primary community—and have been billed as such—as an American Indian. I am also Jewish and Filipino. Oh, and I was raised Catholic. Yes, it seems to me that I indeed must take and learn from those shared histories, but not without braiding them to my Coast Miwok and Southern Pomo heritage and place. They meet, indistinguishable in my blood, as I, and as all of us, must be to the land. I must think like the old timers, my Coast Miwok and Southern Pomo ancestors. That is, I must think of and consider all of us. I need to say my primary community is the future . . .
> If not, won't it be true that in forty-some years our discussions today—about diaspora, holocaust, memory, what is

recoverable and what isn't—will look like a mere tea party under a hailstorm?

Sometimes I feel like a motherless child, the American spiritual goes, *a long way from home*. The old tunes may still tenor the best stories.

Amazing grace—how sweet the sound—
That saved a wretch like me.
I once was lost, but now am found,
Was blind, but now I see.

Medicine Word Warriors

Linda Hogan and Sherman Alexie

> The Swampy Cree say stories live in the world, may
> choose to inhabit people, who then have the option
> of telling them back out into the world again. This all
> can form a symbiotic relationship: if people nourish a
> story properly, it tells things about life. The same with
> dreams. And names.
>
> —Howard Norman, *Who Met the Ice Lynx*

SMALL QUICKENINGS

> Perhaps "between" was, is,
> at the root of my very existence.
>
> —Linda Hogan, *The Woman Who
> Watches Over the World*

Linda Hogan traces her evolutionary Native kinship through mixed bloods
to endangered animals—slaughtered whales, trapped wolves, skinned
bears, sacrificed caribou, scavenger crows. Sutured in the scars of history,
her personal views of Indian evolution, more healing than judging, fuse
with contemporary feminist and biospheric reckonings. This woman's
voice spans tribes and traditional lands, racial and sexual schisms, Native
and Moral Majority fissures. She overlays Darwin with Joseph Campbell,
quotes Loren Eiseley next to Luther Standing Bear. Bringing natural science into a narrative layered with human myth, Hogan seeks a language of
reparation and quickened listening. "Perhaps there are events and things

that work as a doorway into the mythical world," she muses in her collected essays *Dwellings*, "the world of first people, all the way back to the creation of the universe and the small quickenings of earth, the first stirrings of human beings at the beginning of time" (19).

The core thesis of evolutionary biology today, symbiogenesis or serial endosymbiosis theory (SET), refines Darwin's natural selection to advance species as a fusional, rather than fissional model. Pioneering microbiologist Lynn Margulis writes of collaborative adaptation in *Acquiring Genomes: A Theory of the Origins of Species*:

> the co-opting of strangers, the involvement and infolding
> of others—viral, bacterial, and eukaryotic—into ever more
> complex and miscegenous genomes. The acquisition of the
> reproducing other, of the microbe and its genome, is no
> mere sideshow. Attraction, merger, fusion, incorporation,
> cohabitation, recombination—both permanent and cyclical—
> and other forbidden couplings, are the main sources of Darwin's
> missing variation. Sensitivity, co-optation, merger, acquisition,
> fusion, accommodation, perseverance and other capabilities
> of the microbes are not at all irrelevant to the evolutionary
> process. Far from it. The incorporation and integration of
> "foreign" genomes, bacterial and other, led to significant,
> useful heritable variation. The acquiring of genomes has been
> central to the evolutionary processes throughout the long and
> circuitous history of life. (205)

And in 2004, as cited, scientists proved that sono-fusional reactions emit light bursts of nuclear energy intense as the sun—"sono-luminosity"—through the molecular coalescence of hydrogen and oxygen particles. From elements to species so long separated, these may be naturally crossing and coming-together times.

A tribal earth caretaker, mixed-blood Chickasaw from Oklahoma, Hogan works as a spiritual zoologist. Her scientific empathy bridges ecology and native humanism. She writes in *Dwellings*, "Inside people who grow out of any land there is an understanding of it, a remembering all the way back to origins, to when the gods first shaped humans out of clay, back to when animals could speak with people, to when the sky and water were without form and all was shaped by such words as *Let there be*" (80). Linda Hogan calls to her muted ancestors in "Blessings," cited in part earlier:

Chickasaw

chikkih asachi,
they left as a tribe not a very great while ago.
They are always leaving, those people.

Blessed
are those who listen
when no one is left to speak.

Blessing voices still rise out of her damaged father's Oklahoma bottom-lands, magpies and mosquitoes, spiders and salamanders, crawdads and catfish. Blessed in stillness, blessed in attention, blessed in faith, blessed in speaking up after the silencing. In the older sense of a first language of the earth, speech is never lost on those who survive to listen. "How can we listen or see," she writes of bat sonar in *Dwellings*, "to find our way by feel to the heart of every yes or no? How do we learn to trust ourselves enough to hear the chanting of earth? To know what's alive or absent around us, and penetrate the void behind our eyes, the old, slow pulse of things, until a wild flying wakes up in us, a new mercy climbs out and takes wing in the sky?" (28). This poet listens beneath the brain's ceaseless scanning to the Native pulse that Mary Austin called an American rhythm in the land-scape: "Sometimes I hear it talking. The light of the sunflower was one language, but there are others more audible. Once, in the redwood forest, I hear a beat, something like a drum or heart coming from the ground and trees and wind. That underground current stirred a kind of knowing inside me, a kinship and longing, a dream barely remembered that disap-peared back to the body" (D 158).

COMING TO LIGHT

A fence post talks back.
—Dwellings

Hogan has grown from her early poetry in *Calling Myself Home* and *Red Clay*, through *Eclipse* and *Savings*, then broader recognition in *Seeing through the Sun* (American Book Award from the Before Columbus Foundation) and *The Book of Medicines* (finalist in National Book Critics Circle Award), and more recently two novels, *Mean Spirit*

(Pulitzer finalist in 1991) and *Solar Storms* (1995). Her collection of essays *Dwellings* (1996) preceded a third novel, *Power* (1998), about the endangered black panther. She has coedited with Carol Bruchac and Judith McDaniel *The Stories We Hold Secret: Tales of Women's Spiritual Development* (1986). With Deena Metzger and Brenda Peterson, Hogan has gathered literary and scientific essays in *Intimate Nature: The Bond Between Women and Animals* (1998), and philosophical essays, *Face to Face: Women Writers on Faith, Mysticism, and Awakening* (2004). With Brenda Peterson she has coauthored *Sightings: The Great Whale's Mysterious Journey* (2002) and coedited *The Sweet Breathing of Plants: Women Writing on the Green World* (2002). She has published a post-traumatic memoir, *The Woman Who Watches Over the World* (2001), a tribal history with Jeannie Barbour, Amanda Cobb, and David Fitzgerald *Chickasaw: Unconquered And Unconquerable* (2006), and is collaborating on a study of interspecies connections to be called *Between Species*. The poet-essayist-novelist-naturalist has received distinguishing support from the Newberry Library, the Guggenheim Foundation, Yaddo Colony, National Endowment for the Arts, Five Civilized Tribes Playwriting Award, and a Lannan Fellowship. Hogan has settled into teaching at the University of Colorado, where she received an MFA decades before.

Linda Hogan's Irish-American grandmother was an immigrant Nebraska pioneer, her Chickasaw grandfather an Oklahoma horseman. This fusional poet gathers the *native* of her mixed American bloodlines into a singular voice with a gentle humor and graceful imagery. Native verse in Hogan's hands is picked clean. She writes ecological lyrics, grace notes that signal animal crossings and contemplative flights. A reader does not parse these lines so much as ponder them, carefully, quietly, like contemplating stone runes, game paths, star patterns, or lunar cycles. Hogan tries hard to make her poems not sound formally poetic. No end rhymes, no blank verse or syllabic metrics, no stanzaic forms, no big metaphors or grand ideas—lines stripped to essential thought, obliquely slanted, broken-cadenced, elemental as stones in a streambed. A line hangs bone-clean, often bent-kneed, bare and beautifully lean, with the light of awakened consciousness all around it.

> We have stories
> as old as the great seas
> breaking through the chest
> flying out the mouth,
> noisy tongues that once were silenced,

all the ocean's we contain
coming to light.

The poet-essayist works to mend broken connections, reconnecting tribal *arm* to Native *art*. All her relatives are scattered among Chickasaw cousins and westering pioneers, her adopted Lakota daughters Tanya Thunder Horse and Sandra Dawn Protector rescued from toxic broken homes. So, too, as a working naturalist she nurtures wounded raptors back to health and grieves the biospheric desecration of Native land. Her essays meditate gently, forgivingly on frontier atrocities and pioneer arrogations of tribal homelands. She writes as elder women like Mabel McKay tell their lives to succeeding generations, their griefs blossoming in compassionate acceptance, the seasoned heart's forgiveness. This is not born-again sentiment, but sentient faith and sensible reason. Hogan lives the crossings that Silko fictionalizes in Tayo's journey home, that Sarris and Harjo make literature of positively—the misfit mestizo displaced among her kin, globally shell-shocked, praying for peace internally and internationally.

DARWINIAN INDIAN

Can we love what will swallow us when we are gone?
—Dwellings

A fusionist seeks a unified field of hard facts and receptive hearts in America's mixed cultures, the divided arts and sciences. Hogan wonders how to reconcile the specialist and the general reader, how to cross the poet and the prose writer, as a Native essayist how to speak to America at-large. Natural scientists have spanned complex detail and broader context: Charles Darwin and Marie Curie, Loren Eiseley and Jane Goodall. Richard Dawkins unravels human genetics, Stephen Gould clarifies evolution, James Watson spells out the double helix. Even Stephen Hawkings and Brian Greene write cogently of an "elegant" universe strung together by energized molecular webbing. Lynn Margulis explains a global Hypersea of coevolving microbiology. Culture and history need be no less intimidating to the poet-novelist. Charles Eastman and Ella and Vine Deloria Jr. write eloquently on the Lakota. Paula Gunn Allen and Leslie Silko shape mixed-blood essays on Laguna culture. N. Scott Momaday and Sherman Alexie fire the debate on Native culture and intertribal aesthetics. Joy Harjo climbs frontier fences, and Greg Sarris challenges disputed legitimacy.

Among all these fusional voices, Linda Hogan writes quietly, contemplating Native and American crossings in the thick fission of cultural fallout. She is a grandmother storyteller on home and heath, a scientific essayist on relatives and the wilds, an impassioned advocate on ancestral spirits and ecological warrior women. The hundred and one ribs of a golden racer snake in Oklahoma, the five beating hearts of an earthworm, bat radar as sonar location, wolf village as tribal paradigm—Hogan targets the natural daily miracles of Native life shared by all. She is a poet unafraid of populism, a novelist finely grinding a tribal axe, an interspecies essayist "listening to what speaks in the blood."

Dwellings, her naturalist essays, is subtitled *A Spiritual History of the Living World*. Land and thought—where people dwell, what they dwell on—these are personal reflections wandering instinctually through a world of biological mysteries and botanical secrets, bats and caves, mice and icebergs, wolves and cairns, praying for eagle-feather grace, an umbilical cord to her daughters. Synchronous events tie things together and draw this adoptive mother into the delicate web of global kinships. Spirit is no stranger to physiology. Sensing her way by heartfelt sound and common sense, she listens to a world speaking back like bat radar. Hogan considers a hybrid mammal flying at dusk—a hibernating poet-cousin, as Randall Jarrell elsewhere wrote for children *and* adults in *The Bat-Poet*:

> Bats hear their way through the world. They hear the sounds
> that exist at the edges of our lives. Leaping through blue twilight
> they cry out a thin language, then listen for its echo to return. It
> is a dusky world of songs a pitch above our own. For them, the
> world throws back a language, the empty space rising between
> hills speaks an open secret then lets the bats pass through, here
> or there, in the dark air. Everything answers, the corner of a
> house, the shaking leaves on a wind-blown tree, the solid voice
> of bricks. A fence post talks back. (D 25–26)

Hogan sketches travel notes in search of life-forms interdependent with human life—the simple diction of a journal entry in the field, fragments, sketches, participial phrases, thoughts on the go, notes *dashing about*, as Heather McHugh says of Dickinson's hyphenated lines. The Native naturalist sees Mayan sea turtles and flamingos in the Yucatan, reads daybook entries from Luther Standing Bear and Barry Lopez back home. Readers learn something *about* wolves in her narratives—their habits, colorations, survival intelligences, means of communication. In the poems readers *see* as wolves.

Hogan places herself between beings—translating liminal fusions, border crossings, hybrid reconciliations. She lives to remake connections, searching for legitimate treaties between Red and White gene pools, men and women loving the blend of children between them. Exogamy proves the golden rule, ethnocentric endogamy dangerous. She talks to herself, letting readers overhear musings on a world at once personal and cosmic, from adopted daughters to the threat of global holocaust, local racism to frontier atrocity, tendering wounded life-forms to selfless, heroic kindness. She is witness to a green global crisis of deforestation, species extinction, war, cruelty, and indifference. This desecrated lethal environment is rubbing out condor, carrier pigeon, bald eagle, bison, grizzly, and hundreds of species a day. Twenty percent (1,666) of the world's surviving bird species are at risk, the International Council for Bird Preservation estimates, and half the world's 30 million species will go extinct this century. Species are dying at the rate of 150,000 per year, or seventeen per hour, Jared Diamond calculates in *The Third Chimpanzee*. Aborigines asks where are "far-hearted" humans in this poisoning? Far-ranging and focused at once, using both descriptive science and narrative art, Hogan lets out personal rope to draw the reader into the scientific and cultural debates that tense the times, global warming to ethnic cleansing, deforestation to habitats for humanity. Her essayist pace is reflexive and elastic, a supple narrative contrasting with more scoured poetic lines.

CLAN OF CROSSINGS

So we make our own songs to contain these things,
make ceremonies and poems, searching for a new
way to speak, to say we want a new way to live in the
world, to say that wilderness and water, blue herons
and orange newts are invaluable not just to us, but in
themselves, in the workings of the natural world that
rules us whether we acknowledge it or not.

—Dwellings

Honed and shardlike, the poet's preoccupations run thematic and ideological, backgrounding aesthetics. As with the 12,000-year hybridization of corn from wild grass to world staple, Hogan celebrates the *metamorphoses* of growing things, evolutionary adaptations and advances. As with Minnesota wolves and bald eagles, she turns to a world of *totems*-to-be-read for signs of life informing human lives. As with bear and mountain lion, bat and porcupine, she trusts animal *guardians* for natural kinships—Cree *mistebeo* spirits protecting people out-of-sight, arms-length to the left. As with the great mammalian whales, whose offspring appear human at birth, she believes in transformative *changes*, both social and biological. Across the Continental Divide or Terra del Fuego or the frontier, she sees *crossings* as migratory quests—mountain, desert, forest, and water passages as spiritual treks. In Native American reemergence, she takes *journeys* in time, her cultural evolutions ongoing.

As the elders remember, Hogan sees humans and animals in collaborative evolution within an originally unified tribe. She practices a Darwinian Indian bioscience of the animal-in-us-all, from embryonic gills and tails and fine body hair, to the coyote behavior of teenagers, to the cat-like stealth of lovers, to bear and eagle warriors, to the warren behaviors of families and lupine clans, to the spider, snake, and turtle elders. She is a religious realist trusting the guardian spirits in this natural world, as well as the need to protect and to nurse unnaturally threatened organisms. She honors traditions, the ceremonial regards of the ancestors, daily regarded, layering the organic contexts of personal texts.

The poet practices collective art, the everyday sacraments and sayings of shared culture. Poems record story-events that keep readers going. Essays post tribal dailies. Novels chant historical sagas of human lineages. Hogan mediates the spoken song in her work, the lyric speech of everyday life. Her poetics parse the homely measures of breath, pulse, heartbeat, and pace, the vital signs and honest words of plains truth over parlor beauty. Questioning things, she steps forward in her measures freely, naturally, somewhat hesitantly. Her words are temporal lyrics by which Americans live, breathe, speak, and love the common world. In global oral traditions John Foley calls this *Ars gratia vivendi*, "art for the sake of living."

AFTER THEIR KIND

I was the wild thing
she had learned to fear.
—"Mountain Lion"

The Book of Medicines opens with a history of biological evolution, interspecies exchanges interwoven with the beginnings of language and art—all in red motifs of birth, blood, greed, lust, anger, fire, fruit, dawn, sacrifice, redskin, passion, to stop sign. Hematite colorations read as elliptical narratives on a stone wall. Ancient Greeks painted crossroad markers red, plains Lakota stained grandfather *Tunkáshila* stones red, and the Cherokees elected "red" war chiefs. Archaeologists have found a 300,000-year-old marked bison rib in caves of southern France where tribal Europeans painted running red bison on walls—"after their kind," the poet adds. Primitive hunters imaged animals with their own blood, as they were honoring the hunted animal within, compassionate totemic kinship for *Homo erectus*. Out of respect for differences, that alterity defines a first inner awakening, Native American and tribal Eurasian as one primal family: "Love, like creation / is some other order of things."

Women know the menstrual power of blood, Paula Gunn Allen argues. The poet asks whose blood flows in times of sacrifice, and for what reason among hunter or soldier, mother or artist, lover or enemy. "This life in the fire, I love it, / I want it, / this life," the red-skin poem ends in plain assertion, and opens to a section called "Hunger" with flow lines of water, milk, tears, semen, and sweat.

The monosyllabic "Fat" splats down a phonemic ring that echoes through the carved poem titles: "Bear, " "Skin," "Salt," "Map," "Drought," "Milk," "Tear," "Glass," "Drum," "Two," "Gate." Slender chinks mark the slate riprap of disconnected lines falling down the page like broken talus. "Fat" sets off a staccato litany of griefs. For a century, sperm oil, rendered from mountains of whale fat, lighted New England. "Light, Smoke, Water, Land." The smoky slaughter triggered one of many species holocausts. That blood-ocean also loosed unappeasable hunger on the land, bison to bear, animal carnage to Native rape. Estranged whalers at sea lusted for women and dreamed dolphins as mermaids to be sexually abused.

> They were like women,
> they said,
> and had their way
> with them,
> wanting to be inside,
> to drink
> and be held in
> the thin, clear milk of the gods.

This misbegotten atrocity, an ancient misreading of desire, twists out of hunger lust into male violence, abusing the living. Simple diction, wretched arrogance, and stunning lyricism lift the passage above aesthetic verse plane. Line cadences observe talk phrasing; enjambed pauses at the fragmented ends of lines abrupt an easy slide to the plosive image. The last line is Ledaen mother's milk, the nurturing feminine at the mammal's living heart, where displaced male killers batter reentry. And its mothering power is the compassion of adoptions, of caretaking the world, of holding those most vulnerable close and taking them inside. Here in her internal home, the maternal guardian is guarded by her own attempts at tenderness and understanding.

Bare and basic, these lines are constructed from the bone, fat, and gristle of wilderness anatomy. They resist poetic convention with stone-scoured diction, thin skeletal structure, absolute distillation of metaphor to the thing itself—whale, bat, bear, wolf, crow, moose, deer, coyote. As Robert Duncan said of Plato, an idea is a *thing seen*. With iconic minimalism, the line breaks encroach and erode the armature of the poem until there is slim thread left, reduced to simple nouns like *light* or *Mother* or *water*, at times turning on two syllables per line, *and fear, and rain, and fire*. Hers is a transparent diction with few tangibly active verbs, more linking verbs of apposition, transition, and placement. Art reduces to essentials, story in an image, plot as detail. Scrubbed of connectives, constellating points of reference replace metaphors. Scattered verse shards condense lyric to elements of earth, fire, flint, wood, and water.

This poet sings softly with the ghost-heart of an animal protector. An old man rubs her back with bear fat, and she dreams of starving horses eating tree bark and each other's tails. Equestrian becomes Indian victim, warrior woman a BIA-dependent mother on welfare in "Bear Fat": "I slept a hole into my own hunger / that once ate lard and bread / from a skillet seasoned with salt." Three bony dogs lead men into a cave to grow fat on bear grease and wood ash, and the dogs dream their evolutionary descent back to when they were wolves. The poet fears for her own canine wilderness, before the taming of love along with senseless killing, and so she fears love in the clumsy attempt to make wild things love her. Times ago, the old ones say, people spoke with animals, a time of mutual interdependence and interspecies understanding.

These poems turn on a startling simplicity, their directness arresting confusion or complication. Like the bison or the whale, "The bear is a dark continent," only more human, "that walks upright / like a man." Old Man Bear "lives across the thawing river," marks the poet's door with winter claws, and cries when a man shoots it.

Madness is its own country,
desperate and ruined.
It is a collector of lives.
It's a man
afraid of what he's done
and what he lives by. Safe,
we are safe
from the bear
and we have each other,
we have each other
to fear.

Our self is turned back on *it* self like the halibut's eye curving into horizon: not the wild, or the natural, or the primordial other, but "each *other* / to fear." The isolate human, a self severed from animal union, fears the "terrible other" in itself. So *ours* is a fear of our other's fear, a mixed-blood confusion between animal and human, Red and White lineage. Caught between incompatibles, the hybrid poet would be animal-human again. Fear is natural, and humans are born so. If nature is composed of fearful differences, recognizing a mutual alterity at once joins and saves people. She peers into the mountain lion's "yellow-eyed shadow of a darker fear" and sees a shared desperate shyness, turning away from the other's *other*. "I was the wild thing / she had learned to fear."

And so readers journey to a "clan of crossings," beginning with whales near Terra del Fuego, singing across the twenty-foot ocean drop that divides the western hemispheric seas. Then a reader turns to a fetal whale with human face and fingers, then to a child with vanishing gill slits (an embryonic sonogram in the first trimester shows vestigial tail, flippers, and lateral eye sockets tracing to animal-human evolution). The poet says that she "spoke across elements" to her amphibious children, swimming like horses across the river: "Dark was that water, / darker still the horses, / and then they were gone." Animal-human passages, evolutionary changes, mutations and metamorphoses make humans sea creatures on land, wild things grounded, the salt content of human bodies exactly proportionate to salt in the sea. Amphibian breeds are caught between worlds, mixed-bloods or Metis, *mesteños* or mustangs, coyotes or mutts. Hogan voices her own hybrid lament, back through creation stories and beast fables, of shape-changing growth, adaptations, acculturations—the cross-blood alchemy of the natural world "where moose becomes wolf and crow" in "Crow Law":

The temple where crow worships
walks forward in tall, black grass.
Betrayal is crow's way of saying grace
to the wolf
so it can eat
what is left
when blood is on the ground,
until what remains of moose
is crow
walking out
the sacred temple of ribs
in a dance of leaving
the red tracks of scarce and private gods.
It is the oldest war
where moose becomes wolf and crow,
where the road ceases
to become the old forest
where crow is calling,
where we are still afraid.

Line breaks are abrupt as appositions ("worships / walks"), and verbs halt before their subjects ("saying grace / to the wolf"). Anaphoric phrasings whittle the lines down to fragments ("so . . . , what . . . , when . . . , until . . . , is crow") and abbreviate lines to a personal standstill ("It is the oldest war / where . . . / where . . . / to . . . / where . . . / where we are still afraid"). Narrative fracture places the reader zoomorphically inside moose, wolf, and crow. Hers is a poetry of broken kinship, of muted crowing. The shamanic black raptor calls through stripped ribs, lost bone fragments, no/things left but longing, isolation, and need. Aching from hunger, the call may not call back, starving and silent in natural laws of necessity.

Tooth-and-claw necessity is "why war is only another skin," the next poem knows, "and why men are just the pulled back curve of the bow." The hunter's misfortune is to be hungry; his arching need bows a tension to kill, for the deer's "hide / of light" to become, finally, human skin. The hunter is his own prey, the wound a bow of its own internal healing, the sacrificed animal-human. A staggering lyricism shutters forward in matter-of-fact narrative, bunching along in tufts of words turned into light—men in "the pulled back curve of the bow"—the focal mythic perception. In *Dwellings* the poet narrates it simply: "we are the wounders and we are the healers" (151). The classic wound in the bow, Homer to Hogan, seems the apt image to conclude an interspecies parable of understanding the hunt through the artless art of candor, concision, and credibility.

Which leads to the hollow virtue *Te* of "Bamboo," the first Chinese writing scratched on shells, then etched bones, then scored bamboo. "Lord, are you listening to this? / Plants are climbing to heaven / to talk to you." "Map" maps the world's touching words, ice sister to water, salt brother to loss:

> But they called it
> ice, wolf, forest of sticks,
> as if words would make it something
> they could hold in gloved hands,
> open, plot a way
> and follow.

Hogan's poems track essential minims of a neolithic beginning, no less than the petroglyphic panels of La Cieneguilla or the Lascaux bison pictographs of southern France. She holds these primal clusters up for inspection and comparison in the biospheric crisis of postmodernity. The poet knows natural magic and tribal ceremony through scientific observation: that every snowflake centers in a grain of dust, that ice fractally carves away the land, that wolves circle into themselves. "This is what I know from blood: / the first language is not our own. / There are names each thing has for itself, / and beneath us the other order already moves."

"Water is a door," Hogan writes in her memoir *The Woman Who Watches Over the World*, "and you pass through and are beneath" (39). Water invented humans, the old ones say, to move about on land. People are walking reservoirs; words are layered transparencies to fluid origins. The human need for flowing syntactic speech breaks the tongue loose, begging song, even when it betrays the call to truth. The poet returns continually to *women and water*, the mythic and stone-carved glyphs of the Jug Boy quest initiating this study. These ancient origins cannot be named, but flow beneath a monosyllabic speech as ancestral syntax: "so we tell him our stories," the poem "Drought" says of thunder weeping rain, "in honest tongues." The virtue and mystery of this poetry lie in its plain speech, its open prayer for help, slanting into strange reconsiderations of the most basic being and need. Honesty before beauty bears the need of true art, where animals sing the human *through* themselves, here in the shortest and least assuming poem in *The Book of Medicines*.

Once we said thunder
was the old man of sky snoring,
lightning was the old man
striking a match,
but now we only want him to weep
so we tell him our stories
in honest tongues.

A pre-Adamic Lilleth stands in the Garden "Naming the Animals": "wolf, bear, other," as if she made them with lingual tags. Some animals are relegated to crawl, swim, and root like pigs in a wilderness, "where all things know the names for themselves," unspoken or stolen by no (wo)man. Yet inherited names open people, if awkwardly, as speech rounds mouths to being in the true world: "From somewhere I can't speak or tell, / my stolen powers / hold out their hands / and sing me through." Words are passages through the world—not ends in themselves, but messengers from others, beneath and beyond us—made of a ghost world of guardian "others," ancient layers of worlds. We are "made of words," Momaday claims, as we are composed of spirits and ancestral mysteries. Poetry is not a "fabricated thing," as the *Princeton Encyclopedia* defines it, but breath-in-the-pipe, in-standing wind-soul, lyric spiritual passage through narrative time and space.

And so, a guardian "animal walks beside me," the poet says, Algonkian *mistebeo* arm's-length to the left, a protector down on all fours from "the house of pelvic truth" in "The Ritual Life of Animals." The basic drives—hunger, procreation, shelter, touch—come in ritual sacrifice, lowering selves to *be* the sacrificed, the violated, the excreted. Down on her knees, Hogan concludes the section "Hunger" with the smell of her white mother's breast, nipple to her nipple, white milk and red blood fusing in the beginning and end of all journeys. Readers are regeneratively back to the title poem "Hunger," wanting to be inside loving, to drink and be held in the "thin, clear milk of the gods." The poet finds herself gathered by her dead mother in "the thin blue tail of the galaxy," the Milky or Spirit Way—*gone south*, Plains Indians say, to the other world of nurturing heavens beyond the northern lights.

SIMPLE POWERS

Believe the medicine of your own hand.
—Dwellings

The second section, "The Book of Medicines," answers "Hunger" with the natural elements of snow, rain, ice, and cloud—analogues to personal fluids of blood, tears, semen, and sweat. Playing on the homonym "tear" for Chickasaw dresses torn from scraps along the Trail of Tears, Hogan recalls her descent from both pioneer and Native grandmothers:

> They walk inside me. This blood
> is a map of the road between us.
> I am why they survived.
> The world behind them did not close.
> The world before them is still open.
> All around me are my ancestors,
> my unborn children.
> I am the tear between them
> and both sides live.

The poet is the weeping rip that separates White intruder and Red captive through buckskin tears and is sewn together again with falling tears. She is the human who desecrates, the animal who suffers; together she dreams of returning by way of a "circle of revelations" through the mirrored hole of herself to

> . . . the place wind blows through
> when winter enters the room,
> the wounded place
> Raven walked out from.

Born white, grown black in the wilderness reflection of grey storms, Raven, too, would go back to its origins in "Glass,"

> the way glass wants to go back
> to being sand
> and ice wants to return

to being water on earth
as it is in heaven.

The poet's voice is lived "in the cracks between thawing ice" and reaches "all the infinite way down / to where breaking and darkness / are simple powers."

Hogan's prayer touches contemporary global history. She knows that the destruction of Hiroshima was by no means a simple or natural force; still, trumpeter-vine seeds, buried in clay bricks, sprout from the carnage (see Kenzaburo Oe, ed., *The Crazy Iris and Other Stories of the Atomic Aftermath*). So, too, barley still sprouts from Irish ditches where IRA resisters fell with seed rations in their pockets, Seamus Heaney writes in *Preoccupations*. Chickasaw and Cherokee women caressed oak leaves when they left Georgia and carried living roots to Oklahoma on forced removal. The stories of these losses lift descendants out of historically embedded rage, bringing them back from tragedy by taking them all the way through it. "The peaches were green when we left Alabama," the 1830s relocated Creek Itshas Harjo said, "and the wild onions plentiful here when we arrived" (Alexander Posey, *Poems*, in Brandon, *The Magic World* 115).

Skin is humanity's oldest connection, a transparent curtain that both separates and joins others by touch. Just so, the blue skin drum of a mother's womb, embracing the heartbeat itself, stretches through a heated water drum: "and is the oldest place / the deepest world / the skin of water / that knows the drum before a hand meets it." Healing comes through releasing to the elements, accepting what is and has been done, believing in the oldest truths of things. "Earth tells her, / return all lies to their broken source, / trust in the strange science of healing. / Believe the medicine of your own hand." Primal and primeval, water and blood find their nexus flowing down to common fulfillment, letting go, running their course and then lying still.

It is true our lives will betray us in the end
but life knows where it is going,
so does water,
so does blood,
and the full and endless dance of space.

Others connect through the flow of all things. The poem "Two" reminds lovers that "Water falls through our hands as we fall through it." Humans are permeable reality, primarily fluid, conditional, evolving, and adaptive to countless forms of life. "Expect poison from standing water," Blake warned in *The Marriage of Heaven and Hell*. Water, the great mother of the sea, carries humans life within, flowing red with blood. Just so, the faith-healing of Hogan's mother, Nebraska pioneer daughter, sees the poet through her hopelessness. "Nothing sings in our bodies / like breath in a flute." Skin is a shaman's water drum, voice an open flute, skeleton a taut bow, and "this living is such a journey / inside a breaking open world," the poet marvels in "Great Measures." Ours is a world breaking into blossom, as James Wright saw.

With "the weight of living / tugging us down and earth wanting us back," Hogan steps into light, growing inch by inch with her children "like trees in a graveyard." The poet chants mother, daughter, sister: "It is ocean / calling the river, / Water." And ends with "The Origins of Corn" as a sensual dance between man and woman, bringing forth the miracle of another life, to be called by the same Hopi word, "child" and "corn," as cited earlier. Domesticating Mother Corn from wild grass 12,000 years ago, the Mayans and Pueblos today say, *We are corn*. Back home, the Algonquin gift of green corn in 1621 saved English pilgrims from starvation, commemorated in the most American of feast days, Thanks-giving—a treating or joining both sides "at the forest's edge" of Hogan's genetic lineage in conditional peace and bounty. This inclusive dream, beyond the night-sweat tears, encloses *The Book of Medicines*.

Searching Simplicity

so we tell him our stories
in honest tongues.
—*The Book of Medicines*

A mixed-blood writer, conscious of Indian-Anglo schisms, Hogan writes herself together as a modern *Native* American, Chickasaw relocatee to Nebraska pioneer, singing the heart home. Mixed-American, she worries over spiritual dispossessions. Chickasaw descendent, she reads the landscape for signs of damage and living renewal. Hogan listens to the land's rhythms and feels for its wounds, talks with and about plants and especially animals in her poems. Combining spiritual intuition with environmental activism, the poet listens over machines that deaden hearing. She asks blessing, grace, and courage from her totemic guardians—bear, wolf, raven, whale, coyote, blackbird. No less than any spiritual scientist—caretaker of the natural world and the natural part of humans—she listens and observes the Other, even rapacious "far-hearted" men, as aboriginal Bushmen say, for empathic understanding and interspecies exchanges. Her human attentions, beginning with adopted daughters, reach out to *all* her *relatives* as kinsmen, an extended tribal family drawing open the Buckskin Curtain. Stories, places, events, revelations—from animal magic, to historical markings, to strange happenings—tie her people tribally together, from the old days (Coyote Old Man to Darwin), to frontier collisions of *both* her peoples (Trail of Tears to Wounded Knee), to present acculturations (Elizabeth Bishop to Ralph Nader). As a woman, Hogan is particularly concerned about the threats of male violence to the biosphere, whale oil to oil wells, mass slaughter of bison, wolf, and bear to chemical pollution and radioactive waste. Hers is a full and critical agenda. She mourns the raping of land and animals ("they had their way with them"), mindless killing (sport-hunting wild "game" to overseas dirty wars), and men abusing even themselves (love-grief, loneliness, rage, neglect).

What makes this poetry? Not so much rhyme or meter, metaphor or structure, but her *concision* shapes the economy and depth of lyrical thinking. In a phrase, Hogan's *searching simplicity* informs and shapes the verse. As with Greg Sarris letting Mabel McKay's story tell itself, words do not stand between reader and subject. A starving dog remembers it was wolf, a deer turns into a raven eating carrion, a dentist uses Chief Joseph's skull for an ashtray. A Mimbres *kill hole* in the clayware of Native America swallows Ishi, the last of 4,000 Yana. Hogan's narrative points are clear, original, startling, memorable as poetic insight embedded in prose essay. The healing comes, the poet-at-large concludes, when the animal-in-human is regarded as a guardian spirit of this natural world, unnaturally threatened by violence, greed, and ignorance. Healing naturally quickens in the narrative contexts of lyric texts, the ceremonial regards of ancestors observed daily. The everyday sacraments and fluid sayings of poems-as-stories keep humans going on going on.

WORD WARRIOR: SHERMAN ALEXIE

There are so many possibilities in the reservation 7–11,
so many methods of survival. Imagine every Skin on
the reservation is the new lead guitarist for the Rolling

Stones, on the cover of a rock-and-roll magazine.
Imagine forgiveness is sold 2 for 1. Imagine every
Indian is a video game with braids. Do you believe
laughter can save us? All I know is that I count coyotes
to help me sleep.

—Sherman Alexie,
"Imagining the Reservation"

NOBODY'S INDIAN

Consider a young male 'Skin countering Linda Hogan's ecopoetic empathy with essentialist attitude. A Spokane Indian who goes on no spiritual quests to talk with the Great Mystery, no good red roads to meet the White Father. A Coeur d'Alene brother to no guardian wingéd or leggéd, kin to no totemic animal or clan. A brash postmodernist who checks romance with irony, sentiment with sarcasm, pathos with anger, the Family of Man with pop sass. Hogan fuses natural science with social and artistic crossings; translates interspecies dialogue as documentary fiction and homeopathic verse; seeks forgiveness, understanding, tolerance, and grace among the living and the dead—compassionate mother, simpatico feminist, scientific humanist, open-field poet, essayist, and novelist. No less than Russell Means warning White Men to watch where they tread, X-generation Alexie tears the scabs off frontier history. À la Craig Womack's Red Stick purge, he scorns the naiveté of non-Indian liberals. Along with Elizabeth Cook-Lynn, he checks feckless reconciliation with the ongoing facts of poverty, racism, injustice, and dire Indian life expectancies.

Leading the attack on the masses, Alexie holds out for an Indian uprising in the popular arts. Hogan's open heart, Alexie's sharp tongue—no two writers could stand more at odds, more diametrically gendered, more generationally disparate. Sherman Alexie feeds off public controversy—glossy New York magazine articles that taunt White Men who can't drum or dance, trickster movies that turn Westerns inside out and stereotypes upside down, short stories that cut to the ethnocentric chase, novels that fuel fictive race riots in Seattle, poetry that challenges all the rules of form and manner, censored diction and edged syntax. Alexie is truly the *enfant sauvage* of contemporary Native writing, the trickster with wicked lip—nobody's Tonto, nobody's tenth little Indian.

MONEY IS FREE IF YOU'RE POOR ENOUGH

Waiting on LAX Homeland Security, I reread the first of *The Best American Short Stories 2004*, Sherman Alexie's "What You Pawn I Will Redeem" (originally published in *The New Yorker*, April 2003, and republished in *Ten Little Indians*). "Exhausted and cold, I pulled a plastic tarp from a truck bed, wrapped it around me like a faithful lover, and fell asleep in the dirt" (14). Here it was again, 'Skin mainstream hip going on a decade, pop-culture radical, a book a year plus two movies—half magician and half clown, as Thomas Builds-the-Fire says of his lineage in Alexie's *The Lone Ranger and Tonto Fistfight in Heaven*.

Indian castaways, panhandling "warrior drunks" and feisty off-rez women, these street cons hold cardboard slogans on Seattle corners. Theirs are conquered cultures in hock with "built-in pawnshop radar." The *characters* indeed seem cartoon-real—Rose of Sharon, Junior, Real Change, Irene Muse, Honey Boy, nameless Aleuts down by the docks, all incidentally shadowing the narrator. Either they pass out, die, or move back to the rez, the plot skipping around single-minded as a Roadrunner skit. Alexie point-guards a shaggy reality of sound bites just artful enough to snag attention, not overly crafted to distract or to draw the reader unnecessarily into the writing, à la Gerald Vizenor's "survivance" trickster tales: "We Indians are great storytellers and liars and mythmakers, so maybe that Plains Indian hobo is just a plain old everyday Indian" (2). The 2007 novel *Flight* trails a breed orphan named Zits through time, from Little Big Horn insurgent to jet pilot.

ECCE HOMO ROSSO

The real Indi'n story in post-moderno vérité, the "most prodigious" Native writer to date, Alexie told a Chicago Sun reporter asking about his vampish novel *Indian Killer* (October 1996). In the author's own fictive words, "This was the generation of HUD house, of car wreck and cancer, of commodity cheese and beef. These were the children who carried dreams in the back pockets of their blue jeans, pulled them out easily, traded back and forth" (*The Lone Ranger and Tonto Fistfight in Heaven* 142). The young gadfly speaks for a Grunge generation of off-reservation, schooled, born-again Native activists who want to make movies, reclaim tribal rights, update history, play in rock bands, get famous, and be published in high-paying magazines. Notwithstanding anyone's great traditions, why not?

For *Reservation Blues* in 1995, *Granta Magazine* controversially named this 'Skin among the twenty best U.S. novelists. Alexie faced down his critics: "To say I was on the list because I'm an Indian is ridiculous: I'm one of the most critically respected writers in the country. So the *Granta* critics . . . essentially, fuck 'em" (*New City's Literary Supplement*, 31 October 1996). Parodic anti-formalism caches some of Alexie's mass maverick appeal, tribal tradition and ceremony airbrushed aside. "I'm sorry, but I've met thousands of Indians," he told *Indian Artist* magazine (Spring 1998), "and I have yet to know of anyone who has stood on a mountain waiting for a sign." Black Elk in the dust, Momaday remaindered, Mabel McKay dreamless, the 'Skin hipster strikes out on his own deconstructive warpath, no brother to Linda Hogan's lower-case verse or all-nations essays.

In the classic trickster history of Will Rogers, W. C. Fields, Jonathan Winters, Lenny Bruce, or Charlie Hill, Indian improvisator *is* the performing text as stand-up comedian: six-foot-two or so, off-rez *enfant terrible*, born 1966 in Wellpinit, Washington, now living in Seattle and taking the *fin de siècle* postmodernist world by Red Stick storm. Think Native Oscar Wilde. After a century of benign neglect, Indian literature has hit an inflationary spiral with six-figure book deals and million-dollar movies. Some 20 billion pan-tribal dollars in annual casino profits salt the reservation rush. New York publishers have been humping this sassy, talk-back satirist as the last essentialist holdout, a commercially successful Native insurgent mass-marketed to Gen-X hip and liberal guilt. "A slam dunk collection sure to score with readers everywhere," *Publishers Weekly* starred *Ten Little Indians*. "Fluent, exuberant and supremely confident, this outstanding collection shows Alexie at the height of his powers." However critics slant his talent, Alexie can't be ignored.

Urban Red

A breed Spokane and Coeur d'Alene, not just any-body, but 13/16ths blood, according to his poetry, "I write about the kind of Indian I am: kind of mixed up, kind of odd, not traditional. I'm a rez kid who's gone urban" (*Indian Artist*, Spring 1998). Witness a photogenic black mane of hair; dark-framed bifocal glasses; high-school-class-president, book-worm nose—broken six times by bullies, he reminisces in public—with an English Lit college degree from Eastern Washington State (after passing out as a premed student in his anatomy class, twice). His work snaps back wizened with poetic anger, ribald love, whipsaw humor, and heartbreak. Alexie's sister and brother-in-law passed out in a trailer and died by fire when a window curtain blew against a hot plate, a family tragedy replayed in a number of his poems and prose pieces. Alexie's film *Smoke Signals* (coproduced with Cheyenne-Arapaho director Chris Eyre) starts with a firestorm that launches the road movie from Idaho to Arizona. As a boy, Sherman mimed everyone in his family and won't stop talking back. "I was a divisive presence on the reservation when I was seven," the writer told an *LA Times* reporter, 17 December 1996. "I was a weird, eccentric, very arrogant little boy. The writing doesn't change anybody's opinion of me."

Not so much rhymer in the old sense, Sherman Alexie is a circus juggler who can eat apples while juggling, toss off poems and short stories annually, while making movies and cutting records. This college graduate played basketball sixteen hours a day to keep from boozing with his drop-out cronies: Seymour chugging beer as a poet writes verse (up to the last one that kills you) and Lester dead-drunk in the convenience-store dumpster. This comic juggler crosses pain, pugnacity, scavenger laughter, and raw talent.

Artistic grit and ironic survival run inseparable through Alexie's verse, tracing a short lifetime of hoops (a team captain "ball hog" in high school), teenage beer, cable TV, rez cars falling apart, pony dreams, fetal-alcohol-syndrome babies, and fancy-dancing drunks. "You call it geno-cide; I call it economics," Custer snorts in free verse through *Old Shirts & New Skins*. A warm-up for fiction and the movies, Alexie's poetics are wrapped in the politics of Native poverty, torqued metrics, and ethnic protest: dime store Indi'n princesses and back-alley vision questers, 7–11 heroes and Vietnam vets, Marlon Brando and Crazy Horse. "Believe me, there is just barely enough goodness in all of this" (*The Lone Ranger and Tonto Fistfight in Heaven* 144). No cultural-insurance CEO or village doctor, Alexie has the near fatal, comic bravado of surviving an everyday reservation of the mind, where every day is a blow to the stomach and a blaze of understanding. "The ordinary can be like medicine."

Reading Alexie's work triggers recoil from the shock of Indian reality: "*whiskey salmon absence*," the poem "Citizen Kane" ends. Firewater, relocation, vanishing American, the images Natively de-create the poison where food swarms, desperate homing, an absence that starves Indians to death. *Rosebud* is no child's sled in a movie, but a desperately poor Sioux reservation in the Dakotas. The fractured associations make real sense only to a tough-love Indian, as Joyce reads best to a homeless Irishman.

VIRTUAL SHOOTIST

His waggish titles tell all: *The Lone Ranger and Tonto Fistfight in Heaven* marqueed his 1993 short stories to date, after four collections of poetry in half as many years. "The Existential Gunslinger," pundits dubbed JFK during the Bay of Pigs just before Alexie was born, updating the archetypal Westerner—Cortés and Columbus, to John Wayne and the Marlboro Man. The ironic White/Red duo fronts a wilderness paradigm old as Don Quixote and Sancho Panza, Robinson Crusoe and his Man Friday, Leatherstocking and Chingachgook, Old Shatterhand and Winnetou, Buffalo Bill and Sitting Bull, Red Ryder and Little Beaver, Beavis and Butthead. The Western trope of hand-to-hand combat or a brawl "in heaven" raises the frontier humor of American manifest violence to a Christian rapture current as Operation Iraq Liberation (OIL). Terrorists rise up everywhere genocidal dispossession has dumped them, and Ward Churchill stumps justice as some wacky leftist 'Skin. Victor Joseph reminisces:

> Imagine Crazy Horse invented the atom bomb in 1876 and detonated it over Washington, D.C. Would the urban Indians still be sprawled around the one-room apartment in the cable television reservation? Imagine a loaf of bread could feed the entire tribe. Didn't you know Jesus Christ was a Spokane Indian? Imagine Columbus landed in 1492 and some tribe or another drowned him in the ocean. Would Lester FallsApart still be shoplifting in the 7–11? (*Lone Ranger* 149)

Alexie specializes in quips and long, talky, goofy titles, graffiti scrawl as anti-art: "Because My Father Always Said He Was the Only Indian Who Saw Jimi Hendrix Play 'The Star-Spangled Banner' at Woodstock." The national anthem started as an 1812 war song by F. Scott Keyes, and now plays as heroin rock riff in Indian family history. Alexie counterpunches with curt sexual spoof in "The Fun House," on to a conventional title undercut, "A Good Story," his dyadic characters sparring in two-dimensional vaudeville skits. Victor Joseph, the protagonist, narrates many of the twenty-two sketches as stand-in for the author, born hydrocephalic: "I was conceived during one of those drunken nights, half of me formed by my father's whiskey sperm, the other half formed by my mother's vodka egg. I was born a goofy reservation mixed drink, and my father needed me just as much as he needed every other kind of drink" (27).

Julius Windmaker plays basketball all day, and Lester FallsApart passes out in the rez dumpster. Adrian drinks Coors and watches the stopped traffic signal (John Trudell in the movie *Smoke Signals*). Frank Many Horses shoots pool. Simon skips rocks off the highway. Seymour makes bad jokes. Tremble Dancer dances. Thomas Builds-the-Fire, who reappears in the novel *Reservation Blues* and the movie *Fancy Dancer*, plays the bush-league storyteller nobody listens to. Talk is a waste of time. "Junior," Norma Many Horses says with gentle patience, "shut the fuck up." Jimmie Many Horses is simply a 'Skin boyfriend-husband with cancer, and Norma the runaway dancer. Junior Polatkin and Raymond and James crop up in sketch riffs as domestic comedy with local color. Readers meet and lose sight of these figures as though busing through Pine Ridge or Farmington or Spokane on the way to a Sundance Film Festival.

The author calls his short fiction "reservation realism" in the tenth-anniversary revised edition of *The Lone Ranger and Tonto Fistfight in Heaven* (Grove Press, 2005). "I'm a poet who can whine in meter," he confesses at the outset (xxi). Art starts in the streets. A story can be triggered by a scene outside the rez convenience store, a house party that catches fire, a condition like cancer as bad joke in "The Approximate Size of My Favorite Tumor," or simply a recurrent Indian condition— poverty, alcoholism, drug abuse, homelessness, endemic cultural despair. And there's sight-gag schlock with brash one-liners: watching a stopped stoplight, a BB-gun suicide, Jesus Christ's half-brother alive and well on the Spokane Indian reservation. These gimmicks topple Native stereo-types: Victor as self-defeating warrior-chief, Norma as cheap princess, Big Mom as bad medicine woman, Lester as trash ecologist, Seymour as fallen noble savage, Junior as gentle naïf, Jimmie as primitive sage, Thomas as mystic dreamer. Low-comic character types go on with an ongoing frontier history of defeat, five Indian generations falling into the 7–11 dumpster, flaming solar basketball diversions, beer delusions. Today's realism becomes tonight's TV surrealism, a mix of sensational shtick and documentary shock. "'Shit,' my mother said. 'Old Jesse WildShoe choked to death on his own vomit and he ain't anybody's hero'" (32).

ALL KINDS

Alexie deconstructs today's Indian with reverse warrior horsepower. His Native education features Red humor with a savvy savagist twist. "And I laughed because half of me was happy and half of me wasn't sure what else to do" (*Lone Ranger* 50). Survival draws the bottom line, the undercutting humors of irony, parody, caricature, and satire targeting the enemy's ignorance, raising a tribal outcry, banding Crazy Horse to Custer, Joy Harjo to Lou Reed. "There are all kinds of dancing" (*Lone Ranger* 78). This hipster fires from a full, deadly quiver—classic pratfall, the cheek of the desperate, the absurdity of facing despair, the razz of staring down tragedy. "Tonight the mirror will forgive my face." With reservation alcoholism, unemployment, illness, and suicide at a national benchmark, Indians have nothing left to lose, the blues song goes, and they use wild-ass jokes to stave off despair. "There are all kinds of wars." Low comedy grounds the people in reality, wild humor keeps them going for more, a rich desperation imagines anything. "I'm traveling heavy with illusions." The tone is burlesque realism, a performance fiction where characters play their roles, rather than being fated to fail. "That's how I do this life sometimes by making the ordinary just like magic and just like a card trick and just like a mirror and just like the disappearing" (*Lone Ranger* 125).

This is the updated Red humor of old trickster tales, Winnebago Wakdungkaga traveling with his asshole partner and backpacking his epic penis in a box. The ancestral past is a family parody of tragic history, as with the dead father Arnold Joseph (Gary Farmer) retrieved from Phoenix morphing into the movie *Smoke Signals*. Beast fables translate into creation spoofs, as with the mouse up Mama's skirt in "The Fun House." In "A Drug Called Tradition," dream visions come from d.t.'s, magic mushrooms, reservation poverty, personal fantasy and illusion. Teepees and venison shapeshift to trailers and Spam, HUD housing and Diet Pepsi. The sacred word drops down to street improv, satiric riff, and guerrilla theater, virtual Indians in heretical skits. Deadpan Thomas tells his endless story:

> It *is now*. Three Indian boys are drinking Diet Pepsi and talking out by Benjamin Lake. They are wearing only loincloths and braids. Although it is the twentieth century and planes are passing overhead, the Indian boys have decided to be real Indians tonight.
>
> They all want to have their vision, to receive their true names, their adult names. That is the problem with Indians these days. They have the same names all their lives. Indians wear their names like a pair of bad shoes (*Lone Ranger* 20).

No Fucking Apple

Art metastasizes from readymades found on the rez, collages cobbled together, scattershot fragments as kinship chaos. Joking can be poetry in its own diction, rhythm, and insight. The cartoon clarity of all this simplifies, focuses, pokes fun, and plays with the "serious" reader. The satirist checks out sentimental deceptions, targets and drives out unwanted guests, exposes indifference, ignorance, racism, and injustice. The caricaturist bases human nature in reality, pushes the stereotype toward absurdity. "The boy Thomas throws the beer he is offered into the garbage. The boy Junior throws his whiskey through a window. The boy Victor spills his vodka down the drain" (*Lone Ranger* 21). The ironist makes the audience think twice, taking a realistic double take on ordinary assumptions about Indians. "Very fucking Indian" drugs produce some "spiritual shit" that does little good for the down-and-out Noble Savage. "Then the boys sing. They sing and dance and drum. They steal horses. I can see them. *They steal horses*" (21). Parodist of Harjo's wild herd in *She Had Some Horses* and Tapahonso's Diné ponies in *Blue Horses Rush In*, Red Stick Alexie milks sacred mares for 'Skin survival.

Edgy Red dialogue opens the Lone Ranger versus Tonto tales: "Goddamn it. You ain't shit, you fucking apple," says one brother slugging another. This is all-my-fucking-relatives, extended kin inverted, Christian heresy damning the heathen, bad grammar as revolutionary illiteracy ("We don't need no ed-u-ca-tion," goes the X-generation punk song). A "fucking apple" is a stale American icon, Natively red on the outside, Edenically white inside. An essentialist *How*-Indian complex misfires on and off the rez, blood quantum and spiritual octane as Native measuring sticks. And scatology sneaks in—the explosive monosyllable "shit"—the purgative toxins, excremental grounding, and common secret of bodily functions back to Trickster's antics and forward to purgative winters in the blood. Add bestiality and sexuality to the contrary mix, no less than postmodernist descendants of Kokopelli petroglyphs: scared by a fart, a varmint scrams up Big Mom's pant leg, the "ugly mousetrap" of bad male jokes, etc.—no P.C. cultural police in sight.

Native basics are played for laughs—the honest release of shame, repressed desire, pain, and fear. In "The Approximate Size of My Favorite Tumor," comic realism counters artistic manners. "If you say anything funny ever again, I'm going to leave you," Norma threatens her terminal husband. "And I'm fucking serious about that" (*Lone Ranger* 159). Truth deflates pretense, reality brings airs down to earth, honesty bonds humans in common humility.

"Well," I said. "I told her the truth, Simon. I told her I got cancer everywhere inside me."

Simon slammed on the brakes and brought the pickup sliding to a quick but decidedly cinematic stop.

"That ain't nothing to joke about," he yelled.

"Ain't joking about the cancer," I said. "But I started joking about dying and that pissed her off." (157)

In contrast with Tapahonso's sacred tongue-tip words, the lowest narrative denominator resides in the mortal common tongue—a get-down, in-your-face candor that includes censored words and deeds and griefs; an unaffected release that vents spoiled innards; a democratic laughter that would cross cultural boundaries. Is it art? Don't even ask, the corporate publishers snort over royalties. "One thing that I noticed in the hospital as I coughed myself up and down the bed: A clock, at least one of those old-style clocks with hands and a face, looks just like somebody laughing if you stare at it long enough" (168).

INDIAN IN OUR TIME

If Walter Benjamin is right about sailor and farmer being archetypal male storytellers—tales from afar of strange and wonderful Others, stories at home about the extra-ordinary in everyone and the Other within—then Victor and Thomas Builds-the-Fire spin fantasies of now distantly connected to then. The camera pans contemporary diaspora. Riffed myths tie Indians, ancestrally, with the history of trickster-fantasy tales, making up things back through tribal time-and-space. Admittedly, Alexie's fiction is not Momaday's history, myth, or personal lyric—no regressive nostalgia as a cultural slide, elegy singing the open wound. His poetry decries formal indulgence. Neither is Alexie's language carved in Welch's diction, edged and tangible, nor metrically loping across northern plains. His plots in no way resemble Erdrich's three-generational kinship sagas, many voices and multiple narrators, or the visionary realism of connections that save characters—a knowledge that will make or break you, Lulu tells her grandson. This Native maverick is his own man, perhaps closest to Adrian Louis in lyric hard edge and narrative caustic, anticipating Sherwin Bitsui's bravura poetic shapeshifts.

Alexie's sketches make puncture points about surviving history. "The Approximate Size of My Favorite Tumor" faces death with riffs to ease the witnessing. "The Fun House" sets cultural markers for postmodernist

Indians. Jimi Hendrix at Woodstock serves a revisionist vision of the national anthem and third-world resistance. "A Drug Called Tradition" takes a pratfall, and "The Only Traffic Signal on the Reservation Doesn't Flash Red Anymore" turns on a one-pony gag. "Imagining the Reservation" flags the point of it all, a surreal rez dream floating across the page in celluloid technicolor. A far cry from petroglyphs, tribal plots, or metered lyrics, this writer wants to make movies. He admits in *Aboriginal Voices* (May/June 1998):

> But, I mean I really love movies. I always have. I love movies
> more than I love books, and believe me, I love books more than
> I love every human being, except the dozen or so people in my
> life who love movies and books just as much as I do. I mean,
> screenplays are more like poetry than like fiction. Screenplays
> rely on imagery to carry the narrative, rather than the other way
> around. And screenplays have form. Like sonnets, actually. Just
> as there's expectations of form, meter, and rhyme in a sonnet,
> there are the same kinds of expectations for screenplays.

In 1993, the UCLA American Indian Studies Center published *Old Shirts & New Skins* as #9 in the Native American Poetry Series begun in 1975. Old shirts, not stuffed new suits: new 'Skins, Redskins reborn, sloughing "old" skins. There are always two sides to things, bicultural ironies to New Age lies, & the blessed ampersand, hip shorthand to a coded new tongue of the with-it Indi'n poet. There's no text *set* here as such, but more something spilled over, virus or toxin released, a metastasizing anger. A "reservation of my mind," the poet says. The opening epithet again equates, "Anger x Imagination = poetry," in the amplitude & invention of the angry young Indian who says "Survival = Anger x Imagination" in *The Lone Ranger and Tonto Fistfight in Heaven* (150). One shot short of death, Seymour repeats, drink as a poet writes free verse, no matter if "our failures are spectacular." Maverick Trixter talks back. Alexie makes a different kind of poetry for people with differences: "It was not written for the white literary establishment," Adrian Louis says in the Foreword to *Old Skins & New Shirts*. Alexie introduces the 2005 revised edition of *The Lone Ranger and Tonto Fistfight in Heaven*:

> "It's free verse," I said. "And some of them do rhyme. I've
> written sonnets, sestinas, and villanelles. I've written in iambic
> pentameter."

"What's that?"

"It's the *ba-bump*, *b-bump* sound of the heartbeat, of the deer running through the green pine forest, of the eagle singing its way through the sky."

"Don't pull that Indian shaman crap on me," my mother said.

In Alexie's ragged narrative lyrics, a double buckskin language frays at the edges of bicultural America, questions the multiple meanings of reservation, red, risk, Cody & Crazy Horse, Marlon Brando & John Wayne, Christ & Custer who *died for your sins*. The critic is left with notes to bumper-sticker poetics, insult & antagonism, the fractious come-hither. Poetry as disruptive tease, a sideshow of historical truth and poetic hyperbole. Tribal teasing tests boundaries, deepens resilience, ensures survival, bets on renewal, all the scholars from Mary Douglas to Keith Basso agree (Lincoln, *Indi'n Humor*). Start with inventories of abuses, imagined and otherwise: hunger of imagination, poverty of memory, toxicity of history, all in the face of cultural genocide and racial misrepresentation and outright extermination, to challenge musty stereotypes of vanishing, savage, stoic, silent, shamanic, stuporous Indians. Poetry is never bread enough and doesn't pay the bills. Who could quibble about aesthetics in this setting?

Invoking Freud, Mary Douglas says that all jokes test and break form in the *privileged license* of bad behavior ("The Social Control of Cognition"). Alexie pushes against formalist assumptions of what poetry was or ought to be, knocks down aesthetic barriers set up in xenophobic academic corridors, and rebounds as cultural performance for the people. The poet plays off formal technique with mock sonnet, breezy villanelle, unheroic couplet, tinkling tercet, quaky quatrain in any-beat lines. The anti-rhymer trades on surreal images and throwaway metaphors in a drunken villanelle: *Trail of Tears . . . trail of beers*. The rush of his poems is an energy released, stampeding horses, raging fires, stomping shoes: the poet as fast-and-loose sharpster in accretive repetition.

Alexie likes catalogues, anaphoral first-word repetitions, the accumulative power of oral traditions. Agreed, there is something freeing about all this—free to imagine, to improvise, to make things up, to wonder, to rage on. Sharpening wits with quick lip, his poetry runs free of restrictive ideas about Indians, poems, ponies, movies, shoes, dreams, dumpsters, reservations, angers, losses. His lines break free of precious *art* . . . free for what that matters? Readers certainly learn about New

Rez Indi'ns who shoot hoop, stroke pool, fancy dance, drink beer, snag girls, hustle, hitch, rap, joke, cry, rhyme, and dream. Some write everything down in enjambed lines. These Computer *Rad* 'Skins scat verse that does not stay contained in formal repose—does not pull away, or shimmer in the night sky, or intimidate the common reader, but comes on full as a flashpoint that begs visceral response. Cartoonish gag, point-of-view gimmick, more "like" *Virtual Indian.* "There is no possible way to sell your soul" for poetry, Alexie said at a Beverly Hills book-signing (Brentano's, 17 December 1996), "because nobody's offering. The devil doesn't care about poetry. No one wants to make a movie out of a poem." He should know. This loose-lyric trickster has made two movies, *Smoke Signals* and *The Business of Fancy Dancing,* and has cast another from the controversial novel *Indian Killer,* though he has backed away from shooting the film.

Call it a reactive aesthetics, kinetic pop art, protest poetics to involve and challenge late-century readers—much-maligned "liberals" cajoled, battered, insulted, entertained, humored, angered to respond. A poetry that gets Whitey off his easy chair. Tribal jive, that is, road quick, popular, ethnocentric, edged, opinionated, disturbed, fired up as reservation graffiti—à la John Trudell's Venice, CA, rock lyrics, the Cherokee-breed Elvis as "Baby Boom Che." Alexie joins the brash frontier braggadocio of westering America, already out west a long time, an ironic trickster-confidence tradition shared with Whitman, Stein, Mailer, Kesey, Kerouac, Ginsberg, Vonnegut, Bellow, Mamet, and hundreds of tribal mavericks going back tens of thousands of years through Kokopelli carved into basalt cliffs above the Santa Fe River Valley. Huckster, con man, carny barker, stand-up comedian, Will Rogers to Jonathan Winters, Cheech & Chong to Charlie Hill. The impudence of the anti-poetic Red Rapster dares America not to call this poetry. "You'll almost / believe every Indian is an Indian," Alexie carries on.

FRYBREAD . . . SNAKES . . . FORGIVENESS

Firestorm and Fire Sale: Alexie takes the stage as a 7–11 dumpster poet sorting through rags of ribbon shirts, dirty tennis shoes, broken bottles, used condoms, old news and shopping-bag sacks, the debris of the reservation and the litter of city streets. The trickster anti-visionary tips everything sideways. He challenges the myths and stereotypes of Mt. Olympia, truly a Hermes misfit stealing into the Washington pantheon of poets including Roethke, Hugo, Carver, Gallagher, and Waggoner. If Momaday lyricizes the ancestral golden days of warriors and grandmothers, epic migratory events and hollow log origins, Kiowa sisters in the sky and historic cataclysms, Alexie turns to basketball dead-beats and mouthy maidens, a blank tribal past and archaeological dry bones. This now-day hip Indi'n is wrapped in personal history rewriting Native stereotypes for urbanites.

"The Unauthorized Biography of Me" opens his latest verse collage, *One Stick Song* (2000). Rather than song-poems and ceremonial dances from the old days, storytellings and tribal homogeneity, Alexie's province is broken-step performance measures in postmodernist free-verse slam. In both the poetry and the prose, fictive characters like Seymour and Lester bend all the traditional rules. A pan-Indian, broken, solar hoop flames like a sunset basketball across the night sky. Contrary to Nick Black Elk on the Lakota plains, no grandfathers from the six directions, no animal-human transformations, no symbolic creation ("old like hills, like stars") or magical voices ("spoke like singing"). And no transla-tive collaborations or exogamous marriages with non-Indians. The poet projects Crazy Horse of the classroom, Custer of the virtual War Room: no venerable old ones, no cardinal points, no visionary hallucinations. Things are what they are. "This is not a metaphor," he says over and over in the poems. Whites are the accusatory "you" in his "Introduction to Native American Literature." Spun off from Welch, no trickster surre-alism with winter in the blood, no riding Earthboys post-shamanically: rather a user-unfriendly realism to pique his willing audience, a cheeky humor of dis/respect, unpermitted or otherwise. Alexie's world is the post-holocaustal present, dirty with reality, and an insurgent chip-on-the-shoulder blues.

Cross-tribal rival to Sarris, no healing Pomo grannies or mother-less child discovering his heritage, no storytelling as belonging or self-discovery, no Indians among us, but a headstrong boy adrift on the rez and quick to leave for the coastal big city. So, too, a prosey poetry, sto-rytelling riffs and vaudeville poetics, stand-up satire. Genres blur, all but the last-standing lineations. He makes lyric less so, narrative pop art—story *run runs* over lyric *row row*. Harjo's spirit horses purge fear, chant courage, challenge wrong, dare ignorance. Alexie's hip poetics exorcize hurt through anger, ridicule ignorance through parody and sarcasm, sat-irize wrong by debunking faux heroes, from Columbus's accident, to Cortés's plunder, to Custer's folly, the 3 C's of the West. Cheek metasta-sizes in-your-face as the courage to speak up, to talk back, to counter the

Invasion masked as *Discovery of a New World* continuously inhabited some thirty thousand years by two thousand Native tribal cultures now dubbed *Indi'n*. "We don't have a prehistory," says Rochanne Downs, coordinator for the Great Basin Inter-Tribal NAGPRA Coalition to protect tribal sites, in recent *Time* magazine words on Indians. "We have one continuous history" (*Time*, 13 March 2006, 51).

Alexie's poetry is a pickup basketball game in the streets with makeshift tribal teams. No referees, no time clock, no audience, just play for playing. Trash talk, pep talk, team chatter, fancy dribbling and rough rebounding, three-pointers from the perimeter bouncing off the rim or sucking air, slam-dunk motifs with Custer's sins and Crazy Horse's martyrdom at either end of the court. "Am I the garbage man of your dreams?" Alexie's personal witness of injustice takes the public ring in a leftist poetry slam, the poem as a boxing match, a sucker's punch to the reader's nose. Trading insults, will the White man talk back? Can he drum or dance fancy? Will he fess up his father's sins, his mother's misdemeanors? To repeat, this is poetry as revisionist history from an insurgent Indian perspective, reimagining Native devastation, deconstructing tribal heroism, reversing good/bad guy paradigms, cowboys and Indians, the Lone Ranger and Tonto. *Enit?* the tribal marker punctuates the diatribe.

Nothing We Cannot Survive

From Sherman Alexie's first collection of forty poems and five stories, *The Business of Fancy Dancing* (1992), and *The First Indian on the Moon* the following year, his poems skitter like pop tunes through prose riffs of seven verse books in eight years. Or skid to a stop antipoetically: "I hate baseball." Celebrating literally all the *fucking* poets and liars in "Open Book," Alexie rants his latest verse shtick, *One Stick Song* (2000), and chants down the academic thought police ("Sex in Motel Rooms"):

AIDS is a shitty deal for everybody

but it's a really shitty deal for sex in general.
After all, our parents got to fuck

and fuck and fuck and fuck
without the fear of death.

The poet wishes Patsy Cline, Emily Dickinson, Jesus Christ, Mary Magdalene, Sappho, Bruce Springsteen, Voltaire, and Walt Whitman "were Indian." After Alexie's sister died drunk in a trailer fire and his father lost a foot to diabetes, the poet says the hell with the whole damned thing, in diction lower than poetic vernacular has rarely gone:

> . . . fuck
> the amputees and their loneliness, fuck the inadequate
> body that houses me, fuck beauty, fuck the shoe, fuck
> the song, fuck irony, fuck this war and that war, fuck this
> war and that war, fuck this and that, fuck this, fuck
> that, fuck, fuck, fuck, fuck, fuck, fuck, fuck, fuck, fuck.

Ginsberg howled down hypocrisy in the 1950s, "America, go fuck yourself with your atom bomb," but Sherman has one stick left to lose, so he beats the bad syllable for all it's worth. And there's a thin line between poetry and prose in all these rants—repetitions, chants, spaces in the lines, prose only somewhat denser on the page. These riffs skitter a long way from ceremony, carriers of the dream wheel, Christmas at Moccasin Flat, jacklights, books of medicine, and having some horses. *One Stick Song* tapers to blank end-pages.

POST-INDIAN POETICS

Somewhere long ago, Ancestral Pueblos scratched icons in cliff rock; their descendants still tell and sing of ancient origins. Warriors returned from killings with old homecoming myths, and tribes continue to migrate, while winter in the blood chokes ancient storytellers. Tribal generations triangulate into the twentieth and next century. Today the saxophone is not considered a traditional Native instrument, Joy Harjo says, but it will be in a hundred years because I'm playing one. A twenty-first century Native Whitman ahead of everyone, perhaps, writing at breakneck speed in WordPerfect, Sherman Alexie is pecking his stories, poems, and movies into Native and American digital history. One day, his work too may be considered ancestral.

TWELVE

Diné Shapeshifter

Sherwin Bitsui

I see things as arrivals and departures, momentary
specks that glisten and erupt into shards of light,
only to quickly diminish again. It is quite difficult
at times to be present when the poems begin their
journeys and reveal fields where flowers once bloomed.
I am in an inbetween place now. I don't know where
I return to, where the air is thinnest, where I can
collect words again . . .

—10:10 a.m. 16 November 2004,
bitsui.com website

Every Indian writer today has studied Euro-American and global texts
outside tribal traditions, students from the Institute of American Indian
Arts (IAIA) in Santa Fe to the Iowa Writers Workshop, from Dartmouth
University to Sinte Gleska Community College. Native poets, novelists, dra-
matists, essayists, and screenwriters work from the postmodern texts and
rebirthing contexts of over a thousand published tribal writers. Youngest of
this gathering and deeply traditional, the bilingual poet Sherwin Bitsui—a
Many Goats and Bitter Water clan Diné from White Cone, Arizona—writes
in a 2003 Sun Tracks publication, *Shapeshift,* an early classic no less than
Joyce's *The Dubliners* or Momaday's *House Made of Dawn*:

At Deer Springs
Turn signals blink through ice in the skin.
Snake dreams uncoil,

burrow into the spine of books.
Night spills from cracked eggs.
Thin hands vein oars in a canyon bed.
We follow deer tracks back to the insertion of her tongue.

Here is a kind of fractal poetry (broken or fractured) that Alice Fulton admires as the post-formalist freeing of language and imagination ("Of Formal, Free, and Fractal Verse" 470–78). The lines coalesce in idiosyncratic ways, no diction, image, rhythm, or cadence continuous one insight to the next. The verse is radically sequenced in evolving patterns, as with fractal cloud formations (a mackerel sky or juniper bark) all caught up in the ghosted sweep of lucid detail, local image, precise naming, and immediate perception. The poem shifts from one shape to another, surreally: old clan and new trail, truck signal and book spine, iconic snake and local canyon, eggs and oars, deer tracks and matriarchal tongue. Bitsui's is verse-tracking of a different kind, poetry dangerously fresh as the quicksilver trail of a wintry shapeshifter (think of January cat's-paw across moonlit lake water). It's not easy to decode. Someone is signaling an icy turn, but which way? Ova are spilling origins of night, or is the crescent-moon-boat leaking eggs? Libidinously literate snakes uncoil the dark, and "thin hands" devolve to fins as they futilely "vein oars" in a dry canyon wash. Poor directions, bad dreams, dangerous books—backtracking the deer to a probing female tongue: sex, hunting, rowing, reading, and driving all cross in wildly leaping, darkly luminescent images.

If Diné sacred begins at the tongue's tip, to cite Luci Tapahonso, Bitsui's surreal backtracking speaks in split tongues. Internally rhythmic and voweling off-rhymes tie his disparate lines together phonetically: "signals" to begin and "uncoil" to reverse the second line, slur-enjambed to "burrow" and "Night spills" directly underneath in a visual-oral echo, with "vein oars" and "canyon bed" quick to "follow." This poet has an uncanny ear and peripheral vision. Vowels glide through the tongued nasals m and n—"Turn signals blink" to "in the skin." "Snake dreams uncoil" to "spine." "Night spills" toward the bent vowels in "cracked eggs." "Thin hands vein" to "canyon bed," and on into the mini-rhyme cadence reversing vowels in the mouth, "deer tracks back," to the erotic/lingual "insertion of her tongue" voweling down the throat. The poetry here is glutinously fractal, lyrics shaded in echoic howls. What seems to dissipate through fractured images soaks back in open-mouthed vowels, one liquid syllable pooling into another. "Bitsui haunts the edges between cultures, connecting the previously unconnected, finally dissolving the boundaries between worlds," his IAIA teacher Jon Davis blurbs *Shapeshift*.

SHEPHERDING VERSE

Sherwin Bitsui was born in 1975 in Fort Defiance, Arizona, a return stop on the Long Walk. He embodies the incendiary charge, visionary drive, musing spirit, and language passion of an emerging classical poet. Surreal, still traditionally based, "fool-blooded" Navajo, he says (with a Cherokee grandmother!), and Southwest denizen of rez tensions, Sherwin comes from sacred Native landscape, schooled in IAIA Fine Arts. By spring 2005 he had finished a B.A. in Creative Writing at the University of Arizona while editing the Internet arts journal and website RedInk and touring the country giving readings. "I grew up herding sheep in the hills," he says when asked how he became a poet, "daydreaming in summer." Crossing the Sheepskin Divide, Bitsui also saddlepacks Gen-X Grunge and Matrix blogs with retro homage to Jim Morrison of The Doors, eighties rock, and Ramsey Lewis jazz riffs. Bitsui writes image-thick poetry, paints palette-rich canvases, and makes documentary films, but he really wants to complete a novel. If lyric condensation releases as narrative arc, his next shapeshift may be prose fiction.

The generic tension between narrative *run run* and lyric *row row* decenters linear continuity. Crazy-dancing Southwestern deserts, Bitsui is the most radical poet yet considered, his second manuscript-in-progress to date, March 2005, he says the most "disruptive." The poet's range is staggering: ceremonial Diné culture to translated ethnography, TV ads and acid-rock lyrics to reservation politics and a history of colonial dispossession, personal artistic angst to youth crises and aesthetic obsessions and compulsions. His poems borrow from oral songs, dance chants, and creation stories translated by Washington Matthews, David McAllester, and Paul Zolbrod in Beautyway and Coyoteway gatherings. Yet every other Bitsui line bends back on itself, torques against lineation even if it breaks—shaded with historical black holes, reservation dislocations (the Long Walk, Code Talkers, Black Mountain coal disputes, Peabody uranium mining), radio jingles and highway billboards, rodeo emcees and powwow singers, The Doors and The Last Poets, The Beats and Language Poets. There is little *run run* progression in Bitsui's lines, more a fractured series of images that fire discontinuously, like the random discharges of popping corn or a swarm of flies buzzing at different pitches. The reader can't so much *read* the flow line, as cross-reference images discharging as free radicals in space. Conjure a meadow full of different birds all singing their own muses—sparrows chittering, blackbirds hallooing, jays screeching, finches skirring, robins yodeling, grackles squawking, meadowlarks caroling—hear all these together and try to trace, indeed to parse, the various melodies in the melee. Not chorus, nearer polytonal cacophony. No forward-flowing narrative, but lyric flashes firing off each other.

Teaching Arizona teenagers poetry, Bitsui asks them to see lyric diction and lined syntax as shifting frames in a filmscript (fractal petroglyphs in swirling panels). The camera pans from Panavision, to closeup, to fadeaway. Would there be interconnective patterns, he asks students, through the diversely framed perspectives of images? Consider a dozen various-size television sets in an electronics showroom, all tuned to different stations covering the day's news. The stories eventually overlap and corroborate one another more or less, even the commercials, but the immediate effect is white noise, eventually showing patterned discontinuity. Bitsui's verse reads then as embedded news-chaos theory, the poetic roughage of hyperactive images, found fractals.

The poet does not offer set text, sculpted as the lines seem, so much as crystalline catalysts or generative "seeds," he says, to take root and grow in the intercultural landscape. The poems call (through) him; he trusts his audience to do as they will in response to the performance—hair tied back (shorn after graduation), lambent eyes and skin, jeans and an open-neck black shirt, grey-striped suit jacket with a silver-and-turquoise crescent necklace. Call-and-response modulates the interchange, as in ceremonial prayer-song—he chants with his head tilted back, eyes closed, drumstick wrist measuring time, his reading a cadenced performance. No less than Sitting Bull or White Buffalo Calf and the Plains "all-color" *wanekia* of Black Elk's vision, Bitsui serves as pure example of the poet who *speaks like singing*. Just so, the more traditional Apache sculptor Allan Houser etches in stone the trancelike lift of the head and closed eyes among ceremonial chanters (as mentioned earlier, see his collected work in the Smithsonian National Museum of the American Indian on the Washington Mall, a stone's throw from Congress). Vocally edging each syllable a modernist character unto itself, Bitsui's lyric tenor voice modulates pitch two generations away from Allen Ginsberg howling down America, performance poetry that captured the young Navajo's imagination.

At thirty-one, Sherwin Bitsui is a celebrated poet of surreal leaps and shattering light, chosen by the Poetry Society of America among the twenty best 2005 emerging poets nationwide. He has read his work in Italy, Mexico, Canada, South America, and across the United States, where in eight months *Shapeshift* went into a second, then a third printing by March 2005. His collaborative, laptop digital film *Chrysalis* debuted at the 2002 Sundance Film Festival. And he paints like Wassily Kandinsky and Franz Marc of Der Blaue Reiter (Munich, 1907): "I climbed paint strokes to try to reach a world that shifted under the weight of ants" (*IAIA Chronicle*, cited in Bitsui website). No anxiety of influence for this sheepherding young artist, only the fractal imagination of shifting arroyos, soughing winds, passing clouds, and sacred mountains. Still, Sherwin Bitsui has Adrian Louis's outlandish candor, John Ashbury's over-the-top courage, Sherman Alexie's Red Beret sass, Frank O'Hara's wild high jinks, James Welch's dense brilliance, Allen Ginsberg's performance guts. This is quicksilver imagination, Native talent to make the mind jump, metaphorically wilder than any poet considered.

Radioactively charged and formally unstable by ordinary verse standards, Bitsui's poetry leaps as surds in sequence. He thinks through irreducible images. His verse fractals defy pattern and break trail through a contemporary wasteland, sifting pan-Native debris of a White Man's Scorched Earth Burden, Manifest Disdain for Native Rights, Pilgrim's Distress and Regress, Pioneer Annihilation, Westward Hoe and Saber Plow, Barbed Wire Hell, Lethal Freedom for Not Quite All (Dark Skins Unwelcome), Six-Gun Democracy, Death to the Infidel Savage, the Heathen Redskin, the Barbarian Wild Man and his Wanton Squaw. Choose your rez aftershock, go deep and feel the jagged edges.

SHIFTING SHAPES

We are only atoms trailing the carved skull
wrapped inside a sunbeam.
—"Halo"

Shapeshift, Sherwin Bitsui titles his first book of poems, "an inbetween place" from Dinétah to Spellcheck. "Shape'shift," he carefully abrupted the gap between the shaped syllables in UCLA class discussion, March 8, 2005. The vowel shift *a''ih* slides through a glottal stop, indeed a voiceless lateral glide *Sh'sh* of Diné Red English. Take back the endangered "beautiful" word *Shápe'shíft* as a spondaic force, the poet insists, *not* the appropriated Shapeshift*er* kitsch of Tony Hillerman's witchery tales. Still, all are shifting shape these days, this Diné says—American, Native American, Navajo, Bitter Water and Many Goats clans, the poet newly graduated after his "ten-year plan" of a dozen college years. Time shift to space warp, the post-9/11 world and free verse "on fire," *Shapeshift* may be closer to the algebraic poetry of nuclear physics than standard verse alchemy.

To shapeshift is to change form, perhaps to elude, certainly to baffle or to mystify. Shapeshift implies tracking or being tracked—possibly a hunting, detecting, or divining metaphor. The word certainly raises protean questions of identity, pursuit, capture, and release. An animal shapeshifter in Navajo thinking can be a trickster, say a crow or coyote, where the humor of the hunt (disguise, trickery, deception, even thievery) remains basic to desert survival. Laughing at the odds is critical. A shapeshifter can be more dangerous, a witch or demonic figure the Navajo call *Skinwalker*, though the poet wants nothing to do with the virtual fictions that have festered around faux witchcraft. The subject is off-limits for public discourse, certainly taboo for non-Indian pop art. According to Navajo belief, these incestuous ghouls disguised under coyote or wolf hides prey on humans. They seduce victims with narcotic plants, confusing and disorienting and destroying them. To cast spells Skinwalkers hide nail parings or hair strands in graves. They shoot prey with bone or ash from death-contaminated hogans, erase their finger- and footprints, powder them into "corpse poison." Skinwalkers are much to be avoided, even as Tony Hillerman appropriates isomorphic terror in the fictional thriller *Skinwalkers*. Kluckhohn and Leighton's classic *The Navaho* documents a fifteen-year-old Diné testament:

> There is one of them down there towards those hills. They cover
> themselves with a skin of a dog, or a bear. They dig up the dead
> men, then they make them small so that they can fit in the hand
> and take it home. Then they sing and make the small dead man
> get big again. Then they put something on that dries them up,
> and they grind it up. Then they put the powder in a deerskin
> bag and carry it with them even if they don't have their skin on.
> When they put this powder on you, you die. (189)

Do people have defenses against such witchery? In traditional thinking, well-worn fears can be countered with the good medicine of allies, prayers, ceremonies, and guardian spirits. The Diné appeal to the *hozhó* natural good order of all things in the living oral roots of poetry. For example, the difference between Changing Woman, cyclically evolving Navajo creatrix, and horrific shapeshifting hinges on natural and unnatural change—annual life cycles in naturally evolutionary development—as opposed to artificial intrusion and ill-intended meddling. Navajos hold that ignoring right ways to live causes disorderly harm. Don't go against the organic order of things. Wind, water, earth, fire, wood, and stone all form and flow according to their own nature and within nature's larger patterns. So *don't* counter (the given organic) reality, old ones hold the world over, Lao Tsu to Luci Tapahonso. Such are the laws of the way things are and always have been for the People. Still globally, Bitsui says, all beings shift shape to accommodate living in the twenty-first century.

Ill-intended meddlers or witches, according to Diné thinking, mess with things as they are or should be. They contort and distort, cross nature and change natural forms. Witches just can't let things be, as Silko narrates in *Ceremony*, and they try to upset or to reshape or to snuff out natural life. Witches, make no mistake, are up to no good. They shift shape to disorient, attract to deceive, seduce to destroy right ways of behavior and being. This is where traditional words and medicine cross homeopathically. The People say the right way to do anything, *hozhó*, is layered into singing and praying the ways things have always been changing cyclically. *As it used to be long ago may I walk*, the Navajo timelessly sing, as cited in the beginning of this study. Living by *hozhó* brings health and happiness, harmony and beauty.

So Changing Woman changes as the earth *moves* through time, Kluckhohn, McNeley, Matthews, Zolbrod, and others detail (see Witherspoon's *Language and Thought in the Navajo Universe*). "In Navajo origin narratives," Karen Ritts Benally writes, "Changing Woman is a kind of quintessential 'earth mother' who matures and changes like the seasons, always within a process of renewal. It is Changing Woman who creates The People (*Diné*, Navajo) from the epidermis of her own flesh, stabilizes and enriches the world in which they are to live, and provides them with the knowledge and skills necessary for maintaining a good life" ("Thinking Good," in *American Indian Grandmothers* 25). Changing Woman seasonally evolves with the four winds. She ages with grace and beauty, mutating normally, and rebirths with each new life. She accepts all forms of natural balance, harmony, truth, and goodness as *hozhó*. Contrariwise, shape-changers challenge the natural ways of things, disruptive of right order and attitude; they would run the seasons counterclockwise. Shapeshifters slough in and out of recognizable identity, confusing and tricking and thieving other life-forms. Hence shifting shape can be positive in a risky sense (learning, for example, the skills to hunt or to heal or to spell behavior), or wantonly negative in a predatory sense.

As noted, coyotes are just such problematic border-shifters, living on the edges of given orders, feeding on critters and castoffs, mocking their human counterparts. Some Navajos say they have human eyes, even God's eyes, Hope Ryden documents in *God's Dog*. Tribes differ on coyote. Pueblo Natives shun him, Navajos track his ways (see, for example, the curing ceremonies discussed in Karl W. Luckert's *Coyoteway*). Ravens, crows, owls, and blackbirds too can be shamanic raptors playing off human order and surviving on the *de*risive coyote fringe. Like dark comic poets, these creatures live in between the fire and the night, shamanically sliding from shape to shadow. They can either move in the life-affirming (laughing) direction of natural order, or away from the light into the bewitching darkness. Altogether their shapeshifting is dangerously empowering, uncertain and destabilizing—to be emulated only in dire straits, not to be wholly trusted, even then taken with a due human measure of salt, suspicion, and spit. Watch out, the old ones say, around shape-changers.

> Beware! In time they will return, those who were pushed
> beyond our lands. They will come drinking *black water*,
> speaking nonsense, making pictures with a stick, and they will
> claim this land as theirs. They will come like thunder in the sky.
> They will turn brother against brother. When this happens the
> world will soon be turned upside down.
> —Zuni prophesy following the 1540 Coronado Expedition,
> Museum of Indian Arts & Culture, Santa Fe, New Mexico

Sherwin Bitsui's poetry is at once baffling and dangerous, comic and chaotic, survivalist and shamanic—surely to be avoided by insecure readers, feared by faltering lyricists, shunned by mainstream formalists. No less than Ginsberg, Welch, or Alexie, this Navajo shapeshifter upsets all poetic certainty and lyric comfort. Poetry metamorphoses as slippery anagram of history fractured, culture decimated but clinging to the desert, family shattered, clan divided, environment uprooted and despoiled, personal identity inebriate, even schizoid, and verse fractal. These tribal schisms blow-back in the aftershock of the *Discovery*. Zuni elder Edmund J. Ladd blames world imbalances on "coffee drinking, foul talking people who make thunder in the sky with their jet aircraft" ("Here, Now & Always," Santa Fe Museum of Indian Arts & Culture, 2004). In Bitsui's poetry the ideal balance, beauty, goodness, and harmony of *hozhó* is offset by hallucinatory scat and a decreative scattering of linear focus. As in Welch, postmodern poetry rides a Red-earth Removal rez quarter section. Shifting shape to stay upright takes only the first stutter step: there may be no pheasant in the brush after all, only coyote's yawp; no ice on the hot stove, only a hogan smoke hole; no red wheelbarrow in the rain, only an abandoned covered wagon; no house made of dawn or jacklight clearing, not even Earthboy riding the quake of frontier history, only the quicksilver slime of poetic elision. Readers best move carefully and closely through the poems, one at a time. Summation is risky.

REFERENCE MARKS

So Kit Carson killed crops not Navajos.
—Ruth Underhill, *The Navajos*

Open *Shapeshift* to the first page, "Asterisk," meaning *small star* in Greek. The asterisk is a writer's "reference mark," Random House says, "or to indicate omission, doubtful matter, etc." Bitsui sees the asterisk as a sign that blots out or *disappears* things, self-referential sign of something missing. Questionable matter, critical doubt, asterisk is also used as a verb: "to asterisk a word that requires a footnote." There are no footnotes, no guiding stars in Bitsui's poems. Context, subtext, pretext, postlude—the reader must hunt for and fill in the missing Diné data and reconstruct the narrative Red-line, poem by poem, line at a time. There's some explaining to be done, if things are to clear up. Some tracking, perhaps backtracking into Native America, some fessing up, even confessing to do.

Fourteen ninety-something,
   something happened
and no one can pick it out of the lineup,
its rising action photographed
    when the sign said: *do not look*
       irises planted inside here.

No easy images or clear directives, except to say that somewhere in the 1490s Native homelands were "discovered," they say—more precisely, *invaded*—and for five hundred years 50 to 60 million Indians were "rubbed out." Statistics don't lie. Western liberators, Natives say, *discover* indigenous cultures to eradicate them, and 'Skins talk back in mixed voices—Momaday's "The Morality of Indian-Hating" in *Ramparts* (Summer 1964), to Deloria's "Custer Died For Your Sins" in *Playboy* (August 1969), to Alexie's "White Men Can't Drum" in the *New York Times Magazine* (4 October 1991), to Joy Harjo and Gloria Bird's *Reinventing the Enemy's Language* (Norton, 1997). From Columbus through Cortés, Coronado and De Soto to Johns Smith and Rolfe, Lewis and Clark to Kit Carson, the killings have left Indians in shock, dumb, devastated, at a loss for words or actions: "*something* happened." It's a felony no official will finger in the criminal lineup. But yes, they've been photographed in tatters—Geronimo scowling and Ishi smiling, Wounded Knee and the new 1890 reservations, World War I volunteer soldiers and Native citizenship in 1924, the Southwest Harvey Hospitality Houses for Union Pacific tourism and 1934 Reorganization Act powwows, World War II Code Talkers and Ira Hayes at Iwo Jima, Navajo uranium workers dying of cancer and photogenic drunks in Gallup, government commodities and bingo parlors, powwows and halfway houses—but "*do not look*" the verse sign warns. Looking dead into the toxic flash of Native affairs could be hard on the eyes, citizen.

Detaching line break, indent shift: "*irises planted inside here.*"

An ethnic *iris* colors and guards the eye, the word coming from the Greek for all-colors "rainbow." Bitsui may be thinking Noah's Flood or Navajo Beautyway, the promise of no more ethnic cleansing or the arced blessing across a Southwestern desert after life-giving rains. The choice may be Trinity Site or House Made of Dawn, both or neither. In *Strangers to Ourselves*, Julia Kristeva describes that "rainbow of pain" all share after Hiroshima, the global mushroom cloud hanging over love, *mon amour*, first rising over White Sands, New Mexico, from yellowcake mined by Navajo workers in 1945.

But look—
  something lurking in the mineshaft—
a message, ice in his cup,
  third leg uprooted but still walking.
It peers over his shoulder at the dirt road dug into the mesa's skirt,
 where saguaro blossoms bloom nightfall at the tip of
   its dark snout,

and motor oil seeps through the broken white line of
   the teacher's loom.

Contrary impulses push the verse margins. Don't look, but look (rub-
berneck the crash)—is that mineshaft *something* a dying native canary,
as Felix Cohen warned in the 1952 *Handbook of Federal Indian Law*,
or just Frost's poetic ice tinkling in a cup of rotgut? Is Williams's three-
legged local dog still limping along, uprooted, unwanted? They should
have put Indians on wheels, the Winnebago Red Dog said of rez relocation in the nineteenth century (Nabokov, *Native American Testimony*
145). Shapeshifter peers over someone's shoulder at the White Man's
road dug into the mesa's skirt (a sexually intrusive mining track) where
penile cactus petals mushroom by night (a giant Piman saguaro cactus
with thick spiny stems and white flowers). Crankcase oil smears the
broken white line of driving promises and weaving lessons blurred across
classroom margins.

DO WE RAMBLE WHEN WE SPEAK IN TONGUES?

Bitsui shapeshifts in metaphoric chaos, unraveling and leaping trail like
a wired Walt Whitman. Parsing shaggy lines may needle an impatient
culture tracker. The poet remains identifier, spotter, tagger, but never
completer, comforter, or assured critic. The reader must unravel tangled
webs of time, place, and Native identity in a world of nuclear fission and
fractal art.

> *Something,*
> can't loop this needle into it,
> occurs and writes over their lips with thread;
>> barnacles on their swings;
>> fleas hyphened between their noses;
>>> eels asphyxiating in the fruit salad.

Acid-rock images, radioactive poetic meltdown: it's all deconstructing
in a flurry of fractals, proving a disruptive rule that breaks irregular
shapes free of larger patterns refracted at odd angles—clouds mutating,
winds swirling over troubled waters, sands shifting, land eroding, coastlines crumbling, time sagging, stars sliding. Recall "fraction" or literally *broken in pieces.* "I coined the word fractal in 1975 from the Latin

fractus," Benoit Mandelbrot says, "which describes a broken stone— broken up and irregular" (John Gribben, *Deep Simplicity: Bringing Order to Chaos and Complexity* 89). Think of reconstructing a thousand-year-old Mimbres pot from a broken shard, then archaeologically recontextualizing ancestral village life around the pieces, guessing and cussing and discussing the fractured possibilities. Imagine gravediggers in the backyard. Indians are no strangers to disinterring, theorizing, alien social scientists stealing them culturally blind (see Deloria's *Custer Died For Your Sins* and Basso's *Portraits of "The Whiteman"*).

FRACTAL FISSURES

Alice Fulton lifts fractal poetic form from Mandelbrot's studies of chaotic phenomena—earthquakes, neurons firing memories, price jumps in the stock market, turbulent weather, galaxy distribution, the Nile flooding. "To put it simply," the New York poet says, "each part of a fractal form replicates the form of the entire structure. Increasing detail is revealed with increasing magnification, and each smaller part looks like the entire structure, turned around or tilted a bit" ("Of Formal, Free, and Fractal Verse" 475). Chaos yields chronos, given the right angle of vision. Look into the spiral petals of a rose or the coils of a seashell and notice the five-eighths principle of an organically expanding radius in nature's most efficient growth pattern ($1+1=2+1=3+2=5+3=8+5=13$ . . .). A fractal configuration works in substructures that replicate indefinitely— juniper-bark puzzles, riverbed mud cracks, cactus spines, geologic striations. Coastlines fracture and fall asymmetrically into the ocean. At any one moment the shores of the Colorado River, for example, slough into deeper waters; hence boundaries are permeably dissolving, even as the land remains a geologic jigsaw in-process. Just so, a Bitsui verse line abrupts within and ruptures along its edge, as eruptive clump implodes each preceding insight and splintering icon shatters ideation, image to image. The line itself caves toward a dead weight chaos that continually leads on as cultural shorelines fall into the sea. The poem "whispers juniper to the wilderness," Bitsui says in new work, "calling us home."

Still there is *hozhó* hope. Order governs natural disorder, the fractal diviner says, pattern cadences disorderly art. Fulton reassures the reader that "any line when examined closely (or magnified) will reveal itself to be as richly detailed as was the larger poem from which it was taken; the poem will contain an infinite regression of details, a nesting of pattern within pattern" ("Of Formal, Free, and Fractal Verse" 475). The free-form organic sculptor Andy Goldsworthy throws a fistful of snow into the winter wind showering fractals or drops a handful of powdered red clay into a summer brook swirling fractals (see his 2001 documentary film *Rivers and Tides*). Cultures collide and cross. Wassily Kandinsky rides a blue horse through the mesquite, Alexej von Jawlensky adopts a *Yeibicheii* mask, and Franz Marc sets up shop in a hogan.

So for starters, digression, abruption, fragmentation, and discontinuity reveal buried but governing aesthetic forms that certainly *were there*, rather than chaos or patternless "free" verse. Through shifting glyphic stills a viewer imagines the fractal patterns that would have made up an abandoned Navajo *hooghan*. Through slants, cracks, fractures, and fissures, someone might sense the *hozhó* that once made sense, was beautiful, seemed true, balanced good and evil in a fortuitous homing for the old ones. The same hidden structure or *deep song*, as Lorca called it, holds for neoprimitive art or atonal music. Yet *Something* in Bitsui's lines (subject or object or agent-recipient) can't rethread the needle—can barely sew dead lips together with verse string, hardly barnacle their (s)wings, the lines say. *Something* only binarily hyphenates mixed-blood nostrils as Native American fleas, badly asphyxiates Thanksgiving eels in the pioneer fruit salad. "Nits make lice," Colonel Chivington snarls at Sand Creek. Unweaving blankets, sea debris and nitty critters—Thanksgiving gifts (eel and corn) saving the 1621 Puritans at Plymouth—the poet crosses dark, ironic visions of the New World with the devastated Old. *They* are collateral damage in the five-hundred-year war, militant patriots say, to asterisk the hearts and minds of The People.

"Remember, every wrist of *theirs* acclimates to bruises," the out-riding line to the seven-line stanza in four reminds the reader as an after-thought (4 x 7 = 28 lunar phase lines in the moon's fractal pattern, 28 patterned fragments on a turtle shell, province of *Klehanoai* or Moon-Carrier, husband of White Shell Woman, younger sister to Changing Woman, the Diné say). Kinship dictates pattern. Lineage is all. And don't forget, witness-reader, the invaders profit from wounds that don't heal, so never trust the pain of aboriginal insurgents. Broken-branched fingers hover in ghostly gloves around skinned trees.

> Twigs from their family tree flank the glove's aura
> > and asterisk water towers invisible,
> while fragrant rocks in the snout remain
> unnoticed in the bedroom,
> because the bridegroom wanted in,

Pioneers wanted in,
and the ends of our feet yellowed to uranium at the edge of fear.

Shape-changing casts intractable shadows, the fractal image of "asterisk water towers invisible": family trees splintered, clans uprooted, émigré invasions fracturing tribal moieties and vaporizing caches of precious runoff. Think back to La Cienega petroglyphs of breeding women and underground springs in the Ancestral beginnings. The promise of water to the desert remains an asterisk on the disappearing horizon of quick artesian claims, broken treaties, Long Marches, land steals, tourist invasions, rescinded sovereignty, military conscription, diabetes and alcoholism, roadside homicides and open-pit mining, Peabody Coal and Thriftway Convenience Gas.

Something's up someone's nose, "rocks in the snout" intimately invisible, the logic unravels, because Adam wanted back into the Garden. John Rolfe was John Smith's second chance at Pocahontas, his dusky Eve. "Pioneers wanted in, / and the ends of our feet yellowed to uranium at the edge of fear." That is to say, canary miner feet yellowcake to the slow genocide of uranium poisoning at the crevasse of the pit of fear ("Call it an ocean of fear of the dark," Joy Harjo says in *She Had Some Horses*). Make no mistake, readers are looking down into the radioactive holocaust of Native history. *Pioneer* literally means "foot soldier," or those who dig trenches for the troops. Pioneer also tags a plant introduction that takes over the garden. The word Pioneer was used to christen a probe satellite in outer space, as well as christen the earliest "discoverers" of the New World. *Wanting* pioneers got in and dug up everything, Natives counter, and now want to quick-claim outer space.

White Space

[The Navajo in 1868] recognized that life was fragile,
that harmony within oneself and within one's family
could prove elusive, and that contact with others
might provide new benefits or pose unanticipated
dilemmas. Nevertheless, the promise of finding
something better usually outweighed the danger of
discovering something worse. Already it was becoming
a society noteworthy for its members' willingness

to look around the corner and over the next hill,
for their curiosity about what might be gained by
exploration and inquiry, and for their determination to
do something well. Is it any wonder that others might
consider joining such a people—less enamored of
routine and more tolerant of innovation?

—Peter Iverson,
Diné: A History of the Navajos

The second poem is a date only, "1868," no text. "What could I say?" the poet says about an "unnameable" moment of mourning. A page of silence respects the ancestral dead. The date 1868 refers to the Diné "Fearing Times"—five-years desert exile after Kit Carson's volunteers in 1863–64, including vengeful Zuni, Hopi, Ute, and Pueblo gun-bearing recruits, burned the Canyon de Chelly corn, wheat, and peach trees and shot all the goats, sheep, cows, and ponies ("a reservoir of Navajo-haters ready to be let loose," Underhill says in *The Navajos* 117). Soldiers commanded some eight-and-a-half thousand *Lords of the Soil* three hundred miles on the *Long Walk* to Fort Sumner, a fifteen-mile-a-day forced march to the arid wasteland of eastern New Mexico. Fugitive Diné hid in arroyos and canyons, far into the Painted Desert or with other tribes. Dumped on a barren plain of forty square miles, the captives were herded into the "Navajo Corral," counted like sheep, and issued bacon, flour, and coffee. Diné POWs suffered yearly crop failures and Comanche raids, snaring rats, birds, and rabbits and digging wild roots for food. Thousands died walking both ways, half of these from smallpox. "All who go in never come out," a Diné named Herrero complained of the Fort Sumner hospital. General William Tecumseh Sherman said at Bosque Redondo, New Mexico, 28 May 1868, "You have no farms, no herds, and are now as poor as you were when the government brought you here" (Iverson, *Diné* 63). Treaty Day came four days later when the Diné renounced raids and captives. "After we get back to our country," the leader Barboncito promised, "it will brighten up again and the Navajos will be happy as the land, black clouds will rise and there will be plenty of rain" (Iverson, *Diné* 64). Little more can be said about the foot trail, a broken human procession ten miles long, back to Diné Bikéyah.

Enjambed silence—white space, the *unnameable*.

Deluge/drought, Bitsui's poems either spark a fractal firestorm—unstable asterisk icons—or catatonia. "If I could come back as a Superhero," Bitsui mugs in class lecture, "I'd be Captain Asterisk." A reader doesn't know what to expect next, shapeshifting yawp to verbal arrest: drunk talk, schizoid swings, hysterical metaphors, dumb rage, verbose pyrotechnics—or silent space. Keith Basso's linguistic work with Western Apache proves useful in contextualizing the poetry. The Cibecue keep silent out of respect and distance from unknowables, including strangers, showing restraint toward uncertainty and unpredictability ("'To Give Up on Words,'" in *Western Apache Language and Culture*). In cousin Diné crossover, the Navajo remain silent to face absence, anger, mourning, and healing ceremony. To say "1868" or "The Long Walk" or "Fearing Times" speaks for itself, enough said—fused time-space takes on wounded speech flesh, a horrific cultural *chronotope* à la Bakhtin.

GOOD TALK

So you just go around together and don't talk.
At first, it's better that way. Then, after a while,
when you know each other, you aren't shy anymore
and can talk good.

—Teenage Cibecue Apache, Basso
Western Apache Language and Culture

Bitsui's translative verse remains wildly reactive in a bilingual tongue, Red English *inbetween* immigrant and Native dialects, often indecipherable. There are no Diné fricatives for *r* or *f*, Underhill notes in *The Navajos*, but a goodly share of consonant *Sh-sh* as in Shapeshift (123). English turns on nouns, Bitsui says, Navajo works through verbs. Hearing his dad speak Diné through a cell phone gives this son strength away from home at readings in New York or Venice or Los Angeles. Alas, Navajo has thirteen verb tenses, Gary Witherspoon explains in *Language and Art in the Navajo Universe* (21), and 356,200 words for *go*. Kluckhohn and Leighton characterize Diné as "excessively literal" and "almost overneat, overprecise," recalling the "scrupulous symmetry" of a Bach fugue: "The language of The People delights in sharply defined categories. It likes, so to speak, to file things away in neat little packages. It favors always the concrete and particular, with little scope for abstractions" (*The Navaho*). Hence with postbellum asterisk as starry fissile fractal, a Native speaker can't have a Diné noun without verbing something. "Navaho focuses interest upon doing—upon verbs as opposed to nouns or adjectives," Kluckhohn and

Leighton stress. And Bitsui's radical verse certainly verbs things concretely, however hyper-molecular. "I peel the edges of the world toward me and away," Bitsui told my UCLA poetry class (8 March 2005). "I hear the words come into the poem."

Keith Basso's discussion of imagist analogues among the Cibecue Western Apache helps to unpack metaphoric density, to unravel Bitsui's iconic semantics ("'Wise Words' of the Western Apache: Metaphor and Semantic Theory," in *Western Apache Language and Culture*). Non-Indians need to approach language and culture both inside (phon*emic*) and outside (phon*etic*), Basso argues, if they are to parse local linguistic systems and to intuit human universals in speech (27). So, too, fractal poetics may be "old like hills, like stars," Black Elk sees through his purblindness. Creative imaging is Natively critical among Athabascan kin. The linguistic anthropologist takes the case back two-and-a-half millennia to Aristotle, who regarded *metaphor* as the "sign of genius" leaping holes in language to imply "an intuitive perception of the similarity in dissimilars" (*Western Apache* 53). Saying what one means is a start, but metaphorically leaping across muted silence may be genius itself.

Classics jump gaps. Imagine being *inbetween* hyphenated Native-American. Asserting one *thing* to be *some*thing *else* bridges the gap in designative usage: "*Some*thing there *is* that *doesn't love* a *wall*," Robert Frost concludes with chilly abruption, and the contracted verb "doesn't" *spells* the walled "gaps" (*not*'s missing "o" apostrophied). The asterisked gap in the walled line implies holes in the neighbor's folksy argument for adjoining fences. Dickinson metaphorically sees "a certain Slant of light" and holds "Much Madness is divinest Sense—." The poet listens acutely while dashing through the linguistic wreckage of Civil War, Calvinist rapture, patriarchal privilege, and thwarted sentiment: "*Being, but an Ear, / And I, and Silence, some strange Race / Wrecked, solitary, here—.*" Spondaic meter and abruptive metaphor slow the lines to a suspended hyphen.

No less classically lyric in the Southwest, Basso's elder Apache with talking time to master ancient metaphor discover and make up *wise words*. With penetrant wit, these elders find the genius to see where others don't look, the common words to say what can't be told commonly: *ravens are widows* (fringe feeding); *lightning is a boy* (unpredictably shooting here and there, dangerously); *the White man is a carrion beetle* (wasting food left behind); *dogs are children* (disruptive). It is not what things "look like," Apache elders instruct, but "what they do" that encodes things in such *wise* metaphoric *words* (*Western Apache* 59, 65). The World War II Code Talkers spoke in poetic tongues: *shark* for submarine, *hawk* for fighter plane.

Sherwin Bitsui is a fractal image-coder whose metaphors leap to speak "appropriately" *in tongues*, as the Apache say, *not* just correctly by grammarian's rules. The old ones, or ones ancient in their imaginations, Basso notes, discover and master *wise word* metaphors as cultural signs of lingual genius, to say things freshly, perceptively, creatively, memorably.

John Miles Foley calls this distinction of axial "words" from ordinary words the *Immanent Art* of oral poetic performance, "a repertoire of registers," borrowing from Dell Hymes's anthropological linguistics, that works in and through traditional contexts, behind and between verbal signs (*How to Read* 114). The coded registers resonate beyond common language into tribal memory, from Homeric epic, to Beowulf, to Nuyorican Café slam performance, to Serbian bardic song-poem. The Old English bard cries *Hwæt!* or *Lo!* and the epic battle song is off and running. According to Foley, the performative context of text, process not product, "is the performance, the audience, the poet, the music, the specialized way of speaking, the gestures, the costuming, the visual aids, the occasion, the ritual, and myriad other aspects of the given poem's reality" (*How to Read* 60). Just so, Bitsui's fractal images and fractured syntax come through tribal context, ceremonial performance, and distinguished lineage (Aristotle, Shakespeare, Blake, Black Elk, Tapahonso, Welch, Harjo, Momaday, Hogan, Alexie). Difficult to read, yes, and never easy to do, Bitsui's poetry spans *inbetween* ground—deep-rooted, clairvoyant, lucid, arresting, shapeshifting—true to his people, places, and times.

FORKLIFT DIALECTS

If we lose our language, we will lose our breath.
Then we will die and blow away like leaves.

—Mrs. Annie Peaches, Cibecue Apache,
Western Apache Language and Culture

Keep going to the third poem "Atlas," which means world-bearer, mapbook, Arabic for *silk-smooth*. Will what a reader knows or learns have anything to do with *bearing* or *smoothing* what one makes of the lines? "Tonight I draw a raven's wing inside a circle," the poet says, and in a nanosecond the icon "expands into a hand." Nothing stable, all in shapeshifting quickness. Verse country of trickster radicals—wing and hand reaching—black raptor trapped as wild wings in circles: "we thrash against pine needles inside the earthen pot." The shard is cased invisibly in its shattered form, as conversely Ancestral Pueblo pots are broken with "kill holes" to put them down. Discussed in the beginning, a pre-Pueblo congeries of cultures disappeared by 1300 from Mesa Verde, to Chaco Canyon, to Canyon de Chelly, to Monument Valley. From Dinétah to Gallup, Trickster shiftily elegizes handcuffs (pen/penal/penury), protests traffic jams as prisoner of urban rez hours, "and speaks the dialect of a forklift" over cedar-smoke mesas "acred to the furthest block." The forked bilingualism of Red or "Joe Babe" English (boarding-school Navajo in Tapahonso's verse) splits a raptor's tongue, no less than raven jabbering "Atlas." Displacing "forked-pole" hogan construction, BIA reservation Indian housing has been surveyed into suburban plots, squared land with rectangular government hogans (once six-sided to eight-sided mudded log structures with cedar-pole roofs). The HUD housing Projects no longer follow riparian life-ways, wandering arroyos, sky-view mesas, or cool river canyons.

Car headlights flare at sundown as raven's eye Coyote wraps around his own bitten tail, forklifting the world as a foolish mining Atlas bearing all things, "shaped like another reservation— / another cancelled check." Post-traditionally speaking, the circle is broken, sacred hoop scattered, the snake with a canine tail in his mouth. *Rezzed out* Indians, as Bitsui says in passing, have reservations about all this, to be sure, poor survivors of the land surveyance, their reparations in arrears, their accounts bankrupt. The dishwasher dies with red lights flashing through his wrinkled ribbon shirt of quilted ceremonies. The destitute poet muses in his kitchen, ignoring the buzz of Coyote warning of car headlights (snuffed stars from Coyoteway). The dogs lie silenced by the thought of lunar respite, constellations shaking the quivering gourd of ashes (Ancestral Pueblo portent of the atomic bomb scratched into rocks above the Hopi mesas), the Beautyway gone south. Hopi elder Thomas Banyacya's distress mission to the United Nations in 1948, warning of global nuclear holocaust in a precarious time of shapeshifting changes, strikes a far Southwestern cry from "the wonder and the beauty and the strangeness" of Black Elk's Great Vision up north. The film cliché of Indians hearing horses coming through train tracks stains the tawdry romance of the unmade bed. "In the cave on the backside of a lie / soldiers eye the birth of a new atlas," another New World deceit within and underneath the worn map-book of "Indian" Discovery. A naked Native woman straddles an armadillo silhouetting Mother America, as Amerigo Vespucci mapped the New World, and the ant-eating "little armed men" mutter, *"one more mile."* How much farther must Manifest Destiny go, those moving-picture pioneers, the unsettlers displacing rooted Natives, mapping the unmapped home country of Native America, the Diné, the People?

one more mile, they say,
                    one more mile.

PETROGLYPHIC GHOSTS

Tracking critters, taking no game yet, the reader comes to the third alphabetized poem, "Apparition," that begs dazed connection filling in postcolonial blanks.

I haven't _____
since smoke dried to salt in the lakebed,
since crude oil dripped from his parting slogan,
        the milk's sky behind it,
                birds chirping from its wig.

What is it that readers don't see or hear? If the allusion is true, the poet hasn't done something for some time (eaten, slept, written?). Perhaps he has restrained from something dangerous (smoke, drugs, drink?) though a reader doesn't know what, just that the poet hasn't _____ since smoke smudged the dried lagoon, the oil rigger left, and the whitened sky backed birdsong behind a false hairpiece. A tangled mess of missing things. Strange, the mapmaker ponders the mare's nest, how the old ones pecked out their belonging in rocks and prophetically walked through rearview mirrors into a future orbiting around knives circling a galaxy of apparitions. Is this the portent of ancestral petroglyphs, as with the Whirling Logs (swastika), Red Sun (Japanese flag), and Gourd of Ashes (atomic bomb) at Hopi Third Mesa? Where is Hopi Jug Boy, the Southwestern rediscovery of women and water carved into the La Cienega and Chaco Canyon stones? Perhaps September's early fall betrayed a late Indian summer, solar fire only white lies. Or perhaps the other guy burned up the phone book, the poet suspects, blood seeping from memory's light socket, rivering "mud deep when imagination became an asterisk in the mind." Something's certainly messed or missing again, typos and slips of the tongue, the dangerous play of dreaming things up. No footnotes fill in the absence, no explicator beckons in the wings. Tough verse going, watch the match's blue flame, the pyrotech says.

Mention _____,
    and a thickening lump in the ozone layer
    will appear as a house with its lights turned off—
        radio waves tangled like antlers inside its oven,
because *somewhere*
    in the hallway nearest thirst,
        the water coursing through our clans
      begins to evaporate
        as it slides down our backseats—
its wilderness boiled out of our bodies.

Diné of the *Todich'ii'nii* or Bitter Water Clan, born for the *Tl'izilani* or Many Goats Clan (indeed 1975 in Fort Defiance, Arizona, known as "Hell's Gate" to cavalry soldiers in 1851, then a returning way station in the 1868 Long Walk back), Bitsui asterisks global warming (Great White Father in denial) and the coming shutdown of Native homes, their ovens antlered with emergency radio waves (another Auschwitz relocation?). Car seats lose precious rainwater drained from the asterisk reservoirs of a previous poem. The natural world and all its wildness have been boiled like bitter coffee from the people's bodies. *Of* Bitter Water, *for* Many Goats, consider self-introductions in a minor key from Luci Tapahonso. Swirling fractal icons, surreal doesn't begin to speak to the shapeshift here, more a lingual space warp in time. For a Native this slippage signals postcolonial *Apparition*, a prophetic ghostly petroglyph. The nightmare warning won't go away, despite the silencing of Diné tongues. Loose fractals add up to missing song-stories—"shocking, beautiful, sensual," the poet asks of his art.

WEEPING MONGOLIANS

Sherwin's poetry is obscure and different—deep politics. He has passion and *Duenda* present within his paintings and poetry.

           —Jon Davis, Institute of
           American Indian Arts

"The Skyline of a Missing Tooth" breaks the alpha-betic title order. By now a reader can hazard that Bitsui's verse crosses inner and outer cultural senses, micro-shift to macro-warp, with the riddling ease of a star gambler in the old stories. This inner dental loss in a gap-toothed heaven works two ways: a butte sticking up through the sky (bicuspid Shiprock or "Winged Rock")—or a horizon road-cut, maybe arroyo gash (Interstate #40 through Gallup). Either way, there's a fracture in the skyline. "The ice hook untwists inside the whirlwind like a tail." Speaking in split tongue, Coyote bites down on his own—a cycloning broken circle, the ice hook of White intrusion. Raven's rib matches Adam's sin, a rusted core gaffer-taped with Eden's apple skins. Whipped eggs caulk the cement cracks of the gatekeeper's interrogative road. Regurgitive images of penal evil in mass culture filched from movies like *The Exorcist* or *Alien*, *Shawshank Redemption* or *The Green Mile* italicize the lines with celluloid prophesy: *"The fourth generation of bees flee the unlocked mouth."*

"You there," the interrogator challenges the reader with Native worm hook, "you there," land bridge to the old ways, "your apathy grows like gray hair in these untied shoes." Pale moccasins sink through the comfort zones of cultureless suburbia. A reductionist crossing straits theory fills "the quarried pockets of the pilgrim": all Natives are émigrés, the anthros opine in cultural countershift. All are interlopers, all newcomers taking plants and minerals from the New World (corn and tobacco fields, gold and silver, turquoise and coal, oil and obsidian, hydrogen and uranium beds). *Your people speak like weeping Mongolians,* nameless anthros whine in "The Northern Sun." Everyone came from somewhere else, the émigré homeboys rationalize, even Native Americans long ago. The caged wren almost sits comfortably in her BIA penal zone. "Motor oil trickles from the harpooned log." The images cross and startle, New England whale oil lighting a city on the hill, Linda Hogan laments, to SUV black gold in Oklahoma oil fields. All gone south. "The Milky Way backbones the nervous system of the stream the deer sips." Reflecting light off the sun's neck, a sunflower of lice, *"This is where I broke the ice."* The poet rhymes the land bridge back to the old ways—the People stoned down, fleeing, their hair unbraiding from fan belts of disinterred internal-combustion engines. A surreal cliché settles over ruptured pioneer film-trails west: *"One twin kissed the other in the uncovered wagon."* *Nostos* or returning home may be the core fractal pattern.

Witnesses envision all this through ravaged and troubled, deranged and prophetic *Indian* eyes, neckties unraveling, rain clouds eclipsing the sun, the nightmarish suburbs gloving the gilled evolution of First Americans. The images so impact and overlay and embed mystery that MLA crowbars from critical hell cannot detach them. The dishwasher poet works at his sink, plates leaping from the lies that layer them, a vengeful spear driven under the pilgrim's skirt: "*the skyline of a missing tooth.*" Where does the abscess, the abuse come clean?

STILL BLUE

Your children shall learn paper.
—General William T. Sherman,
Fort Sumner, 1868

"At Deer Springs" came up earlier, backtracking oral tradition to the father clan Bitsui was *born for* at Deer Springs. Trek on to "The Eyes of the Executioner." Still no summaries—random fractals, or overriding chaos theory? At least readers know that *Somebody killed Something,* as Alice suspected of Wonderland Jabberwocky. "*No his fist did not become eggs, / his eyes are still blue.*" Enough to say that this is Red English or *being John,* the Diné say, language poetry through a frayed Sheepskin Curtain—nonsensical jibber-jabber, random metaphoric associations, wild image clusters, absurd crossings and broken synapses. And the blue-eyed boys still gun-barrel things, Sand Creek to Iraq. This Indian is talking back in lingual string theory. His "Official Blog" records for Wednesday, 1 September 2004, 9:14 p.m.:

Where have you gone poems? With your dreams of babies,
elevators that shout moonlight, the mountains that tumble
in and out of your sleep? All I have now are these strings of
matter. Vermont here in this knot, the Rez here tied around
a lump of coal, the inbetween places after closing time: lumps
in the throat, all here, around my waist, I hold in, what must
be held out.

Returning home (the old Native quest), the poet realizes "the islandless sea inside the ear of man." Darwinian Indian origins deafen the chartless discoverers "who stretched barbed wire over these grey hills" (the classic Navajo double-loom weavings of Two Grey Hills and the fencing of Native pastures of plenty). With an evolutionary shell to his lips, the poet trumpets the circling palomino that trampled the gap-toothed sky and bit the sun in two, holographic portent of a resurgent Native apocalypse, four ponies and a pale rider to come.

BITTER WATER

> They learned agriculture from the Pueblos,
> sheepherding from the Spaniards, weaving from the
> Pueblos and traders, silverwork from the Mexicans,
> and new costumes from the Spaniards and Americans.
> —Ruth Underhill, *The Navajos*

Make room for one unlineated romp in this verse-skein of surprises, a prose-poem loosening eidetic intensity and fractal density. "The Northern Sun," the poet's "signature" poem, could refer to the alleged Athabascan origins of the Arizona Diné, who migrated southwest some eight hundred years ago, emigrating over the Siberian land bridge thousands of years ago. Don't look back, the instructions say on the poet's waking body, but he confesses a heritage: "I wear a mask made from the map of Asia." Ravine or cliff, Pontiac hood piece or Jeep Cherokee SUV, even Custer's luckless horse Comanche at the Little Big Horn images the Vanishing (Noble/Savage) American returned for a revised look at each mesa intimately named *brother, sister,* or *friend* by his grandfather (in the *Shadow-Catcher,* 1904, Edward Curtis scrimmed Navajo riders disappearing into the horizon as "The Vanishing Race"). All the while the lines are dis-lineating, sprawling across and down the page like Whitman gone berserk, until the images rein in the running on. Is this poetically cricket? Momaday's conjunctions indicate a harmonizing and balancing *hozhó,* as discussed earlier by way of Witherspoon and others; Bitsui's conjunctions signal chaotic override. "After this, you will reach to scratch your back and feel nothing but a black hole, spiraling like the agitator in an empty washing machine." The reader slides back into the fractal mix of narrative lyrics that rock in hexameter (so lineated), the poet chanting to musical backup:

> The cigarette ignites the bedsheets, and I write my last sentence.
> Lamp shades cover me; my eyelashes wriggle in my pants pockets.
> *Your vocabulary is like the breakfast menu of a science convention.*
> Bricks ripple underfoot, the moon reveals her daughter
> for the first time in 28 days, born with fists instead of hands.

The verses run like imploded logorrhea, a recovering John Berryman in delirium tremens, a fox stealing pens from the henhouse of his hospital ward, putting on and down a White therapist/anthropologist who says

Diné people *speak like weeping Mongolians*. Are the handcuffs coming off, the asterisks filling in? Memory hits like a rifle butt against the road. "The last time I saw the sun reflected red, I was pulling a screaming baby from her clutching, drunk mother on Highway 77 at noon." Homebrew still smells of sunrise yeast rising. Skimming America by air, all this Indian poet wants is decent coffee and a good look at the Washington Monument, as Sherman Alexie asks no less in *One Stick Song*. No generics, only specifics: "The cab driver asked if I was American Indian, I said, *No, I'm of the Bitter Water People*."

NAME CATCHERS

Hence a single Navaho will have as many as seven
or eight different names which are current in a region.
In white society only authors, actors, and criminals
use aliases.

—Kluckhohn and Leighton, *The Navaho*

With the satiric quips of a latter-day Sherman Alexie crossing the spondaic leaps of a lost-son James Welch, this Native scrabbles his Book of Nightmares à la Galway Kinnell, his early vatic model. "What's there but rum and Coke?" Grim rez realities bracket the Red ghetto: "Bottle walls standing knee-deep in confusion and rat traps disguised as dream catchers?" Back-home stories still teeter on Grandma's cracked lips, burning leaves in her last harvest. The all-night sweats of the extra-Native poet see Coke cans bleeding sugar in obese high schools, a blender of steamed blood "rising from the necks of hemorrhaging antelopes." As a *hooghan* policeman siphons the spit can of a medicine man singing his last four songs, the poet-singer feels "the gravel in my veins soften." His free verse maps precision prose strikes. Metaphoric fallout takes on collateral damage, the Native Fall, the Discovery and Invasion as bimillennial shock-and-awe of Native ways, hearts, and minds. It's been a long walk, brother, and a longer war. A Diné mother tells Ruth Underhill in *The Navajos*, "I hate to send this boy to school. I know I say goodbye. He would come back a stranger."

Moving more quickly, skip over "Red Light" of lightning twice striking Coyote, a grace note of brevity, and "She Was Not Invited" about the abandoned old ones—matriarchs as bag ladies, clans of homeless grandmothers, shelters for Native unborns and unwed women. "Trickster" always dickered there, before the winged one exploded with bathwater in mid-sentence. Coyote peeked when he shouldn't, waiting "in the waiting room of the resurrection of another Reservation," looking for air pockets at the paragraph's end. Constructed by anthros, the Bering Straits toll-booth stands a leap away from lyric respite at the ruckus end, "blue horses grazing northward in the pre-dawn." Harjo had some razored horses, Tapahonso heard blue horses rush in, and the Diné counted their blessings in ponies. Bitsui pauses for a quietist moment of reservation reflection in chanted imagist palettes, Blessingway oral tradition translated by Berard Haile, ghostlike across ethnographic anthologies (quoted in Momaday's *House Made of Dawn* 170 and Astrov's *The Winged Serpent* 183):

My horse has a hoof like striped agate;
His fetlock is like a fine eagle plume;
His legs are like quick lightning.
My horse's body is like an eagle-plumed arrow;
My horse has a tail like a trailing black cloud.
I put flexible goods on my horse's back;
The Little Holy Wind blows through his hair.

His mane is made of short rainbows.
My horse's ears are made of round corn.
My horse's eyes are made of big stars.
My horse's head is made of mixed waters
(From the holy waters—he never knows thirst).
My horse's teeth are made of white shell.
The long rainbow is in his mouth for a bridle,
And with it I guide him.
When my horse neighs, different-colored horses follow.
When my horse neighs, different-colored sheep follow.
I am wealthy, because of him.

He Had Some Horses

Bitsui's poems canter on, patterns off-center. Hopping "Blankets of Bark," a sisterly lament, fractals mutate through more shapeshifting icons: "The Sun Rises and I Think of Your Bruised Larynx." Sunrise is Southwestern prayer time asking blessing and scattering corn pollen in a trail for the day. The title also resurrects Hemingway's postwar elegy at the end of *The Sun Also Rises*, Jake muttering to Lady Brett's sentiment stopped by a traffic cop, "Isn't it pretty to think so?" If the sun sets twice on lost generations, as Ecclesiastes warned, can it also rise Red a second time?

> Sister,
> blue like the larynx of rushing rainwater,
> I think of you when I squeeze static from the river's bent elbow.

Daughter of "female rain," the Navajo say, a sister's bruised larynx invokes a damaged voice, the elbowing static of impaired speech, a stutter or palate defect. Red brother counts backwards to nothing, following her scampy, reverse-sun dance around "steel-rimmed America" (ceremony always turns clockwise) and back home "with back spasms and a foaming mouth." As with Erdrich's love-medicine sisters and boarding-school runaways, the old *nostos* isn't going so well for estranged siblings. "My child, you have returned to us," Bitsui's grandmother still chants in unpublished poems. Returning to the big (Rio Grande) river brings up a loose shoe burial where Navajo names are no misnomers, where the elders saw refineries and pipelines replace foot trails and rivers, where IHS rez doctors delivered tongueless infants with asterisk fingers.

The poems course to their beginnings. A mud-caked sun petals this sister's cupped hands, and raven "browned by winter moon's breath" shape-changes into a horse head carved from coal "found in your grandmother's clenched fist." The dangerous instabilities of these images—trickster raven turned horse head, a nameless grandmother's coal-gripping fist, silent fingerless babies (radioactive fallout?), a sister wounded in the throat—recall Welch's "wet, black things" of the lunar-slipping night when Blackbird confesses his incestuous crime in "Surviving." Only Bitsui finds no ellipsis for surviving, just a clenched ancestral fist. "To stay alive this way, it's hard. . . ."

BREATH BELOW ZERO

I've turned on all the lights, but these walls are still
lined with furry shadows. I pick axe words from the
ceiling and crack stanzas between my teeth. My mouth

is a grave of mud. A bird weaves a nest of water from
childrens' hair. Dreams stung into jewels roll off my
pillow when the train shoots through the city's veins.

—bitsui.com blog, 20 October 2005

"Bodies Wanting Wood" carries the grace note of minimal lyric, the fractal
trail of the wind in human fingertip revealing how humans were made
(see Matthews' *Navajo Legends*, more recently Zolbrod's *Diné bahane'*).
Wind is breath, and breath is "in-standing wind" or soul, as noted with
Simon Ortiz's breathing poetics. Diné speech, the out-breath of Holy
Wind within, ex-presses the soul in sound back to the Creator. James Kale
McNeley writes of *Holy Wind in Navajo Philosophy*, "Nílch'i, meaning
Wind, Air, or Atmosphere. . . . gives life, thought, speech, and the power
of motion to all living things and serves as the means of communication
between all elements of the living world" (1). But here in Bitsui's verse
prayer, the wind's trail sleeps between fingers, and when released, blows
a fiery-winged locust swarm into town—Native Revelations with adjacent mayhem and justicing Apocalyse. Across the page, "*Nazbas*" answers
with the *zero* or infinite nothing of revisited Edenic Expulsion:

> It came whispering in broken English,
> a stutter,
> a twig tweezed from the small of the back.
> > *He reached to pull the apple from her mouth.*
> Was it *asphyxiation*?

The poet is again speaking in prophetic tongues, *as-phyx-i-a-tion*, a five-
syllable, Romanized, rocking word that suggests Eve choked on the apple
or Adam strangled her.

> Should she have leaned away
> and not let her hair slip through the cracks in the book?

Paradise is lost each time an American reads Milton's fall poem. Did
lit crit talk gag Changing Woman? "Was it just theory?" or a crack in the
asterisk of Original Sin?—God's Will that we fall, *Nazbas* or zero, the poet
wonders, counter-reflecting lingual mirrors of faces waking in a snow drift.
Winter bleeds in first breath. The enemy's language has to be remade, as Joy
Harjo and Gloria Bird gather Native women's voices across Indian Nations,
the creation theories rethought in Native kitchens. Who gets what portion

of the lamb of God, "who gets to speak English as a second language?" This dilemma is kin to Paul Celan writing German verse in the viscid tongue of the Auschwitz assassins who butchered his parents. Poetic risk here, verse cost in the face of holocaustal genocide (can poetry be written after 97 percent extermination?). And so too the marketing tedium of public airwaves: *"Dogs lap rainwater on television during conversations of drought."* Is global warming really drying up the Southwestern deserts, even more than dehydrating Phoenix or Los Angeles or Farmington? Are the reborn angels of White land grabs hustling the runoff? Memory fails. Translations steal the breath and soul of words, "voices within voices pecking eyelids with velvet beaks." The Native is on his knees to the dry water hole putting "damp, white earth" into his collapsing veins.

GOAT RIB CLIFFS

> One horse eats five times as much as a sheep and the
> sheep are starving. You must sell some horses.
> —1929 U.S. Government Navajo Directive

Is there no relief? "You have to jump off the cliff," the poet told my class, "and see if you sprout wings." The mute turtle courage of the heart and the energy crisis of the Arctic National Wildlife Refuge lead to another rivering poem, and still another about De Soto buried in the Mississippi mud. Then a title whiplashes "The Gravitational Pull of a Fishbowl," originally published as an IAIA student poem in the 1998 anthology *Moss Moon*.

> I look into the lens of a fishbowl,
> where my days branch toward the gravity
>   of footprints leading away into
>   the thick green plaster of moss on stone.

A college Diné poet has charted his own tracks through the postmodern poetic wilderness. "I bleed my left arm, / carving deep gills at the entrance of light."

"The Scent of Burning Hair" takes no prisoners in excoriating self-examination at 5 a.m. "I have either become a black dot growing legs, / running from the blank page, / or the mud that is caked over the keyhole of a church hiding its bandaged eyes." And there in bed before sunrise, "when everyone discovers razors in the womb of this land," the sun will decide which rivers to cover "with skin and leaves / and which should remain as goat ribs submerged in sand smelling of diesel engines." T. S. Eliot got no closer to the tumid river in his own *fin de siècle* Waste Land.

NAMELESS RIDERS

How many sheep does it hold?
—Barre Toelken, "The 'Pretty
Language' of Yellowman"

"The Hoof in My Soup Glistens" with an arresting grace note: "*A cheetah has been pulled from its skin,*" nothing linked and everything (fractal?) to do with flayed Native ways and spilled soup gone abruptively before. Then comes a pivotal concept, "Trans-lation?" Native names quit breathing in the last Hollywood episode filmed in Monument Valley— Diné ghosts made "butterflies freeze on the forks of their tongues." Raymond Stedman's *Shadows of the Indian* exposes the clichés of vanishing Indians, but safe to say languages were the first to go.

When you have ten names for snow,
What is the temperature of each vowel in *photosynthesis*?
And will winter run-off green the deserts again after so much dusty
mistranslation?
Because—*They* were listening,
They had ears in the marrows of their fist,
They heard the last horse snort under its
nameless rider.
Pale mustang, paler rider, save grace for the last verse in this
American elegy

WATERLESS

Psychologically, they lived in the Middle Ages.
—Ruth Underhill, *The Navajos*

"Halo" prays humbly to rain, child, moon, mesa, hawk, sun, stone, mothers and fathers, concluding—

We are only atoms trailing the carved skull wrapped inside a sunbeam.
Dawn.

Bitsui pushes Native icons over a verse envelope in "The Noose in My
Dream," the suicidal nightmare chanting, "I heard songs when the cactus
wren sipped nectar from the tongue of a cricket." No less shifty the poet
westers on, "a sailboat anchored to a dying whale," and on to the resurrective "uncovered wagon" where a woman going west licks a white fish brow
and marries her broken-lipped husband, the aftershock of Hieronymus
Bosch. Update to a highway homicide: "*She gripped the steering wheel
so tight that they buried her with it.*" The poet drives home "imagining
a man suckling milk from the cliffs of Canyon de Chelly" and dreaming
"the awakening of knives inside grandmother's cabinet." The ever-present
rearview mirror reflects a storm plane landing with speechless passengers,
"calling a nation to drink water from the river / underneath the race barrier." As in Welch's *Winter in the Blood* or Silko's *Ceremony*, this water-
kin cry is old as the myths of Osiris and the Fisher King, newly ripped off as
Compassionate Conservatism—the Clear Air, Clean Water, and Healthy
Forest Initiatives (lifting pollution controls and clear-cutting sanctions)—
all illusions and lies in translation. Jug Boy lies broken in pieces. Leave no
living Native behind, the born-again Custers and Chivingtons chant, no
lie untold.

Perplexed That We Even Have a Tongue

Shapeshift staggers toward home, still, in the final eight poems of varying
lines and line lengths. "Umbilicus," a second "signature" poem, Bitsui
says, argues centripetally against going outside the four-mountains home
box, "and all of us / in these classrooms were speared by the shepherd's
single gray tooth." The poem was inspired by his grandmother's stories
of running away from boarding school when she and her sister were
abused for speaking their mother tongue. More kidnapping fractals,
more crossed images of postmodern culture war and Native signs, ana-
grams of violence in the questionable asterisk of the sunrise. Gunpowder
scents the curio shop of raven-circled inmates "in the entrails of clouds
swelling under the belt of the Orion nebula." So the poet makes another
"Offering" of hillcrest fire, winter-counting thirteen annual moons.
The spondees grind away, as in Welch's surviving confession. "*Fins grip
flint lodged between my fingers.*" The poet follows with winter in his

Athabascan blood. *"The snow won't cover these pages."* What survives? "Coyote bones curl over river rocks and crumble into salt." Trickster's yip is missing, another casualty in the list of asterisks.

> A tree line slopes over bodies
> casting shadows between the pages of closed books.

The White culture fix is in, ghosts out, shadows over dead asterisks on the page. Bitsui's verse closes down with a slurry of stutter-step abruptions, line breaks, syntactic spaces, broken synapses, failed rhymes, and all-night-sweats.

Nearing the end, the cold war constricts the poet's voice in "Bullet Wet Earth" after a late summer, winter-in-the-blood monsoon.

> My shoulders hang like a rainstorm over a bed that has become desert
>> as I have become:
>>> a dehydrated shadow born with scratches in his throat.

With a diagnosed heartache and raspy larynx, the poet drives across the Southwest listening to the wind, even more erratically than Erdrich's Lipsha in *Love Medicine*.

> I cover these pages with my fist.
> Imagine skin meeting the lens of a camera.
>> Hear a voice coming from the roots in the basket, saying:
> "Come closer,
> swallow a handful of air,
>> pour water over your feet,
>> you have become a ghost without hands."

The baptismal Skinwalkers call homesick Diné back "to be suckled by black stones." Is this good or bad medicine?

In his mother-clan speech, muttering *"Nahasdzáán,"* the bilingual son remembers her asking, *"Do we ramble when we speak in tongues?"*

> The dusk, the dawn, everything in between: a mistake.
> The morning,
>> her toothache,
> the shovel dulled in daylight—
>> all digging fire from shallowing rivers.

"The Four Directions of a Lie" leads to that recurrent worry of "Drought," a five-page, slug-it-out song through a dry-drunk Navajo day. Women and water desiccate as cold stone carvings.

> Where am I when I follow the satellite east?
> Does the sun know that a rock soaks in a bowl of rice somewhere
> on the other side of my palm? Does the sky recognize its feet
> when it is covered with light bulbs instead of the eggs of red ants?

Images mix from time's cradleboard, a clock wrapped in a white sheet, through angry moths shaking their fists and autumnal newspapers. Eyes cross in "*the shadows of crushed grapes.*"

Poetics get no easier. Cinder blocks throb under Diné feet swallowing fishhooks. The nightmare noose returns as a deer shaking dust from its eyelids. Travelers keep "the rain in Styrofoam boxes at the bus station." Walking out one evening in "Song," W. H. Auden heard the glacier knock in the cupboard, the desert sigh in the bed, the crack in the teacup open "a lane to the land of the dead." Bitsui follows poetic suit with sibilant cutting tools, Auden's *scissors* and Frost's *axe*, cherished American-English diction:

> When one dreams of a mouth covered in white chalk,
> speaking only in English,
> it is a voice that wants to be cut free from a country whose veins
> swim with axes and scissors.

Shards of cultural debris gather around a downed Native Hamlet in the reverse anxiety of Anglo influence:

> Listen, the gravediggers unfold the earth's bandages
> and remove vacuum cleaners filled with killed pottery and
>   broken arrowheads

Indians are forced to survive on cherts of the Invader's tongue:

> *Read this,*
> *understand their language,*
> *or sleep in a bottle of broken nails for the rest of your life.*

In the basements of their tribal homes, children find no parents, no paper or address books, only familial cinders:

So a reader begins shifting through the ash of burnt hooves
   in a field of rust,
        but finds only broken glass,
            coat hangers,
                 and the shoes of a dying priest.

And in the follow-up shortest, perhaps simplest poem in the book, "I Don't Remember," the poet can't re-member "horses / running / from glass / over / broken glass / into broken glass." The bicultural mirrors cracked, the translative transparencies shattered, where is the *hozhó* of the old chants, as in the "War God's Horse Song"?

Before me peaceful,
Behind me peaceful,
Under me peaceful,
Over me peaceful,
All around me peaceful—
Peaceful voice when he neighs.
I am Everlasting and Peaceful.
I stand for my horse.

Fractal Survival

"Chrysalis," Greek for "little gold," harbors a butterfly pupa for aerial rebirth. Think again of renascence. The verse worm turns into a winged rainbow, circling back to the iris of the opening poem, "Asterisk" or little star. *Chrysalis* is also the green waiting room for a shapeshifter's debut as digital filmmaker. Neither falling leaves nor kneeling horse will flower wantonly, but ash cocoons this desert poet where "the language is a dying thing, / covered in blankets, / beaten with forks and spoons." Ancient Diné expires with the old ones in the hogans. Everyday waste-land detritus litters this midden, no less than Welch's winter blood farther north—"a shot glass of tears tucked between the legs of a veteran"—his tongue wristwatched to the hour of hunted children. "How young I was to read the passages of the Bible," the poet laments, nor can he stop "the red squaw from selling her jewelry in aisles of restaurants serving leaves and grass." Free-verse Whitman pawn for New Age wannabes, a lonely deathwatch seizes the moment:

And no, there is no one here.
This casket: the seed of a blood clot.

In Native boarding school Hansel and Gretel nibble bread dipped in gun-powder, get their raven hair cut short and wrists snapped with rulers: "their whispers metamorphose into a new chrysalis of thought."

What if . . . they didn't? Something withholding is sprouting on their lips, not the English slick of "an oil-soaked dictionary," but hooves now as raptor talons, crickets laughing all around, a rebirth of AIM and Red Power and Native Cultural Insurgency.

NOT ABOUT SADNESS

A tourist gazing at the throng in blue jeans and
cotton frocks inquired, "Where are the Indians?"
—Ruth Underhill, *The Navajos*

The Santa Fe Institute of American Indian Arts, now an accredited four-year college, educates its own in resistance to co-option and reac-culturation to Native traditions, a radically conservative renaissance or reawakening. Here a 1999 Truman Capote Creative Writing IAIA Fellowship shored up Sherwin Bitsui in 1999. The Academy of American Poets distinguished him nationally in *American Poet*, no. 15 (Fall 1999). A 2000–01 Witter Bynner Poet's Award took the poet home to Arizona. A 2002 Academy of American Poets Student Poetry Award kept him going at the University of Arizona, an institution awarding Master's and Doctoral degrees in American Indian Studies.

"Antelope are gnawing into the walls of the city. / And *those* Indians are braiding yucca roots into the skin of their scalps again." Their raven hair grows back, and they wash it in the old yucca-root ways. Runaways from reservation boarding schools follow the long walk back home through IAIA and the U of A to Native re-education. As for the ashes of Beat accul-turation, "eyeless dogs barking in hailstorms" will *howl* over a valley of "weeping dishrags" with paired owls from the east "carrying the night between them," warning the people of arid winds that suck them dry.

"And no," the poet says, "this is not about sadness," not mute grubbing "for nectar in the thinning bones of shadowless thieves" on the cross. His is birthing revolution, reawakening to Native Blessings and Beautyways.

All poetic life-forms lead back positively to Changing Woman, the earth mother seasonally shapeshifting, the eternally changing, ever balancing rhythms of *hózhóni*. *Shapeshift* is finally not irrecoverable loss, but cyclical gain and reconnective tribal kinship in the face of disbelief. So far it's neither the death of the Diné tongue, nor accommodations silenced bilingually, but a Red English renaissance in fractal and freed Navajo verse:

> This is not about the rejection of our skin;
> the mud dries as it is poured into our ears.
> But the linguist still runs his hands up the length of our tongues,
> perplexed that we even have a tongue   at all.

The largest living Native language pool in the States—approaching 300,000 Southwest sovereign citizens, according to the 2004 Census Bureau, with 178,014 speaking the language at home—Diné is nowhere near dying out, or giving up, or giving in to *Bilagáana* ways, not while Navajo poets like Luci Tapahonso, or Laura Tohe, or Rex Lee Jim, or Nia Francisco, or Gloria Emerson, or Norla Chee, or Rhiana Yazzie, or Sherwin Bitsui are writing. The Diné make American English their own poetic second language. For starters, check the literary racks or the Internet for *RedInk Magazine*.

Name as our own

> Our child, you have returned to us.
> Our child, you have returned to us.
> —Sherwin Bitsui manuscript

"I still want to eventually write a novel, which I'm finding out is harder than it looks," Bitsui says on his website, 24 September 2004. "First of all, I have a very short attention span, secondly, my thoughts trail in and out like flashing lights, and I'm somewhat of a daydreamer slacker type, and I listen to depressing 80's alt rock music and, I can't think of a story that hasn't already been written." Will Bitsui begin where *Finnegan's Wake*, or *Gravity's Rainbow*, or *House Made of Dawn*, or *Ceremony* leave off? Will he outwit Gerald Vizenor with shapeshifting shenanigans, circle Ray Young Bear's reservation surrealism, trot over Sherman Alexie's hip trixters? "But this might really mean that I've all the ingredients to write a novel about a Navajo renegade/hipster rebel who can't seem to make ends meet. Who, after years of herding sheep for his grandma, finds the woman of his dreams sipping 'Ocean' martinis in a Gallup bar." And in an Immaculate Dream sequence, still in manuscript but offered at readings, a young Diné on the borders of the mind, *inbetween* lyric and narrative, dreams of office clerks holding signs *Free me,* and corn again in people's bellies, and sunlight plateaus with deer running out. In this novel everyone walks the streets knowing their clan, and everyone speaks Navajo, the phone ringing throughout, the Native dreamer choosing which tree to chop down first.

> Strange, how they burrowed into the side of this rock.
> Strange . . . to think,
> they "belonged"
> and stepped through the flowering of a future apparent
> in the rearview mirror,
> visible from its orbit
> around a cluster of knives in the galaxy closest to
> the argument. ("Apparition")

Speak Like Singing has come a distance from ancestral petroglyphs, ceremonial dance-songs, and narrative lyric, as readers approach the leaping, luminous voices of Native peoples still here. Contemporary American poetry shifts all the margins: Jorie Graham swarms, John Ashbury parses a convex mirror, Carolyn Forché divides the country between us, James Welch rides the Earthboy allotment, N. Scott Momaday stands in the presence of the sun. Sherwin Bitsui shapeshifts among all these voices—postmodern, surreal, political, and/or fractal. Like a young Alexie or Berryman, Welch or Ginsberg—raw with talent, soaked in genius, starkly vivid as an Arizona arroyo—Bitsui writes *freely* what he *sees*, radical associations everywhere, and what he believes, Hemispheric Natives to Global Nations. This tribal singer pays homage to the ancestors, with humility before the insecurity, instability, and sheer disbelief of poetry in our time.

Sherwin Bitsui says he does not write for an audience—maybe for the Masters, Talking God to Homer to Lorca, Diné to all cultures; maybe for the teachers who inspired him, Jim Davis and Arthur Sze at IAIA to Joy Harjo, Luci Tapahonso, and Simon Ortiz across the Southwest; maybe for some extended self who listens when he's lonely; or maybe just for the ecstatic beauty and high of the craft. Bitsui believes in getting a poem right, even if it takes a year or more. Every word counts, as with endemic Diné concision and concreteness; every line matters just the way it lays out on the page. Bilingually code-switching between tongues, the poet is troubled that those who speak Diné cannot read or write their Native tongue, that those who read and write Diné cannot speak it.

Navajo is not at all like English, Bitsui explains, not a linear linguistic progression of subject-verb-object, but a flow of movable morphemes where the speaker moves words around without losing meaning. The poet pictures *Shapeshift* as sculpted horizontal striation. He asks his listeners to close their eyes and see *through* his filmic images—the cascade of mutations, the metamorphic coyotes and butterflies and ravens, the intuitive leaps through a real Diné world of 1868, *Yeibicheii* dancers, uranium mines, Beautyway chants, car wrecks, Code Talkers, dishwashers, lovely frustrated poets at midnight, wannabe novelists, abstract painters, dime-store drunks sick on Ocean Spray and airplane glue, the last high, the most recent low, the crash, the rush, the logorrhea of free-form wordplay. Sherwin Bitsui is a poet respectful of classics and moderns alike in all cultures, Bosch to Chagall, *Beowulf* to *Star Wars*, curious about other work, learning his trade on the way, alive to the world. His family had not been *over* the horizon until he went away to school, Bitsui says, and he calls home just to hear them speak Diné. He blogs America on 31 December 2005, 7:46 p.m.:

Happy New Year, you out there with one hand on the wheel, a kettle of thoughts boiling at land's end in your head. I toast you. It's been a wild year. I can't wait to sit awhile and think back on what all has happened. . . . I, the son of a time seemingly erased, am plotting my way to reenter this confused house again. There are so many stones left unturned, so many paths untravelled, I am happy to have met you, out there, on the high roads in the Rockies, in cafes, on a dirt road on a reservation somewhere, in the back of our minds, still witnessing what we have left behind. Be well this year!

Welch's desert descendant, Harjo's kick-ass kin, Alexie's homeboy, Tapahonso's Navajo bro, Bitsui is nobody's minion, no one's fool. Looking over his shoulder, he says a "beautiful innocence" lights his early work in *Shapeshift*, seasoned radiance to come. As with other 'Skin writers, schooling (the right Native kind) does not deaden or silence the tribal voice, but allows lyric to spring forward between cultural differences, spawning a new fractal gathering of its own Native and appropriated literary resources. "Asterisk," "Atlas," "Apparition," and all the clustering poems that follow shift shape through the oppressor's alphabet like wild creatures hunting game down arroyos. There will be more tracks and radical tracts to come.

You can't say *poet* in Diné to a non-English-speaking grandma and aunt, Sherwin Bitsui says on his website, 8 September 2004, 8:38 a.m., nor speak of "other attributes, such as mania, hysteria, and high carbohydrate intake. So this journey's yours now, future Native artists. We've got a whole lot to uncover and name as our own."

Select Bibliography

This book is intended for the layman,
not for the carping professional.
—Clyde Kluckhohn, *Mirror for Man*

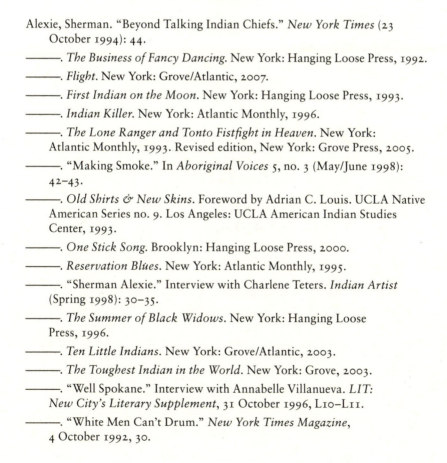

Alexie, Sherman. "Beyond Talking Indian Chiefs." *New York Times* (23 October 1994): 44.

———. *The Business of Fancy Dancing.* New York: Hanging Loose Press, 1992.

———. *Flight.* New York: Grove/Atlantic, 2007.

———. *First Indian on the Moon.* New York: Hanging Loose Press, 1993.

———. *Indian Killer.* New York: Atlantic Monthly, 1996.

———. *The Lone Ranger and Tonto Fistfight in Heaven.* New York: Atlantic Monthly, 1993. Revised edition, New York: Grove Press, 2005.

———. "Making Smoke." In *Aboriginal Voices* 5, no. 3 (May/June 1998): 42–43.

———. *Old Shirts & New Skins.* Foreword by Adrian C. Louis. UCLA Native American Series no. 9. Los Angeles: UCLA American Indian Studies Center, 1993.

———. *One Stick Song.* Brooklyn: Hanging Loose Press, 2000.

———. *Reservation Blues.* New York: Atlantic Monthly, 1995.

———. "Sherman Alexie." Interview with Charlene Teters. *Indian Artist* (Spring 1998): 30–35.

———. *The Summer of Black Widows.* New York: Hanging Loose Press, 1996.

———. *Ten Little Indians.* New York: Grove/Atlantic, 2003.

———. *The Toughest Indian in the World.* New York: Grove, 2003.

———. "Well Spokane." Interview with Annabelle Villanueva. *LIT: New City's Literary Supplement,* 31 October 1996, L10–L11.

———. "White Men Can't Drum." *New York Times Magazine,* 4 October 1992, 30.

Allen, Paula Gunn. "'The Grace that Remains'—American Indian Women's Literature." *Book Forum* 5 (1981): 376–82.

———. *The Sacred Hoop: Recovering the Feminine in American Indian Traditions.* Boston: Beacon Press, 1986.

———. *Shadow Country.* Native American Series, no. 6. Los Angeles: American Indian Studies Center, UCLA, 1982.

———. *Spider Woman's Granddaughters: Traditional Tales and Contemporary Writing by Native American Women.* Boston: Beacon Press, 1989.

———. *The Woman Who Owned the Shadows.* San Francisco: Spinster's Ink, 1983.

Allen, Paula Gunn, and Kenneth Lincoln, eds. Native American Supplement to the *Jacaranda Review* 6 (Winter/Summer 1992): 53–111.

Anati, Emmanuel. "Valcamonica Rock Art: A New History for Europe." *Studi Camuni* 13. Valcamonica, Italy: Edizioni del Centro, 1994.

Anschuetz, Kurt F., et. al. *"That Place People Talk About": The Petroglyph National Monument Ethnographic Landscape Report.* Santa Fe, NM: National Park Service, 2002.

Arana, Marie, ed. *The Writing Life: Writers on How They Think and Work.* A Collection from *The Washington Post* Book World. New York: The Washington Post, 2003.

Arnold, Katie. "The Ways of Means" on Russell Means. *Santa Fean* (November 2005): 38–48.

Astrov, Margot, ed. *The Winged Serpent.* 1946. Reprinted as *American Indian Prose and Poetry.* New York: Capricorn, 1962.

Auden, W. H. *The Dyer's Hand and Other Essays.* New York: Random House, 1962.

Austin, Mary. *The American Rhythm: Studies and Reëxpressions of Amerindian Songs.* New York: Houghton Mifflin, 1923, 1930. Reprint, New York: Cooper Square, 1970.

Bachelard, Gaston. *The Poetics of Space.* Translated by John R. Stilgoe. Boston: Beacon Press, 1994.

Bakhtin, M. M. *The Dialogic Imagination.* Translated by Caryl Emerson and Michael Holquist. Edited by Michael Holquist. Austin: University of Texas Press, 1981.

———. *Rabelais and His World.* Translated by Helen Iswolsky. Cambridge, MA: MIT Press, 1965. Reprint, Bloomington: Indiana University Press, 1984.

Barnes, Jody, Crystal Henry, Tvli Jacob, Mary Shakesspeare, Tianausdi Shenandoah, De Armond Williams, eds. *Moss Moon: New Work from the Institute of American Indian Arts, 1997–1998.* Santa Fe, NM: Institute of American Indian Arts, 1998.

Basso, Keith H. *Portraits of "The Whiteman": Linguistic Play and Cultural Symbols among the Western Apache.* Cambridge: Cambridge University Press, 1979.

———. *Western Apache Language and Culture. Essays in Linguistic Anthropology.* Tucson: University of Arizona, 1990. "'To Give Up on Words'" originally published in *Southwestern Journal of Anthropology* 26, no 3 (1970): 213–30. "'Wise Words' of the Western Apache: Metaphor and Semantic Theory" originally published in *Meaning in Anthropology*, ed. Keith Basso and Harry Selby (Albuquerque: University of New Mexico Press, 1976).

———. *Wisdom Sits in Places: Landscape and Language among the Western Apache.* Albuquerque: University of New Mexico Press, 1996.

Benally, Karen Ritts. "Thinking Good: The Teachings of Navajo Grandmothers." In *American Indian Grandmothers: Traditions and Transitions*, ed. Marjorie M. Schweitzer. Albuquerque: University of New Mexico Press, 1999.

Bender, John, and David E. Wellbery, eds. *Chronotypes: The Construction of Time.* Stanford, CA: Stanford University Press, 1991.

Benjamin, Walter. *Illuminations.* [1955]. Second edition translated by Harry Zohn and edited by Hannah Arendt. London: William Collins Sons, 1972. See especially "The Task of the Translator" and "Storyteller."

Berryman, John. *John Berryman: Collected Poems, 1937–1971.* Edited by Charles Thornbury. Noonday/Farrar, Straus and Giroux, 1989.

Bierhorst, John. *In the Trail of the Wind: American Indian Poems and Ritual Orations.* New York: Farrar, Straus and Giroux, 1971.

Bitsui, Sherwin. *Shapeshift.* Sun Tracks vol. 52. Tucson: University of Arizona Press, 2003.

———. "The Gravitational Pull of a Fishbowl." In *Moss Moon, New Work from the Institute of American Indian Arts*, ed. Jody Barnes, Crystal Henry, Tvli Jacob, Mary Shakesspeare, Tianausdi Shenandoah, De Armond Williams. Santa Fe, NM: Creative Writing Program, Institute of American Indian Arts, 1998.

Bloomfield, Leonard. *Sacred Stories of the Sweet Grass Cree.* Anthropological Series of the National Museum of Canada, Department of Mines, Bulletin no. 60. Anthropological Series no. 11. Ottawa: F. A. Acland, 1930.

Boas, Franz. *Keresan Texts.* Publications of the American Ethnological Society, vol. 8, part 1, 1928. New York: AMS Press Reprint, 1974.

Boer, Charles. *The Homeric Hymns.* Athens, OH: Ohio University Press, 1970.

Borafoux, Pascal. *Van Gogh: The Passionate Eye.* [Gallimard 1987]. Translated by Anthony Zieloulka. London: Thames and Hudson, 1992.

Borges, Jorge Luis. *Selected Poems.* Edited by Alexander Coleman. New York: Viking Penguin, 1999.

———. *This Craft of Verse.* Charles Eliot Norton Lectures, Harvard University, 1967–1968. Cambridge: Harvard University Press, 2000.

———. "*The Divine Comedy.*" In *The Poets' Dante: Twentieth-Century Responses*, ed. Peter S. Hawkins and Rachel Jacoff. New York: Farrar, Straus and Giroux, 2001.

Bowra, C. M. *Primitive Song.* New York: The World Publishing Company, 1962.

Brandon, William, ed. *The Magic World: American Indian Songs and Poems.* New York: William Morrow, 1971.

Brinton, Daniel G. "Native American Poetry." In *Essays of an Americanist.* Philadelphia, 1890.

Brock-Broido, Lucie. *Trouble in Mind.* New York: Knopf, 2004.

Brooks, James F. *Captives & Cousins: Slavery, Kinship, and Community in the Southwest Borderlands.* Chapel Hill: University of North Carolina Press, 2002.

Brown, Calvin S. *Music and Literature: A Comparison of the Arts.* Athens: University of Georgia, 1948.

Brown, Dee. *Bury My Heart at Wounded Knee.* New York: Holt, Rinehart, and Winston, 1970.

Bruchac, Joseph. *Survival This Way: Interviews with American Indian Poets.* Sun Tracks vol. 15. Tucson: University of Arizona Press, 1987.

Buffalo Bird Woman. "Waheenee: An Indian Girl's Story Told by Herself to Gilbert L. Wilson." *North Dakota History: Journal of the Northern Plains* 38, no. 1–2 (Winter/Spring, 1971).

Carruth, Hayden. *Effluences from the Sacred Caves: More Selected Essays and Reviews.* Ann Arbor: University of Michigan Press, 1983.

Carver, Raymond. *A New Path to the Waterfall.* New York: Atlantic Monthly, 1989.

———. *What We Talk About When We Talk About Love.* New York: Knopf, 1981.

———. *Where I'm Calling From.* New York: Atlantic Monthly, 1988.

———. *Where Water Comes Together with Other Water.* New York: Random House, 1985.

———. *Will You Please Be Quiet, Please?* New York: McGraw Hill, 1976.

Celan, Paul. *Todesfuge* ("Death Fugue"). In *Paul Celan: Poems*, trans. Michael Hamburger. New York: Persea Books, 1980.

Chanoff, David. "Guided by Voices: The Work of a Ghostwriter." In *The Writing Life: Writers on How They Think and Work*, ed. Marie Arana. A Collection from *The Washington Post* Book World. New York: The Washington Post, 2003.

Churchill, Ward. *From a Native Son: Selected Essays on Indigenism, 1985–1995.* Cambridge, MA: South End Press, 1996.

Clements, William M. *Native American Verbal Art: Texts and Contexts.* Tucson: University of Arizona Press, 1996.

Coleridge, Samuel Taylor. *Complete Works.* 7 vols. Edited by W. G. T. Shedd. New York: Harper & Brothers, 1853, 1884.

Coltelli, Laura. *Winged Word: American Indian Writers Speak.* Lincoln: University of Nebraska Press, 1990.

Conrad, Joseph. *The Nigger of the Narcissus.* London: Dent, 1897.

Cook-Lynn, Elizabeth. *Anti-Indianism in Modern America: A Voice from Tatekeya's Earth.* Urbana: University of Illinois, 2001.

Cronyn, George W. *The Path on the Rainbow.* [1918]. Reprinted as *American Indian Poetry.* New York: Ballantine, 1991.

Curtis, Natalie Burlin. *The Indians' Book.* New York: Harper, 1907.

Day, A. Grove. *The Sky Clears: Poetry of the American Indians.* New York: Macmillan, 1951. Reprint, Lincoln: University of Nebraska Press, 1964.

Dawkins, Richard. *The Selfish Gene.* Oxford: Oxford University Press, 1976.

Deloria, Vine, Jr. "Custer Died For Your Sins." *Playboy* (August 1969): 131–32, 172, 175.

———. *Custer Died For Your Sins: An Indian Manifesto.* New York: Macmillan, 1969.

———. *God Is Red.* New York: Grosset and Dunlap, 1973.

———. *We Talk, You Listen: New Tribes, New Turf.* New York: Delta, 1970.

Deloria, Vine, Jr., and Clifford M. Lytle. *The Nations Within: The Past and Future of American Indian Sovereignty.* New York: Pantheon, 1984. Reprint, Austin: University of Texas, 1998.

DeMallie, Raymond, ed. *The Sixth Grandfather: Black Elk's Teachings Given to John G. Neihardt.* Lincoln: University of Nebraska Press, 1984.

DeMallie, Raymond J., Jr., and Robert H. Lavenda. "*Wakan:* Plains Concepts of Power." In *The Anthropology of Power: Ethnographic Studies From Asia, Oceania, and the New World.* New York: Academic Press, 1977.

Demetracapoulou, Dorothy. "Wintu Songs." *Anthropos* (Vienna) 30 (1935): 483–94.

Densmore, Frances. *Chippewa Music–II,* Bureau of American Ethnology Bulletin 53, Washington, DC: Smithsonian, 1913.

———. *Teton Sioux Music.* Institution Bureau of American Ethnology, Bulletin 61. Washington, DC: Smithsonian 1918. Reprint, New York: Da Capo Press, 1972.

Dewar, Elaine. *Bones: Discovering the First Americans.* New York: Carroll and Graf, 2002.

Diamond, Jared. *Collapse: How Societies Choose to Fail or Succeed.* New York: Viking/Penguin, 2005.

———. *Guns, Germs, and Steel: The Fates of Human Societies.* New York: W. W. Norton, 1997.

———. *The Third Chimpanzee: The Evolution and Future of the Human Animal.* New York: HarperCollins, 1992.

Dickinson, Emily. *The Complete Poems of Emily Dickinson.* Edited by Thomas H. Johnson. Cambridge, MA: Harvard University Press, 1955.

Dobyns, Henry F. "Estimating Aboriginal American Population: An Appraisal of Techniques with a New Hemispheric Estimate." *Current Anthropology* 7 (1966): 395–449.

Dobyns, Stephen. "Aspects of the Syllable." *The Writer's Chronicle* (Association of Writers & Writing Programs) 38, no. 4 (February 2006): 56–64.

Douglas, Mary. "The Social Control of Cognition: Some Factors in Joke Perception," *Man* 3 (1968): 361–76.

Driver, Harold E. *Indians of North America.* [1961]. 2nd revised edition. Chicago: University of Chicago Press, 1969.

Ellis, A. N. "Reflections of an Interview with Cochise." *Kansas State Historical Society* 13 (1913–14).

Erdoes, Richard, and John (Fire) Lame Deer. *Lame Deer, Seeker of Visions.* New York: Simon & Schuster, 1972.

Erdoes, Richard, and Alfonso Ortiz, eds. *American Indian Myths and Legends.* New York: Pantheon, 1984.

Erdrich, Louise. *The Antelope Wife.* New York: HarperCollins, 1998.

———. *Baptism of Desire.* New York: Harper & Row, 1989.

———. *The Beet Queen.* New York: Holt, 1986.

———. *The Bingo Palace.* New York: HarperCollins, 1994.

———. *The Blue Jay's Dance.* New York: HarperCollins, 1995.

———. *Books and Islands in Ojibwe Country.* New York: National Geographic, 2003.

———. *Four Souls.* New York: HarperCollins, 2004.

———. *Jacklight.* New York: Holt, Rinehart and Winston, 1984.

———. *The Last Report of Miracles at Little No Horse.* New York: HarperCollins, 2001.

———. *Love Medicine.* New York: Holt, Rinehart and Winston, 1984.

———. *The Master Butchers Singing Club.* New York: HarperCollins, 2003.

———. *Original Fire: Selected and New Poems.* New York: HarperCollins, 2003.

———. *The Painted Drum.* New York: HarperCollins, 2005.

———. *Tales of Burning Love.* New York: HarperCollins, 1996.

———. *Tracks.* New York: Holt, 1988.

————. "Where I Ought to Be: A Writer's Sense of Place." *New York Times Book Review*, 28 July 1985, 1, 3–4, 23–24.

Ewers, John C. *The Horse in Blackfeet Culture*. Bureau of American Ethnology Bulletin #159. Washington, DC: Smithsonian, 1955.

Finnegan, Ruth. *Oral Poetry*. Cambridge: Cambridge University Press, 1977.

Fleck, Richard F. *The Indians of Thoreau: Selections from the Indian Notebooks*. Albuquerque: Hummingbird Press, 1974.

Fletcher, Alice C. *Indian Story and Song from North America*. Boston: Small Maynard, 1900. Lincoln: University of Nebraska Press, Bison Reprint, 1995.

Foley, John Miles. *How to Read an Oral Poem*. Urbana: University of Illinois Press, 2002.

Fonseca, Harry. *Harry Fonseca: Earth, Wind, and Fire*. Santa Fe, NM: Wheelwright Museum of the American Indian, 1996.

Fogarty, Mark. "Census Bureau Releases Annual Snapshot." *Indian Country Today*, 23 November 2005, D4.

Frost, Robert. *The Complete Poems of Robert Frost*. New York: Holt, Rinehart and Winston, 1949.

Frye, Northrop. *Anatomy of Criticism*. Princeton, NJ: Princeton University Press, 1957.

Fulton, Alice. "Of Formal, Free, and Fractal Verse: Singing the Body Eclectic." In *Twentieth Century American Poetics: Poets on the Art of Poetry*, ed. Dana Gioia, David Mason, and Meg Schoerke, 469–78. New York: McGraw-Hill, 2004. Originally published in *Poetry East* 20–21 (Fall 1986). Collected in *Conversant Essays: Contemporary Poets on Poetry*, ed. James McCorkle, 185–93. (Detroit: Wayne State University Press, 1990).

Geertz, Clifford. *Local Knowledge: Further Essays in Interpretive Anthropology*. New York: Basic Books, 1983.

Gimbutas, Marija. *The Language of the Goddess*. San Francisco: Harper & Row, 1989.

Goldsworthy, Andy. *Rivers and Tides: Working with Time*. Directed by Thomas Riedelsheimer. Documentary film. Germany, Finland, UK: A&E Production Company/New Video Group, 2004.

Grant, Campbell. *Canyon de Chelly: Its People and Rock Art*. Tucson: University of Arizona, 1978.

Greene, Brian. *The Elegant Universe: Superstrings, Hidden Dimensions, and the Quest for the Ultimate Theory*. New York: W. W. Norton, 1999.

Gribbin, John. *Deep Simplicity: Bringing Order to Chaos and Complexity*. New York: Random House, 2004.

Grinnell, George Bird. *Blackfeet Lodge Tales: The Story of a Prairie People*. 1892. Reprint, Lincoln: University of Nebraska Press, 1962.

Guss, David M., ed. *The Language of the Birds: Tales, Texts, and Poems of Interspecies Communication*. San Francisco: North Point, 1985.

Haile, Berard. *Blessingway*, Version I. Told by Slim Curly, Crystal, New Mexico. Manuscript 112–14. Flagstaff: Museum of Northern Arizona, 1932.

———. *Blessingway*, Version II. Told by Frank Mitchell, Chinle, Arizona. Manuscript 112–15. Flagstaff: Museum of Northern Arizona, 1939.

———. *Blessingway*, Version III. Told by River Junction Curly. Manuscript 112–16. Flagstaff: Museum of Northern Arizona, n.d.

Hallowell, A. Irving. *Culture and Experience*. Philadelphia: University of Pennsylvania, 1955.

———. "Ojibwa Ontology, Behavior, and World View." In *Teaching from the American Earth: Indian Religion and Philosophy*, ed. Dennis and Barbara Tedlock. [1975]. New York: W. W. Norton, 1992.

Harjo, Joy. *How We Became Human: New and Selected Poems, 1975–2001*. New York: W. W. Norton, 2002.

———. *In Mad Love and War*. Middletown, CT: Wesleyan University Press, 1990.

———. "The Language of Tribes." Interview by Ray González. *The Bloomsbury Review* 17, no. 6 (November/December 1997): 18–20.

———, ed. *Ploughshares* 30, no. 4 (Winter 2004–05).

———. *Secrets from the Center of the World*. Stephen Strom, collab. Sun Tracks vol. 17. Tucson: University of Arizona, 1989.

———. *She Had Some Horses*. New York: Thunder's Mouth Press, 1983.

———. *The Spiral of Memory: Interviews*. Edited by Laura Coltelli. Ann Arbor: University of Michigan, 1996.

———. *The Woman Who Fell from the Sky*. New York: Norton, 1994.

Harjo, Joy, with Gloria Bird. *Reinventing the Enemy's Language: Contemporary Native American Women's Writings of North America*. New York: Norton, 1997.

Hass, Robert. *Twentieth-Century Pleasures: Prose on Poetry*. New York: Ecco/HarperCollins, 1984.

Hawkins, Peter S., and Rachel Jacoff, eds. *The Poets' Dante: Twentieth-Century Responses*. New York: Farrar, Straus and Giroux, 2001.

Heaney, Seamus, trans. *Beowulf: A New Verse Translation*. New York: Farrar, Straus and Giroux, 2000.

———. *Preoccupations: Selected Prose, 1968–1978*. New York: Farrar, Straus and Giroux, 1980.

Hillerman, Tony. *New Mexico, Rio Grande and Other Essays*. New York: HarperCollins, 1993.

———. *Skinwalkers*. New York: Harper & Row, 1988.

Hitt, Jack. "The Newest Indians." *New York Times Magazine*, 21 August 2005.

Hogan, Linda. *The Book of Medicines*. Minneapolis: Coffee House, 1993.

————. *Calling Myself Home*. Greenfield, NY: Greenfield Review, 1978.

————. *Dwellings: A Spiritual History of the Living World*. New York: W. W. Norton, 1995.

————. *Eclipse*. Native American Series, no. 6. Los Angeles: UCLA American Indian Studies Center, 1984.

————. *Mean Spirit*. New York: Atheneum, 1991.

————. *Power*. New York: W. W. Norton, 1998.

————. *Red Clay: Poems and Stories*. Greenfield, NY: Greenfield Review, 1991.

————. *Savings*. Minneapolis: Coffee House, 1988.

————. *Seeing Through the Sun*. Amherst: University of Massachusetts Press, 1985.

————. *Solar Storms*. New York: Simon & Schuster, 1995.

————. *The Woman Who Watches Over the World*. New York: W. W. Norton, 2001.

Hogan, Linda, with Carol Bruchac and Judith McDaniel. *The Stories We Hold Secret: Tales of Women's Spiritual Development*. Greenfield CT: Greenfield Review Press, 1986.

Hogan, Linda, Deena Metzger, and Brenda Peterson, eds. *Face to Face: Women Writers on Faith, Mysticism, and Awakening*. New York: North Point Press, 2004.

Hogan, Linda, Deena Metzger, and Brenda Peterson, eds. *Intimate Nature: The Bond Between Women and Animals*. New York: Fawcett/ Ballantine, 1998.

Hogan, Linda, and Brenda Peterson, coauthors. *Sightings: The Grey Whale's Mysterious Journey*. Washington DC. National Geographic, 2002.

Hogan, Linda, and Brenda Peterson, coeds. *The Sweet Breathing of Plants: Women Writing on the Green World*. New York: North Point, 2002.

Howard, Richard. *Alone with America*. New York: Atheneum, 1980.

Hughes, Ted. *Winter Pollen: Occasional Prose*. Edited by William Scammell. New York: Picador, 1994.

Huizinga, Johan. *Homo Ludens: A Study of the Play-Element in Culture*. [1938, 1944]. Reprint, Boston: Beacon Press, 1955.

Hyde, Lewis. *The Gift: Imagination and the Erotic Life of Property*. New York: Vintage/Random House, 1983.

————. *Trickster Makes This World: Mischief, Myth, and Art*. New York: Farrar, Straus and Giroux, 1998.

Iverson, Peter. *Diné: A History of the Navajos*. Albuquerque: University of New Mexico Press, 2002.

Jarrell, Randall. *The Bat-Poet*. New York: Macmillan, 1964.

Jung, C. G., Carl Kerenyi, and R. F. C. Hull. *Introduction to a Science of Mythology: The Myth of the Divine Child and the Mysteries of Eleusis*. London: Routledge, 1970.

Katanski, Amelia. *Learning to Write "Indian": The Boarding-School Experience and American Indian Literature*. Norman: University of Oklahoma Press, 2005.

Kazin, Alfred. *An American Procession: Major American Writers, 1830–1930*. Cambridge, MA: Harvard University Press, 1984.

Kenison, Katrina, and Larrie Moore, eds. *The Best American Short Stories 2004*. New York: Houghton Mifflin, 2004.

Kluckhohn, Clyde. *Mirror for Man: The Relation of Anthropology to Modern Life*. Tucson: University of Arizona Press, 1949.

Kluckhohn, Clyde, and Dorothea Leighton. *The Navaho*. Rev. ed. Garden City, NY: Doubleday, 1962.

Kristal, Efraín. *Invisible Work: Borges and Translation*. Nashville, TN: Vanderbilt University Press, 2003.

Kristeva, Julia. *The Kristeva Reader*. Edited by Toril Moi. New York: Columbia University Press, 1986.

———. *Strangers to Ourselves*. Translated by Leon S. Roudiez. New York: Columbia University Press, 1991.

Kroeber, Alfred L. "California Basketry of the Pomo." In *The California Indians: A Source Book*, ed. R. F. Heizer and M. A. Whipple, 329–31. Berkeley: University of California Press, 1971.

Kroeber, Alfred L. *Handbook of California Indians*, Bureau of American Ethnology Bulletin 78, Washington, DC: Smithsonian, 1925.

Kroeber, Theodora. *Ishi in Two Worlds: A Biography of the Last Wild Indian in North America*. 1961. 2nd edition Berkeley and London: University of California Press, 1976.

Krupat, Arnold, and Brian Swann, eds. *Everything Matters: Autobiographical Essays by Native American Writers*. New York: Random House, 1998.

———. *Here First: Autobiographical Essays by Native American Writers*. New York: Modern Library/Random House, 2000.

Kunitz, Stanley. *Next-to-Last Things: New Poems and Essays*. Boston and New York: Atlantic Monthly Press, 1985.

Lao Tsu. *Tao Te Ching*. Translated by Gia-Fu Feng and Jane English. New York: Vintage, 1972.

Lawrence, D. H. *Mornings in Mexico*. [1927]. Reprint, London: Heinemann, 1956.

———. *Phoenix: The Posthumous Papers of D. H. Lawrence*. Edited by Edward D. McDonald. [1936]. Reprinted in *The Spell of New Mexico*, ed. Tony Hillerman. Albuquerque: University of New Mexico Press, 1976.

Lee, Harold. "Humans, Birds Share Vocal Learning Genes." UCLA *Daily Bruin*, 13 April 2004, 3.

Lemonick, Michael D., and Andrea Dorfman. "Who Were the First Americans?" *Time* magazine, 13 March 2006, 45–52.

Lincoln, Kenneth, with Al Logan Slagle. *The Good Red Road: Passages into Native America*. San Francisco: Harper & Row, 1987. Reprinted as a University of Nebraska Bison paperback with a new Epilogue, 1997.

———. *Indi'n Humor: Bicultural Play in Native America*. New York and Oxford: Oxford University Press, 1993.

———. *Native American Renaissance*. Berkeley: University of California Press, 1983.

———. *Sing with the Heart of a Bear: Fusions of Native and American Poetry, 1890–1999*. Berkeley: University of California Press, 2000.

Locke, Kevin. *Lakota Wiikijo Olowan: Lakota Flute Music by Kevin Locke*. Brookings, SD: Featherstone Tape Cassette, n.d.

Lorca, Federico García. *In Search of the Duende*. Translated and edited by Christopher Maurer. New York: New Directions, 1998.

Lodge, David. *Consciousness and the Novel*. Cambridge, MA: Harvard University Press, 2002.

Lord, Albert B., with Milman Parry. *The Singer of Tales*. New York: Atheneum, 1974.

Louis, Adrian C. *Blood Thirsty Savages*. St. Louis: Time Being Books, 1994.

———. *Vortex of Indian Fevers*. Evanston, IL: TriQuarterly Books, Northwestern University Press, 1995.

Luckert, Karl W. *Coyoteway: A Navajo Holyway Healing Ceremonial*. Tucson: University of Arizona Press, 1979.

Machado, Antonio. *Selected Poems*. Translated by Alan S. Trueblood. Cambridge, MA: Harvard University Press, 1982.

Malotki, Ekkehart. *Kokopelli: The Making of an Icon*. Lincoln: University of Nebraska Press, 2000.

Mandelbrot, Benoit. *The Fractal Geometry of Nature*. New York: W. H. Freeman, 1977, 1983.

Margulis, Lynn. *Symbiotic Planet: A New Look at Evolution*. New York: Basic Books, 1999.

Margulis, Lynn, and Dorian Sagan. *Acquiring Genomes: A Theory of the Origins of Species*. New York: Basic Books, 2003.

Matthews, Washington. *Navajo Legends*. The American Folklore Society. Boston and New York: Houghton Mifflin, 1897.

————. *Navajo Myths, Prayers, and Songs.* University of California Publications in American Archaeology and Ethnology, vol. 5. Berkeley, 1907.

————. *The Night Chant, A Navajo Ceremony.* Memoirs of the American Museum of Natural History, vol. 6. New York, 1902.

Mattina, Anthony. *The Gold Woman: The Colville Narrative of Peter J. Seymour.* Translated by Anthony Mattina and Madeline de Sautel. Tucson: University of Arizona Press, 1985.

Mayhall, Mildred P. *The Kiowas.* Norman: University of Oklahoma Press, 1962.

McAllister, H. S. "'The Language of Shamans': Jerome Rothenberg's Contribution to American Indian Literature," *Western American Literature* 10 (February 1976): 293–309.

McHugh, Heather. *Broken English: Poetry and Partiality.* Hanover, NH: Wesleyan University Press, 1993.

McMaster, Gerald, and Clifford E. Trafzer, eds. *Native Universe: Voices of Indian America.* Smithsonian National Museum of the American Indian. Washington, DC: National Geographic Society, 2004.

McMurtry, Larry. *Reading Walter Benjamin at the Dairy Queen: Reflections at Sixty and Beyond.* New York: Simon & Schuster, 1999.

McNeley, James. *Holy Wind in Navajo Philosophy.* Tucson: University of Arizona Press, 1981.

Merwin, W. S. *Selected Translations, 1968–1978.* New York: Atheneum, 1979.

Milosz, Czeslaw. *A Book of Luminous Things: An International Anthology of Poetry.* New York: Harcourt, Brace, 1997.

Momaday, N. Scott. *The Ancient Child.* New York: Doubleday, 1989.

————. *Conversations with N. Scott Momaday.* Edited by Matthias Schubnell. Jackson: University Press of Mississippi, 1997.

————. *House Made of Dawn.* New York: Harper & Row, 1968. Reprint, Perennial Library, 1989.

————. *In the Presence of the Sun: Stories and Poems, 1961–1991.* New York: St. Martin's Press, 1992.

————. "A Love Affair with Emily Dickinson," *Santa Fe Viva,* 6 August 1972.

————. *The Man Made of Words: Essays, Stories, Passages.* New York: St. Martin's Press, 1997.

————. "The Morality of Indian Hating." *Ramparts* (Summer 1964): 30–40.

————. *The Names.* New York: Harper & Row, 1976.

————. *The Way to Rainy Mountain.* [1969]. Albuquerque: University of New Mexico Press, 1976.

Monroe, Mark. *An Indian in White America.* Edited by Carolyn Reyer, with an Afterword by Kenneth Lincoln. Philadelphia: Temple University, 1994.

Mooney, James. *Calendar History of the Kiowa Indians*. U.S. Bureau of American Ethnology, 17th Annual Report, 1895–96, pp. 141–444. Washington, DC, 1898.

Moulard, Barbara L., and Bill Schenck. *Re-creating the Word: Painted Ceramics of the Prehistoric Southwest*. Santa Fe, NM: Schenck Southwest Publishing, 2002.

Mumford, Lewis. *The City in History*. New York: Harcourt, Brace, 1961.

Nabokov, Peter, ed. *Native American Testimony: An Anthology of Indian and White Relations, First Encounter to Dispossession*. New York: Thomas Y. Crowell, 1978. Reprint, New York: Harper & Row, 1979.

———. *Where the Lightning Strikes: The Lives of American Indian Sacred Places*. New York: Viking, 2006.

Nabokov, Peter, and Lawrence Loendorf. *Restoring a Presence: American Indians and Yellowstone National Park*. Norman: University of Oklahoma Press, 2004.

Neihardt, John G., trans. *Black Elk Speaks: Being the Life Story of a Holy Man of the Oglala Sioux*. 1932. Reprint, Lincoln: University of Nebraska Press, 2000. Foreword by Vine Deloria Jr.

———. *John G. Neihardt, Flaming Rainbow*. Three long-playing records of Neihardt readings. Los Angeles: United Artists Records, 1973.

Neruda, Pablo. "Towards an Impure Poetry." In *Caballo verde para la poesía* (Madrid), no. 1 (October 1935): 1–3.

Niatum, Duane. *Carriers of the Dream Wheel: Contemporary Native American Poetry*. San Francisco: Harper & Row, 1975.

———. *Harper's Anthology of 20th Century Native American Poetry*. San Francisco: Harper & Row, 1988.

Noble, David Grant. *Ancient Ruins of the Southwest: An Archaeological Guide*. 1981. 2nd revised edition. Flagstaff: Northland Press, 2000.

———, ed. *In Search of Chaco: New Approaches to an Archaeological Enigma*. Santa Fe, NM: School of American Research Press, 2004.

Norman, Howard A., trans. *Who Met the Ice Lynx*. Ann Arbor, MI: Bear Claw Press, 1978.

———. *The Wishing Bone Cycle: Narrative Poems from the Swampy Cree Indians*. New York: Stonehill, 1976. Second edition expanded to include *Who Met the Ice Lynx* and *Why Owls Die With Wings Outspread*. Santa Barbara: Ross-Erikson, 1982.

Oe, Kenzaburo, ed. *The Crazy Iris and Other Stories of the Atomic Aftermath*. New York: Grove, 1985.

Okpewho, Isidore. *African Oral Literature: Backgrounds, Character, and Continuity*. Bloomington: Indiana University Press, 1992.

Ortiz, Alfonso. "Ritual Drama and the Pueblo World View." In *New Perspectives on the Pueblos*, ed. Alfonso Ortiz. Albuquerque: University of New Mexico Press, 1972.

———. *The Tewa World: Space, Time, Being and Becoming in a Pueblo Society*. Chicago: University of Chicago Press, 1969.

Ortiz, Simon J. *Fight Back: For the Sake of the People, For the Sake of the Land*. Albuquerque: University of New Mexico, Institute for Native American Development, 1980.

———. *Fightin': New and Collected Stories*. Chicago: Thunder's Mouth Press, 1983.

———. *Going for the Rain*. New York: Harper & Row, 1976.

———. *A Good Journey*. Berkeley, CA: Turtle Island, 1977.

———. *Howbah Indians: Stories*. Tucson: Blue Moon Press, 1978.

———. *Out There Somewhere*. Sun Tracks vol. 49. Tucson: University of Arizona Press, 2002.

———. "Song, Poetry, and Language." In *Survival This Way: Interviews with American Indian Poets*, ed. Joseph Bruchac. Sun Tracks vol. 15. Tucson: University of Arizona Press, 1987.

———. "Song, Poetry, and Language—Expression and Perception." In *Genocide of the Mind: New Native American Writing*, ed. MariJo Moore, 105–18. New York: Thunder's Mouth Press, 2003.

———. *Speaking for the Generations: Native Writers on Writing*. Tucson: University of Arizona Press, 1997.

———. *Woven Stone*. Sun Tracks vol. 21. Tucson: University of Arizona, 1992.

Owens, Louis. "Motion of Fire and Form." In *Here First: Autobiographical Essays by Native American Writers*, ed. Arnold Krupat and Brian Swann. New York: Modern Library/Random House, 2000.

Parsons, Elsie Clews. *Kiowa Tales*. American Folk-Lore Society, New York: G. E. Stechert, 1929. Reprint, New York: Kraus Reprint, 1969.

———. *Laguna Genealogies*. Anthropological Papers of the American Museum of Natural History, vol. 19, part 5. New York: The Trustees, 1923.

———. *Notes on Ceremonialism at Laguna*. Anthropological Papers of the American Museum of Natural History, vol. 19, part 4. New York: The Trustees, 1920.

———. *Pueblo Indian Religion*. Vol. 2. Chicago: University of Chicago Press, 1939.

———. *Tewa Tales: Memoirs of the American Folk-Lore Society*. New York, 1926. Reprinted with a new Foreword by Barbara A. Babcock. Tucson: University of Arizona Press, 1994.

Patterson, Alex. *A Field Guide to Rock Art Symbols of the Greater Southwest*. Boulder, CO: Johnson Books, 1992.

Patterson-Rudolph, Carol. *On the Trail of Spider Woman: Petroglyphs, Pictographs, and Myths of the Southwest*. Santa Fe, NM: Ancient City Press, 1997.

———. *Petroglyphs & Pueblo Myths of the Rio Grande*. Revised edition. Albuquerque: Avanyu Publishing, 1993.

Pierce, T. M. *New Mexico Placenames: A Geographical Dictionary*. Albuquerque: University of New Mexico Press, 1965.

Pinker, Steven. *The Language Instinct: How the Mind Creates Language*. New York: William Morrow, 1994.

Porcupine Singers: Traditional Lakota Songs. Canyon Records Vintage Collection, vol. 16. Phoenix: Canyon Records Productions, 1997.

Porter, Joy, and Kenneth M. Roemer, eds. *The Cambridge Companion to Native American Literature*. New York: Cambridge University Press, 2005.

Posey, Alexander Lawrence. *Poems*. Topeka, Kansas, 1910.

Pound, Ezra. *ABC of Reading*. New York: New Directions, 1960.

———, trans. *Confucius: The Great Digest, The Unwobbling Pivot, The Analects*. New York: New Directions, 1969.

Princeton Encyclopedia of Poetry and Poetics. Edited by Alex Preminger. Princeton, NJ: Princeton University Press, 1974.

Pulitano, Elvira. *Toward a Native American Critical Theory*. Lincoln: University of Nebraska Press, 2003.

Ramsey, Jarold, ed. *Coyote Was Going There: Indian Literature of the Oregon Country*. Seattle: University of Washington Press, 1977.

Rose, Wendy. *Academic Squaw: Reports to the World from the Ivory Tower*. Marvin, SD: Blue Cloud Press, 1978.

Rothenberg, Jerome, ed. *Shaking the Pumpkin: Traditional Poetry of the Indian North Americas*. Garden City, NY: Doubleday, 1972.

Rourke, Constance. "The Indian Background of American Theatricals." In *Literature of the American Indians: Views and Interpretations*, ed. Abraham Chapman. New York: New American Library, 1975.

Ryden, Hope. *God's Dog: A Celebration of the North American Coyote*. 1975. Reprint, New York: Penguin Books, 1979.

Sarris, Greg. "Culture and Memory: What Has Been Lost? What Can Be Recovered?" Lecture to the Jewish Community Center of San Francisco, 15 May 2005.

———. *Grand Avenue: A Novel in Stories*. New York: Hyperion, 1994.

———. *Keeping Slug Woman Alive: A Holistic Approach to American Indian Texts*. Berkeley: University of California, 1993.

———. *Mabel McKay: Weaving the Dream*. Berkeley: University of California, 1994.

———. "On the Road to Lolsel: Conversations with Mabel McKay." *News from Native California* 2, no. 4 (September/October 1988): 3–6.

———, ed. *The Sound of Rattles and Clappers: A Collection of New California Indian Writing*. Tucson: University of Arizona, 1994.

———. *Watermelon Nights*. New York: Hyperion, 1998.

Schaafsma, Polly. *Rock Art in New Mexico*. Santa Fe: Museum of New Mexico Press, 1992.

Schmidt, Michael. *The First Poets: Lives of the Ancient Greek Poets*. New York: Alfred A. Knopf, 2005.

Schubnell, Matthia. *N. Scott Momaday: The Cultural and Literary Background*. Norman: University of Oklahoma, 1985.

Sewall, Richard B. *The Life of Emily Dickinson*. Cambridge, MA: Harvard University Press, 1974.

Shanley, Kathryn W., ed. "Native American Literature: Boundaries and Sovereignties." *Paradoxa*, no. 15 (2001).

Silko, Leslie. Biographical note. In *The Next World: Poems by 32 Third World Americans*, ed. Joseph Bruchac. Trumansburg, NY: The Crossing Press, 1978.

———. *Ceremony*. New York: Viking, 1977.

———. *Laguna Woman*. Greenfield, NY: Greenfield Review Press, 1974.

———. *Storyteller*. New York: Seaver Books, 1981.

———. *Yellow Woman and a Beauty of the Spirit: Essays on Native American Life Today*. New York: Simon & Schuster, 1996.

Simic, Charles. *Wonderful Words, Silent Truth: Essays on Poetry and a Memoir*. Ann Arbor: University of Michigan Press, 1990.

Slifer, Dennis. *Signs of Life: Rock Art of the Upper Rio Grande*. Santa Fe, NM: Ancient City Press, 1998.

———. *The Serpent and the Sacred Fire: Fertility Images in Southwest Rock Art*. Santa Fe: Museum of New Mexico Press, 2000.

Slifer, Dennis, and James Duffield. *Kokopelli: Flute Player Images in Rock Art*. Santa Fe, NM: Ancient City Press, 1994.

Soens, A. L. *I, the Song: Classical Poetry of Native North America*. Salt Lake City: University of Utah Press, 1999.

Spicer, Jack. "On Spoken Poetry." In *Twentieth-Century American Poetics: Poets on the Art of Poetry*, ed. Dana Gioia, David Mason, and Meg Schoerke. New York: McGraw-Hill, 2004.

Spier, Leslie. *Havasupai Ethnography*. Anthropological Papers of the American Museum of Natural History, vol. 29. New York, 1928.

Spindon, Herbert J. *Songs of the Tewa*. Exposition of Indian Tribal Arts. New York, 1933.

Standing Bear, Luther. *Land of the Spotted Eagle*. [1933]. Lincoln: University of Nebraska Press, Bison Books, 1978.

———. *My People the Sioux*. Edited by E. A. Briminstool. [1928]. Lincoln: University of Nebraska Press, Bison Books, 1975.

Stedman, Raymond William. *Shadows of the Indian: Stereotypes in American Culture*. Norman: University of Oklahoma Press, 1982.

Stegner, Wallace. *Wolf Willow: A History, a Story, and a Memory of the Last Plains Frontier*. [1955]. New York: Viking, 1973.

Stephenson, Dave. "America's Urban Youth and the Importance of Remembering." In *Genocide of the Mind: New Native American Writing*, ed. MariJo Moore. New York: Thunder's Mouth, 2003.

Swann, Brian, ed. *Coming to Light: Contemporary Translations of the Native Literatures of North America*. New York: Vintage, 1994.

———, ed. *On the Translation of Native American Literatures*. Washington, DC: Smithsonian Institution, 1992.

———. *Recovering the Word: Essays on Native American Literature*. Berkeley: University of California Press, 1987.

———, ed. *Smoothing the Ground: Essays on Native American Oral Literature*. Berkeley: University of California Press, 1983.

———, ed. *Song of the Sky: Versions of Native American Songs and Poems*. Foreword by Paula Gunn Allen. New York: Four Zoas, 1985.

———, ed. *Wearing the Morning Star: Native American Song-Poems*. New York: Random House, 1996.

Swann, Brian, and Arnold Krupat, eds. *Recovering the Word: Essays on Native American Literature*. Berkeley: University of California Press, 1987.

Talayesva, Don C. *Sun Chief: The Autobiography of a Hopi Indian*. Edited by Leo W. Simmons. New Haven, CT: Yale University Press, 1942.

Tapahonso, Luci. *Blue Horses Rush In: Poems and Stories*. Sun Tracks vol. 34. Tucson: University of Arizona Press, 1997.

———. *A Breeze Swept Through*. Albuquerque: West End, 1987.

———. *One More Shiprock Night*. San Antonio: Tejas Art, 1981.

———. "The Radiant Curve: Navajo Ceremony in Contemporary Life." In *Native Universe: Voices of Indian America*. Smithsonian National Museum of the American Indian. Washington, DC: National Geographic Society, 2004.

———. *Sáanii Dahataal/The Women Are Singing*. Tucson: University of Arizona Press, 1993.

———. *Seasonal Woman*. Santa Fe, NM: Tooth of Time Books, 1982.

Tatham's Characters Among The North American Indians. Annual of Biography and Obituary. London, 1820.

Taylor, Timothy. *The Prehistory of Sex: Four Million Years of Human Sexual Culture*. New York: Bantam Books, 1996.

Tedlock, Dennis. *The Spoken Word and the Work of Interpretation*. Philadelphia: University of Pennsylvania Press, 1983.

Todorov, Tzvetan. *Mikhail Bakhtin: The Dialogical Principle*. Translated by Wlad Godzich. Theory and History of Literature, vol. 13. Minneapolis: University of Minnesota Press, 1984.

Toelken, Barre. *The Anguish of Snails: Native American Folklore in the West*. Logan: Utah State Press, 2003.

———. "Poetic Retranslation and the 'Pretty Languages' of Yellowman." In *Transitional Literatures of the American Indian*, ed. Karl Kroeber. Lincoln: University of Nebraska Press, 1981.

———. "The 'Pretty Language' of Yellowman: Genre, Mode, and Texture in Navajo Coyote Narratives." *Genre* 2 (September 1969): 211–35.

Treuer, David. "Smartberries: Interpreting Erdrich's *Love Medicine*." *American Indian Culture and Research Journal* 29, no. 1 (2005): 21–36.

Turner, Frederick W., III, ed. *The Portable North American Indian Reader*. [1973]. New York: Penguin, 1977.

Underhill, Ruth. *The Autobiography of a Papago Woman*. Menasha, WI: American Anthropological Association, 1936.

———. *The Navajos*. Norman: University of Oklahoma Press, 1956.

———. *Singing for Power: The Song Magic of the Papago Indians of Southern Arizona*. Berkeley: University of California Press, 1938.

Valéry, Paul. *The Art of Poetry*. Introduction by T. S. Eliot. Bollingen Series, vol. 45, no. 7. Princeton, NJ: Princeton University Press, 1958.

Vestal, Stanley. *Sitting Bull: Champion of the Sioux. A Biography*. 1932. Reprint, Norman: University of Oklahoma Press, 1956.

———. "The Works of Sitting Bull, Real and Imaginary." *Southwest Review* 19 (April 1934): 265–78.

Vizenor, Gerald. *The Darkness in Saint Louis Bearheart*. St. Paul, MN: Truck Press, 1978.

———, ed. *Summer in the Spring: Ojibwe Lyric Poems and Tribal Stories*. Minneapolis: Nodin Press, 1981.

———. *Wordarrows: Indians and Whites in the New Fur Trade*. Minneapolis: University of Minnesota Press, 1978.

Vogel, Virgil J. *American Indian Medicine*. Norman: University of Oklahoma Press, 1970.

Voth, Henry R. *Hopi Material Culture*. Barton Wright. Flagstaff: Northland Press, 1979.

———. *Traditions of the Hopi*. Field Museum of Natural History Publication 96, Anthropological Series 8. Chicago, 1905.

Weaver, Jace, Caig S. Womack, and Robert Warrior. *American Indian Literary Nationalism*. Albuquerque: University of New Mexico Press, 2005.

Welch, James. Interview with Kay Bonetti, April 1985. Audiotape. Columbia, MO: American Audio Prose Library.

———. Interview with Kate Shanley, 12 July 2000, *Paradoxa 6*, no. 15 (2001): 17–37.

———. *The Death of Jim Loney*. New York: Harper & Row, 1979.

———. *Fools Crow*. New York: Viking, 1986.

———. *The Heartsong of Charging Elk*. New York: Doubleday, 2001.

———. *Indian Lawyer*. New York: W. W. Norton, 1990.

———. *Riding the Earthboy 40*. New York: World, 1971. Reprint, New York: Harper & Row, 1976; Penguin, 2004.

———. *Winter in the Blood*. New York: Harper & Row, 1974.

Welch, James, with Paul Stekler. *Killing Custer: The Battle of the Little Bighorn and the Fate of the Plains Indians*. New York: Norton, 1994.

Welsh, Andrew. *Roots of Lyric: Primitive Poetry and Modern Poetics*. Princeton, NJ: Princeton University Press, 1978.

Wiget, Andrew, ed. *Handbook of Native American Literature*. New York and London: Garland Publishing, 1996.

Williams, William Carlos. *In the American Grain*. New York: New Directions, 1925.

Winn, James Anderson. *Unsuspected Eloquence: A History of the Relation between Poetry and Music*. New Haven: Yale University Press, 1981.

Witherspoon, Gary. *Language and Art in the Navajo Universe*. Ann Arbor: University of Michigan, 1977.

Womack, Craig S. *Red on Red: Native American Literary Separatism*. Minneapolis: University of Minnesota, 1999.

Wright, Anne, ed. *The Delicacy and Strength of Lace: Letters Between Leslie Marmon Silko and James Wright*. St. Paul, MN: Greywolf, 1986.

Wright, Charles. "Mondo Orfeo." In *A Short History of the Shadow: Poems*. New York: Farrar, Straus and Giroux, 2002.

Wright, James. *James Wright: Collected Poems*. Middletown, CT: Wesleyan University Press, 1971.

Wyss, Hilary E. *Writing Indians: Literacy, Christianity, and Native Community in Early America*. Amherst: University of Massachusetts Press, 2000.

Yeats, William Butler. "Why the Blind Man in Ancient Times Was Made a Poet." [1906]. In *W. B. Yeats: Selected Criticism*, ed. A. Norman Jeffares. London: Macmillan, 1964.

Young Bear, Ray A. *Black Eagle Child: The Facepaint Narratives*. Singular Lives: Iowa Series in North American Autobiography. Iowa City: University of Iowa Press, 1992.

———. *Winter of the Salamander*. New York: Harper & Row, 1980.

Zolbrod, Paul. *Diné bahané: The Navajo Creation Story*. Albuquerque: University of New Mexico Press, 1984.

———. *Reading the Voice: Native American Oral Poetry on the Written Page*. Salt Lake City: University of Utah Press, 1995.

About the Author

Kenneth Lincoln grew up in northwest Nebraska south of Wounded Knee, where his great-grandparents homesteaded along the North Platte River and ranching sandhills. Graduating from public high school in Alliance, Nebraska, he went to Stanford University for a degree in American Literature, to Indiana University for a doctorate in Modern British Literature, and to UCLA where he has taught Contemporary and Native American Literatures for thirty-eight years. In spring 1969, Lincoln was adopted into the Oglala Sioux by the Mark Monroe family of Alliance and given the Lakota name Mato Yamni. Beginning with *Native American Renaissance*, *The Good Red Road*, and *Indi'n Humor*, he has published six books in American Indian Studies, chaired the country's first interdisciplinary master's program in the field, and written novels, poetry, and personal essays about Western Americana.

Index